Constructing the Stalinist Body

Constructing the Stalinist Body

Fictional Representations of Corporeality in the Stalinist 1930s

Keith A. Livers

LEXINGTON BOOKS
Lanham • Boulder • New York • Toronto • Oxford

LEXINGTON BOOKS

Published in the United States of America
by Lexington Books
An imprint of The Rowman & Littlefield Publishing Group, Inc.
4501 Forbes Boulevard, Suite 200, Lanham, Maryland 20706

PO Box 317
Oxford
OX2 9RU, UK

British Library Cataloguing in Publication Information Available

Library of Congress Cataloging-in-Publication Data

Livers, Keith A., 1963–
    Constructing the Stalinist body : fictional representations of corporeality in
the Stalinist 1930s / Keith A. Livers.
        p. cm.
    Includes bibliographical references and index.
    ISBN 0-7391-0773-9 (cloth : alk. paper)
    1. Russian literature—20th century—History and criticism. 2. Utopias in
literature. 3. Ideology and literature. 4. Body, Human, in literature. 5. Mind
and body in literature. I. Title.
PG3026.U8L58   2004
891.709'372—dc22
                                            2004014464

Printed in the United States of America

♾™ The paper used in this publication meets the minimum requirements of American
National Standard for Information Sciences—Permanence of Paper for Printed Library
Materials, ANSI/NISO Z39.48-1992.

Contents

Acknowledgments   vii

Introduction: Stalinism Embodied   1

1   Turning Men into Women: Andrei Platonov in the 1930s   27

2   Mikhail Zoshchenko: Engineering the Stalinist Body and Soul   91

3   Lev Kassil': The Soccer Match as Stalinist Ritual   153

4   Conquering the Underworld: The Spectacle of the
Stalinist Metro   189

Conclusion: Stalinist Bodies on Display   237

Bibliography   247

Index   257

About the Author   267

Acknowledgments

I would like to express my thanks to the following people for the help, understanding, and patience that they showed during my researching and writing of this book. First of all, I owe a great debt of gratitude to Sydney Monas for his careful reading not only of this manuscript but of everything else I have written while at the University of Texas. His many insights, commentary, and enthusiasm were an essential part of this project and were a genuine inspiration to me throughout the process. I would also like to thank Hana Pichova, Joan Neuberger, and Lida Oukaderova for their patient reading and rereading of the manuscript. I am grateful to Hana not only for her friendship and support, but for the wealth of practical advice and guidance she has given me over the years. I am also indebted to Joan Neuberger for her advice on this project and her help on matters relating to Russian cinema. My friendship with Lida—particularly our many spirited conversations about Russian literature and culture—have enriched me in too many ways to enumerate. I would like to thank the office staff in the Department of Slavic Languages at the University of Texas. Finally, gratitude and much love to my very good friend Stacey Thompson, who helped me make it through many of the more trying moments of book writing.

Introduction

Stalinism Embodied

"In a conversation with me, Lazar Moiseevich [Kaganovich], advised me to take care of my health. He stood up and pulled his belt out, away from his waist, 'See how trim I am? If I can tell from my belt that I'm starting to put on weight, I immediately get down to work on my gymnastics. The party needs my health, my organism—I have to keep them in working condition.'"

—Vladimir Petrovich Stavsky

"But all the sounds had ceased. The events, it seems, had retreated into the center of the bodies of those who were sleeping."

—Andrei Platonov (*Happy Moscow*)

Taken from sources that are politically and spiritually nearly diametrically opposed, the two quotes above mirror the profound interpenetration of the human body with the twin realms of ideology and mythology that were the very core of Stalinist culture. The first quote comes from the anguished diary of Vladimir Petrovich Stavsky (written in 1938). A party hack known as the "'executioner of Soviet literature,'" he denounced Osip Mandelshtam—an act which led to the poet's arrest and execution—in addition to authorizing the arrests of a number of members of the Soviet Writers' Union.[1] The second quote is from Andrei Platonov's unfinished novel *Happy Moscow*, which was sporadically written between 1933 and 1936 but remained unpublished until a year after the Soviet experiment had already ended in 1991. An allegory of Stalinist construction during the '30s, *Happy Moscow* likens the socialist metropolis to the body of the novel's heroine—a parachutist and metro builder named Moscow Chestnova. Reflecting with varying degrees of polemic Stalinist culture's push to create an ideologically uniform social body, such major authors as Andrei Platonov,

1

Mikhail Zoshchenko, and Mikhail Bakhtin—to name only a few—situate the ideal self as well as the ideal society deep within the bowels of the human organism. Likewise, many of the most visible construction projects of the time serve either directly or indirectly as metaphors for a radical reconfiguring of the body politic. The building of the Moscow metro is a prime example. Begun in the early '30s as part of the socialist reconstruction of Moscow, it was widely viewed as emblematic of a utopian society that was already beginning to take shape. The following example from Demian Bednyi's long poem "Moscow" illustrates the point. Using the dramatic imagery of the period, which often portrayed socialist construction in terms of a mythological contest between nature and Bolshevik technology,[2] the poet describes the building of the Moscow Metro in 1935 as a kind of ontological tête-à-tête. What Bednyi and others depicted as an encounter between a femininely passive nature and the phallic thrust of socialist technology must ultimately be understood allegorically—as a metaphor for the wholesale restructuring of human nature undertaken by Stalinism. Not surprisingly, this process is one that impinges directly on humanity's most enduring link to the natural world—that is, on the human body, on its organs and limbs: "After all, isn't it time/ To dig an arterial beneath the ground./ And so in the soft, solid ground/ At Kalanchevka and at Hunter's Chase./ On the Sands and at Pokrov/ The giant drills crunch./ The earth-digging machines wheeze. . . . But in a year, when you/ disembowel the insides/ And the speedy Metro,/ Runs down its main course/ When the rewards will rightly/ Write you into our heroic fame/ I will sing [your praises] to the whole Union!"[3]

This book examines the remarkable, indeed, unprecedented fusion of private bodies and state ideology as reflected in a number of works from the Stalinist '30s. In order to demonstrate the remarkable breadth of the phenomenon, I have intentionally *not* limited my discussion to those masterworks already familiar to the educated reader. Thus in addition to such well-known works as Platonov's *Happy Moscow* or Zoshchenko's *Before Sunrise*, the present study looks at the writing of a lesser-known (but nevertheless extraordinarily influential) author of children's literature, Lev Kassil'. According to Omry Ronen, Kassil''s many books "realistically molded the lives of urban teenagers in the Soviet Union, from soccer to the formation of 'secret societies.'"[4] For the same reason I include a chapter on the representation of the Moscow Metro, the Stalinist superproject that engendered collectively authored encomia such as the commerative volumes *How We Built the Metro* (1935) and *Stories of the Metro Builders* (1935), as well as individual polemics in such works as Bulgakov's *Master and Margarita* or Platonov's *Happy Moscow*.

As the still expanding field of body studies has repeatedly shown, the human body is as much an invention of culture—a fluid projection of broader cultural ideologies and myths—as it is a self-evident manifestation of physiology. The body, as Robert Romanshyn notes, is "always metaphorical in its relation to the world and symbolic in its inherent power to unite self and world in a richly textured field of meaning."[5] Likewise, David Hillman and Carla Mazzio remark that the "spatially imagined body was perhaps the most common vehicle for the making of social and cosmic metaphors in early Modern Europe."[6] Meanwhile, both of these authors stress the predominance of the corporeal fragment in the cultural imagination of early modern Europe. Throughout this period, they argue, the body *part* provided a potent metaphor for the overwhelming sense of spiritual and social fragmentation that marked the passing of the medieval Christian understanding of the body (politic) as unified and whole.[7] The example of Russian culture confirms this model, even as it departs all the more sharply from it. Here, too, the body is no less frequently pressed into service as a means of portraying the body politic. Yet this is where the similarity ends. For as Aleksandr Etkind explains in his monograph *Khlyst: Sects, Literature and Revolution*, Russian folk and sectarian culture (as well as the high culture that would later be influenced by it) invariably emphasized not corporeal fragmentation but the communal body as a means of overcoming societal disunity and strife.[8]

A particularly dramatic example concerns the founding of the so-called *Khlysty* sect during the first half of the seventeenth century. In 1631 a runaway soldier named Danila Fillipovich threw the Orthodox holy books into the Volga River and proclaimed himself leader and deity of a new religion. The *Khlysty* replaced traditional Orthodox practice with rituals aimed at creating a collective body. In this manner the "body of written culture" was replaced in the religious practice of the unlettered with the body as such.[9] Similarly, in formulating the rhetoric of the *raskol* (the sect of Old Believers who rejected the liturgical reforms of Patriarch Nikon in the mid-seventeenth century), the Archpriest Avvakum employed corporeal metaphors as one of his main weapons. In a petition to the tsar in which he describes a vision, Avvakum depicts the Tsar Aleksei Mikhailovich's sins as pus-filled sores that have covered his entire stomach. Meanwhile, Avvakum portrays himself as the "mystical body of the world: 'and my arms and legs were great, and in addition I was wide and spacious . . . and had spread out, and afterwards God placed inside me the sky, the earth and all the creatures.'"[10]

Yet the image of the ideal community as body, which for Avvakum remained a metaphor (no matter how literally it might have been taken), is realized in the extreme rituals of bodily mutilation practiced by Russia's most radical sect—the so-called *skoptsy*, or castrates. Employing surgical rather than ritual means, they realized their communal ideal by physically removing the most enduring obstacle to collective subjectivity, that is, the sex organs.[11]

For both of these sects, sex (because of its organic ties to the institutions of family and property) stood in the way of their members' cherished objective of "spiritual communism."[12] Hence the need for an entirely unmetaphorical, surgical intervention. A similar urge to organize the ideal community in the guise of a unified body social will make itself felt much later, in the writings of such prominent Russian philosophers as Nikolai Fedorov and Sergei Bulgakov. Particularly in the case of the latter the philosophical casus belli is the putative hyperindividualism of Western social thought. Polemicizing with Max Weber's Protestant Ethos, Bulgakov argues that the true aim of economic activity is the creation of a collective, mystical body.[13] Not far away from this, Nikolai Fedorov (in his voluminous *Philosophy of the Common Cause*) had earlier advocated scientifically resurrecting the bodies of the dead as a means of repealing the "unbrotherly" state of human relations and thereby achieving spiritual unity.

Finally, it should be noted that the corporeal utopianism of such projects (whether in the unprecedented religious practices of the *skoptsy* or in Fedorov's unorthodox dream of scientifically resurrecting the dead) significantly shaped the communal ideology of the postrevolutionary era.[14] This is most evident in the writing(s) of the *Proletkul't*, a movement which in the years after the revolution aspired to produce strictly proletarian and collectivist forms of consciousness.[15] In this manner—one might argue—the watershed of 1917 encouraged many writers and cultural figures to take the rhetoric of the prerevolutionary years to its logical, maximalist conclusion, clothing in flesh and blood what had previously been a mere figure of speech. Yet unlike the religious sectarians, such *Proletkul't* figures as Aleksei Gastev foresaw a proletarian body collectivized not through exotic religious ritual but in the sublime cathedral of labor. And if the *khlysty* or the castrates strove to replace individual sex with a collective orgasm, in Gastev's poem the same goal is attained through a quasi-sexual orgy of communal labor.

One of the hot-button issues for all of such utopias is the "woman question." What, in other words, is the place of women in the dreams of utopian collectivity elaborated above? This question will prove particularly relevant for the authors and texts of the present study, where attitudes range from ambivalent acceptance to outright hostility. In her book *Space, Time and Perversion: Essays on the Politics of Bodies*, Elizabeth Grosz describes the distinct ways in which men and women have historically been portrayed in terms of their relationship to space. Among others, she notes the male push to achieve mastery and dominion over the entire spectrum of social space, while simultaneously relegating woman to a position of ontological secondariness. Within the masculine cosmos, Grosz writes, women emerge as the embodiment of the domestic or natural that man must purge in order to represent himself as "above-the-mundane." In order to "sustain this fantasy of auto-production and pure self-determination . . . men have had to use women as the delegate of men's materiality."[16] This conceptual sleight of hand is not without consequences, however, since the phantom of woman as the "body to be mastered" never ceases to hover around the edges of the male fantasy of transcendence. The ideological and cultural discussions about sexuality and the feminine which punctuated the postrevolutionary '20s were similarly misogynistic and—one might say—similarly haunted. As Eric Naiman notes, they represent a clear outgrowth of the prerevolutionary philosophical tradition (e.g., Fyodorov, Bulgakov, and Berdiaev) which bundled woman, sexuality, and nature into a single conceptual node that stood in stark opposition to the civilizing and spiritualizing agency of Man.[17] And there is no shortage of examples from the period (both in terms of artistic output and broader ideological debates) that demonstrate the mutual antagonism of the utopian (male) collective and the image of Woman.[18] For an example, let us turn to one of Andrei Platonov's earliest stories, a piece entitled "A Story About Many Interesting Things" (1923). In it the protagonist Ivan sets out on a journey to transform the world with the help of a woman referred to as the Caspian Bride, who is strongly reminiscent of the Eternal Feminine sought after by Solov'ev and the second-generation symbolists. Yet when another character—an engineer—invites Ivan to accompany him on an interstellar journey, he tells Ivan to "leave your girlfriend here—so she won't fence your eyes off from the world and tear your soul in two."[19] For Platonov—as for many of his like-minded contemporaries such as Babel or Olesha—the utopian collective can be created but only at the cost of excluding Woman from its ranks.

It will perhaps come as no great surprise to the reader that with the advent of the Stalinist utopia in the 1930s the same tendency to project utopia onto the body once again became a significant feature of public and private discourse. Here, perhaps even more than in the preceding decade, the body (its limbs, organs, and other parts) stands in the foreground as the ideological and mythological arena in which the Stalinist dream of a realized utopia is violently played out. As Lars T. Lih writes, by the mid-1930s, according to the official mythology, "the virtuous community had triumphed in real life because the foundations of socialism had been laid in the Soviet Union and the waverers had all been won over."[20] And on the level of cultural mythology, the result of this shift toward "utopia found" was a carefully cultivated sense of social unity enacted in almost corporeal terms of physical closeness and warmth. As Aleksandr Gol'dshtein remarks, the official image of a country in which the social and ontological barriers separating individuals had finally "withered away" was energetically promoted throughout the public sphere. Take, for example, Ilya Ehrenburg's 1935 novel *Without Pausing for Breath*, in which a woman suddenly senses her closeness to the people around her as a result of being able to speak to her husband (who is stationed somewhere in the Arctic) by radio.[21] Likewise, in Grigory Alexandrov's immensely popular 1936 musical *Circus*, the Soviet Union appears as a joyous, familial collective comprising every possible nationality and ethnicity. Here even a white (American) circus performer with her mixed-race child could find safe haven. This sense of Stalin's Soviet Union as a kind of extended patriarchal family is further evidenced by the broad application of kinship terms to define the country in relationship to itself and to the outside world. Thus the Soviet Union reemerges as "the Motherland," even as it becomes possible to speak of "sister republics" and "fraternal peoples."[22] Naturally, the head of this imagined community is none other than the "father of nations" himself, that is, Stalin. Whether imagined or real, the appeal of such a relationship was such that the Stalinist "living" utopia (as opposed to the mechanistic ones of the previous decade) appeared suffused with the animating warmth of love — a love which at its highest level allowed the individual subject to unite with the "leader" in a kind of mystical union.[23]

Stalinist culture's striving toward festive familial collectivity is demonstrated, among others, by its attempts to promote an official carnival culture. Complete with laughter, masks, and an erotically charged atmosphere, "carnival" was clearly the order of the day. And while such celebrations were ultimately far from spontaneous, the desire on the part of the official ideology to orchestrate a feeling of collective corporeality seems beyond doubt.[24] Of course, mass spectacles had been an effective propaganda tool since the revolution. In the years immediately following 1917 they were used to "revive the pathos of revolution . . . its collectivist, iconoclastic spirit," while at the same time providing the masses with a "status-quo affirming myth of origins."[25] Yet the mass spectacles of the '30s were noticeably bereft of any such (even symbolic) iconoclasm. Instead, they concentrated on the sensation of physical closeness and corporeal unity necessary to produce the image of a totally integrated body politic — of what would soon become known as the great family of Stalinism. Within this broader phenomenon there were a number of locales where a sense of mythic unity was actively forged, such as the physical culture parades, various sporting events (e.g., soccer), and the numerous parks of culture and rest parks that sprang up during the period. Of these the park merits particular attention. Not simply generic grassy or wooded areas, the many Parks of Culture and Rest that came to dot the landscape of the Soviet Union of the 1930s fulfilled a twofold function. The first was didactic: the parks' abundant statuary endeavored to provide the visitor-spectator with a coherent narrative of Stalinist ideology and myth. Take for instance, the myth of Chapaev (the famous civil war hero), which was tirelessly reproduced in materials ranging from bronze to porcelain, in miniature statuettes and in statues measuring as much as eight meters. The Stalinist Park of Culture and Rest, notes Zolotonosov, "was to be read the way one reads a book or an ideological primer."[26] The second function was to create a sense of communal physicality, such that the constant sensation of the Other's body would allow the visitor to festively immerse him- or herself in the carnival "we."[27] That these two functions are, to some extent, contradictory is not surprising. For just as the Stalinist coming-to-consciousness narrative mediates between "spontaneity" and "consciousness,"[28] so, too, the function of the Park of Culture and Rest lies in modulating between the ideal of supreme, statuary stasis and that of ceaseless movement (i.e., the carnival body). A natural corollary of this festive carnival body were the no less boisterous show trials of the mid-to-late '30s, which pursued the same goal of social cohesion via rituals of collective purgation. And it is certainly no accident that these rituals employ a language that calls to mind the emunctory processes most closely associated with the human body. As Lars T. Lih writes, the "demand for purification gives rise to a strong filth vs. purity opposition in the rhetoric of the trial: 'A foul-smelling heap of human garbage' contaminates a land 'illumined by the sun of the Stalinist constitution.'"[29]

In many ways the image of collective corporeality described above recalls Bakhtin's preoccupation with the festive communal body in his famous *Rabelais and His World* (1939). To be sure, Bakhtin's relationship to the surrounding Stalinist culture was an extraordinarily complex one. As recent scholarship demonstrates, his celebration of the carnival body mirrors the contours of Stalinist ideology and myth, at the same time that it subjects the reality of the Terror to a relativizing historical analysis. Thus even as it suggests an alternative to the deadening monologism of Stalinist stasis, Bakhtin's "carnival" can also be read as an intimate portrait of the culture's inner workings.[30] For instance, the precipitous swings from praise to blame,[31] the cult of "pregnant death" which gives birth to the new by killing off the old—all of this can be viewed as a metaphor for Stalinist culture of the 1930s. Meanwhile, Bakhtin's carnival festivities, with their sudden crownings and dethronings, recall nothing if not the atmosphere of the Stalinist show trials.[32] Yet unlike Stalinist carnival, whose ritual purges were ultimately aimed at shoring up the claims of a monologic ideology, Bakhtin portrays the carnival festivities as part of an unending, fundamentally unfinalizable process. For him there is no possibility of ideational or bodily purity; only the ceaseless back and forth of opposing ideologies. Within this contest Stalinism as a historical epoch emerges not as the final telos but as only one amid a host of possible outcomes. The effect is such that in Bakhtinian carnival Ideology sheds its monolithic, statuary quality, just as the *body* politic relinquishes its claim to classical perfection and purity. In this regard, Bakhtin's carnival body is not unlike that described by the first author of this study, Andrei Platonov. For Platonov—like Bakhtin—never ceases to emphasize the excessive, "excremental" aspect of the human body, precisely that which has been ejected in order to produce the illusion of statuary perfection.

The totalizing reach of Stalinist culture, its desire to become what Groys has termed a *Gesamtkunstwerk*, produces a situation in which (collectivist) ideology intrudes into the most private places of human psychophysiology. Indeed, even the public toilets of the many Parks of Culture and Rest became—as Zolotonosov notes—an essential part of a larger architecture of surveillance. The Soviet human being, writes the critic, "is not to be left unsupervised, and his collectivism must always be trained."[33] More to the point, this totalizing quality signalled an unprecedented heightening of the Stalinist subject's desire to become ideologically coherent and continent. Following Slavoj Žižek, one might say that all Stalinist subjects—even Stalin himself[34]—were implicated in a process of reforging, the point of which was to raise the empirical, flesh-and-blood individual up to a higher order of symbolic and social identification. This unprecedented incursion of official ideology into the private lives of Soviet citizens is perhaps best summed up in a famous statement made by Stalin during the first All-Union Conference of the Workers of Socialist Industry given on February 4, 1931. Here the leader remarks that "it is time to put an end to the putrid policy of not meddling in production. . . . It is time to adopt a new policy appropriate for the current period: a policy of meddling in everything."[35] What emerges from this is a situation in which the dividing line between public ideology and private life is significantly blurred. The bulk of recent scholarship confirms this, pointing toward a broad attempt on the part of the Stalinist regime to create the impression of an unprecedented rapprochement between individual and state. Thus for many a Stalinist subject the fantasy of ideological incorporation would play itself out at the most minute levels of self-constitution. The case of the Stalinist hack writer Aleksandr Afinogenov provides an eloquent case in point. As Jochen Hellbeck notes, during the early 1930s Afinogenov had established himself as one of the most successful Soviet playwrights.[36] In fact, he was so successful that he regularly corresponded with Stalin, whom he considered to be his literary mentor. During the latter half of the decade, however, Afinogenov's plays came under increasing fire from the critical establishment and the playwright was accused of reflecting Soviet society through a "distorted mirror."[37] The year 1937 brought with it the promulgation of the new Stalinist constitution, which claimed to lay the foundation of a still purer form of socialist society, as well as a wave of political purges intended to clean out the remaining elements of social corruption. This sparked a kind of parallel, "internal" purge on the part of

Afinogenov, whose diary entries from the year 1937 become a potent means of "inner purification."[38] Summing up the complex relationship between political purge and individual self-purification, Hellbeck writes: "The Stalinist purges emerge in this light not as an expression of absolute estrangement between state and society but as an intense synergetic link between individuals and the state, in which the respective agendas of social purification and individual work on the self culminated and fused."[39]

A similar case concerns the Soviet endocrinologist Aleksei Zamkov, whose work with a substance called "gravidan" (made from the urine of pregnant women) aroused considerable interest throughout the 1930s. The only difference is that Zamkov's project took the same metaphor to its logical conclusion, literally endeavoring to create a new species of the Stalinist body. Working at a factory clinic in Voronezh, Zamkov injected workers who had complained about fatigue and poor health with the drug and achieved apparently "miraculous" results.[40] Indeed, Zamkov's success not only in restoring the workers' energy levels, but also in enabling them to work longer and more efficiently captured the interest of the Kremlin leaders themselves.[41] Whatever the actual effects of the drug, it is clear that its seemingly miraculous qualities were intimately intertwined with the ideology of Stalinist culture itself. Thus, for instance, the ubiquitous rhetoric of purging translates readily into a miracle drug that purifies the body of its "internal corruption"—for, as Eric Naiman notes, the Stalinist subject was inclined to see his or her ailment not as the product of a broader political and social pathology but in terms of a strictly internal, corporeal dysfunction.[42] In this regard, the comments of one of Zamkov's correspondents (a certain Olga Sotnik) are quite instructive.[43] Sotnik tells the story of a woman who willfully transforms her womb into "something like Dneprostroi." What on the surface might appear to be a rather outré comparison (the womb with Dneprostroi!) is, in fact, quite commonplace and merely recapitulates Stalinism's obsession with reversing the course of nature.[44] Likewise, in his *Youth Restored* Mikhail Zoshchenko tells the story of an aging professor who miraculously transforms his ailing body into that of a much younger man, and like Sotnik Volosatov accomplishes his aim by rechanneling the body's natural "inertia." More importantly, in both cases the reforging of old into new is portrayed as akin to the fairy-tale events that were a permanent fixture of Stalinist mythology. Thus Sotnik writes: "We live in a time, when the fairy-tale is being transformed into life, dreams into reality."[45] And in the commentary section of *Youth Restored* Zoshchenko points out that Volosatov's recovery is linked to the much larger rejuvenation of Soviet humanity currently taking place under Stalin: "In this case, it is extremely interesting to note that not only individual people but even an entire people . . . can be shifted to a different speed, even if it is a rather unusual one."[46] Similarly, in his 1939 novel entitled *The Goalkeeper of the Republic*, the children's author Lev Kassil' preaches the rechanneling of its Jewish and Russian protagonists' "watery" (i.e., chaotic) nature as central to the Stalinist project of producing the New Man. The odd man out—as far as the present study is concerned—is surely Andrei Platonov, whose novel *Happy Moscow* (1933–1936) casts a dark shadow of doubt on Stalinism's optimistic plans for reforging (human) nature. Here the "different speed" that Zoshchenko invokes as a metaphor for Stalinism's aspiration to set forward the evolutionary calendar is offset by a lingering sense of nature as eternal and, indeed, unchanging. Thus a relatively minor character in the novel—a designer of high-speed aircraft and utopian dreamer named Muldbauer—reflects: "Better to finish with the bothersome fun of living on Earth. Let old Stalin direct the speed and thrust of human history beyond the point of the Earth's gravity" (*Happy Moscow*, 22). Meanwhile, the protagonist closest to the author himself (i.e., the engineer Sartorius) later muses that "what is destined for liquidation can sometimes prove to be not only the most durable of all, but even doomed to eternal existence."[47]

To be sure, what all the authors who appear in this book have in common is precisely their *un*common fascination with the body and its place in realizing the claims of Stalinist ideology. Yet it is equally clear that their approach frequently appears inconsistent—as if governed by competing or even incompatible metaphors. To a large extent, this mirrors the ideologically hybrid character of Stalinist culture itself. As most scholars seem to agree, the period of the Stalinist '30s was wedged squarely between the experimentation and upheaval of the previous decade and a pressing need to normalize the character of economic and social life throughout the Soviet Union. Yet "normalization" brought with it more than a simple shift from the iconoclastic free-for-all of the '20s to the rehabilitation of hierarchy and patriarchy characteristic of the Stalinist '30s. To be sure, the advent of high Stalinism during the '30s signaled a new preoccupation with borders, boundaries, and norms of every kind.[48] At the same time, Stalinist culture does not simply abandon the previous era's orientation toward the temporally distant utopia of the future. Rather it proclaims itself the historical *telos* toward which all of human history is inexorably moving.[49] This conflation of contradictory perspectives produces a strange bifurcation of Stalinism's temporal outlook.[50] On the one hand, the loudly trumpeted image of "socialism achieved" portrays the present as a limpid mirror of the soon-to-be-realized utopian future. On the other, the culture's revolutionary core hesitates to declare history's transformative project at an end.[51] The future is now, as the saying goes, yet in its ambivalent relationship to the present the latter still manages to preserve its status as the ideal against which reality is measured and judged.

Stalinist culture's modal schizophrenia runs like a red thread through the ideology and rhetoric of the period. Thus rather than privilege exclusively that which was temporally, spatially, or ontologically marginal (as the previous era had done so aggressively), Stalinism emphasizes its unique status as a mediator between various extremes (e.g., center and periphery, past and present, or high and low).[52] By contrast, the utopian scenarios of the '20s avant-garde were—as Boris Groys notes—invariably inclined to locate the ideal society in a single space, either on the surface of the earth or in the heavens. For obvious reasons, the latter seems to have been preferable. Thus El Lissitzky dreamed of apartment buildings with enormous leg-like struts hovering high above the streets of Moscow.[53] Such scenarios are perhaps best described as "homotopias," since they automatically exclude the possibility of conceptual discord. In other words, in spatial, temporal, and even gender terms, the '20s utopia is fundamentally removed from the profane chronotope of the present. Thus the Chevengur common in Platonov's novel of the same name is both all-male and spatially entirely apart. By the 1930s this model had already been discredited, however. In place of the homotopia of the '20s, the Stalinist '30s gave birth to what might be called a revolutionary "heterotopia"—one that intentionally blurs the distinction(s) between the ideal society of the future and its less-than-ideal incarnation in the present. In an analogous vein, in his book *Stalin as Writer* Mikhail Vaiskopf speaks of the fundamentally mixed or eclectic character of Stalinist ideology. Stalin's genius, according to the critic, lay in his ability to fuse organic, vitalist metaphors (which reflected the agrarian roots of the country's largely rural population) with metaphors that would appeal to the technophilia of its urban citizenry. Indeed, the rhetoric of both Stalin and of Stalinism as a cultural phenomenon bears this out, modulating freely between images taken from the vegetable and industrial realms.[54] The writers who constitute the subject of the present study were, of course, not immune to Stalinism's "miscegenation" of metaphors. For instance, much of Andrei Platonov's writing of the '30s seems to have been animated by a somewhat quixotic desire to reconcile the antithetical realms of utopian technology and everyday life. Thus in his 1936 short story "Fro," the author endows his heroine of the same name with an unusual ability to mediate between the "feminine" realm of nature and the "male" world of technology and industry. One could make a similar case for Mikhail Zoshchenko, whose later works such as *Youth Restored* and *The Sky-Blue Book* draw equally on the enlightenment and voluntarist strains within Stalinist ideology and myth. Thus it is not only the "iron formulas of science" that guarantee the Stalinist subject's ability to reform her- or himself, but also the mysterious, hidden powers of the mind. Finally, in the rhetoric that accompanied the construction of the Moscow metro, praise of Bolshevik technology goes hand in hand with its denigration in favor of such "unscientific qualities as daring, will-power, spirit, etc."

As the comments above seek to demonstrate, the authors and narratives presented here reflect a wide spectrum of acceptance and resistance to Stalinism's *Gesamtkunstwerk*. What all share in common, beyond their preoccupation with the body and its role in articulating a new, collectivist subjectivity, is their connection to the ideology and mythology of the Stalinist '30s. The first of these is Andrei Platonov, who provides the subject matter for the first chapter. Born into a poor working-class family, Platonov was an enthusiastic supporter of the Bolshevik cause from the outset.[55] The writer's close ties to revolutionary ideology are abundantly clear from both his essays and fiction of the early 1920s. Whether in the *Proletkul't* verse of A. Gastev or in the later NEP-era discussions surrounding sex, early Soviet ideology was inclined to see the (implicitly male) body social as embroiled in a life-or-death struggle with a sexualized Other, whether feminine nature, an ideologically contagious bourgeoisie, or Woman herself.[56] And with few exceptions, Platonov's writing of the early '20s reprises this misogynist, antinaturalist stance, painting the road to utopia as a contest between male consciousness and feminine sexuality.[57] Still, what allows Platonov to stand out even in such relatively immature works is his striking ambivalence. For even in his ideologically most hard-boiled essays, the writer preserves a core of uncertainty that prefigures the startling revision(s) of these same ideas that will occur in his later fiction. As Eliot Borenstein notes, the rigid oppositions that form the core of Platonov's essays have an unusual ability to "reverse polarities." "The natural suddenly turns into the mechanical, . . . and even men are, on occasion, transformed into women."[58] It is precisely this ability of the writer's cherished ideas to reverse polarity, such that men are "transformed into women," that—I would argue—provides a convenient conceptual bridge between the writer's early work of the '20s and his fiction of the 1930s.

If Platonov's writing of the early '20s views sexuality and the body as twin evils to be banished from the proletariat's "kingdom of consciousness,"[59] his works from the latter half of the decade serve to complicate the picture. The short work "Antisexus" (1926) provides a clear case in point. Here the author takes the postrevolutionary era's obsession with rechanneling eros to its logical and, indeed, grotesque conclusion.[60] All too often the ideological and intellectual establishment had equated sexuality and biology with "flawed" female physiology. Platonov, who himself had been complicit in this, now parodies the notion. Thus in the story the sex act is neatly replaced by an electromagnetic device meant to regulate the "chaotic" flow of desire. Reflecting the predominance of the biomechanical ideal throughout the early '20s, the (female) body is replaced with a more perfect, scientifically ordered mechanism.[61] This only slightly veiled allusion to a kind of glorified "masturbation machine" reflects what has been described as the ideological core of the avant-garde project. As Igor' Smirnov remarks, the world of the Russian avant-garde was inclined to exaggerate its own autonomy in both the temporal and spatial senses.[62] In essence, its world was one entirely bereft of the Other. Consider, for instance, Khlebnikov's characterization of the future world language as *samovityi* ("autoreferential"), the *auto*biographies of such futurists as Osip Brik and Vladimir Mayakovsky, and, last but not least, the parodied *auto*erotic ideal in Platonov's "Antisexus." Finally, the all-male utopias, which Platonov embodied more dramatically than any author of his time,[63] are nothing if not an extension of this same ideal. Meanwhile, it is precisely in such works as "Antisexus" and in most of his writing of the late '20s that Platonov debunks the "auto-erotic" utopianism of the avant-garde and of early postrevolutionary ideology. Moreover, in a dramatic volte-face the female body that had appeared so problematic and thus been marginalized throughout Platonov's early work is rehabilitated in his writing of the '30s. How are we to understand this sudden about-face on the writer's part? Borenstein mentions Platonov's disenchantment with NEP, his withdrawal from the Communist Party, and finally, the practical reality of having to adjust to family life.[64]

To be sure, these factors played a significant role in Platonov's change of heart, yet the larger story of the author's retreat from utopia is more complicated still. It concerns not only the author's personal evolution away from long-held beliefs, but his ambivalent relationship to Stalinist ideology. This relationship, as the first chapter demonstrates, was one of simultaneous acceptance and rejection. The acceptance is hardly surprising, given the regime's active promotion of the present as a kind of utopia found. What's more, the Stalinist revolution of the early '30s adopted as "part of the 'official' Soviet culture" the very utopian ideals that Platonov himself had espoused in the early '20s.[65] Yet ultimately this shift proved to be a disastrous one for the writer, since the profound ambivalence of his mature writing could now be read only as an affront to the very utopia whose beginnings had already been firmly put in place. Not surprisingly, it is precisely during this period that Platonov ran afoul of the literary establishment. His publication in 1931 of a satirical piece entitled "For Future Use: A Poor Peasant's Chronicle" earned him vicious condemnation at the hands of Fadeev, condemning him to virtual silence until 1934.[66] Still, the temptation to embrace unambiguously the ideals of his youth remained. In this regard, Platonov is perhaps no different than such prominent contemporaries as Zoshchenko, Pasternak, or Akhmatova. For these authors and poets—as for Platonov himself—the desire to be included in Stalinism's quest for the fairy-tale-come-true could neither be totally resisted nor entirely embraced.[67] Thus Platonov's embrace of the female body, of sexuality, and of family appears to echo the widespread revalorization of private life undertaken by Stalinism itself. For the culture at large this meant, among other ideas, a new tolerance and even encouragement of luxury items and pleasures that had once been viewed with suspicion as signs of "bourgeois abundance and well-being."[68] At the same time, the image of the female body (particularly in its connection to fertility and child-bearing) that had been marginalized, indeed even demonized during the previous decade, once again takes up a central place in the cultural imagination.[69] There is no better illustration of this than the famous 1930s statue by Vera Mukhina, which was created to symbolize the new Stalinist "union of the worker and the peasant."[70]

Not coincidentally Platonov's fiction of the '30s and '40s elevates the image of woman, particularly in her maternal role, to a place of particular distinction.[71] Yet we would be remiss to view this *merely* as a gesture of acquiescence on Platonov's part, just as it would be shortsighted to simply ascribe this sea change to the author's growing conservatism.[72] Indeed, the writer's preference for female or strangely transgendered protagonists can easily be read as a challenge to the most important aspects of the Stalinist worldview. Despite its widely touted claim of being the synthesizer of all opposites (and thus embodying the very essence of dialogue),[73] Stalinism as worldview was rigidly monologic.[74] This is particularly true of its relationship to biology, where, according to Igor' Smirnov, the natural invariably plays the part of a hostile (implicitly feminine) Other to be purged, transcended, or redeemed by male technology and reason.[75] Yet as chapter 1 demonstrates, in such works as *Dzhan* or *Happy Moscow*, Platonov dismantles the Socialist Realist cliché of a femininely passive nature waiting to redeemed by ideology, even as it retreats from the Stalinist ideal of a totally transfigured body politic. Indeed, the author's works of the '30s stress not so much the utopian conquest of nature and the natural as the necessity of coexisting with it.

The image of Woman has a special part to play in this. For in *Dzhan*, *Happy Moscow*, and elsewhere, Platonov depicts the female body as a means of reconciling the utopian desire for transcendence with the mundane exigencies of the everyday. More importantly, for the mature Platonov it is precisely woman who embodies the peculiar coupling of raw physicality and spiritual transcendence that constitutes the central paradox of the human condition. An ideal embodiment of Bakhtinian dialogue, she is both filth *and* cleanliness, high *and* low, self *and* other. By the same token, in the novella *Dzhan* Platonov suggests that the male hero's quixotic search for a permanent refuge from the ravages of the physical world ultimately leads only to disaster. Far more preferable is the practical ("mixed") strategy of a young nomad woman who is forced to make *every place* her home, thus eliminating the distinction between cosmos and chaos—sacred and profane: "She probably had to consider every place her house and immediately become accustomed to it; otherwise, if she put off her need and care until the moment when she would have her own home, she would have become a pauper, impoverished from negligence and would have perished from the filth of her body."[76] More dramatically still, in *Happy Moscow* the heroine Moscow Chestnova comes to symbolize the paradoxical, indeed even mystical cohabitation of filth/excrement/disease and so on and spirituality within the human body. The result can be described only as a kind of immanent transcendence—an immortality *in* and *of* the body. Consider the following episode in the novel where Chestnova is seriously wounded while working to build the new Moscow metro. Emphasizing the same coexistence of filth and transcendence mentioned above, Platonov's narrator remarks that despite the abundant filth that had burrowed into her fresh wound, the "surrounding intact body looked gentle and tanned, and the curves of late innocence were so fresh and full that this worker surely deserved immortality."[77] Not merely a polemic with the stultifyingly monologic worldview of Stalinism, such works as *Dzhan* or *Happy Moscow* strive ultimately to dismantle the very antagonism of matter and spirit that underpins much of Western thought. By the same token, these and other related works must be seen not only as an argument against the "utopia found" of Stalinism, but as a broader, more ambitious attempt to redefine the very character of utopia, turning "no-place" into every place.

Chapter 2 deals with one of Platonov's most prominent contemporaries and a writer who has often been compared to him—Mikhail Zoshchenko. The grounds for comparison are significant indeed. Both authors are best known for having written using the idiom and, to some extent, ideology of their semi-literate heroes. Both ran afoul of the literary establishment for their satirical, insufficiently tendentious portrayals of Soviet reality, and both shared a deep spiritual link to Gogol. And the list goes on.[78] Yet more important than the striking similarity of their early careers are the differences that mark the artistic and philosophical outlook of both writers during the Stalinist '30s. If in his *Happy Moscow* Platonov portrays the failure of the Stalinist *Gesamtkunswerk*, Zoshchenko's writing of the same period arrives at nearly the opposite conclusion. Thus in June of 1933, while Platonov was working on the first chapters of *Happy Moscow*, Zoshchenko's *Youth Restored* began to appear in serial form in the journal *Zvezda*. The two works are such polar opposites that one can hardly avoid the impression that one represents a response to the other. Certainly, Platonov could not have overlooked the noisy public discussion of *Youth Restored* that accompanied its publication—a discussion that attracted

numerous writers, scholars, physiologists, and even the likes of Gorky himself.[79] Moreover, one can imagine that the author of *Happy Moscow* was that
much more attentive to the fate of Zoshchenko's book given that it embodied
many of the ideas that he himself had professed (but since dramatically re-
vised) in his early essays and fiction.[80]

Most important—for Zoshchenko at least—was the idea of engineering a
new, scientific body to replace the flawed creation of nature. Whereas the persona of Platonov's essays of the early '20s looks forward to a distant future
time in which consciousness will fully dominate the lower bodily functions,
the Zoshchenko of *Youth Restored*, *The Sky-Blue Book*, and *Before Sunrise*
endeavors to provide his readers with a blueprint for an ideologically reengineered body in the Stalinist *present*. This endeavor mirrors Zoshchenko's
private obsessions, as well as the passions of the broader public arena. As numerous scholars and critics have noted, from the beginning of his career as a
writer Zoshchenko was unusually preoccupied with matters of health (both
physical and psychological), which in turn reflects the author's long battle
with chronic depression.[81] And in this regard, it is probably no accident that
many of Zoshchenko's works from both the '20s and '30s project an ambivalent interest in both medicine and doctors.[82] Still, the author's career-long interest in the healing arts became particularly acute during the 1930s. Surely
this is no coincidence. For it was during this very period that Zamkov was
supposedly able (using the "miracle drug" gravidan) not only to raise the general "tone" of the human organism,[83] but even to produce a new species of socialist superworker. Likewise, both the Stakhanovite movement that rose to
prominence in the middle of the decade as well as the grandiose experiments
in "reeducating" supposed criminal elements at the Baltic-White Sea Canal
construction were directed at producing the so-called New Man.[84]
Zoshchenko himself was more than a casual participant in the process, becoming a member of a writers' brigade organized by Gorky to commemorate
the achievements of the Baltic-White Sea Canal construction project. The result of his work was a biographical piece entitled "Story of a Reforging,"
which chronicled the putative rehabilitation (by means of forced labor) of a
professional swindler and thief named Abraham Rottenburg.[85] In addition to
being published in the Belomor volume itself, the piece also appeared in September of 1933 in *Literary Leningrad* under the title "Youth Restored"—only
half a year before the longer work of the same title would begin to be published in serial form in *Zvezda*. Thus the author's personal quest for self-healing and the larger public pursuit of a purified body politic emerge as two sides
of the same coin.

Zoshchenko scholars have traditionally divided the author's career into two
distinct periods: the comic writing of the '20s and the more serious works of

the '30s.[86] Recent criticism has added an important corrective to this idea, characterizing the writer's entire oeuvre as the literary projection of a single worldview. This worldview was—according to Alexander Zholkovsky—shaped in large measure by Zoshchenko's multiple fears, phobias, and obsessions, as well as by the writer's quixotic quest to find stability and order in what seemed to be a fundamentally unsettled cosmos. While Zholkovsky performs the monumental task of tracing these issues through the entire corpus of Zoshchenko's work, his approach does little to address the intersection of Zoshchenko's personal mythology with its ideological environment. Chapter 2 seeks to correct (at least partially) this omission by examining the manner in which Zoshchenko's works of the '30s and '40s reflect not only the architectonics of the writer's internal "spiritual city," but also the ideological architecture of Stalinism, which encompassed and informed it. It seeks to articulate, in other words, how Zoshchenko's attempts at rationalizing his own psycho-physiology are intimately intertwined with the broader culture's promotion of a purified, ideologically regenerated body politic.

One of the primary myths of Stalinist civilization concerns the broadly orchestrated "struggle with nature,"[87] and even more specifically the rejection of humankind's connection to biology.[88] While the literary doctrine of Socialist Realism mandated that the course of rivers be reversed and even the flow of time itself accelerated, the culture's approach to anatomy proved to be no less radical. An eloquent example of this is the remarkable frequency of physical mutilations in Stalinist literature,[89] most of which serve to mark the hero's passage from the profane world of primordial nature into the ontologically higher realm of civilization and technology. In Zoshchenko's writing of the '30s, as well, there is an abundance of woundings (both real and symbolic) in which the author's various alter egos part with this or that body part as a prelude to achieving emotional stability. Thus in the commentary section of *Youth Restored* the author—himself afflicted with depression and melancholia—visits a doctor who was cured of his neurasthenia after losing the use of his legs following in an accident. While Zoshchenko dismisses this type of "cure" as exacting too high a price, it nevertheless remains clear that such "amputations" are not unlike the cures that Zoshchenko himself proposes in such works as *Youth Restored* or *Before Sunrise*.[90] What would appear to be the writer's ambivalent attraction to "castration" must be understood not merely as the product of Zoshchenko's individual psyche, but of a larger, collective pathology that played itself out in the bodies of countless Stalinist subjects. Meanwhile, the only cure for this social pathology was, as Eric Naiman points out, one that brought about the partial death of the subject her- or himself. Thus Zamkov's miraculous elixir was effective precisely because it allowed people to forget (in essence, to *amputate*) those parts of their psyche that had been traumatized by Stalinism's repressions. The tragedy of Zamkov's work lay in the fact that for his patients "murder and healing were not only not incompatible but often led to the same result."[91] A similar case could be made for Zoshchenko's strategies of autotherapy during the '30s and '40s. For these, too, were often enough predicated on the annihilation of the very subject they were meant to cure—what Zholkovsky aptly terms Zoschenko's method of "death therapy."[92]

Without a doubt the most ambitious of Zoshchenko's attempts at self-healing is to be found in the lengthy autobiographical work *Before Sunrise* (1943). It is here that the author undertakes not merely to investigate but to exorcise the fears and phobias that had pursued him throughout his life. Attempting to fuse Freudian psychoanalysis with Pavlov's theory of conditioned response, Zoshchenko pursues a cure that is nothing if not a microcosm of the Stalinist subject's dilemma vis-à-vis the project of self-reform. For if Afinogenov and other Stalin-era subjects had used their diaries as laboratories for the creation of the Stalinist soul—endeavoring to raise their profane personal selves to the level of socialism's sacred narrative—Zoshchenko, too, uses his private memories (Freud) only to bolster Stalinism's call for totalizing self-mastery and control (Pavlov). Thus the first half of the work is taken up with stories of the writer's childhood, adolescence, and adulthood, told almost as if he were lying on the analyst's couch. By contrast, the second half of *Before Sunrise* undertakes to interpret these story-vignettes through the prism of Stalinist ideology. And by this point Zoshchenko's highly selective account of how he vanquished his melancholy using the tools of reason and self-control all but replaces the decadent Freud with a more robust, politically correct Pavlov. One need hardly stress that these tools (i.e., reason and self-control) were the same implements by means of which the vast majority of Stalinist subjects were enjoined to "rationalize" their disorderly lives.[93] Applying the Stalinist myth of Reason and Civilization overcoming a benighted Nature to his own biography, Zoshchenko finally pronounces himself cured: "I emerged the victor. I became different after the battle. . . . There arose a new life, absolutely unlike the one that had existed before. Sometimes my foe attempted to take back his positions. Still my reason controlled all his actions and these attempts ceased."[94] To be sure, one might well come away from *Before Sunrise* with the impression that Zoshchenko had indeed managed to cure himself, especially if we consider the triumphant tenor of the writer's paean to Reason in the second half of the work. Yet this victory is ultimately a Phyrric one. For the writer is healed only at the cost of ignoring much of what is contained in the stories that constitute the text of his life. In other words, Zoshchenko's miraculous cure in *Before Sunrise* entails nothing less than the death of subject himself—which is to say, his passage from the troublesome world of desire(s) to the sublime realm of Ideology.

If the second chapter concerns the configuration of the individual author's body as a microcosm of the state, chapter 3 examines rather the processes whereby the Stalinist collective body is created and maintained. The focus is Lev Kassil''s 1939 novel for adolescents *The Goalkeeper of the Republic*. A paean to soccer, male friendship, and life within Stalinism's extended family, Kassil''s portrayal of happy collectivism in the *Goalkeeper of the Republic* stands in marked contrast to the anguished reflections on the dilemma of the intellectual outsider vis-à-vis the collective of such authors as Isaac Babel or Yurii Olesha. In Babel's *Red Cavalry*, for instance, the narrator Lyutov's status as an intellectual and a Jew remains fundamentally incompatible with his desire to merge with the (Russian) Cossack collective. Moreover, the core ambivalence of the text precludes any possibility of its achieving resolution or closure, which is borne out by the cycle's "dual ending," where the narrator is at once a Jew ("The Rebbe's Son") and a would-be Cossack ("Argamak").[95] Likewise, the final lines of "The Rebbe's Son" demonstrate that the fantasy of remaking oneself as part of the revolutionary collective is incompatible with the more enduring reality of physiology: "And I, who could hardly contain the storms of my imagination in an ancient body, I accepted the last breath of my brother," Lyutov says of the Jewish revolutionary Ilya Bratslavsky.[96] Yet the *Goalkeeper of the Republic*, published more than a decade after Babel's cycle appeared in 1923–1925, proves precisely the opposite. If Lyutov's dilemma of nonacceptance results from his "Semitic inheritance," the transformationalist narrative of Stalinist ideology declares the ancient rule of nature and biology at an end. Indeed, the Stalinist body politic is one in which the cultural and even physiological differences that separate Jew from Cossack are triumphantly, *dialectically* resolved. Hence, the culture's promotion of itself as a single, transbiological family in which racial and other differences have simply withered away. In this regard one need only recall Grigory Alexandrov's immensely popular 1935 musical *Circus*, with its vision of Soviet society as a racially tolerant, multiethnic family that includes Russians, Ukrainians, Jews, Georgians, and even a small black child from America! Kassil', who himself was Jewish and one of whose protagonists in the novel is a Jew, reproduces this pathos.

Embodying the consciousness-versus-spontaneity dialectic that was one of the founding myths of Stalinist culture, according to Katerina Clark,[97] Kassil''s *Goalkeeper of the Republic* describes the curious friendship of two diametrically opposed protagonists: a *bogatyr'*-like Russian named Kandidov and an intellectual Jew named Karasik. The dialectic presupposes—as Clark and others have shown—the rechanneling of the spontaneous hero's excess energy and enthusiasm into socially useful forms under the tutelage of a politically and ideologically conscious mentor figure. Meanwhile, it is easy to recognize in Clark's conceptual paradigm a dynamic that runs throughout the culture of the Stalinist '30s. Stalinism, as I have already mentioned, modulates freely between organic and mechanistic metaphors. Its enthusiasm for "feminine" images of fertility, fecundity, and the like is matched only by its obsession with "male" rationality and (self)-control.[98] Thus in Grigory Alexandrov's 1938 musical *Volga-Volga* the grassroots enthusiasm of a group of amateur musicians from the Volga is coupled with classical precision and form in order to produce the sentimental-patriotic hit "Wide is My Native Land"—a song that quickly became an icon of Stalin's Soviet Union. Kassil''s novel, too, thematizes the spontaneity-versus-consciousness dialectic by combining images of Dionysian excess (Kandidov) and Apollinian restraint (Karasik).[99] Centered around one of the most important locales within the Stalinist *polis*,[100] Kassil''s novel portrays the soccer stadium as an allegory of Stalinist subjectivity. For it is in the stadium that the mythical extremes of chaos and order are merged to produce the Stalinist superbody. In a description that is nothing if not laden with symbolism, Kassil' describes the soccer ball placed at the center of the stadium as bursting with highly compressed air from within, yet tightly bound by leather from without. It is not difficult to recognize in this description the contours of the ideal Stalinist subject. Bound by tight straps of discipline, he or she nonetheless remains overflowing with love for the State—for the chastizing hand of the Father. As Kassil' writes of the spectators who fill the stadium: "The spectator of our stadiums is . . . noisy but disciplined."[101] By depicting the Stalinist body politic as the perfect synthesis of enthusiasm and discipline, Kassil', writing in the late '30s, overcomes the ambivalence about the communal body that Isaac Babel, writing in the '20s, could not. Thus the unresolvable contradictions (Jew versus Cossack, spirit/intellect versus strength, etc.) at the core of the *Red Cavalry* cycle finally achieve closure in the tender camaraderie of two lifelong friends—Kandidov and Karasik.

Chapter 4 looks at what is possibly the most visible and enduring utopian project of the Stalinist era: the Moscow metro. And like the corporeal narratives of such individual authors as Zoshchenko or Kassil', the collectively authored narrative of the Moscow metro is intimately bound up with questions of physiology, body, and body politic. An engineering and architectural feat of truly remarkable proportions, the Moscow metro was no less remarkable in its capacity as one of the foremost ideological and rhetorical projects of the Stalinist '30s.[102] Conceived as part of the grandiose reconstruction of Moscow undertaken by Stalin, Kaganovich, and others during the early '30s,[103] the Moscow metro stood out among such sister projects as the Moscow-Volga Canal (to which it was most often compared) in terms of its ability to capture the public imagination. Indeed, Stalin's sister-in-law described the newly constructed *metropoliten* as "an underground paradise."[104] This is hardly surprising, for in addition to the unusually lavish architecture that adorned every station, the metro was loudly trumpeted in both print and other media as a harbinger of the socialist world to come.[105] As such, its palatial architecture was significant primarily as a metaphor for the new architecture of human relations that would soon materialize under Stalin. Thus the newspaper *Workers' Moscow* writes in 1935: "Here we see a new order, and new behavioral norms are crystallizing, norms free of the crude habits that are still far from being cast off in our lives above ground."[106]

As Boris Groys remarks, the Moscow metro was the utopian project par excellence, on a par with the construction of St. Petersburg at the beginning of the eighteenth century. The fact that the metro was built deep under ground—in some locations so deep that it was initially thought to be technically unfeasible—makes it akin to the founding of St. Petersburg on a swamp.[107] In both instances, the quality of *u-topia* (i.e., of a place radically opposed to mundane topography of the world above ground) points up the utopian quality of both the Petrine and the Stalinist historical narratives.[108] The present chapter takes this idea a step further, situating the contemporary "metro narrative" within Stalinism's portrayal of utopia building as a mythological contest between Bolshevik technology and daring, on the one hand, and recalcitrant nature, on the other. In this sense, the struggle to reconstruct the underground mirrors the broader attempt to restructure human nature undertaken at the same time. Meanwhile, the implications of this "reconstruction" were hardly lost on the metro's contemporaries, such as Andrei Platonov or Mikhail Bulgakov.[109] Like the battle of chaos and culture described in Pushkin's "Bronze Horseman" (1833), the struggle to build the Moscow metro was fought against a heavily mythologized foe: the *watery* soil of the Moscow underground. As such, the Kaganovich metro (as it was then called) aspires to reclaim the "feminine" underground ("Moist Mother Earth") in the name of "masculine" technology. In this sense, one might even say that metro project requires the death of the feminine.[110] The following excerpt taken from a contemporary account makes the point admirably. In it the earth is shown as dressed in watertight clothing, the function of which is to protect the fledgling underground from its (the earth's) treacherous seepage: "We don't need a sick metropoliten. And that's why we're dressing our underground Moscow ["Moscow" is feminine in Russian] in sturdy, good, stable clothing."[111] By contrast, the ideal of the reclaimed underground projects stability and statuary perfection. Indeed, the Revolution Square station provides a model of the Stalinist ideal of a "sculpted" body politic. Its statues represent a broad spectrum of Soviet humankind forever frozen in a series of ideal poses and postures. In this gallery of Stalinist types, "the female swimmer only swims, the worker only works, the border guard only guards, etc."[112] In this manner, the Moscow metro provides a perfect metaphor for those Stalinist subjects (the later Zoshchenko comes to mind) who aspired to make their bodies into something resembling the famous Manizer statues that adorned Revolution Square station. For in this "underground paradise," which was free of the ideological imperfection and incontinence that still plagued the world above, the Word had indeed become flesh.

NOTES

1. *Intimacy and Terror: Soviet Diaries of the 1930s*, ed. Véronique Garros, Natalia Korenevskaya, and Thomas Lahusen, tr. Carol A. Flath (New York: The New Press, 1995).

2. Katerina Clark, *The Soviet Novel: History as Ritual* (Chicago: University of Chicago Press, 1985), 100.

3. Quoted in Dietmar Neutatz, *Die Moskauer Metro: von den ersten Plänen bis zur Grossbaustelle des Stalinismus*, bd. 33 (Köln: Böhlau Verlag, 2001), 553.

4. Omry Ronen, "Detskaia literatura i sotsialisticheskii realizm," in *Sotsrealisticheskii kanon*, ed. Hans Günther and Evgenii Dobrenko (Sankt-Peterburg: "Akademicheskii proekt," 2000), 972.

5. Dennis Patrick Slattery, *The Wounded Body: Remembering the Markings of Flesh* (Albany: State University of New York, 2000), 9.

6. David Hillman and Carla Mazzio, "Individual Parts," introduction to *The Body in Parts: Fantasies of Corporeality in Early Modern Europe* (London: Routledge, 1997), xiii.

7. Ibid.

8. A. Etkind, *Khlyst: Sekty, literatura i revoliutsiia* (Moskva: Novoe literaturnoe obozrenie, 1998), 95.

9. Ibid., 79.

10. Ibid.

11. Ibid., 95.

12. Ibid., 71.

13. Ibid., 23.

14. A. Etkind, *Khlyst*, 71.

15. Eric Naiman, *Sex in Public: The Incarnation of Early Soviet Ideology* (Princeton: Princeton University Press, 1997), 65.

16. Ibid., 122.

17. See Eric Naiman, *Sex in Public*, 37.

18. Eric Naiman, *Sex in Public*, chapter 5 (181–207).

19. Quoted in Eliot Borenstein, *Men without Women: Masculinity & Revolution in Russian Fiction: 1917–1929* (Durham: Duke University Press, 2000), 222.

20. Lars T. Lih, "Melodrama and the Myth of the Soviet Union," in *Imitations of Life: Two Centuries of Melodrama in Russia*, eds. Louise McReynolds and Joan Neuberger (Durham: Duke University Press, 2002), 190.

21. Aleksandr Gol'dshtein, *Rasstavanie s nartsissom: Opyt pominal'noi ritoriki* (Novoe literaturnoe obozrenie, 1997), 185.

22. Ibid., 35.

23. Boris Groys, *Utopiia i obmen* (Moskva: Znak, 1993), 66–67.

24. Sheila Fitzpatrick, *Everyday Stalinism: Ordinary Life in Extraordinary Times: Soviet Russia in the 1930s* (Oxford: Oxford University Press, 1999), 95.

25. Katerina Clark, *Petersburg, Crucible of Cultural Revolution* (Cambridge: Harvard University Press, 1995), 132–33.

26. Mikhail Zolotonosov, *Slovo i telo: Seksual'nye aspekty, universalii, interpretatsii russkogo kul'turnogo teksta XIX-XX vekov* (Moskva: "Ladomir," 1999), 253.

27. Ibid.

28. Katerina Clark, *The Soviet Novel*, 126.

29. Lars T. Lih, "Melodrama and the Myth of the Soviet Union," 200.

30. Boris Groys, *Die Erfindung Rußlands* (München: Carl Hanser Verlag, 1995), 66.

31. Alexandar Mihailovic, *Corporeal Words: Mikhail Bakhtin's Theology of Discourse* (Evanston: Northwestern University Press, 1997), 203.

32. Boris Groys, *Die Erfindung Rußlands*, 66.

33. Mikhail Zolotonosov, *Slovo i telo*, 690.

34. Žižek writes (*The Sublime Object of Ideology* [London: Verso, 1994], 105–10), for instance, that Stalin's name (Russian for "made of steel") refers not to "some steeley, inexorable characteristic of Stalin himself: what is really inexorable and steely are the laws of historical progress, the iron necessity of the disintegration of capitalism and of the passage to socialism in the name of which Stalin, this empirical individual, is acting—the perspective from which he is observing himself and judging his activity. We could say, then, that 'Stalin' is the ideal point from which 'Iosif Vissarionovich,' this empirical individual, this person of flesh and blood, is observing himself so that he appears likeable.'"

35. Quoted in *Andrei Platonov: Vospominaniia sovremennikov: Materialy k biografii*, eds. N. V. Kornienko and E. D. Shubina (Moskva: Sovremennyi pisatel', 1994), 323.

36. Jochen Hellbeck, "Writing the Self in the Time of Terror," in *Self & Story in Russian History* (Ithaca: Cornell University Press, 2000), 71.

37. Ibid., 72.

38. Ibid., 75.

39. Ibid., 75.

40. Eric Naiman, "Diskurs, obrashchennyi v plot': A. Zamkov i voploshchenie sovetskoi sub"ektivnosti," in *Sotsrealisticheskii kanon* (Sankt-Peterburg: Akademicheskii kanon, 2000), 629.

41. Ibid.

42. Ibid., 631.

43. Ibid., 632.

44. Azhaev's novel *Far From Moscow* provides an ideal illustration. As Lahusen notes, in writing his novel Azhaev "reversed the topography, undoubtedly for both strategic and 'dialectical' reasons. If the novel was even to see the light of day, maps had to be blurred to mislead the enemy, and nature had to be reengineered to allow one of the great Stalinist constructions to go *left*" (*How Life Writes the Book:Real Socialism and Socialist Realism* [Ithaca: Cornell University Press, 1997], 21).

45. Ibid.

46. Mikhail Zoshchenko, *Sobranie sochinenii v 3-kh t-kh*, v. 3 (Leningrad: Khudozhestvennaia literatura, 1987), 113.

47. Ibid., 64.

48. Katerina Clark, *Petersburg*, 281. See also Hans Günther, "Sotsrealizm i utopicheskoe myshlenie," in *Sotsrealisticheskii kanon*, 43. In this regard, Bakhtin's theory of the chronotope, with its tethering of literary genre to the categories of time and space, may well have been prophetic, as Clark suggests. For the Stalinist era itself not only witnessed a renewed preoccupation with problems of genre, but moved unambiguously to embrace time as the central category around which the literary text unfolds. "Literature and plays," writes Clark, "were reordered around sequences of events in time, biographism returned, including biographies of major historical figures" (*Petersburg*, 282).

49. Vladimir Papernyi, *Kul'tura "Dva"* (Ann Arbor: Ardis, 1985), 46.

50. Irina Gutkin, *The Cultural Origins of the Socialist Realist Aesthetic: 1890–1934* (Evanston: Northwestern University Press, 1999), 36.

51. Ibid.

52. Katerina Clark, *Petersburg*, 283.

53. Boris Groys, *Die Erfindung Rußlands*, 158.

54. Mikhail Vaiskopf, *Pisatel' Stalin*, (Moskva: Novoe literaturnoe obozrenie, 2001), 342.

55. Thomas Seifrid, *Andrei Platonov: Uncertainties of Spirit* (Cambridge: Cambridge University Press, 1993), 4.

56. See Eric Naiman, *Sex in Public*, 69, 128, 198.

57. Eliot Borenstein, *Men Without Women*, 193.

58. Ibid., 194.

59. Mikhail Zolotonosov, *Slovo i telo*, 466–67.

60. As Zolotonosov notes (*Slovo i telo*, 472), Platonov's "Antisexus" serves to parody the entire spectrum of contemporary discourse about sexuality, including the popular misconceptions about the socially harmful effects of onanism, the equally popular notion of rechanneling sexual energy into labor energy, and finally A. V. Nemilov's theory of the "biological tragedy of woman."

61. On a deeper level, however, Platonov's sketch seeks to overturn the entire homotopic or "masturbatory" ideal that constitutes the very core of the avant-garde project. And in this regard one can take serious issue only with Zolotonosov's claim that "Antisexus" represents a surreptitious attempt on the writer's part to promote a kind of masturbatory, autofellatial ideal (Mikhail Zolotonosov, *Slovo i telo*, 458). Platonov, argues Zolotonosov, essentially inhabits the same tradition of equating art and autoerotic activity that stretches from Rousseau's *Confessions* to Barthes's *Pleasure of the Text*. More important still, the social situation of the early Soviet subject is such that self-sufficiency in sex (masturbation) becomes symbolic as the last refuge of personal freedom and creativity (Mikhail Zolotonosov, *Slovo i telo*, 458).

62. Igor' Smirnov, *Psikhodiakhronologika: Russkaia literatura ot romantizma do nashikh dnei* (Moskva: Novoe literaturnoe obozrenie, 1994), 197.

63. Eliot Borenstein, *Men Without Women*, 193.

64. Ibid.

65. Thomas Seifrid, *Andrei Platonov: Uncertainties of Spirit*, 133.

66. Ibid., 134.

67. A. Zholkovskii, *Mikhail Zoshchenko: Poetika nedoveriia* (Moskva: "Iazyki russkoi kul'tury," 1999), 310. See also Alexander Zholkovsky, "The Obverse of Stalinism," in *Self and Story in Russian History*, eds. Laura Engelsteiner and Stephanie Sandler (Ithaca: Cornell University Press, 2000), 62.

68. Sheila Fitzpatrick, *Everyday Stalinism*, 91.

69. Mikhail Zolotonosov, *Slovo i telo*, 605–7.

70. Irina Gutkin, *The Origins of the Socialist Realist Aesthetic*, 113.

71. Hans Günther, "Liubov' k dal'nemu i liubov' k blizhnemu: Postutopicheskie rasskazy A. Platonova vtoroi poloviny 1930-kh gg.," in *Strana filosofov Andreia Platonova: problemy tvorchestva, vyp. 4, iubileinyi* (Moskva: IMLI RAN, "Nasledie," 2000), 310.

72. N. V. Kornienko, commentaries to Andrei Platonov, *Zapisnye knizhki: Materialy k biografii* (Moskva: IMLI RAN, Nasledie, 2000), 375.

73. Boris Groys, *Die Erfindung Rußlands*, 67.

74. Aage A. Hansen-Löve, "Von der Dominanz zur Hierarchie," *Wiener Slawistischer Almanach*, no. 47 (2001): 22.

75. Igor' Smirnov, "Sotsrealizm: Antropologicheskoe izmerenie," *Novoe literaturnoe obozrenie*, no. 15, (1994): 33.

76. Andrei Platonov, *Schastlivaia Moskva, povesti, rasskazy, lirika* (Moskva: Gud'al Press, 1999), 421.

77. Andrei Platonov, *Happy Moscow*, 99.

78. Zoshchenko's connection to Gogol was a lifelong preoccupation. The case for Platonov is less obvious but nevertheless significant. Indeed, no less an authority than Gorky wrote of Platonov "there is something in your psyche, as I recall it—a similarity to Gogol'" Quoted in L. Anninskii, "Otkrovenie i sokrovenie: Gor'kii i Platonov," *Literaturnoe obozrenie*, no. 9 (1989): 8.

79. N. V. Kornienko, "Zoshchenko i Platonov: Vstrechi v literature," *Literaturnoe obozrenie*, vol. 1, no. 249 (1995): 50.

80. Ibid.

81. See A. Zholkovskii, *Mikhail Zoshchenko: poetika nedoveriia*, 73ff.

82. Ibid., 90ff.

83. Eric Naiman, "Diskurs, obrashchennyi v plot'," 629.

84. Sheila Fitzpatrick, *Everyday Stalinism*, 75.

85. Cynthia A. Ruder, *Making History for Stalin: The Story of the Belomor Canal* (Gainesville: University Press of Florida, 1998), 81.

86. Thus even Linda Hart Scatton, while alluding to the broad continuity between Zoshchenko's work of the '20s and '30s, buttresses her claim only by referring to certain stylistic similarities: "Clearly, Zoshchenko's longer works are no longer funny, but they do exhibit the same tendencies towards staccato, anecdotal arrangement of material and the same uncomplicated sentence structure which characterizes the short stories" (*Mikhail Zoshchenko: Evolution of a Writer* [Cambridge: Cambridge University Press, 1993], 7).

87. Katerina Clark, *The Soviet Novel*, 100.

88. Igor' Smirnov, "Sotsrealizm: Antropologicheskoe izmerenie," 30.

89. Igor' Smirnov, *Psikhodiakhronologika: Psikhoistoriia russkoi literatury ot romantizma do nashikh dnei*, 253.

90. Aleksandr Zholkovskii, *Mikhail Zoshchenko: poetika nedoveriia*, 212.

91. Eric Naiman, "Diskurs, obrashchennyi v plot'," 631.

92. Aleksandr Zholkovskii, *Mikhail Zoshchenko: poetika nedoveriia*, 212.

93. Jochen Hellbeck, "Writing the Self," 74. See also Bernice Rosenthal, "Sotsrealizm i nitssheanstvo," in *Sotsrealisticheskii kanon* (Sankt-Peterburg: Akademicheskii proekt, 2000), 66.

94. Mikhail Zoshchenko, *Sobranie soch.*, v. 3, 689.

95. Eliot Borenstein, *Men Without Women*, 114.

96. Isaak Babel', *Sochineniia*, v. 2 (Moskva: Khudozhestvennaia literatura, 1990), 129.

97. Katerina Clark, *The Soviet Novel*, 124ff.

98. Vladimir Papernyi, *Kul'tura "Dva,"* 144–54.

99. Aleksandr Gol'dshtein's argument that Kassil' was pursuing a synthesis of the Russian demos and Jewish intellect in order to restrain the violence of the powers-that-be misrepresents what is (on Kassil''s part) an entirely unproblematic, ideologically correct position.

100. Aleksandr Gol'dshtein, *Rasstavanie s nartsissom: Opyty pominal'noi retoriki* (Moskva: Novoe literaturnoe obozrenie, 1997), 208.

101. Lev Kassil', *Vratar' respubliki* (Moskva: Sovetskii pisatel', 1939), 175.

102. Mikhail Ryklin, "Metrodiskurs," in *Sotsrealisticheskii kanon*, 714.

103. *Metro: sbornik, posviashchennyi pusku moskovskogo metropolitena*, ed. L. Kovalev (Moskva: "Rabochaia gazeta," 1935), 1.

104. Quoted in Dietmar Neutatz, *Die Moskauer Metro*, 563.

105. Ibid., 565.

106. Quoted in Dietmar Neutatz, *Die Moskauer Metro*, 565.

107. Boris Groys, *Die Erfindung Rußlands*, 157.

108. Ibid.

109. As Natasha Drubek-Meier notes ("Rossiia—pustota v kishkakh mira," *Novoe literaturnoe obozrenie*, no. 9 (1994): 264), the mutilation of the beautiful Moskva Chestnova's body in Platonov's novel *Happy Moscow* can easily be read as a thinly veiled commentary on the destruction wrought by Kaganovich's reconstruction of Moscow, all the more so since one of the characters in the novel—the engineer Bozhko—seems to based on the figure of Kaganovich.

110. Mikhail Zolotonosov, *Slovo i telo*, 633.

111. P. Lopatin, *Pervyi sovetskii metropoliten* (Moskva: Moskovskii rabochii, 1935), 74.

112. Mikhail Zolotnosov, *Slovo i telo*, 611.

Chapter One

Turning Men into Women: Andrei Platonov in the 1930s[1]

Like the early Proletkul't fantasies of collective (male) bodies merged together in orgiastic celebrations of labor, the young Andrei Platonov's vision of the future communist utopia looked forward to the day when the human organism would be purged of its natural imperfections, perhaps the greatest of which was the urge to copulate and procreate. The idealized body of the future would no longer be held hostage by "feminine" sexuality, Platonov speculated. Rather it would be guided by the exclusively male quest for consciousness and truth. Accordingly, the larger body politic would reflect the predominance of an all-male collective, along with the rationalist, technocratic values it exemplified. If women were invoked at all, it was only as a kind of ontological foe—the abject Other—against which the fledging utopia had continually to be defended and secured. Yet almost from its inception Platonov's all-male utopia would be continuously haunted by what it sought most vigorously to repress—"desire and the feminine."[2] By the mid-1920s what had begun as a campaign to uproot the twin evils of sexuality and procreation gave way to the author's parody of his own ideas as demonstrated in such works as "Antisexus" and others. A similar kind of parody—though enacted on a much larger, ontological scale—lies at the core of Platonov's most important works of the late '20s such as *Chevengur* and *The Foundation Pit*. In these masterworks of twentieth-century dystopianism, the relatively localized conflict between sexuality and "truth" of the author's earlier works matures into a series of anguished reflections on the very possibility of realizing the utopian dream.

It has been suggested that utopianism at the most basic level derives from a desire to fuse the transcendent with the everyday—to join together the eternally opposed realms of matter and spirit.[3] Platonov's unique contribution to the genre's undoing lies, in the words of one critic, in creating a "series of

27

ontologically vivid parodies of the genre in which the fusion routinely fails to take place."[4] The perennial standoff between these two realms in the author's work can comfortably be explained in terms of the consciousness-versus-spontaneity dialectic that Katerina Clark has identified as one of the quintessential cultural paradigms of Soviet and, indeed, Russian culture.[5] Sufficiently broad to encompass numerous other binaries such as Slavophiles and Westerners, or the philosophical distinction between subject and object, the most prominent variant of the myth (which coincides with the period of the first five-year plan) concerns the struggle between culture and nature. Reencoded in terms of the gender distinction mentioned earlier (such that nature is identified as feminine matter, while culture is portrayed as masculine endeavor), it is this particular incarnation of the myth that seems most relevant to Platonov.[6]

Unlike the canonical Soviet novel with its projection of the inevitable triumph of culture and technology over nature, Platonov's works of the late '20s chronicle not victory but rather the disastrous consequences of the struggle. Interpreting the myth in ontological rather than political terms, the pathos of both *Chevengur* and *The Foundation Pit* revolves inescapably around the failure of the utopian ideal to materialize—that is, to become reified. Thus the material substrata of existence remain untouched by the animating warmth of spirit, while base matter becomes the void that condemns the ideal to entropy and finally death.[7] In the *Foundation Pit*, this is conveyed by the image of a utopian shelter for the proletariat turned grave, which ultimately devours its single most important inhabitant, a child mascot and representative of the future utopia named Nastia. At the heart of these and similar works we see a nearly irremediable antagonism between spirit and body (or culture and nature), such that base matter and all it encompasses is rejected as hostile to the territory of the self proper. Yet the attempt to redeem or transform matter ultimately ends in disaster—with what one might describe as a catastrophic return of "return of the repressed." In the *Foundation Pit*, for instance, the utopian house for the proletariat remains conspicuously unbuilt, while the resurgent (profane) time of the present—not that of the radiant future!—relentlessly marks the digging of a grave-as-house for communism's youngest inhabitant (i.e., the mascot Nastia).

Platonov's early affinity for the male machine-utopia coupled with his distaste for biology leads Borenstein to speak of a distinct "necrophiliac" orientation in the writer's work of the '20s. His male characters' rejection of sex and nature, their affinity for graves, and preoccupation with machines and other devices that have no analogue in nature seem to recall Erich Fromm's claim that the necrophile loves "not only corpses, but war, destruction, commerce . . . , and machines." And if Platonov's "necrophiliac" heroes appear overly preoccupied with *living* machines, they are no less fascinated by the image of their *dead* mothers. For these "the mother becomes not only the symbol of the earth, home, and life, but also the representation of 'death and chaos' to which all life must eventually return."[8] While much of Platonov's writing of the '20s can thus be viewed in terms of its implicit or explicit "necrophilia," the opposite might well be said of the author's writing beginning in the latter half of the '30s. Drawing once again on Fromm, one can speak of a pronounced *biophiliac* (i.e., the love of women, the organic) tendency in Platonov's later writing. Thus Zakhar Pavlovich's preoccupation (in *Chevengur*) with making "useless things," coupled with his secret desire to to unearth his mother,[9] yields to the urge in such later characters as Nikita Firsov ("The River Potudan'") to make children instead of things—even as he discards his dream of returning to the maternal womb.

The germ of this later shift in Platonov's writing can be traced back to one of the author's earliest and most mysterious essays. Entitled "The Soul of the World" (1920), it stands apart from Platonov's early nonfiction in that the ideas it puts forth are curiously absent from the essays that immediately follow it.[10] To be sure, it echoes the standard gender dichotomy of Platonov's essays, where woman is likened to the physical world awaiting transfiguration via the conscious, truth-seeking aspirations of spiritual man. What stands out is the essay's positive valorization of woman as a *self-transcending* outgrowth of nature. Particularly interesting with regard to the problematics of Platonov's later prose is her ability to blur the boundaries between ontologically incompatible realms, such as the upper and the lower.[11] Like Divine Sophia in Orthodox Christianity, woman's role here is that of a mediator who knits together the extremes of heaven and earth. Accordingly, *she* (rather than *he*) represents for Platonov the locus within which matter and spirit are definitively merged. For it is woman, precisely because of her biological attachment to "flawed" nature, who is most conscious of the fallen state of the world and therefore most at pains to overcome it. As Platonov writes in "The Soul of the World," "Woman distills the ugliness and horror of the earth through her own blood." And much later in his unfinished novel *Happy Moscow* (1933–1936), the writer will likewise portray Woman—in the guise of his heroine-cum-Sophia manqué, Moscow Chestnova—as a kind of ontological paradox, where humankind's innate desire to transcend its "chthonic" origins is reluctantly reconciled with the poor but undeferrable needs of the body.

In her book *The Powers of Horror: An Essay on Abjection*, Julia Kristeva remarks that within the confines of a monotheistic, monologic worldview, in order for the body to participate in the symbolic order it must erase any "trace of its debt to nature: it must be clean and proper."[12] The legal-phallic-linguistic establishment, in other words, arises out of a mythological articulation of the

body. The realm of the "clean and proper"—forever synonymous with paternal law—is set apart from the improper and dirty (i.e., maternal authority).[13]
In stark contrast to this paradigm, Platonov's work of the mid-to-late 1930s
seems to recall rather the archaic symbolic structures of so-called primitive societies. This type of thought, according to Bataille, is characterized by its unusually weak prosecution of the principle of exclusion. One of the many striking similarities between Bataille and Platonov is their keen interest precisely
in those marginal elements that have been excluded (rendered abject) from ho-
mogenous social and ideological structures—which is to say, their waste products.[14] In the case of Platonov it seems clear that this interest reflects a strong
desire on the part of the writer to contest Stalinism's push for extreme social
cohesion, predicated as it was on the violent expulsion of what it had deemed
to be society's "human waste." Yet even more than this, Platonov's champi-
oning of the abject suggests a deeper desire to strike at the exclusionary logic
underpinning the very rhetoric of cohesion (whether sociological, philosophical, or linguistic).[15]

Dirt, filth, and excrement, by dissolving the boundaries between discrete
realms, represent the greatest obstacle to the purist fantasy of social and linguistic cohesion. As Paul Hegarty notes in connection with Bataille's *The
Story of the Eye*, "Dirt breaks down the barriers between individuals, between
individuals and their morals, and breaks down the codes of society as it
breaks with the discontinuity of individuals."[16] Similarly, in Brahmanism the
notion of the remainder (i.e., food or sacrificial remains) is thoroughly ambivalent. As Kristeva remarks, "The remainder appears to be coextensive with
the entire architecture of non-totalizing thought. In its view there is nothing
that is everything; nothing is exhaustive, there is residue in every system—in
cosmogony, food, ritual, and even sacrifice, which deposits, through ashes for
instance, ambivalent remains."[17] The writing of the later Platonov betrays a
similarly "non-totalizing" kind of logic. Here abundant images of waste and
filth act to erode the same overarching oppositions that had been most prominent in his earlier work.[18] And is it any surprise, given his early essay "The
Soul of the World," that Platonov repeatedly chooses Woman (more precisely,
the female body) as a means of undermining the purist's dream of cohesion?
For woman's body produces—in Platonov's eyes—filth and waste *at the
same time* that it gives birth to the desire to transcend the "ugliness and horror of the earth."

By contrast, the phallus—according to Platonov—is that which engenders
the future through a continual process of self-purification and transcendence.
"Man is like a cock," the author writes in his notebooks for the years
1931–1932. "[H]e casts aside filth and produces the future."[19] Not accidentally, Platonov's late-career embrace of "waste matter" coincides precisely

with his retreat from the (ambivalent) utopianism of his earlier works. In what can only be described as an impressive volte-face, the "tyranny of the phallus" yields to an unprecedented feminization of his prose during the mid-to-late '30s.[20] Neither develepment can be properly grasped outside the context of the broader cultural atmosphere. It is no secret that the Stalinist '30s witnessed a cardinal shift away from the asceticism, iconoclasm, and mechanistic collectivism that were the hallmarks of the revolutionary '20s. And Platonov's embrace (reluctant, to be sure) of the *hic et nunc* is not entirely at odds with the aggressive resurgence of patriarchy and traditional values that set this decade apart from its predecessor. Likewise, the author's persistent undercutting of boundaries appears—if only superficially—to echo Stalinism's promotion of itself as the greatest synthesizer of opposites.[21] Still, Platonov's foregrounding of the feminine is far from serving the needs of patriarchy. After all, notwithstanding the gender-inclusiveness of Mukhina's famous statue, Stalinist ideology saw woman as occupying a position inferior to that of the ideologically dominant male (witness the clear juxtaposition of the girl-parachutist with the boy-pilot in Alexandrov's *Circus*).[22] Platonov undermines this hierarchy either by an outright privileging of the female, as in the case of *Happy Moscow*, or by paradoxically conflating genders in the image of the androgyne, or "(she)-male."

This sea change in Platonov's thought appears to coincide with the author's journey in 1934 to the deserts of Central Asia. Here the almost unpublishable Platonov might well be compared to Osip Mandelshtam, whose trip to Armenia in 1930 brought about a return to the music of poetry following an extended period of silence. Given the choice of traveling with other writers' brigades to such exotic locales as Georgia or Dagestan, Platonov nevertheless settled on Turkmenistan. Yet unlike many of his lesser contemporaries for whom travel to Asia or Armenia promised a simple encounter with the exotic Orient,[23] Platonov chose Turkmenistan for reasons that were firmly anchored in his own biography. One can imagine, for instance, that in addition to obvious political considerations, the author's long-standing professional interest in land reclamation provided a significant motivation for his decision.

Marking the beginning of Platonov's shift from a "necrophiliac" to a "biophiliac" stance, the trip seems also to have sparked an interest on the part of the writer in renegotiating the traditional juxtaposition of Europe and Asia.[24] Typically, this relationship was such that Europe appeared to exemplify all that was "historical" and "rational," whereas Asia embodied everything mystical, ahistorical, and irrational.[25] Platonov's notebook entries serve to undermine such an "either-or" narrative, however, conjuring up an Asia that occludes the very possibility of clear-cut distinctions. Echoing the Bataillian understanding of dirt as the great reconciler, the writer paints a portrait of Turkmenistan in which the lines of demarcation between conceptually and ontologically opposed realms erode. The writer's portrayal of the Eastern bazaar seems particularly noteworthy, since it prefigures Bakhtin's slightly later celebration of the carnival fairground precisely for its near-mythological ability to unsettle rigidly hierarchical structures—whether social, philosophical, or linguistic. Thus in his notebooks Platonov describes the bazaar as a place not so much of commerce, but of community and communion—as a locus where self and other coalesce. And this image will prove of considerable significance to the writer in conceptualizing the philosophical framework for such works as *Dzhan* or *Happy Moscow.*

The first of these (the novella *Dzhan*) was published in 1934. Written immediately upon Platonov's return from Turkmenistan, it draws on the writer's impressions of the desert and its inhabitants to signal a retreat from the (ambivalent) utopianism of his earlier writing. And like so many of Platonov's works, the novella represents a veritable grab bag of different myths. Drawing on a broad spectrum of mythological and historical figures—from Prometheus and Christ to their contemporary incarnation in Lenin—it polemically engages with the "coming-to-consciousness" and "Great Stalinist family" narratives characteristic of Socialist Realism.[26] The hero of the novel, Nazar Chagataev, is of mixed Russian and Turkmen descent—perhaps reflecting Stalinist culture's aspiration to become the ultimate "melting pot" of nations. A kind of latter-day Moses, Chagataev is called upon to save his nomad kinsmen from oblivion, even as he labors to write them into the Stalinist narrative of "happiness found." Platonov's achievement lies in the subtle manner in which he both undermines and transforms Chagataev's civilizing mission. By renouncing the telescopic perspective of the visionary in favor of bodily closeness and compassion, the writer spotlights not only the conquest metaphor at the heart of Stalinism's "grand narrative," but the aggressive, universalizing tendency of language as such.

As Hutchings remarks, Platonov's *Dzhan* shuttles back and forth between the universalizing pretensions of philosophical/metaphorical language and a more "humane" mode that honors the claims of the singular, embodied event above all else. The author resolves this standoff using alternating strategies of "miscegenation" and incest," understood in both the literal and figurative senses.[27] While the former term clearly models the relationships that Chagataev enters into over the course of the novel in a literal sense (for Ksenia he is half-Turkmen, for Aydym half-Russian), its symbolic thrust is no less crucial. Miscegenation as metaphor evokes the need to "maintain an irreducible difference between subject and object when one person encounters another" (i.e., distance).[28] By contrast, incest (Chagataev has a quasi-incestuous relationship with both Ksenia and Aydym, since both girls are variously portrayed as daughters and lovers) underscores the concomitant need to bridge the divide between self and other through rituals of bodily contact and desire. Ultimately, neither extreme (distance or closeness, transcendence or immanence) can flourish without the other. What the novella as a whole achieves is a dialogic merging of these—just as in *Happy Moscow* Moscow Chestnova's body will consistently erode the antinomy of purity and filth. On the one hand, Chagataev's *distance-vision*, which stems from his place outside the tribe, proves essential for the Dzhan's survival. It is Chagataev who brings the outside (Bolshevik) world to the insular, nearly prehistorical Dzhan, and it is he who—in concert with the author—renders the tribal body worthy of narration by infusing it with his Word.[29] At the same time, it is only by forgoing the perspective of epic distance in favor of contiguity that Chagataev manages to allow the tribal Dzhan to continue existing as irreducibly unique, singular individuals. Ultimately eschewing the grand pose of a Lenin or a Stalin, Chagataev "saves" his people in a manner that suggests rather the bodily self-sacrifice of Christ. Perhaps not accidentally, Platonov's image of Chagataev seems to recall the Christology of the early Bakhtin. As in Bakhtin's early essay "Towards a Philosophy of the Act" (1919–1924), in *Dzhan* the figure of Chagataev-cum-Christ symbolizes the fundamental interpenetration of disparate but interconnected realms—the "miscegenation" of divine and human which occurs through Christ's descent into the world.[30]

Perhaps the most eloquent expression of the novella's philosophy and thematics concerns the problem of vision. Conceptualizations of the eye have variously emphasized its role as an instrument of communication with the outside world. or as a metaphor for mastery and domination. On the one hand, the eye symbolizes consciousness as the natural outgrowth of self-perception.[31] On the other, in Galenic theory, where it is "both sovereign and implicitly male": the eye "engenders the visible world by its projection of spiritual substance, the 'pneuma' that flows through the hollow optic nerve, exciting the surrounding air and translating it into a receptive body made 'sympathetic.'"[32] The visionary stance of the Socialist Realist hero owes much to the latter understanding. *He* (almost never *she*) negotiates the cosmos precisely through an act of all-encompassing, masterful vision. Thus one of the commonplaces of Socialist Realist literature is the image of the "gaze from the train," which pairs the phallic thrust of Bolshevik technology with the eye's aspiration to master "ever new spaces, materials and worlds."[33] The importance of such visual mastery is exemplified by none other than the premier architect of utopia himself: Stalin. Thus a relatively late Socialist Realist painting by Fedor Shurpin entitled *Morning of Our Motherland* (1949) shows the monumental leader against the backdrop of "utopia found." Towering god-like above his creation, Stalin looks upward and outward toward a distant place located outside the frame of the picture.[34] Likewise, Platonov's Nazar Chagataev is at the outset of his civilizing mission to the Dzhan imbued with a kind of hyperexalted vision—that is, with the will to remake the world after his own image. As if mimicking the sublime gaze described above, Chagataev views the world from a supernal bird's-eye perspective: "He had climbed up high now, high up the mountain of his own mind, from which could be seen all this summer world warmed by the setting evening sun" (*Dzhan*, 331). By the same token, the hero is blind to anything that departs from his *idea*. On the way to rejoin his tribe in Turkmenistan, Chagataev passes a train station where he sees posters of party leaders (including Lenin) whose projections of a radiant future seem to be confirmed by the surrounding bustle of socialist construction. What the protagonist does not *see*, however, are those stations where the dreary canvas of the everyday departs from socialism's optimistic tableau: "Chagataev saw no empty stations, without any people, where only exiles could have lived"[35] (*Dzhan*, 344).

While the Bolshevik hero is repeatedly shown peering intently at the world around him, the virginal Dzhan exhibits a near-total absence of vision.[36] Indeed, the dream-like condition that envelops both Chagataev's kinsmen as well as the surrounding desert causes both to appear blind. Thus the narrator describes Chagataev's mother's oneiric state by focusing specifically on her unseeing eyes: "Her eyes were of such a helpless and pale color that there remained in them no strength for seeing,—they had no expression, as if they were blind or had fallen silent."[37] Unlike Chagataev who exemplifies Moscow's transformational zeal, the Dzhan remain indifferent to the world around them. They exist in a kind of precultural, pre-Oedipal state, still indistinct from the "Great Mother" (i.e., nature). Hence their blind in-*difference* to the larger cosmos. According to Kristeva, the advent of speech ("narratability") is contigent precisely upon the repression of maternal authority—upon the subject's removal of himself from an archaic state of oneness with the Ur-mother.[38] Unlike Chagataev, for whom the separation from the Mother-land is long since past, the primordial Dzhan have yet to undergo such a passage.[39] Mired in a state of perpetual and mute in-*difference*, the tribe's members prove incapable not simply of narrating but occasionally even of speaking. Like the babble of infants or toddlers, the speech of the Dzhan is best described as a kind of infantile *zaum'*. Thus in one instance Chagataev listens to a member of his tribe whose words remained "incomprehensible because there was nothing but sounds in them."[40]

Ultimately the hero's rush to inscribe his people into the Stalinist narrative of "paradise found" encounters stiff resistance from the very bodies of the Dzhan themselves. Hardly surprising, if one considers one of Platonov's most important essays of the early '30s. Entitled "About the First Socialist Tragedy" (1934), it was originally intended for publication as part of the collective work "Two Five-Year Plans" organized by Gorky. In it the writer criticizes the revolution's simplistic fantasy of transforming nature into the handmaiden of human desire. Drawing on his real-life experiences in the field of land reclamation, Platonov characterizes the relationship between technology and nature as a fundamentally dialectic one. Rather than passively submit to humankind's transforming ambitions, nature resists and even counters these in a dialogic game of give and take.[41] Chagataev's relationship to the Dzhan is no different. Metaphorically speaking, it represents the same pitched battle between technology and nature.[42] Yet unlike the Stalinist portrayal of an unambiguous triumph of science over nature, the results of Chagataev's efforts in "reclaiming" the Dzhan prove decidedly mixed. Not so much a one-sided victory, they point toward a manifestly dialogic situation in which the patriarchal savior figure is himself transformed by the very people he aspires to save.[43]

The change undergone by Chagataev lies in his rejection of epic vision in favor of a Christ-like pose of self-renunciation. Rather than attempt in godlike fashion to remake the Dzhan, he shares his body with the tribe in a symbolic ritual of community and communion. This relationship, as Stephen Hutchings suggests, bears more than a passing resemblance to Bakhtin's understanding of the connection between an author and his characters. The common philosophical inheritance shared by both Platonov and Bakhtin is such that for both the writer and the critic "the relationship of an author to the hero he endows with body is one in which the hero's inner life is . . . both maintained intact, yet lovingly completed ("завершен") from without."[44] Chagataev's relation to the Dzhan reflects the same delicate intermingling of individual freedom with the authorial urge to "lovingly complete." Most dramatically expressed in the novella's complex visual thematics, the dialogic posture of the hero-as-author vis-à-vis his people is evident in Chagataev's gradual abandonment of the role of Bolshevik patriarch and *visionary*. In a scene that mirrors the opening of the novella (where Chagataev had been described ascending the "mountain of his mind"), he now "ascends" to a high terrace only to watch his people disperse before his eyes.[45] The visual imagery of the passage serves to deconstruct the telescopic pathos predominant throughout the early scenes of *Dzhan*. Having infused his people with new life, the transformer-hero now renounces the very surplus of vision that would allow him to foresee the end of the narrative he has himself set in motion. And what Platonov underscores is precisely Chagataev's inability to *see* several of the tribe's members, as well as his readiness to cede the prerogative of vision to the Other: "Не было *видно* тех, которые ушли через Усть–Урт на

север и на восток. . . . Но самим людям *виднее*, как им лучше быть"
[my emphasis].[46] In stark contrast to the typical Stalinist patriarch, Chagataev
grants his fellow tribesmen the status of full-fledged individuals, equal in
their ability to *see* to the "savior" himself.[47]

The relationship between the savior Chagataev and the Dzhan brings to
mind yet another important cultural (and only partially mythological) icon of
the time: that is, Aleksandr Pushkin.[48] In his 1938 essay on Pushkin and
Gorky, Platonov evokes a relationship between the artist and the people that
is equally dialogic and which emphasizes the poet/prophet's Christological
aspect. Here the great nineteenth-century poet is paradoxically portrayed—à
la Chagataev in *Dzhan*—as authoring the Russian *narod* even as he himself
is produced by it. Bypassing the top-heavy Socialist Realist paradigm of wise
fathers tempering and molding their unruly sons, Platonov's Pushkin is simultaneously the people's prophet/savior *and* a projection of their collective
spirit. Similarly, just as Chagataev "saves" the Dzhan not by subsuming them
within an abstract, universalizing narrative but by literally sharing his flesh
and blood, Platonov's Pushkin is not only the people's protector but their
"sacrifice." The sacrificial aspect of Platonov's Pushkin is evident in the lines
from Pushkin's "The Prophet" that Platonov quotes. The source of true genius, the writer opines, lies outside of the self proper—in the realm where self
and Other coalesce. Accordingly, in his depiction of the poet's fiery transfiguration it is the traumatic but sublime opening-up of the body to the world
outside the self that Platonov stresses. To be sure, it is the poet/prophet's *individual* word that is called upon to "sear the hearts of men," yet at the same
time Platonov remarks that "genuine, fiery power enters us from outside,
from the great and magical world; 'the coal, glowing with fire' is not ignited
in the singular, lonely heart of humans, the 'coal' is ignited in the general
world."[49]

At once striking and unsettling, Platonov's characterization of the dialogic
relationship between the spiritual leader and the masses demonstrates the author's distance not merely from Stalinist ideology but from the very "totalitarian" countenance of language itself. We see this, among others, in the
writer's attempts at unsettling metaphor as the mode of choice within aesthetic and philosophical discourse. According to Hutchings, the advent of
metaphor signals the breakdown of the primordial unity of the universal and
the particular. And in *Dzhan* it (i.e., metaphor) models a situation in which the
singular event is rendered subordinate to the universalizing grasp of the
mind.[50] To put it another way, metaphor marks the moment where the body's
singular essence is redeemed within the leader's imperious, all-encompassing
gaze. The linguistic equivalent of Chagataev's distance-vision ("he ascended
high now, up the mountain of his mind"),[51] metaphor represents the mode pre-

ferred not only by Stalinist ideology, with its wealth of totalizing myths, but by "conquest-oriented aesthetic language."[52] Platonov's polemic with this kind of totalizing language is mirrored in his use of metonymy as a kind of humane alternative to the "conquest-oriented" aesthetic described above.[53] And here metonymy acquires a broad philosophical resonance, becoming emblematic of an aesthetic language that replaces the subsuming logic of metaphor with metonymy's emphasis on continuity and coexistence. This strategy results, among others, in the decidedly unaesthetic—indeed sometimes even grotesque—effect of Platonov's prose, which insists on combining as equal things that are logically or aesthetically incompatible. How else, one might ask, can the writer draw the seemingly ludicrous parallel (as he does in the essay "Our Comrade Pushkin") between Pushkin and the contemporary Stalinist shock workers? Yet if we set aside for a moment the obvious political considerations and follow the logic of Platonov's thought, the enthusiasm of a Stakhanovite might well be perceived as equal to the inspiration of Russia's greatest poet.

Platonov's ambitious poetics of rapprochement is visible throughout his *Dzhan* and represents nothing less than an attempt on the author's part to "resolve" the perennial standoff between the abstract idea and its incarnation within individual human bodies. This idea is most forcefully suggested by the visual problematics that lie at the core of the work. Thus if Chagataev is simultaneously both Russian *and* non-Russian, his female counterpart in the novella, Ksenia, is not accidentally described as having two different-colored eyes—eyes that "watched painfully, like two close but unacquainted people."[54] Moreover, the narrator's paradoxical suggestion of a "close distance" seems emblematic of the relationship itself, since Chagataev is symbolically both related and unrelated to Ksenia. A still more dramatic example of Platonov's unsettling poetics of conflation is to be found at the end of the novella, where the narrator describes the phenomenon of the Eastern bazaar. In this vignette we see distinct echoes of the author's seminal essay "On the First Socialist Tragedy." There he had described the relationship between technology and nature as one based on the principle of dialogue rather than profit, as a relationship where neither side exists in isolation from or at the expense of the other. Likewise in *Dzhan*, Platonov portrays the commerce of the Eastern bazaar not as a means of achieving financial gain but as an eternal dialogue between distinct yet fundamentally intertwined forces.[55] In both instances, the relationship is such that neither side "conquers" the other. As an aside, one might note that the author's description of the Eastern bazaar is vaguely reminiscent of the institution of the *potlach* as performed in certain "primitive" societies. According to Paul Hegarty, these rituals serve to fuse economic and social exchange in such a way that the obligation to give rather than to accumulate wealth provides the basis for a potentially endless orgy of gift-giving and expenditure.[56] Similarly, in Platonov's *Dzhan* the image of the Eastern bazaar suggests that the purpose of commerce is not to reap profit but rather to engage with the Other in the open-ended game of quid pro quo that is the everyday:

> They put in front of each other ancient five-kopeck pieces and unknown coins, iron buttons, tin name plates, hooks, old nails and pieces of metal, military cockades, empty turtles, dried lizards, tiled bricks from ancient buried palaces, and these sellers were waiting for buyers to come and acquire their goods for their need. The women traded in *chebureks*, knitted wool socks, drinking-water and last year's garlic. Having sold something, a woman would buy a piece of tin plate for herself from the old men to adorn her dress or a shard of ceramic tile to give to her child as a toy. With their take the old men would buy chebureks, drinking-water or tobacco. Trading was on a *tit-for-tat basis*, with neither profit nor gain [my emphasis].[57]

A corollary of this can be found in Platonov's notebook entries for the years 1934–1935 that deal with the Eastern ritual of hospitality. As Hans-Dieter Bahr notes, the symbolic significance of (European) hospitality rests—among others—in the implicit understanding of a dialogic exchange between equal subjects. In contrast to commercial transactions where one object is exchanged *for* or *against* another, the institution of hospitality presupposes a ritual exchange of gifts *with* one another. In other words, hospitality brings about a suspension of traditional subject-object relations.[58] Similarly, in ancient Greece the term "xenos" refers to one who is Other, while at the same time enjoying all the rights and privileges of the host himself.[59] Indeed, one senses a certain ambiguity at the very heart of the phenomenon of hospitality itself, since the Latin words for "guest" (*hospes*) and "enemy" (*hostis*) are etymologically related.[60] Likewise, as Anne Dufourmantelle remarks in her commentary on Derrida's lectures on hospitality, the "hostis" or "guest" "responds to hospitality in the way that the ghost recalls himself to the living, not letting them forget. To the pacified reason of Kant, Derrida opposes the primary haunting of the subject prevented by alterity from closing itself off in its peacefulness."[61] For Platonov the image of the "guest" (*gost'*) is similarly ambiguous. He or she is at once opposed and necessary to the self for its fulfillment and completion. Indeed, the "guest" is not so much a person as it is an emblem of dialogically configured selfhood per se. By the same token, in Platonov's notebooks of the period the role of the "guest" can be played by anything that is marginal or Other with respect to the self—beginning with waste matter or feces and ending with the savior of humankind himself.[62] At one point, for instance, the writer remarks that Asia represents the "guest" (i.e., the Other) of Europe.[63] Developing what seems to be a rather curious image, Platonov emphasizes the importance of Asia as a crucible of spirituality over the impoverished rationalism and materialism of Europe.[64] Likewise, in his depiction of Christ Platonov underscores the latter's absolute and necessary alterity with respect to human laws and institutions. It is precisely this radical "otherness," the author reflects, that renders him ideal as a savior figure vis-à-vis humankind. And here one cannot but recall the *iurodivyi* (fool in Christ) so crucial to the Russian literary and cultural tradition. From Pushkin to Olesha the image of the holy fool serves to expose the exclusionary logic (segregating "clean" from "unclean") that constitutes the hallmark of an unjust society. "By plunging into the midst of 'polite society' naked or with the carcass of a dog strapped to one's waist, the *iurodivyi* forces the issue of his own degradation and marginalization," writes David Bethea.[65] For Platonov, too, the kenotic Christ's "holy foolishness" places him at the very margins of what is deemed acceptable or decent: "The guest of humankind—was himself not a human being, b[ecause] he was absolutely ignorant of humanity and acted in opposition to society's laws, like a madman, like someone who was better or . . ."[66]

Depicted as a place where self and other coalesce, the Eastern bazaar personifies the strategy of mixing and compromise employed to great effect by Platonov throughout his *Dzhan*. What, after all, is Chagataev's mission to reclaim the Dzhan if not compromise par excellence? For while the hero succeeds in keeping the tribe from extinction, he does not yet manage to subsume its members within Stalinism's narrative of utopia-found. And even as their fate comes to mirror a larger, universal narrative, the Dzhan themselves remain firmly tethered to their nameless place of origin. Indeed, Platonov's poetics of connecting and linking (metonymy) ultimately allows Chagataev to view the impoverished Turkmen desert and its inhabitants as homologous with the distant beacon of culture and science that is Moscow. It is precisely this shift from "conquest" to "coexistence" that enables the hero to reclaim his tribe without obliterating their originary essence.[67] Anticipating the metonymic poetics that will be used to even more unsettling effect in *Happy Moscow*, Chagataev finally concludes that the desert of Sary-Kamysh represents a continuation of the same "important cause" as the ideological project promoted by the center: "Chagataev felt with surprise that it was possible to exist together with only animals, with soundless plants. . . . Even here in the poor nature of Ust'-Urta, on the ancient floor of Sary-Kamysh there was an important cause for all of human life" (*Dzhan*, 415). Likewise, at the end of *Dzhan* a less visionary Chagataev will conclude that "happiness" dwells in the unfinished here and now as much as it does in the vanishing point beyond the horizon: "Still it seemed to him that, despite all the calamities, here a happy life was or was beginning, and that it was possible in a small people, in four huts, as much as it was beyond any horizon" (*Dzhan*, 414). The paucity of distinction between Asian desert and European Moscow—between the realms of nature and culture—is linked to the mirage theme developed within the novella, and appears to derive from Platonov's observation of local landscapes while in Turkmenistan. One description in particular prefigures the conflation of high and low that will become the hallmark of such works as *Happy Moscow*. In his notebooks for the year 1935 Platonov paints a picture of the Turkmen desert that emphasizes the optical illusion of a convergence between heaven and earth. Extrapolating from this image of spatial chiaroscuro, Platonov suggests that linear, or "clock," time—the sine qua non of any teleological narrative such as that of Stalinism[68]—is nowhere inherent in nature: "Nowhere does the sky come so close to meeting the earth as it does in the desert. It simply merges with it and is hardly distinguishable from it, especially at dusk, in the heat, and at night, during the undefined time when you see that time is a clock, a mechanism and not the activity of nature. There is no such thing as time, and the space of the things of the air and the earth is unclearly distinguished, as it should be" (*Notebooks*, 170).

If anything, Platonov's *Dzhan* seems to suggest that time in *nature* reflects the nonlinear, biological cycle of life and death. Accordingly, Chagataev's imagination of salvation as forward flight away from the "meager, flat place of the earth" must be seen in conjunction with the image of the Eastern bazaar as the emblem of cyclical, seasonal time. Here, according to Platonov, time moves in such a way as to erode the pathos of Stalinism's soteriological narrative: "Here lay dried apricots in smallish bags, dried melons, untanned lamb skins, dark carpets, woven by women in their long isolation, with a representation of the entire portion of humankind in the form of a sad repeating drawing."[69] It is no accident that the carpets represent the work of women, for throughout the novella these come to symbolize (both in their work and through their very physiology) the idea of life as ceaseless repetition. To the extent that she mirrors nature in its originary condition, woman symbolizes a state of pure immanence. Vera (whose painting negates the male fantasy of a messianic flight away from one's origin) is the first to express a "pessimistic" vision of life as eternal return.[70] In response to Chagataev's naive admonition of Vera to give birth as quickly as possible, so that her child can become an "inhabitant of the future happiness," she responds that perhaps the child will be "an eternal sufferer." In the same vein, Platonov's narrator reflects that suffering is so firmly anchored in the human condition that in order to remove it one would have to destroy the organism itself.[71] And it hardly seems accidental that this pessimistic principle is associated with the heroine Vera's body, for more than anyone else woman-as-nature exemplifies the "biological tragedy" of humankind:

If all of the sudden there were to be some sudden need, she would have given away all of her belongings to some neighbor woman. That good deed would have consoled her somewhat and along with the diminishing of her possessions it would also diminish the dimensions of her suffering soul. But then she would have to give away her body down to its last bit. . . . Despair, anguish and need can be compressed inside a person right down to the smallest crevice: they only go out with one's dying breath.[72]

Platonov's retreat from the ambivalent utopianism that had characterized such masterworks as *Chevengur* and *The Foundation Pit* to a more conciliatory, "biophiliac" position in his writing of the mid-to-late '30s represents a repudiation of the profoundly solipsistic or "onanistic" worldview of the earlier Russian avant-garde. As Zolotonosov demonstrates, that worldview was one in which the function and pathos of eros remained overwhelmingly self-referential.[73] Platonov's "Antisexus" (1927) eloquently illustrates the point, using the image of a mechanism said to be able to satisfy a person's libidinal desires in order to parody the decade's preoccupation with sexual abstinence and sublimation.[74] The author's writing of the '30s takes this implicit criticism several steps further, however; for here the focus is not so much on auto-erotic pleasures but rather on a fundamental, ontological coupling of self and other. Accordingly, the (female) body is no longer scorned as an impediment to achieving transcendent selfhood. Instead it serves—to be sure, not always comfortably—as a bridge between the extremes of bodily immanence and spiritual transcendence. Is it possible that this understanding came about in the wake of the author's trip to Turkmenistan? Perhaps so. For more than any other place, the desert as evoked in Platonov's notebooks and his *Dzhan* emerges as a locale of near mystical ambivalence. Simultaneously manifesting both emptiness *and* plenitude, it is the void that brings forth great riches.[75] Similarly—and no doubt by analogy—in contemporary works such as *Happy Moscow* the woman's body recalls the same desert, shuttling restlessly back and forth between the extremes of chthonic chaos (emptiness) and cosmic order (plenitude).

Platonov's characterization of emptiness as plenitude recalls the negative theological tradition within Eastern (Orthodox) Christianity, according to which divinity can be attained only by passing through the void. Within this tradition "God appears as a 'no.'"[76] Perhaps no less mystical, Platonov's writing of the '30s singles out Woman for her paradoxical ability to bridge the extremes of filth and cleanliness, that is, to mediate between the "ugliness and horror of the earth" and that which aspires to transcend it. In both *Dzhan* and *Happy Moscow* the prominence of the female body coincides (not accidentally) with the author's embrace of an accomodationist stance vis-à-vis the ideal, as opposed to his earlier attraction to utopia proper. In contrast to the revolutionary (male) fantasy of bodily and social purification, Platonov's heroines manifest a more tolerant approach to the unclean—what Bataille describes as the meandering "movement from refuse to the ideal, and from the ideal to refuse."[77] For these, cleanliness is an ongoing process rather than an irreversible fait accompli.[78] No longer the path toward corporeal or societal perfection, cleanliness represents the immediate, undeferrable need of the body in the *hic et nunc*. It is not the promise of "no-place" ("u-topia"); rather it is the imperative of every place.[79] Of the homeless Khanom, Platonov's narrator notes symptomatically: "Probably she had to consider every place home and immediately accustom herself to it. Otherwise, if she put off her need and care until the moment when she had her own dwelling her clothes would have been reduced to rags, she would have fallen into poverty from neglect and she would have perished from the uncleanliness of her body."[80] Likewise, at an earlier point in the novella, while describing Ksenia's dirty hands, the narrator makes clear that the habit of cleanliness is one that can be acquired only over time: "Chagataev shook the strange hand, childish and womanly. The hand was sticky and dirty ['нечистая'], because it takes children a while to become accustomed to cleanliness ['чистота']."[81]

Although it has been argued that the first version of the novella mirrors the full-blown (anti)utopianism of Platonov's earlier works such as *Chevengur* or *The Foundation Pit*,[82] recent criticism has elected to emphasize what might be called its hybrid or postutopian tenor. It has been suggested, for instance, that even the first, unrevised version of *Dzhan* remains rather ambiguous with regards to the utopian ideal. Ideologically indeterminate at best, it fuses together the pathos of utopian construction (implicit in Chagataev's masterful intent to "reclaim" or re-member the tribe for the future) with the hero's final refusal to subsume the latter within the very totalizing narrative that spurred his civilizing mission.[83] In this Platonov seems to anticipate the conclusions that he would later draw in his seminal essays on Pushkin. In the first of these—topically entitled "Our Comrade Pushkin" (1936)—Platonov pairs the broad, utopian gestures of the cultural/mythological hero with the unremarkable needs of individual bodies, such as those of the "little people" Evgenii and Parasha from Pushkin's *Bronze Horseman*. By contrast, such works as *The Foundation Pit* do not so much concede the coequality of the particular vis-à-vis the universal as they demonstrate the calamitous failure of the latter to be instantiated within the former. A similar poetics of coequality is evident in the "Socialist Realist" ending to *Dzhan* that Platonov penned after receiving criticism of the first manuscript from *Red Virgin Soil* and Gorky's almanach *Two Five-Year Plans*.[84] In contrast to the first ending, the second signals—in addition to the successful collectivization of the Dzhan—the rehabilitation of the (female) body that would distinguish such later works as *Happy Moscow* and

Fro. In a move that is nothing short of revolutionary, Chagataev takes the "unclean" hand of his daughter/lover Ksenia (is it by accident that her name derives from the Greek word for "hospitality," or *xenia*?) into his own. Thus the hand of the male hero merges with that of the same Woman whom Platonov and many of his contemporaries had hoped to exclude from the revolutionary-utopian brotherhood.

The dramatic coupling of revolutionary man with the "unclean" feminine at the end of Platonov's Socialist Realist *Dzhan* undoubtedly owes a great deal to the broader cultural climate. Among others, it reflects (albeit idiosyncratically) the resurgence of patriarchal and traditionalist values that accompanied the rise of Stalinism during the 1930s. According to one critic, this sea change manifests itself in the appearance of core cultural myths, such that "the technological utopia gives way to a synthesis of the machine and the garden through the marriage of the He-Worker and the She-Peasant (epitomized by Vera Mukhina's well-known sculpture)."[85] More than a case of cynical accomodationism, Platonov's own coupling of the "He-Worker" with the "She-Peasant" mirrors a need shared by the writer with the culture at large to distance oneself from the previous decade's unrelenting asceticism. Yet Platonov takes Stalinist culture's selective rehabilitation of the feminine several steps further, according Woman pride of place in an unorthodox wedding of the "She-Peasant" to the "He-Worker."[86] The roots of this rapprochement stretch back to Platonov's early career—to an essay entitled "The World Soul." In it Platonov had praised woman's body for its unique ability to reconcile the ideal with the real.[87] Much later this would engender the implict (and sometimes explicit) desire of some of Platonov's protagonists to acquire the characteristics of the other sex. Thus in his notebooks for the year 1935 Platonov contemplates an ending to *Happy Moscow* in which the protagonist Sartorius is transformed into a woman. Like the divine Sophia, she or he would become the savior of the world: "For H[appy] Moscow/ 'Sartor[ius] at the end of his reincarnations is convinced that in order to complete his life['s] task and in order to satisfy his own further love it is essential for him to become Moscow, and with his [turni] reincarnation into her, the woman—the savior of the world—he ends and the novel ends."[88] Of course, this does not actually occur in the unfinished work, though it is noteworthy that Sartorius's new surname at the end of *Happy Moscow* ("Gruniakhin") seems to be formed from the feminine name "Grunia."[89]

As Eliot Borenstein has shown, the peculiar brand of homoerotic collectivism that allows Platonov's *Chevengur* to stand out even vis-à-vis such openly homoerotic works as Babel's *Red Cavalry* or Olesha's *Envy* is not merely a function of communist ideology. Instead it appears to derive from a deeper species of attachment, such that the "men of Chevengur appear unusually preoccupied with the bodies of other men."[90] Platonov's work of the

mid-to-late '30s goes to nearly the opposite extreme. Far from being resettled to the ontological margins of an all-male utopia, women prove essential to the project of reconciling all with everything—of redefining "utopia"
as contiguous with human physiology. This is perhaps clearest in
Platonov's notebooks for the year 1935, where the writer attempts—among
others—to redefine the notion of collectivism in terms of the feminine (or,
more specifically, *maternal*) urge to preserve one's immediate family and
kin.[91] Notably, Platonov's conservatism echoes the recrudescent traditionalism of Stalinist culture, within which the archetype of the mother acquires
particular prominence.[92] Reassessing the "selfish" feminine pull toward
hearth and home, the author now views woman's domesticity almost as a
variant of Fyodorov's project of re-membering the dead so as to unite the
living: "The petty anxiousness, thriftiness, economicality, pedantic tedious-
ness, even voraciousness,—all of that is, in a woman, nothing more than
compensation for the other part of her soul, which contains the urge to preserve her kin, fear for those close to her, etc. A detailed, s[o] to s[peak], concrete reflection, a fencing in and saving of the world."[93] And on the next
page of his notes Platonov attempts to justify the collectivization of agri-
culture by representing it in feminine terms: "The kolkh[oz] movement possesses many purely feminine traits: a society based on a neighborly sense of
family. It seems hard and difficult, but just take away one neighbor woman
from another and she will grieve even more, perhaps, than if she had lost
her family. A neighbor woman is necessary for . . . the whole of life and for
the soul."[94]

   It has been suggested that Platonov's use of incest motifs in *Dzhan* signals
the author's retreat from the abstract model of brotherhood envisioned by Fyodorov toward a privileging of bodily intimacy as a means of securing kinship.[95] By contrast, in earlier works such as *Chevengur* the boy's relationship
to his father had been invoked as the "key to his ability to forge affiliative, or
social bonds later in life."[96] Yet in Platonov's later works it is often the mother
(*not* the father) who embodies the stability of the familial hearth. This in obvious contrast to the stock portrayal of Stalin as the transcendent *paternal*
principle underpinning the unity of the Soviet body politic. Indeed, if
Platonov's *Dzhan* is any indication, it is not so much the model of the transbiological Great Soviet Family that the writer proposes (notwithstanding the
Socialist Realist ending of *Dzhan*), but a synthesis of feminine immanence
and masculine transcendence. This might well explain the frequency of cross-
dressing and cross-gendered episodes in at least several of Platonov's shorter
works from the '30s. For instance, in the short story "Semion" (1936–1937),
a young boy reacts to the death of his mother not only by dressing in women's
clothing but by gradually taking over the role of his deceased parent. More-

over, the boy's transformation is prefigured by a gender ambiguity that pre-dates the death of his mother:

> "Let me be the mother, there's no one else." . . . Then Semion took his mother's
> house-coat-dress and put it on himself over his head. . . . Now, wearing the dress,
> . . . Semion looked as much like a boy as he did like a girl,—equally. If he grew
> a bit, one could take him for a girl, and a girl is the same thing as a woman, and
> that's practically a mother.[97]

Most importantly, cross-dressing as the "miscegenation" of gender traits produces a hero who is decidedly androgynous. Semion resembles a girl as much as he does a boy, his identity becoming that much more confused by his decision to take the name "Ksenia" instead of "Semion" at the end of the piece. An outgrowth, first and foremost, of Platonov's personal mythology, the image of the boy-as-girl/mother surely recalls the fascination of numer-ous early-twentieth-century cultural and literary figures with the myth of the androgyne, as well as much older myths. According to ancient Greek legend, man and woman represent estranged halves of a single, primordial whole.[98] More recently, Dostoevsky, Solov'ev, Berdiaev, Bakhtin, and others had seen in the transgendered (wo)man the ideal of future humanity.[99] Platonov's own interest in the idea is obliquely realized in his 1936 screenplay entitled "Father-Mother." In it the writer uses crossgendering to evoke the mytho-logical, transgendered unity that is the androgyne.[100] In one scene a charac-ter is seen undergoing a painful treatment for venereal disease. His outcries are heard by two other protagonists, and what is most striking about their conversation is the description of what appears to be castration in oddly crossgendered terms: "Zhenia: 'Are they performing an abortion on him or something?' Bezgadov: 'Something like that.' Zhenia: 'Have you ever had one?' Bezgadov: 'No. I gave birth.'" A similar (if less drastic) instance of an-drogynous imagery occurs in the short story "The Clay House in the Uezd Garden" (1937). Here the story's young protagonist decides to leave his fa-ther and become a father himself. Most notably, the young boy's confused account of his "new" family includes a mixing of sexual attributes: "Then I'll start giving birth to children and I'll be with them until death itself. Let them have a father, since I don't."[101]

Platonov's gradual coming-to-terms with the feminine, wherein woman's body emerges as a locus of rapprochement rather than an ontological imped-iment, culminates in the writer's most "biophiliac" work—the unfinished novel *Happy Moscow*. Composed sporadically between 1933 and 1936, the novel debunks not only specific aspects of Stalinist cultural ideology, but many of the philosophical suppositions that underpin the very rationalist core of Western thought. And what might seem at first glance to be little more than a polemic with the commonplaces of 1930s culture (e.g., its fascination with flight, the construction of the Moscow subway) represents, in point of fact, an argument with the conceptual basis of 1930s utopianism. One of the pillars (if not *the* pillar) of Stalinist transformationalism was its ritualized "struggle with nature," whose theater stretched from the frozen wastelands of the Arctic to the Moscow underground and beyond. Like the earlier *Dzhan*, *Happy Moscow* disputes the revolutionary-theurgic worldview that viewed (human) nature as amenable to radical, unilateral improvement. Drawing on that tradition, Stalinism envisioned its "struggle with nature" as the triumph of a latter-day Peter the Great (i.e., Stalin) masterfully asserting his will over a benighted, passive nature. Human beings, it was believed, could be released from their biophysical inheritance through a simple negation of the biological Other.[102] And even as numerous ritualized journeys from periphery to center modelled the transition of Stalinist subjects from "spontaneousness" to "consciousness" by leaping over the intermediate terrain,[103] so, too, the ascent of human nature from biological necessity to cultural freedom was imagined as a single quantum leap.

Yet for Platonov the outcome of the struggle remained decidedly unclear. Witness his 1936 essay "About the First Socialist Tragedy." The relationship between nature and technology, Platonov reflects, is dialogic and therefore tragic. Neither nature nor humanity can secure genuine selfhood without the continual resistance and intrusion of the Other.[104] And perhaps more than anyone else, woman symbolizes this dialogue; for as the author makes clear in his 1920 essay "The World Soul," the female body straddles the divide between nature and culture. By rising above her essence, woman "distills the ugliness and horror of the earth through her own blood."[105] The tragedy of this relationship, as Platonov's *Happy Moscow* demonstrates, is that while the ancient reign of nature invariably resists woman's transforming aspirations, it does not cease to engender the desire for transcendence.[106] In order to access the kingdom of culture, woman must renounce her connection to biology and nature. Yet the very gesture of separation spurs an even more potent realization of one's essential connectedness. As one of the main characters of *Happy Moscow* (Sartorius) puts it, describing what amounts to an endless cycle of immanence-in-transcendence: "He was saddened by the sadness and poverty of life, which was so helpless that it would almost continually have to be distracted from the consciousness of its true situation."[107]

The trajectory of the novel as a whole bears this out. The first draft, composed in 1933, depicts the already adult heroine's engineering feats (she is testing a new kind of ball bearing at the Institute of High Speeds) very much in the spirit of Platonov's earlier unchecked enthusiasm for technology and Stalin's claim that "during the period of reconstruction technology solves everything."[108] Yet Platonov immediately abandoned this beginning. Instead he set about to write the prehistory of the heroine who had grown up without her mother,[109] connecting Moscow's passion for technology to her alienation from her maternal and biological origins. In this sense, Chestnova presents us with a confusion of genders. Perhaps not accidentally, since early-twentieth-century culture's fascination with the female acrobat/flier appears to derive precisely from the fact that she is "different from her own femininity."[110] As Mary Russo points out, the significance of the female acrobat/stuntwoman lies not so much in the fantasy of transcendent flight as it does in the idea of overturning "the limits of the body, especially the female body."[111] Hence, one imagines, the humorous allusions in Alexandrov's film *Circus* (1936) to Marion Dixon's plump double Raika, who must give up cream cakes in order to be able to perform an important aerial stunt with the film's leading man.

In the final version of the novel Moscow Chestnova's conscious life begins at the very moment when the little girl awakens from "monotonous sleep" (on a "monotonous" and "foul" autumn night) to the sound of gunshots signalling the outbreak of revolution. Subsequently, Platonov reflects that as an adult whenever Moscow recalled this moment she would hasten to change her life. Exposed early in life to the "monotony" of nature, Moscow later becomes the archetypal Platonovian hero-transformer, and the perfect illustration of the author's tragic dialectic. Woman, he suggests, cannot negate her "biological Other," since the desire to do so springs from the bosom of nature itself—from the heroine's awareness of its timeless "monotony." This is most evident in the eerie chiaroscuro of the novel's first line, where darkness and light bleed together in an image of the anonymous bearer of the revolution's Promethean aspirations: "A dark man with a burning torch ran through the street on a tiresome night amid late autumn" (*Happy Moscow*, 9). Revolution appears not as political fact but as a Promethean challenge to the tyranny of the ancient Earth-Mother. Yet ultimately the resurgent "chthonic" nature of the world will reassert itself. For at the end of *Happy Moscow* we learn that the "dark man with a burning torch" was none other than Komiagin (a figure exemplifying the eternally unreconstructed realm of nature), while the man who fired the shot marking the beginning of the revolution is exposed as a passing hooligan.

Happy Moscow begins with a flurry of images evoking Stalinist culture's rush to transform the ancient edifice of human existence, to carve a "window into the cosmos."[112] Not surprisingly, since it was precisely in 1933 that a literary campaign (entitled "Proletarian Moscow awaits its artist") was undertaken to portray the transformation of the ancient Russian city into the model hub of socialist humanity.[113] The new Moscow promised a complete departure from the past, as Katerina Clark notes. And if the claim was repeatedly

made that "'all of Moscow is under scaffolding,'" it was only to stress that
the city was "in a chrysalis from which a diaphanous butterfly will emerge,
bearing no resemblance to its former, grublike state."[114] Platonov, who had
written to Gorky three times asking to be included in the campaign without
receiving an answer, responded himself by approaching a publisher with his
project for a novel entitled *Happy Moscow*.[115] The heady optimism of the
Stalinist '30s—its aspiration to overthrow nature even as it molded ancient
Moscow into the New Jerusalem[116]—is reflected in the novel's opening. The
narrative begins with a description of Moscow Chestnova's "lucid and ascending" life as reflected in a short composition written by the heroine as a
young girl. In it Moscow imagines the relationship between nature and humankind as an ontological contest between emptiness and plenitude. In this
she merely echoes the mythology of Stalinist culture itself: "They're teaching
us to use our minds now, and the mind is in the head, outside there's nothing"
(*Happy Moscow*, 10).[117] Likewise, in a scene depicting the best of the contemporary generation of Stalinist youth-heroes, a builder of superfast planes
named Mul'dbauer confidently posits the existence of a stratospheric
paradise—"a particular layer of the atmosphere somewhere between fifty and
a hundred kilometers up, where there existed electromagnetic light, and temperature conditions such that any living organism would not grow tired and
die but would be capable of eternal life among the violet space. This was the
'heaven' of the ancient people and the happy land of the future ones: beyond
the distance of the low-lying bad weather there really was a blessed land"
(*Happy Moscow*, 26).

Yet for Platonov himself it is not the ethereal heights that prove most attractive. Instead it is the middle ground that arugably achieves greatest resonance in his writing of the period.[118] Indeed, the dramatic scene in which
Moscow sets her parachute on fire during a risky stunt proves not only the
naivete of Stalinist culture's stratospheric aspirations, but the essential
connectedness of ether and earth. To be sure, the image of Moscow Chestnova plunging earthward signals the failure of the Stalinist project of conquering gravity, even as it sets in motion the *katabasis* of the novel's second half. Yet the paradoxical imagery of the episode invites a more
nuanced reading. To view the scene as an instance of simple parody or car-
nivalization is to ignore its deeper philosophical resonance.[119] As Moscow
Chestnova plummets earthward beneath her burning parachute, she discovers the similarity of things that only *appear* to be opposed. Like Sophia
whose function is as a "bond" or a "mediator" in Orthodox Christianity,
Moscow Chestnova becomes the "middle ground" stretched between the
opposed poles of heaven and earth.[120] Indeed, Platonov's heroine seems to
echo the popular (among the gnostics) representation of the World Soul as

a woman whose body connects the lower regions of creation to the ethereal upper realm.[121] Indeed, she is not unlike those creatures of "an earlier archaic history" who were viewed as "divine monsters who mediated the natural and cosmic world."[122]

The rigid hierarchy of social, political, and other structures within Stalinist culture points toward a spatial pathos that was overwhelmingly vertical.[123] Much like Platonov's hero(ine)-transformers, it too dreamed of "putting an end to the tiresome bother of life on earth" and "propelling the speed and pressure of human history beyond the pale of the earth's gravity" (*Happy Moscow*, 22). By contrast, in *Happy Moscow* it is none other than the ethereal, airborne heroine who experiences the downward pull of gravity. Thus Chestnova confronts the unconscious truth that Stalinism's privileging of ethereal "consciousness" had overlooked. The coveted ether, the writer reflects, is not merely a void ("outside there's nothing") waiting to be colonized by an intrusive (male) presence.[124] And of the plummeting heroine the narrator notes: "She flew with burning cheeks and the air tore crudely at her body, as if it were not the air of heavenly space but a heavy dead substance. One could hardly imagine that the earth could be harder and more ruthless. 'So, that's what you're really like!' Moscow Chestnova thought unexpectedly, disappearing downward through the dusk of the fog. 'You're only soft so long as we don't touch you.'"[125] Is this not a picture-perfect illustration of the dialectic described in Platonov's essay "About the First Socialist Tragedy"? For even as technology burrows into the earth hoping to transform it, "it [the world] squeezes us in response with an equal force."[126]

The importance of the middle ground as a hyphen or connector in *Happy Moscow* is demonstrated by the abundance of thresholds that populate the novel. These serve primarily to mediate between utopian distance and quotidian closeness, as if thematizing the very trope of metonymy. Naturally, given Platonov's early asceticism, the image of reproduction looms large among such thresholds. In the following excerpt, the biological cycle which unites male and female (androgyny!) through childbearing prefigures the novel's broader emphasis on spatial contiguity. If ever so briefly, lovemaking and children are envisioned as that which knits together heaven and earth:

> Later Moscow watched from above as the rooftops of the neighboring old houses began to fill up with people. Families went out onto the iron rooftops by way of the attics, laid out blankets and lay down to sleep in the fresh air, placing their children between the mother and the father. Meanwhile, brides and bridegrooms went off to be alone in the ravines of the rooftops, somewhere between a fire-escape and a pipe. Not closing their eyes till daybreak, they were lower than the stars and higher than the multitude." (*Happy Moscow*, 15)

Elsewhere the novel's privileging of spatial contiguity is associated with the fence, which in *Happy Moscow* erodes rather than deepens the fissure between ideal and real.[127] In one scene the surgeon Sambikin arrives at a newly constructed institute devoted to the search for longevity and immortality. As if deconstructing the wall separating utopian endeavor from mundane existence, the narrator points out that the still unfinished institute with its clutter of building materials is isolated from a nearby residential building by nothing more than a fence of "child-like proportions" which "had begun to tilt and lean over completely" (*Happy Moscow*, 18). Unlike the engineer-transformer Prushevskii in *The Foundation Pit* who dreams in vain of moving beyond the wall that separates scientifically ordered reality from the dark kingdom of nature, the surgeon Sambikin in *Happy Moscow* mounts the diminutive fence separating the utopian institute from a residential building in order to hear a musician play Beethoven. In its emphasis on the contiguity of disparate realms, Platonov's narrative rejects the idea of a metaphysical firewall between the other- and the this-worldly that had marked his earlier work. For even if the world-weary musician does not see the institute's search for immortality as a continuation of his own music, the narrative itself portrays these activities as fundamentally linked: "Opposite, on the other side of the fence, they were building a medical institute that would search for longevity and immortality, but the old musician was unable to understand that this construction was a continuation of Beethoven's music, and Moscow Chestnova did not know what was being built there" (*Happy Moscow*, 26).[128]

Ultimately, even the most incompatible realms are collapsed in Platonov's willfully paradoxical narrative. Needless to say, the tension between eros and the utopian quest had always been a prominent feature of the author's writing. In *Happy Moscow* the case would seem to be no different. Continuing the tradition of Solov'ev and Berdiaev, both of whom viewed the sex act as little more than a prelude to a higher species of absolute (communal) love, Platonov's heroine remarks to Sartorius in a moment of candor and despair that "love cannot be communism" (*Happy Moscow*, 28). Likewise, the author's description of a restaurant Moscow visits one evening abounds in surreal images of circularity, repetition, and claustrophobic closure. These conspire to portray eros—and with it the self imprisoned within the confines of ego—as an ontological blind alley. In the enclosed place of the heart and the head (which the image of the spherical restaurant merely amplifies), life is divested of its greater, transcendent purpose, becoming what Berdiaev had once characterized as "evil infinity." Yet Moscow Chestnova's revolutionary fantasy of moving beyond the everyday round—"So live according to the straight line, without a subject or circle" (*Happy Moscow*, 37), is undercut by the very physiology of the heroine herself. As woman she *is* the biological cycle of life and death that brackets each human existence: "We live and die on the bosom of woman . . . that's how it's supposed to be according to the subject of fate, according to the circle of happiness" (*Happy Moscow*, 37). This despite the fact that Moscow's breasts are anything but round or feminine (her companion describes them as peering forward like "two metal punches"). Moreover, the image that Chestnova chooses to describe her escape from the prison house of desire is itself thoroughly ambiguous. Staring outside the window of the restaurant the next morning, Moscow sees a tree, whose outstretched limbs hold forth the promise of a linear journey without end or return. Yet the narrator notes that the momentum of the tree's journey is quickly exhausted at the point where it "had neither the strength nor the means to go farther" (*Happy Moscow*, 38). A metaphor for the dilemma of woman as such, the tree models the Stalinist heroine's quixotic desire to escape the vegetable kingdom. Unfailingly rooted in terra firma, woman seeks transfiguration only to be reminded—often abruptly and violently—of her ancient ties to Mother Earth. And just as the parachuting heroine had earlier succumbed to the weight of gravity, so Moscow Chestnova now dreams of flight, all the while remaining firmly tethered to the chthonic underworld.[129]

One of Platonov's best-known short stories of the period ("The River Potudan'") paints a similar picture. Here, too, the writer concludes that the path of self-transcendence runs precisely through the "filth" of the human body—with no hint given of a utopian otherworld. Published in 1937 in a collection of the same name, the story portrays a young man's struggle to come to grips with his sexuality and his relationship to his father. Platonov's "River" is rich in Oedipal motifs. Both father and son are at times interested in the same woman, and the protagonist Nikita Firsov repeatedly fantasizes about returning to the eternal "no-place" (*u-topia*) of his dead mother's womb. Yet by the end of the story Nikita successfully negotiates the conflict, literally taking over the *place* of his father. It is noteworthy that while the latter initially resists—in a key scene he laments the fact that his son is preparing to marry the daughter of the woman he himself did not have the courage to wed—the father ultimately cedes his place to the younger generation, thereby acknowledging the importance of biological/natural law. As in *Dzhan* or *Happy Moscow*, the revolutionary-utopian fantasy of blocking nature and time—an Oedipal urge of the first order—yields to another kind of Oedipal drama, one in which the Fyodorov-like patriarch must agree to be reintegrated into the matrix of biological law.[130] Meanwhile, the ideal of an exclusively male kinship implicit in the Fyodorovian patriarch's attempts to keep his son unmarried and at his side yields to the principle of bodily closeness and contact symbolized by Nikita's relationship with his wife, Lyuba.[131] Particularly noteworthy is the fact that in

Platonov's "River . . . " the hero attains maturity precisely by affirming his biological (sexual) self—a self that incorporates, rather than excludes, the female Other. Thus at the end of the tale Firsov knocks on Lyuba's window (reprising the gesture of knocking on his father's window from the beginning of the story) as if to underscore the substitution of biology, sexuality, and family for the timeless no-place of the all-male utopia.

One of the most potent metaphors for the revolution's sweeping aspiration to remake life on earth was the image of Archimedes's lever. Originally, Archimedes had boasted that given a lever and the proper point of support he could move the entire earth. In a famous quote Trotsky added a revolutionary corrective to Archimedes's ambitious claim. He remarked that while Archimedes himself possessed neither the lever nor the power to perform such a feat, the victorious revolution had, in fact, provided humankind with a new fulcrum—though it was still necessary to construct the levers.[132] In *Happy Moscow* Platonov polemicizes with this idea, offering the scale (in lieu of the lever) as a more just means of ensuring happiness on earth. Thus toward the end of the novel a not entirely reformed Sartorius/Gruniakhin contemplates the ideas of Archimedes and the Alexandrian Heron. Both figures had theorized that the golden rule of mechanics would bestow untold benefits on humankind. Nature's bounty, they believed, could be extracted with a minimum of effort, using mere cunning and trickery as the necessary lever and fulcrum:

> Therfore, it was not so much labor as trickery, cunning and a soul primed for enjoying happiness that determined the fate of humankind. Archimedes and Hero of Alexandria had long ago rejoiced over the golden rules of science, which promised widespread bliss to humanity. After all, using only a single gram on one end of an uneven lever it was possible to raise a ton, even the entire globe, according to Archimedes' calculations. And Lunacharsky even proposed igniting a new sun if the present one were to prove insufficient, or just boring and ugly. (*Happy Moscow*, 55)

Having been seduced in his youth by the pull of Archimedes' lever himself, Platonov now polemicizes with the idea, suggesting that it must be weighed against the law of the dialectic, which reminds us that "we dig inside the world and it squeezes us in response with equal force."[133] Thus the same Sartorius–Gruniakhin who initially exults over the possibility of "swindling" nature by means of the golden rule quickly retracts his enthusiasm when a co-worker named Arabov applies the golden rule of pleasure to his personal life. For Arabov not only ruins his marriage but inadvertently causes the death of his son: "He wanted to revel in a young beauty, he wanted to bear love not as an obligation with his wife alone but as pleasure."[134] In this one can hear a distinct echo of Platonov's earlier essay "About the First Socialist Tragedy," where the author had negatively equated the pleasure principle so often maligned by earlier Bolshevik ideology with the very core of the revolution's Promethean myth.[135] Thus the naïve fantasy of "igniting another sun" implicit in Stalinist transformationalism gives way to a more nuanced, dialogic understanding of the relationship between technology and nature—one based not on the desire for conquest but the need for coexistence: "The dialectic is probably an expression of stinginess, the difficult-to-master coarseness of nature's construction, and it is only thanks to this that humanity has been able to be educated historically. Otherwise, everything would have ended a long time ago on earth, like a child playing with candy, which has melted, and the child did not even manage to eat it."[136]

In *Happy Moscow* Platonov underscores the inadequacy of various revolutionary-transformational fantasies by replacing the metaphor of Archimedes's lever with that of the scale. And it would seem to be no accident that it is precisely Sartorius—the utopian engineer par excellence—who comes to acknowledge the superiority of the scale over the lever. Upon taking up a new position at the Republic Scales Trust, he reflects that "everywhere, at all times and in all spaces, the most universal and indispensable machine has been the balance. Balances are as old as weapons, and it may be that they are one and the same—what is a balance but a sword from the battle, laid across the crest of a rock, so that the victors can divide up the booty justly?" (*Happy Moscow*, 65). Here the ultimate emblem of mastery and conquest, the warrior's sword, renounces its intrusive (male) thrust, instead becoming a means of justly mediating competing claims. Unlike Archimedes's lever or the golden rule of mechanics, both of which presuppose a fundamental inequality between the claims of humanity and nature, the scale represents not only justice but a cosmic equilibrium—the loose logic of give-and-take inherent in any relationship between equals. In both *Dzhan* and his essay "About the First Socialist Tragedy," Platonov had proposed a relationship between self and other that rejected the idea of profit and functioned according to the principle of a universal "tit for tat."[137] It is this same idea—that of a fair apportioning—that is implied in the image of the sword-cum-scale. Elsewhere, this same idea takes the form of "sharing." Curiously, Platonov uses it not merely to denote interpersonal relations, but more generally to evoke a state of corporeal harmony, one in which all the body's organs and parts share equally in the common task of maintaining life. Thus the narrator in *Happy Moscow* speaks of the sword-as-scale as a means of "justly dividing/sharing the spoils between victors" (*Happy Moscow*, 30). More to the point, the ending of Platonov's "River Potudan'" makes clear that the resolution of Firsov's sexual dilemma coincides with a particular kind of bodily equilibrium, since the hero's heart is finally able share its blood with poor but necessary pleasure: "Nikita did not experience as a result of his close love with Lyuba a higher joy than he had ordinarily known. He simply felt that his heart was sharing its blood with poor but necessary pleasure."[138]

Yet as Platonov makes clear, the desire to circumvent the dialectic—to reap untold benefits with the help of Trotsky's lever or, as in the case of Kostia Arabov, to pursue pleasure unencumbered by obligation—is everpresent in humankind's fantasies of *zhiznetvorchestvo* or "life-creating." Indeed, this idea is implicit in the very name of the French Komsomol girl whom Kostia Arabov prefers to his wife. For the name Bessonee-Favor is taken from the famous Bessonee-Favor water pump. And throughout Platonov's oeuvre images of water, pumping, and sluices are synonymous with the utopian project as such.[139] In *Happy Moscow*, as elsewhere, such attempts to "pump out" nature's riches are invariably offset by the greater weight of tragedy. Thus while working to construct the Moscow metro—where large amounts of ground water literally had to be pumped out of the individual shafts[140]—Moscow Chestnova will lose her leg in a tragic accident. Likewise, Arabov will buy his pleasure with Bessonee at the cost of his son's untimely death:

> You've heard about the golden rule of mechanics. Some people thought they could use this rule to outwit all of nature, life itself. Kostya Arabov also wanted to have with you, or out of you—how should I put it?—something, some sort of free gold. . . . But he didn't get very much . . ." "Not much, that's right," Bessonee agreed. "So, how much did he get? Not more than a gram! But to balance it he had to pile a whole ton of burial earth on the other end of the lever, burial earth that is lying there and crushing his son." (*Happy Moscow*, 56)

As I have already mentioned, the structure of Platonov's *Happy Moscow* as a whole follows a downward trajectory, from the noumenal heights to the tragedy of unreconstructed matter.[141] We need only follow the fates of the novel's protagonists to sense the gravity underpinning the novel. At the end of the novel Sartorius takes on the identity of a thirty-one-year-old counter attendant named Gruniakhin, going to work as a kitchen manager at an unimportant factory on the outskirts of Moscow. And after her accident in the bowels of the Moscow metro, Moscow Chestnova becomes simply "Musia," a name that cements the heroine's association (in the second half of the work) with filth and waste.[142] Similarly, Sartorius's earlier utopian notion of "pumping" the basic life force from food directly into the human organism yields to the much less glamorous task of kitchen duty. Gruniakhin's new job makes him responsible for weighing and distributing food: "He was in charge of preparing portions of bread for lunch, weighting out the meat and the amount of vegetables to go in to the pot, so that everyone would get their fair share"

(*Happy Moscow*, 54). Thus the Stalinist project of reforming nature is rejected in favor of a more traditional, almost "feminine" pragmatism.[143] Likewise, in the short story "The Clay House in the Uezd Garden" (1936), the protagonist Iakov Savvich goes from creating "useless," utopian machines (often associated with swindling or cheating) to working on the most banal everyday objects: "He no longer looked for the opportunity to make only strange mechanisms that slaked the desire of the dark soul but worked on everything he was given: pails, pie dishes, iron clamps, hinges for hanging wooden gates and various other things."[144]

This shift from "useless" to "useful" things signals a new understanding of biology and nature as ultimately more enduring than the entire panoply of revolutionary means designed to surgically improve them. Though by no means celebratory or jubilant, Sartorius's remark that "what is destined for liquidation can sometimes prove to be not only the most durable of all, but even to be doomed to eternal existence" (*Happy Moscow*, 30) casts a shadow of doubt over the life-transforming pathos of both pre- and postrevolutionary ideology. At the same time, Platonov's retreat from Stalinism's utopian dream coincides with an attempt to articulate a compromise position where the "no-place" of utopia and the every-place of quotidian existence might coexist.[145] Its decidedly unheroic tenor notwithstanding, the novel's (unfinished) ending hints at just such a possibility. In particular, Gruniakhin's shift from a posture of technocratic mastery to one of meek humility at the end of the novel suggests the importance of *self*-transcendence as a viable alternative to Stalinism's conquest of (human) nature. Following in Dostoevsky's rather than Trotsky's footsteps, Platonov sees the transformation of a "carnivorous" and egoistical Sartorius into the long-suffering Gruniakhin as the true path toward happiness.[146] In this regard, the hero's transformation reminds us of the one undergone by Chagataev in the earlier *Dzhan*. In both cases the search for a distant utopia falters when confronted with the needs of individual bodies anchored in the here and now:

> Matryona Fillipovna's second son would watch his mother quarrel with his new father with indifference, since his mother always got the best of his father. But once when Ivan Stepanovich grabbed his wife's hands because she had started to dig into his throat with her nails the boy warned him: "Comrade Gruniakhin, don't go beating up mom! Otherwise, I'll run your gut through with an awl, you son of a bitch! . . . It's not your house, so don't go getting any ideas!" Gruniakhin immediately came to his senses. Gruniakhin lost control unexpectedly, and then only from sharp pain. Matryona Fillipovna stood in front of him in the hot sweat of despair, exhausted, and working herself up with the entire zeal of her heart. She was protecting her husband from debauchery and ensuring his marital fidelity. Ivan Stepanovich listened, suffered and learned. At night as he lay next

to his wife he thought that this was exactly as it should be. Otherwise, his greedy, fickle heart would have worn itself out and perished in fruitless attachment to various women and friends—in perilous readiness to rush headlong into the thick of all the richness that was taking place on earth. (*Happy Moscow*, 57–58)

In his fiction of the latter half of the 1930s and particularly in *Happy Moscow*, Platonov seems inclined to view the body not as an impediment to be overcome but as a repository of resilience, perhaps even immortality. This view coincides with a cardinal shift in the author's understanding of humankind's relationship to the natural world and of the utopian project. As one critic notes, the protagonists of Platonov's earlier works had sought knowledge through domination and destruction, while those of the author's later prose acquire it by identification and compassionate understanding.[147] No doubt the most startling expression of such ontological empathy concerns the "lowest" manifestations of corporeal existence, such as waste, filth, excrement, dirt, and the like, which make up the fecund thematic core of the novel. As if forcing the reader to re-examine the very relationship between filth and purity—or emptiness and plenitude—Platonov portrays the body's base effusions as contiguous with the "beautiful person" itself.[148] Thus in the very first pages of the novel, the image of food passing through the heroine's digestive tract provides a metaphor for the cosmic homology of high and low, food and filth, scatology and eschatology, that will be played out throughout this and other works.[149]

Both in his stories and his notebook entries of the time Platonov develops the filth-as-food conceit, repeatedly portraying the abject as an object of keen interest and sometimes even affection. In the short story "Among Animals and People," for instance, one of the protagonists (Ivan Alekseevich) picks up a woman's handkerchief that is covered with blood and tests the bloodstain with his tongue.[150] And in his notebooks for the year 1934 Platonov notes the following detail about a Turkmen girl who will later become the heroine of his short story "Takyr": The crows of the steppe sit on telegraph poles. After a train passes by they swoop down onto the tracks and devour the garbage (*otbrosy*). This is how they live in the naked steppe. Dzhumal' also lived this way for a time."[151] Finally, in the first pages of *Happy Moscow* an enthusiastic Moscow Chestnova's reflects on her body's near magical ability to transform filth into health, vigor, and beauty: "Next, Moscow would wash, wondering at the chemistry of nature which transformed ordinary, meager food (and what filth had she not eaten in her life!) into the rosy purity and blossoming spaces of her body" (*Happy Moscow*, 15).[152] In stark contrast to Stalinist culture's promotion of a statuary body sculpted to house the ideally static citizen,[153] Platonov portrays Chestnova's (im)pure organism as a model of grotesque openness. Indeed, it is this same bid for "openness" in an era of statuary closure that would lead the author to repeatedly portray the unfinished, "grotesque" self as ideal: "For Moscow/Sart(orius): "It's impossible to be one and the same person; too great a grief comes of it, too, etc.""[154]

Nowhere is the connection between "clean" and "unclean" rendered more explicit than in the short story "The River Potudan'," in which the protagonist Nikita Firsov is made to undergo a kind of ritual defilement before he can embrace physicality and with it sexual desire. Echoing the philosophically more ambitious *Happy Moscow*, this tale of sexual maturing links food and feces in ways that fundamentally dissolve the boundaries between high and low—between pure and impure. As in the earlier *Dzhan* and his notebooks, here, too, Platonov depicts the marketplace as a locus where opposites merge and the self is "resurrected" through its contact with the Other. Indeed, it is hardly an exaggeration to speak of resurrection here, for Nikita's journey to the bazaar is at least partially modelled on traditional Russian Orthodox figures, such as that of the "holy fool"[155]—a figure with strong roots in the Eastern Orthodox tradition of "negative theology." As is the case with the holy fool, Firsov is forced through this experience of the bazaar's underworld to embrace the unclean. In order to eat, he must either clean out latrines (*otkhozhee mesto*) or sweep up various kinds of waste matter and filth. The unsettling effect of Platonov's conceit (i.e., conflating clean and unclean) is exacerbated by his use of double entendre, as in one scene in which Nikita is told by his boss to "completely clean up the public toilet."[156] Not unlike Moscow Chestnova whose body turns "unclean" things into "cleanliness" and "purity," through his work at the bazaar Nikita Firsov turns feces into food[157]: "In his tidy state apartment, from the room and the kitchen—the guard gave the deaf-mute some cold cabbage soup with lumps of fat in it to eat out of a pot, and after the grub he told him to get the broom, the shovel, the scraper, and the bucket with lime from the entryway and completely clean up the public place." Finally, it bears noting that the term for "latrine" in Russian contains the word for "place" (*mesto*). And it is precisely the absence of a "place" in the *hic et nunc* that propels Firsov's "utopian" desire to reenter the maternal womb. Perhaps it is no accident, then, that at its conclusion the story affirms not the "no-place" of utopia but the "public place" or latrine, even as it charts the hero's difficult journey from the otherworldly Potudan' to the concrete physicality of the marketplace.

In a later scene the hero encounters his father in a latrine just as he is about to lock up for the night and hears his father's voice from inside. "Don't be in such a hurry to lock up, there! . . . Or do they steal goods from here too?" Here, too, the distinction between waste matter and that which is valuable or "good" is purposefully rendered imprecise. Finally, in one of the key scenes of the story we discover that in the hero's absence his wife Lyuba had attempted to drown herself in the river Potudan' but was later revived by several fisherman. The Russian word for "drowned" (*utopilas'*), which points toward the utopian leanings of both characters,[158] is intentionally juxtaposed to the word "resuscitate" or "revive" (*otkhazhivat'*). The similarity of the verb "otkhazhivat'" and the Russian words for "waste" (*otkhody*) and "latrine" (*otkhozhee mesto*) makes clear a structural/thematic truth underlying the entire story. For both Nikita and his wife convalescence or "resurrection" can occur only as a result of being reunited with the "chthonic" underbelly of existence as embodied in various kinds of waste matter and filth. Elsewhere Platonov reflects that "filth" represents the natural milieu from which all life arises. Thus in his notebooks for the year 1934 the author writes: "The first time a plant is produced from the seed of the father-mother, but the second time it is produced from the soil, which consists of the dust of the father-mother. . . . We arise on the dust of our fathers!"[159]

In *Happy Moscow* the idea that the unclean represents an essential element within the dialectically configured structure of redemption is taken to its logical conclusion. As in the "The River Potudan'," here, too, the dialogic nature of reality is conveyed through an obscure logic that conflates incompatibles. Consider the following scene, in which Moscow Chestnova first meets her future husband (the quintessentially chthonic Komiagin). Platonov's description of Komiagin's threadbare clothing suggests that filth and longevity are not only *not* mutually exclusive but that they represent two sides of the same coin. In stark contrast to the image of a purified body (politic) promoted by Stalinist ideology,[160] the author of *Happy Moscow* suggests that filth may prove to be the ultimate refuge of immortality. In this respect, it is significant that the author zeroes in on Komiagin's clothes. For if Sartorius (whose Latin name means "tailor") begins the novel as the model architect of utopia, he ends it by rejecting Stalinism's push to *re-tailor* the ancient fabric of life on earth. And in the case of Komiagin, there is simply no way to distinguish between the fabric of the protagonist's coat and the dirt that holds it together, protecting and warming the human being inside: "The reservist's clothes were as worn as the skin on his face and they warmed the man only thanks to the long-lasting filth that had eaten its way into the decrepitude of the cloth" (*Happy Moscow*, 23). Likewise, in his description of Sartorius's trip to Krestovskii market, Platonov describes the nineteenth-century clothing sold there as testimony to the tenacity of a nearly indestructible past. And if it is true that the author uses images of filth and excrement to suggest the possibility of a "bathroom communism,"[161] here the threadbare clothing of the past reminds us of an equally primitive species of communism—the communism of the coat:[162]

"An unclean air hung over the crowded gathering of standing and muttering people. . . . Old clothing cut in the nineteenth-century fashion, which had been saturated with powder and preserved for decades on a cautious body, was being sold here. There were winter coats that during the time of the revolution had passed through so many hands that the width of the globe was too small to measure the length of their journeys between people. (*Happy Moscow*, 53)

This idea is picked up once again after Moscow loses her leg in a construction accident. Among others, the description of Chestnova's maiming reflects the high price in corporeal terms that Stalinist reconstruction exacted from individual human bodies. For if Moscow Chestnova symbolizes the city of Moscow (i.e., the body politic) brutally "reforged" by Stalin, Kaganovich, and others, then her wounding exemplifies the painful sacrifice that such "reconstruction" required of the entire society.[163] Still, such woundings are far from uncommon within the rhetoric of Socialist Realism, which simultaneously preached the body beautiful and its mutilated, sacrificial equivalent as ideals worthy of emulation.[164] Without being too flippant, let me suggest that Platonov's unusual take on the matter consists in combining these two, in maintaining that the heroine's body could be *both* crippled *and* sublime in the same breath. Thus what he emphasizes—beyond the wounding itself—is the peculiar resiliency and freshness of the surrounding organism. Unlike Stalinist ideology which held these two apart as competing ideals, Platonov intuits that filth and purity, disease and health inhabit the human body in equal measure. And in a final blow to aesthetic and logical norms, he shows his heroine to be "immortal" at the very moment when she is most mortal. It is tempting to see in this a nod to Dostoevsky's Zosima, whose rotting corpse is scandalous only for those who have lost touch with the mystery of the Russian soil. For the truly faithful the elder's decomposing body represents an essential part of the "mythic cycle of birth-death-regeneration that is the soul of the Christian mystery":[165]

Sambikin examined her leg. Under pressure, blood was gushing out of it and was slightly frothed. The bone was shattered along the entire cross-section and various kinds of filth had eaten their way into the wound. But the surrounding whole body possessed a tender brown color and such a fresh, puffy form of late innocence that the miner-woman merited immortality. (*Happy Moscow*, 42)

In what is surely one of the most unusual scenes in the novel this same grotesque quality is underscored by Sartorius's loving reflections on the coextensiveness of human beauty with the waste products of the body. As in "The River Potudan'," where the protagonist's prolonged contact with the natural cycle of eating/defecation allows him to see spiritual love and sexual desire as compatible, so too in *Happy Moscow* the implicit logic of defilement allows the twin realms of filth and cleanliness to abut one against the other. And this is not unlike the very act of writing itself. As Kristeva notes, the process of writing closely resembles such rites of defilement, reminding one "through the linguistic signs . . . of the demarcations that precondition and go beyond them." Indeed, the archaic/maternal nature of the authority that one encounters in pressing beyond the paternal Name or Logos has always been known to great writers, from Gustave Flaubert's "I am Madame Bovary" to James Joyce's Molly and—I would add—Platonov's Moscow Chestnova.[166] Chestnova, too, reflects the archaic authority that predates the name of the Father. Thus, while carefully examining Moscow's excrement, Sartorius notes that "now neither Moscow Chestnova herself, nor anything about her, however dirty, could have made Sartorius feel in the least squeamish, and he could have looked at the waste products of her body with the greatest of interest, since they too had not long ago formed part of a splendid person."[167]

Platonov's conceit recalls—among others—Sergei Bulgakov's notion of the universal "communism of life." For Bulgakov speaks of the fundamental identity of animate and inanimate matter in nature, which is foregrounded in the act of eating. This as opposed to the implacable logic of separation postulated within the natural sciences. By extending the logic of his argument, the Russian philosopher comes to view even pathology as implicated in the mechanism of life.[168] Likewise, for the male protagonists of *Happy Moscow* the "pathological" effusions of Moscow Chestnova's body are imbued with their own measure of life. In the scene just mentioned, Sartorius admires the heroine's excrement. In a parallel episode, another admirer—this time the surgeon Sambikin—embraces the heroine from the other end. And it seems quite clear that for Platonov the mouth and the anus, food and feces, represent part of the same mechanism of life: "He kissed her on the mouth; the suffocating odor of chloroform was coming out of her, but now he could breathe anything at all that she exhaled from herself" (*Happy Moscow*, 43).[169]

The figure of the alimentary canal which brings together food and feces, high and low, is variously embodied throughout *Happy Moscow*. Initially, it appears as the "pipe" that Moscow Chestnova becomes while plunging earthward beneath her burning parachute. Later the same image resurfaces in the guise of a dead woman, whose intestinal tract contains food and feces separated by an empty space that both Sambikin and Sartorius agree represents the site of the human soul. And finally the blocked tunnel of the newly constructed Moscow subway where Moscow Chestnova loses her leg during a construction accident is nothing if not a subterranean echo of the same pipe or canal. In each instance Platonov demonstrates that the high cannot remain segregated from the low—a truth that unfolds with particular gravity in the

depths of the Moscow underground. As I will demonstrate later, the canonical metro narrative invariably portrays the newly constructed Moscow subway as symbolizing the unequivocal victory of the noumenal heights over the
city's "chthonic" underneath. For instance, in his *Metro: Miracle beneath
Moscow*, Lev Kassil' contrasts the brightly lit marble and granite stations of
the completed metro with the "raw, dank and uninviting bowels" negotiated
by L. Kaganovich and his engineers during their initial descents into the
fledgling underground. More importantly, the author notes that the ethereal
architecture of the Moscow *metropoliten* "which beckons towards the heights
rather than underground" stands in direct contrast to the gloomy maws of its
European counterparts.[170] Roughly the same can be said of the socialist workers who daily emerged from Moscow's underbelly. The *komsomol'tsy* who
were the project's undisputed vanguard were said to represent a new generation of Stalinist Homo sapiens—unfailingly optimistic and upward-looking.
Thus in one *Izvestiia* article from 1935, a young Komsomol shockworker who
like Moscow Chestnova went from parachuting to working on the subway appears "fresh, clean, neatly dressed . . . displaying her beautifully curled hair
for the cameras."[171]

Yet Platonov's cameo of the subway highlights the dark side of Stalinism's
lucid narrative. In this sombre retelling, the ambitious attempt to burrow into
the earth undertaken by Kaganovich and company brings disaster rather than
triumph—a disaster that will eventually cost Moscow Chestnova her leg.
With it the utopian attempt to reach into the "the last hiding-place of a man's
insides" so as to "clean out the pus that had accumulated there drop by drop
over the centuries" (*Happy Moscow*, 39) enters a blind alley. This is literally
the case, since Moscow is trapped and almost killed in what Platonov describes as a "blind passageway." And far from emptying out the entrails of the
underground (Platonov's quasi-scatological metaphor should not go unappre-
ciated), Moscow herself is overcome by the very "filth" she had sought to
eliminate. As in the case of the heroine's earlier ill-fated parachute jump,
here, too, gravity gains the upper hand, while Chestnova's body becomes an
emblem of the impossibility of banishing disease and darkness entirely from
the bowels of Mother Earth.[172]

The final and most important embodiment of the "pipe" lies at the very
heart of the novel, in the image of the sewage pipe that symbolizes the intestinal tract of the Stalinist polis. A variant of the mythological world-tree, the
sewer pipe symbolically weds the upper world of flight and utopian striving
to the nether realms of copulation and defecation. As elsewhere in Platonov's
novel, the function of the pipe as a passageway, as a continuum that collapses
extremes, is central. So central is the pipe to the novel's spatial topography,
in fact, that in one instance the narrator maps out the nocturnal events of the

residential building in relation to this scatological variant of the *axis mundi*: "Sartorius leaned his head against the cold sewage pipe that Moscow had once embraced and heard the intermittent sound of filth flowing down from the upper floors" (*Happy Moscow*, 111).

Beyond the symbolic function of knitting together the upper and lower worlds, the sewage pipe serves to portray the Stalinist body politic as engaged in an endless round of defecation. This alone is controversial, notwithstanding Stalinist culture's preoccupation with social hygiene. The Russian term for "sewage pipe" (*kanalizatsionnaia truba*) is obviously related to the word for "canal" (*kanal* in Russian). Among the most prominent Stalinist construction projects were such undertakings as the infamous White Sea Canal (1934). The symbolic function of the latter (which in some cases proved more enduring than their practical usefulness) was not merely to rechannel nature's chaotic flood, but to ritually purge and purify those elements of Soviet society that had been deemed "hostile" or "alien." By contrast, Platonov's scatological imagery suggests that the human body can never purge itself entirely of the filth that courses through it. As the convalescent Moscow Chestnova remarks of her hair, "she . . . washed her hair every day because she constantly felt that there was dirt in her hair and even cried from vexation that the dirt would not go away" (*Happy Moscow*, 44).

Indeed, time itself may be said to function in a manner analogous to that of the city's iron intestines. The work of the clock is, according to Platonov, like that of a conduit that allows the present to filter safely into the future and the past. As in "The River Potudan'," where the renewal of the biological and temporal cycle proves crucial to the hero's final recovery, here, too, we see a radical break with the "temporal anxiety" that had marked the writer's earlier work. In such novels as *Chevengur* the utopian impulse to block time's passage results in a permanent apocalypticism, according to one critic.[173] And in the *Foundation Pit* the tyranny of Chronos at the end of the novel (Nastia is "devoured" by the grave that Chiklin spends fifteen hours digging) signals the demise of the utopian project. Platonov's *Happy Moscow* presents an altogether different scenario, one predicated on the hero's renunciation of the quest for timelessness and his or her acceptance of a life anchored in the present.[174] Here it is only the unfettered passage of time from present to past, like the constant flow of excrement through the sewage pipe, that averts the catastrophe of temporal blockage. Likewise, in *Dzhan* the writer spells out the disastrous consequences for the (woman's) body of the utopianist's inclination to mortgage the moment against the promise of future paradise. Khanom, Platonov writes, would "perish from her body's filth" if she "deferred her need and care until the point when she had a dwelling of her own"[175]:

But all the sounds ceased. The events, it seemed, had retreated deep into the bodies of the sleepers. But at the same time the pendulums of the grandfather clocks in the rooms were striking loud enought for all to hear, as if they were a production mechanism of the greatest importance. And, indeed, the task of the pendulums was of the utmost importance, for they drove off the accumulating time, so that gloomy and happy thoughts passed without obstruction through the human being, without stopping and being able to destroy him altogether. (*Happy Moscow*, 53)

If the Stalinist utopia sought nothing less than to purge human nature of its ontological underbelly, Platonov's *Happy Moscow* suggests rather that the body can never be entirely free of the things it (r)ejects or renders abject. Filth, excrement, even disease represent a naturally occurring (if regrettable) facet of organic life, according to Platonov. Indeed, they inhere in the very fabric of the body and cannot be removed except by annihilating the organism itself.[176] This becomes clear in the scene in which the surgeon Sambikin operates on a young boy with a brain tumor. Like Mikhail Bulgakov, whose 1927 novella *Heart of a Dog* clearly rejects the revolutionary-theurgic project of reworking (human) nature, Platonov suggests that the body is more enduring—more "ancient," if you will—than the revolution's optimistic fantasies of remaking it. At a key moment Sambikin stops the surgery in midstream, after it has become clear that it would be impossible to destroy all of the microorganisms infecting the boy's brain without destroying his body as well.[177] Thus the same "pus" that according to Sartorius would have to be banished from the body (*Happy Moscow*, 39) in order for it to be scientifically redeemed is shown to be deeply rooted in the core of human physiology. And here a comparison with the famous early-twentieth-century zoologist and microbiologist Ilya Mechnikov (whose work was well known to such figures as Bulgakov, Zoshchenko, and Kharms) seems in order, for the latter attributed the brevity of human life to the presence of certain poisonous microbes inhabiting the large intestine.[178] Yet just as Mechnikov realized the unfeasibility of removing or shortening the large intestine in order to free the body of these poisonous organisms,[179] Platonov's Sambikin suddenly grasps the futility of his situation; he cannot destroy all of the "pus-bearing bodies" in the boy's brain:

As he removed the streptococci there were fewer and fewer of them but Sambikin switched over to stronger microscopes that showed that the number of pus-bearing bodies, while quickly decreasing, was not altogether disappearing. . . . "Pack the wound and bandage it!" he commanded, for in order to completely destroy the streptococci it would be necessary to cut to pieces not only the child's entire head but his entire body down to his toes. (*Happy Moscow*, 20)

This description makes explicit what remains implicit throughout much of the novel. For Platonov, disease, like filth, excrement, or the remainder, represents a sort of ontological shadow or fold set deep in the fabric of the organism. That this lining cannot be excised from the body precisely because it *is* the body emerges clearly from the narrator's unusual comparison of the young boy's tumor to "a second wild head sucking out his ailing life."[180] Particularly noteworthy in this instance is Platonov's use of circular imagery. Earlier the author had used such images in his cameo of a restaurant "orgy" in order to evoke the inescapable tragedy of biological life—Berdiaev's "bad infinity." Thus "every voice in it sounded twice, and suffering was repeated" (*Happy Moscow*, 37). A similar strategy functions here. Caught in an anaesthesia-induced delirium, the young patient sees negative mirror images of his mother, sister, and pet cat. The boy's pathological-prophetic vision symbolizes the "closed circuit" of human psychophysiology, where the antagonistic poles of chaos and order, nature and culture are forever fused together. Played out cyclically throughout human history, and, ultimately within the body itself, this "tragedy" will not admit the linear, one-sided resolution proposed by Stalinist ideology. Indeed, the negligible distinction between chaos and order in the novel is evident in the narrator's description of the young boy's head. Steadily eroded by a pus-filled tumor, the fragile bone membrane of the skull barely manages to shelter the brain inside. This clearly echoes the earlier fence of "child-like proportions" that separated the utopian institute from a dilapidated residential building. Thus Stalinism's aspiration to turn the human body into something like *Dneprostroi*—that is, a monument to Bolshevik technology's triumph over nature—yields to a more ancient order. Like eternally feuding twins, nature and culture are, according to Platonov, entwined in a dialogue that is neither chaos nor cosmos but *chaosmos*:

> In the midst of changing clothes and thinking, he heard a noise in his left ear. The pus in the child's head was chemically eroding and eating away at the last bone plate that protected his brain. The mist of death was already spreading through the boy's mind; life was still hanging on beneath the membrane of bone, but there was not more than a fraction of a millimeter's thickness left and the weakening bone was vibrating beneath the pressure of the pus. (*Happy Moscow*, 19)

The notion that health and disease are hopelessly entwined in the human organism is implicit in the surgeon Sambikin's macabre project of using the recently deceased as potential reservoirs of longevity for the living. Recalling experiments with life prolongation that were popular throughout the 1930s,[181] Sambikin/Platonov's project betrays a distinct philosophical underpinning. The surgeon's idea rests on the paradoxical notion that animate and inanimate matter, life and death, are not mutually exclusive. And as grotesque as it might seem, the surgeon's curious undertaking recalls—among others—Vernadskii's concept of the biosphere, which was of considerable interest to the author during the early 1930s.[182] More remotely Sambikin's dream echoes the ancient Egyptian myth according to which Isis was able to conceive a son by retrieving the miraculously preserved life force of her dead husband Osiris. Thus the surgeon theorizes that "at the moment of death some kind of hidden sluice must open in the human body, and that from it there flows through the organism a special fluid which poisons the pus of death and washes away the ash of exhaustion, and which is carefully preserved all through life, right up to the moment of supreme danger. . . . Only death, when it rushes through the body, can break the seal on that reserve of concentrated life" (*Happy Moscow*, 49). Grotesque only in its extreme literalization (at one point the narrator notes that Sartorius "smiled a little at Sambikin's naivete: nature was too difficult, by his own reckoning, for such instant victories, and could not be confined within a single law" [*Happy Moscow*, 68–69]), Sambikin's idée fixe nevertheless throws into relief Platonov's own project in the novel. This project is perhaps best summed up by the philosophical excursus in which Sambikin explains that the secret of human (as opposed to animal) consciousness lies in the ability of human beings to negotiate dualism. According to the surgeon, this occurs because while it had previously been assumed that the brain governed only higher functions, leaving the spinal cord to control the lower functions and the heart, it turns out that both the brain and the spinal cord participate freely in operations assigned to the other.[183] In response to Sartorius's objection that animals, too, are inherently dualistic, Sambikin remarks that it is not dualism per se which defines the phenomenon of consciousness but rather the uniquely human ability to overcome it by synthesizing opposite impulses. Notably, Sambikin describes this synthesis of opposites in terms of the copulation metaphor that in one form or another had become predominant in Platonov's writing of the '30s:[184]

> It was necessary to become accustomed to coordinating, merging two thoughts in a single impulse. One of them rises from below the earth itself, from deep in the bones, while the other descends from the heights of the skull. It is necessary for them always to meet at the same moment and to come together, one wave against the other, to resonate with one another. . . . I'm so terrified of being alone at this moment! The eternal copulation of two passions that warms my head. (*Happy Moscow*, 32)

According to Igor' Smirnov, the tendency to represent opposites as dialectically compatible became a commonplace in the literature of the Stalinist period. For the culture and ideology of the '30s any conflict between opposites is comfortably resolved by dialectically reconfiguring seemingly contradictory elements.[185] Likewise, Boris Groys contends that the mythological telos of the

Stalinist "master narrative" lay in the overarching unity of all opposites.[186] In Socialist Realist texts this manifests itself in the relative ease with which a task can be resolved if only the hero(ine) approaches the problem "dialectically." To begin with a rather extreme example, in Fedor Panferov's novel *Mother-Volga* one protagonist claims that matter, even after having become inanimate, is capable of reentering a state of animateness via a simple change of environment. Biology, it is argued, can achieve immortality even in the profane present—in the proleptically charged *hic et nunc*. Similarly, a person need only possess sufficient willpower in order for any obstacle of (human) nature to be surmountable.[187] Thus in Petr Pavlenko's *Happiness*, Stalin unrealistically advises a Crimean gardener to create varieties of lemons and grapes that would grow in the harsh northern climate, saying: "Get them accustomed to harsh conditions, don't be afraid. You and I are southerners but we feel alright in the north, too."[188] One of the most dramatic variations of this idea concerns the ubiquitous motif of physical mutilation (usually of the legs) in Stalinist texts, where the protagonist's disability miraculously fails to prevent him from returning to work.[189] Thus in a short piece about the construction of the Moscow subway entitled *Metro: Miracle beneath Moscow* a worker named Lushnik injures his foot while working underground. Yet when he finds out after two weeks of convalescing that his shift is falling behind without him he simply returns to work and ignores the injury.[190]

Platonov's relationship to this phenomenon is at first glance somewhat confusing. As Clark has shown, Stalinism drew liberally from the fund of ancient myths and rituals, the rite of initiation or *incorporation* being one of the most compelling of these. Here the individual suffers mutilation or even token death in order to win acceptance into the ideological collective and with it access to a higher plane of consciousness.[191] Platonov's texts of the period are not immune to such mythological imagery—witness the sublimely mutilated heroine of *Happy Moscow*, Moscow Chestnova, or even the author's portrayal of Pushkin as the people's "sacrifice." To be sure, a certain amount of protective mimicry was not uncommon for authors and cultural figures of the time. The example of Akhmatova in the 1930s provides a case in point. "Locked in mortal combat with Stalin the supreme villain," Zholkovsky writes, Akhmatova's public and private persona acquired many of the most significant characteristics of Stalinist totalitarianism.[192] While Platonov's imagery appears to echo the masochistic underpinnings of the culture, particularly as embodied in its promotion of ritual mutilation, on the whole its pathos points elsewhere. Rather than portray suffering as the price of entering the community of the blessed, Platonov sees it as an inescapable facet of the human story.[193] And if Gorky had enjoined Zoshchenko to write a work that would "mock suffering," eventually leading the latter to compose his famous

Keys to Happiness, Platonov seems to have discarded those very keys. In *Dzhan*, *Happy Moscow*, and elsewhere, the author portrays suffering as intrinsic to human psychophysiology ("despair, anguish and need can remain compressed in the human organism right down to the last crevice: only a person's final breath draws them out")[194], and in this the writer seems to mock rather than celebrate "happiness." Ultimately Platonov owes more to Dostoevsky than to Gorky, particularly to the latter's understanding of consciousness as the by-product of suffering, without which there can be no narrative, no history. Mocking the naively optimistic worldview of Stalinism (within which suffering was merely an episode), Platonov remarks in his notebooks: "Any sort of ordering, 'happiness,' etc., of the world is [the result of] hyperbolic imagination, the philosophy of the clerk. The art of war is also 'clerkism.'"[195] And in the same notebooks he suggests, now explicitly invoking Dostoevsky, that "a living person is one within whom pain is *healing*. Anyone else is not alive (those who don't know pain)."[196]

Likewise, in *Happy Moscow* Platonov uses the same dialectic cynically exploited by Socialist Realism not as a means to transcend physiology but rather to embrace the body, even in its ailing and mutilated state. In the typical Stalinist text the dialectic functions as little more than conceptual legerdemain, as a means of reconfiguring the negative as positive. Take, for instance, the example of Olesha's screenplay *A Stern Youth* (1936), in which the protagonist assures a female friend that beauty is "dialectical," since all it takes in order for an ugly person to appear beautiful is for that person to be loved by someone else. By contrast in *Happy Moscow* the dialectic reminds the reader that tragedy (i.e., ugliness) constitutes an inalienable, indeed, essential *part* of the "beautiful person." Thus when Moscow Chestnova enters a residential building where Komiagin lives she sees a poster that—read metaphorically—appears to equate selfhood with mutilation: "Along the corridor walls there hung posters from MOPR, the Savings Bank Administration, directions for taking care of a baby, a person in the form of the letter 'Я' shortened by one leg" (*Happy Moscow*, 17).[197] To a certain extent, this idea mirrors the complexity of Platonov's own psyche. Indeed, a fellow author and close friend of Platonov's (L. Gumilevskii) notes in a letter to the writer in 1941 that "during the entire time of our acquaintance . . . you have treated yourself like a person afflicted by an accidental sickness, . . . or the loss of limbs during a tram accident."[198] Yet there is more at play here than simple pathology. In Platonov's fiction of the period, the loss of limbs (either voluntary or involuntary) most often serves as a vehicle for self-transcendence. One need only recall Chagataev in *Dzhan* or Sartorius/Gruniakhin in *Happy Moscow*. More broadly, Platonov's understanding of "tragedy" mirrors the kenotic tradition within Russian Orthodoxy. For at its most basic level the Orthodox *imitatio*

Christi requires one to actively assimilate and incorporate the ontological Other (i.e., filth, waste, chaos, etc.) necessary for the dialogic completion of the self. No doubt it is in this spirit that the poster representing the "Я" with a shortened leg should be understood.[199] In the same vein Platonov describes an anonymous mountain dweller's readiness to sacrifice his body for the ailing Moscow Chestnova: "'Take it, my Russian daughter,' the old peasant told her. 'I'm sixty, so I'm giving you my fingernail. If I were forty, I would have brought you my finger, and if I were thirty, I also would have cut off my leg, the leg you don't have'" (*Happy Moscow*, 43). Finally, the rather unusual idea that one might preserve a degree of "wholeness" even in a mutilated and limbless state is conveyed—among others—by a disturbing dream that Moscow Chestnova has while under anesthesia. Cannibalized by the animals and people surrounding her, in her dream the heroine fantasizes about a place where she can "survive" or "remain intact" (*utselet'* literally means "to remain whole" in Russian) in the form of "a miserable creature made of a few dry bones" (*Happy Moscow*, 43). And even in this instance, where the image itself is overwhelmingly negative, Platonov's paranomasia nonetheless suggests that one can survive *intact* even if the body is tinged with disease or death.

While Moscow Chestnova is certainly the most visible of Platonov's crippled-yet-immortal protagonists, there are others who qualify as close cousins—if not siblings. The figure of Zarrin-Tadzh in the short story "Takyr" (1934) is one. Like many of the heroes/heroines of Platonov's later work, Zarrin Tadzh transcends death not by conquering it but by literally absorbing it into her flesh and blood. And it is certainly no accident that the writer's retreat from the Fyodorovian/postrevolutionary project of "conquering death" should coincide with a relative increase in the number of heroines (as opposed to *heroes*) in his prose.[200] For as early as 1920 Platonov had written (in "The Soul of the World") that woman distills "death" through her own blood, which is to say, not from a point outside of the body but from within the very prison house of physiology. At a key point in the story Platonov compares his heroine to a tree that had withstood the onslaughts of nature by drawing them into its own body, thus domesticating and taming the hostile Other. This as opposed to Stalinism's declaration of an all-out war against the natural: "It must have been that when the river flooded it thundered against the tree's roots with great boulders, but the tree ate these enormous rocks into its body, surrounded them with patient skin, assimilated and rendered them habitable and kept on growing, having meekly raised up alongside itself the very thing that was to have destroyed it."[201]

This idea is taken to its logical conclusion in Platonov's cameo of Tatiana Larina in his essay on Pushkin and Gorky. Like her predecessor Zarrin-Tadzh, Platonov's Tatiana *incorporates* suffering, using grief as an instrument for self-transformation. Here the writer continues in the Dostoevskian tradition that prizes meekness over power or conquest, locating genuine strength in the "conquest" of ego. After all, at the end of Pushkin's *Eugene Onegin*, according to Platonov, "Tania is in a position of power but refuses when she is given power." Instead she "finds the strength of her happiness and salvation in her own life development that *assimilates all grief* [my emphasis]."[202] And more to the point, the heroine's physical wounding (her legs are broken) becomes the site of her transfiguration and immortality: "She, Tatiana, resembles a mysterious creature from an old fairy tale that crawled on the ground, and its legs were broken so that the creature would perish—then it found wings in itself and ascended above the low place where it had been assigned to die."[203]

Notably, the fate that Platonov envisions for "Tania" carries over to the great poet himself. This was nothing less than a slap in the face of the Stalinist *sotsial'nyi zakaz* ("social command"). For Stalinism's idolatrous worship of Pushkin had all but turned the poet into a Slavic incarnation of Nietzsche's superman, one who could survive on an Arctic ice floe with the shipwrecked Cheliuskinites (if not physically then at least in spirit) or even pilot a fighter plane.[204] Meanwhile, Platonov was more interested in Pushkin's credentials as a tragic hero. Thus in his essay on Pushkin and Gorky Platonov celebrates the idea of "sacred mutilation" that in Pushkin's "The Prophet" marks the transformation of profane individual into sacred prophet.[205] For Pushkin and Platonov alike physical maiming functions as the essential mark of the prophet's status as God's chosen one.[206] And here we would do well to recall the image in Platonov's *Happy Moscow* of the "Я" ("I") that had lost a limb during a traffic accident. Clearly, for both Pushkin and Platonov prophetic selfhood is realized through a painful process of bodily inscription. In other words, the self can rise to the level of language—that is, of narratability—only by being physically maimed.[207] Perhaps this is why in a play about the life of the young Pushkin that Platonov completed shortly before his death in 1951 (entitled *The Lycée Pupil*) the author has Pushkin refer to himself as "an invalid."

That Platonov should produce his own version of the Pushkin myth during the '30s is no surprise. The great nineteenth-century poet was mythologized by both Dostoevsky and numerous Silver Age figures as a new species of universal man, capable of resolving even the most prickly conundra of Russian life.[208] And the energy of that myth survived well into the first half of the twentieth century. For Stalinism Pushkin appeared to embody not only the great literary and cultural pedigree it craved for itself, but the quintessence of healthy, accessible, and life-affirming art mandated within Socialist Realism. The boisterous, all-union celebrations of the anniversary of Pushkin's death in 1937 only serve to confirm this. Indeed, even as skeptical a writer as Mikhail

Zoshchenko was not above celebrating Pushkin precisely for his sunny, life-af-firming countenance. Not so Platonov. Drawing on the tradition of personal-ized appropriations of Pushkin's image associated with the Silver Age, Platonov foregrounds the sense of prophetic martyrdom overshadowed by Stal-inism's celebration of an optimistic "Bolshevik Pushkin." More importantly, by creating an image of the poet that spotlights the artist's ability to overcome the crippling effects of his encounter with state power, Platonov at the same time envisioned the means and manner of his own eventual triumph. Like the mysterious fairy-tale creature whose legs had been broken so that it would die, Platonov's "literary body" was repeatedly mutilated by the attacks of estab-lishment critics. In fact, the writer uses this image quite openly in a letter (writ-ten in 1937) to one of his most vehement detractors, a certain A. Gurvich: "My 'literary torso' was taken, so to speak, and critically prepared. As a result of this 'experiment' the following ingredients were recovered from my (after all) hu-man body: one dog, four nails, a pound of sulphur and a clay ash-tray."[209] At the same time, Platonov's portrayal of Pushkin's Tatiana and of Pushkin him-self as triumphant "invalids" opens up the possibility that the writer might him-self ascend above the place where he had been assigned to die.

Platonov's suggestion of an "immortality in the flesh" speaks to the heart of his literary and philosophical project—a project that aspired to reintegrate the ejecta of the utopian dream back into the hearth of being. It is here that we can begin to grasp the deeper meaning of *Happy Moscow*'s unusual, of-tentimes unsettling imagery. How, for instance, are we to understand Sam-bikin's strange claim that "the vital tension of a person who is being con-sumed by death is so great that a sick person is often stronger than a healthy one, while a dead person is more vigorous than the living" (*Happy Moscow*, 42)? Odd as it might seem, Platonov's portrayal of the ailing body as more re-silient—more ripe for immortality, as it were—than a healthy one provides the writer with a means of self-rehabilitation not envisioned by Stalinist ide-ology. Of course, one might object that this is the route taken by Ostrovsky's Pavel Korchagin, who becomes a Bolshevik saint precisely because of his fantastically mortified body. Yet in Korchagin's case mutilation and even death are redeemed by the promise of a future without either, one where the vicissitudes of the flesh would be no more. Ultimately, this does not differ substantially from the ideal preached by Mikhail Zoshcenko, whose quest for physical and spiritual healing led him to imagine a body (preferrably his own) miraculously transformed by Stalinist science and reason. By contrast, Platonov arrived at a corporeal ideal that was, in many ways, the "obverse of Stalinism."[210] To be sure, this ideal echoes the writer's attempts to negotiate a place for himself within the Stalinist utopia—a process that from the very outset could only be imagined in terms of physical and spiritual mutilation.[211]

At the same time, Platonov's paradoxical vision of an "immortal mortality" reflects a much broader desire (one shared by his prominent contemporary Mikhail Bakhtin) to create a new species of philosophical and artistic language. Based not on the twin gestures of exclusion and identity that had traditionally defined linguistic and philosophical coherence, this language sought the elusive *coincidentia oppositorum*—the connectedness of all with everything.

Like Joyce's *Finnegan's Wake* or Bataille's *The Story of the Eye* (1928) Platonov's writing of the mid-to-late '30s (i.e., *Dzhan, Happy Moscow*, and others) collapses the strictures of Aristotelian logic. An enthusiastic proponent of dualism with all its triumphs and discontents in his early years, the mature Platonov—not unlike Joyce or Bataille—represents reality as comprising filth and purity, disease and immortality in equal measure. For this reason, one cannot help but wonder if it was not this very quality that Platonov found most compelling in the protean figure of Pushkin. Invalid yet immortal, the image of Pushkin's crippled prophet (or that of Tatiana Larina) provided Platonov with a "way out," with a means of contextualizing the tragedy of the moment within a greater sense of "chaotic order" ("chaosmos?"). Perhaps it was this realization that would later inspire the writer to compose the following lines about the young Pushkin, reflecting all the while on uneven contours of his own fate: "All the qualities of a great poet, including the so-called negative qualities, are inclined toward the greatest fulfillment of their purpose in life."[212]

The suggestion has been made that Platonov's work can be divided into two distinct periods, just as the writer himself might be separated into two Platonovs. The first of these periods ends in 1934 with the ascendancy of Socialist Realism in the literary realm and a shift in Platonov's writing toward a more conformist aesthetic that will remain a constant in the author's work until his death in 1951.[213] Likewise, it has been suggested that for a three-year period in the late 1930s Platonov finally capitulated before the demands of the Stalinist utopia—as witnessed by such works as "Among Animals and Plants" (1936) and "The Voice of the Father" (1939).[214] While it is certainly true that one can speak of two different Platonovs, it is not necessarily the case that in his later writing Platonov caves in to Stalinist ideology. Indeed, far from acquiescing to the voice of the Father, such seminal works as *Dzhan*, "The River Potudan,'" and *Happy Moscow* firmly renounce the demands (both existential and philosophical) of the aggressive patriarchy that lay at the core of Stalinism. In her *Powers of Horror: An Essay on Abjection*, Kristeva suggests that the "legal, phallic, linguistic establishment" (in short, the order of the Father) manifests itself in a series of strict prohibitions meant to segregate the "clean and proper self" from its abject Other. At the same time, there exist those more ambivalent systems of thought within which "abjection and high purity" are seen as coequal, and where an archaic Maternal authority "on the nether side of the proper Name" predominates.[215] In renouncing his earlier quest for the ideal "no-place" (i.e., the all-male utopia, Fyodorov's abstract brotherhood, etc.), Platonov is increasingly drawn in his writing of the 1930s to the poor but necessary "every-place" of the *hic et nunc*. And it is no accident that this "every-place" is most closely associated with Woman and Woman's body. For Platonov s/he symbolizes the double-edged process of transcending nature even as one remains tragically tethered to it—of dialogic coexistence rather than monologic conquest. And it is this novel quest for reconciliation and compromise that colors much of Platonov's work after 1934. While such a stance surely contributed to the author's ability to survive the rigors of Stalinism, it cannot be equated with capitulation. Rather it seems to resemble what Kharms described in 1939 as the curious ability of an intelligent person to "exploit the blows of fate and with each blow get closer to the desired goal."[216]

NOTES

1. This chapter represents a significantly expanded version of my article entitled "Scatology and Eschatology: The Recovery of the Flesh in Andrei Platonov's *Happy Moscow*," *Slavic Review* 59, no. 1 (2000): 154–81.

2. Ibid.

3. Gary Saul Morson, *The Boundaries of Genre: Dostoevsky's "Diary of a Writer" and the Tradition of Literary Utopia* (Austin: University of Texas Press, 1981), 86.

4. Thomas Seifrid, "Platonov, Socialist Realism, and the Avant-Garde," in John Bowlt and Olga Matich, eds., *Laboratory of Dreams: The Avant-Garde and Cultural Experiment* (Stanford, 1996), 240–44.

5. Katerina Clark, *The Soviet Novel: History as Ritual* (Chicago: University of Chicago Press, 1981), 167–76.

6. Eliot Borenstein, *Men without Women: Masculinity & Revolution in Russian Fiction: 1917–1929*, (Durham: Duke University Press, 2000), 197.

7. Thomas Seifrid, "Pisat' protiv materii: o iazyke *Kotlovana* Andreia Platonova," in N. V. Kornienko and E. D. Shubina, comps., *Andrei Platonov: mir tvorchestva* (Moscow, 1994), 306.

8. Ibid., 259.

9. Ibid., 255, 259.

10. Ibid., 214.

11. Borenstein writes (*Men without Women: Masculinity & Revolution in Russian Fiction: 1917–1929*, 213) that "it is she who 'brings heaven down to earth,' at the same time raising 'man' (cheloveka) to new heights."

12. Julia Kristeva, *The Powers of Horror: An Essay on Abjection,* trans. Leon S. Roudiez (New York: Columbia University Press, 1982), 102.

13. Ibid., 72. Note that Kristeva in the above-mentioned essay and Luce Irigaray both regard the maternal or feminine as that which is excluded from the symbolic order (and hence from the very opposition of mind/matter) but which serves as the precondition of that same order. As Judith Butler notes (*Bodies that Matter: On the Discursive Limits of "Sex"* [New York: Routledge, 1993], 184), the feminine is "what must be excluded for that economy to posture as internally coherent."

14. Thomas Seifrid, "Smradnye radosti marksizma: Zametki o Platonove i Batae, *Novoe literaturnoe obozrenie,* no. 32 (1998): 56–57.

15. Ibid., 99. Similarly, Seifrid remarks ("Smradnye radosti," 57) on the abundance of terms and images used by Platonov (particularly in *Chevengur* and *The Foundation Pit*) to symbolize those who have been excluded from the social hierarchy. Eric Naiman also suggests ["Communism and the Collective Toilet: Lexical Heroes in Platonov's *Happy Moscow*," *Poetics: The Journal of the British Neo-Formalist Circle* 26 (Autumn, 2001): 100] that Platonov's scatological play in *Happy Moscow* represents a kind of extreme version of Solov'ev's idea of *sobornost'*, which he playfully designates as "*ubornost'*" or "the collectivity of the toilet."

16. Paul Hegarty, *Georges Bataille: Core Cultural Theorist* (London: SAGE Publications Ltd, 2000), 116.

17. Julia Kristeva, *Powers of Horror*, 76.

18. Keith Livers, *Scatology and Eschatology*, 161.

19. Andrei Platonov, *Zapisnye knizhki: Materialy k biografii*, ed. N. V. Kornienko (Moscow: IMLI RAN, "Nasledie," 2000), 102. Note that this conversation which concerns cleaning and purification takes place in a bathhouse.

20. See Keith Livers, "Scatology and Eschatology," 161. See also Hans Günther, "Liubov' k dal'nemu i liubov' k blizhnemu: Postutopicheskie rasskazy A. Platonova vtoroi poloviny 1930-kh gg.," in *Strana filosofov Andreia Platonova: Problemy tvorchestva, vyp. 4, iubileinyi* (Moscow: IMLI RAN, "Nasledie," 2000), 310–11.

21. Boris Groys, "Die gebaute Ideologie," in Peter Noever, ed., *Tyrannei des Schönen: Architektur der Stalin-Zeit* (München: 1994), 18.

22. See John Haynes, *New Soviet Man: Gender and Masculinity in Stalinist Soviet Cinema* (Manchester: Manchester University Press, 2003), 81–82.

23. V. Chalmaev, *Andrei Platonov: K sokrovennomu cheloveku* (Moscow: Sovetskii pisatel', 1989), 382.

24. Jan Peter Locher, "Rasskaz Platonova 'Takyr' i tema vostoka," in *Strana filosofov Andreia Platonova: problemy tvorchestva, vyp. 4, iubileinyi* (Moscow: IMLI RAN, 2000), 289.

25. Andrei Platonov, *Zapisnye knizhki*, 379.

26. See Katerina Clark, *The Soviet Novel*, 167–76, 114–54.

27. Stephen Hutchings, "Remembering of a Kind: Philosophy and Art, Miscegenation and Incest in Platonov's 'Dzhan,'" *Russian Literature* LI (2000): 59.

28. Ibid., 164.

29. The tone is perhaps somewhat inappropriate here. In contradistinction to such latter-day saviors as Lenin and Stalin, Chagataev's saving of the tribe is not predicated on

subsuming the Dzhan within an all-encompassing idea. Rather, it resembles a Christ-like act of bodily self-sacrifice and self-renunciation. At the same time, it resembles either Christ's miraculous feeding of the multitudes, or the Last Supper, in which Christ gives (symbolically) his own flesh and blood to his disciples in an act of communion. The latter idea is suggested by a rather peculiar scene in *Dzhan*, in which Chagataev is portrayed as a kind of twin of the bird he kills. The bird is subsequently eaten by the tribe not so much for its nutritional value but as a step toward community and communion: "It lay on Chagataev's body in the same position in which it had fallen: its breast on the breast of the person, its head on his head, with its beak burrowed deep in his hair, and with its black helpless wings spread broadly on both of his sides" (Andrei Platonov, *Schastlivaia Moskva, povesti, rasskazy, lirika* [Moscow: Gud'ial Press, 1999], 386). Note: All translations are my own and all references to *Dzhan* will be from this edition.

 30. See Alexandar Mihailovic, *Corporeal Word: Mikhail Bakhtin's Theory of Discourse* (Evanston: Northwestern University Press, 1997), 78.

 31. Thus the "idea" (from Greek *idein* or "to see") emerges from an act of perceiving, according to Sergei Lobanov-Rostovsky ("Taming the Basilisk," in *The Body in Parts: Fantasies of Corporeality in Early Modern Europe*, eds. David Hillman and Carla Mazzio [New York: Routledge, 1997], 202).

 32. Ibid., 198. Significantly, Lobanov-Rostovsky goes on to note that in Galenic theory "the eye imposes a form on the visible world, much as the male endows the flesh with spiritual form in classical theories of the act of sexual generation" (199).

 33. Viacheslav Kuritsyn, *Liubov' i zrenie* (Moscow: Solo Aiurveda, 1996), 73–74. And as Alfred Boime notes of the implied perspective in such early American paintings as Asher Durand's Progress (*The Magisterial Gaze: Manifest Destiny and American Landscape Painting, c. 1830–1865* [Washington, DC: Smithsonian Institution Press, 1991], 75–76), "Within this fantasy of domain and empire gained from looking out and down over broad expanses is the subtext of metaphorical forecast of the future. The future is given spatial location in which vast territories are brought under visual and symbolic control." Likewise, one can argue that in Socialist Realism the gaze of the Bolshevik grasps the future proleptically, endowing it with concrete spatial coordinates over which the eye holds dominion.

 34. Jan Plamper, "The Spatial Poetics of the Personality Cult," in *The Landscape of Stalinism: The Art and Ideology of Soviet Space*, eds. Evgeny Dobrenko and Eric Naiman (Seattle: University of Washington Press, 2003), 86.

 35. Likewise, as Kuritsyn points out (*Liubov' i zrenie*, 74), in V. Azhaev's novel *Far from Moscow* (1948), the protagonist Koshkin takes a train to the Soviet Far East to work on a construction site. As he draws closer to the site he envisions the minutiae of construction in terms of the larger narrative of socialist construction, imagining the empirical in terms of the ideal.

 36. Thus Platonov's narrator remarks of the landscape—deprived as it is of the hero's vision—"Everything was unchanging and as before, but indifferent to Chagataev, as if it had gone blind without him" (*Dzhan*, 348).

 37. Ibid., 360 (all translations mine).

 38. Julia Kristeva, *The Powers of Horror*, 72.

39. This is best illustrated by Chagataev's mother Giul'chatai's peculiar reaction to her son's return. While Nazar is asleep she kisses him all over his body, checking to see if he remains "whole" after his long absence. The son's reaction is one that attempts to subvert any reversion to the earlier state of undifferentiation between mother and child: "He opened his eyes. The old woman began to kiss him on the neck, his chest, through his clothes, on his arm, crawling with her face over the person, and she checked and examined from close up all of his body. Were all of his parts whole or not, or had something been sacrificed to sickness or lost during his absence" (Andrei Platonov, *Dzhan*, 359). The state of "eternal nature" with which the subject must ultimately part in order to attain true selfhood is also symbolized by the image of Vera fantasizing her child's desire to be born: "She wrote that her child was nearing the world, that it was thinking something inside her body, because it was often moved around and was unhappy. 'But I caress him, I stroke his stomach and, bending my face closer to to him,' wrote Vera, 'I say: What do you want? It's warm and quiet for you in there, I try not to move much, so you don't get irritated,—why do you want to leave me?'" (Ibid., 347).

40. Ibid., 364.

41. "The relationship between nature and technology is a tragic one. The goal of technology can be summed up as follows: 'Give me a point of leverage, and I can turn the world upside down.' Yet the structure of nature is such that it does not like to be cheated. True, the world can be turned upside down by using the necessary kinds of levers, yet in order one would lose in terms of distance and time required by the long lever that the victory would be practically useless. This is a rudimentary aspect of the dialectic. Let us take a contemporary fact: the splitting of the atom. It's the same problem. The universal hour will come when we, having spent on the destruction of the atom x amount of energy will receive x + 1 as a result, and will be so satisfied with this paltry gain because it, an absolute gain, was achieved by artificially changing the very rules of nature, i.e., the dialectic. Nature holds itself closed. It is only capable of functioning tit-for-tat—and even with a gain for its own side, while technology strains to do the opposite. The external world is protected against us by means of the dialectic" (*Andrei Platonov: Vospominaniia sovremennikov: materialy k biografii*, comps. N. V. Kornienko, E. D. Shubina (Moscow: Sovremennyi pisatel', 1994), 320–21.

42. The connection between Platonov's article and *Dzhan* is borne out on the level of imagery. Thus in "About the First Socialist Tragedy," Platonov remarks that if it were not for the dialectical relationship between nature and humankind, "the world would have been completely destroyed by humans long ago," for human appetites are essentially inexhaustible, like the impatient desire of child for candy: "Otherwise everything on earth would have ended a long time ago, like a child playing with candies, which melted in his hands even before he had time to eat them" (Andrei Platonov, *Vospominaniia sovremennikov: materialy k biografii*," 320). Not surprisingly, Platonov uses the same image to describe the impatient visionary Chagataev in *Dzhan*, as if to suggest that his transforming efforts will meet with the same resistance from the "natural" tribespeople: "Even in childhood he would also stomp with his bare feet onto the earth, and would be covered in tears from inconsolable frenzy and would threaten passers-by when he saw food on the other side of the glass and

couldn't eat it immediately" (Andrei Platonov, *Schastlivaia Moskva, povesti, rasskazy, lirika*, 336).

43. V. Chalmaev, *Andrei Platonov: K sokrovennomu cheloveku*, 397.

44. Stephen Hutchings, "Remembering of a Kind: Philosophy and Art, Miscegenation and Incest in Platonov's *Dzhan*," 60.

45. It is interesting to note that the god-like stance of the Stalinist visionary, which allows him to take in the entire landscape with his gaze, is steadily diminished over the course of the novel. Thus in a scene towards the end of the novella Chagataev no longer ascends a mountain but rather a hillock so as to see the mud houses of his tribe: "Having slept through the daytime heat in the silence of some moist pit, in the evening Chagataev once again set out and by the morning of the next day he approached Ust'-Urt. He quickly mounted a hillock so as to see the the mud houses of his tribe more quickly" (*Dzhan*, 427).

46. Ibid., 414.

47. A more typical stance for the Stalinist hero is illustrated by the "visionary" surgeon Sambikin in the following episode in Platonov's *Happy Moscow*: "Sambikin's discovery had made him happy. He still believed it was possible to ascend in one bound to a mountain peak from which times and spaces would become visible to the ordinary grey gaze of man" (*Happy Moscow*, 68).

48. See commentary to A. Platonov, *Zapisnye knizhki*, 375n45.

49. A. Platonov, "Pushkin i Gor'kii," in *Sobranie soch. v 3-x t-kh*, v. 2 (Moscow: Sovetskaia Rossiia, 1985), 305.

50. Stephen Hutchings, "Remembering of a Kind: Philosophy and Art, Miscegenation and Incest in Platonov's *Dzhan*," 57.

51. Thus in one scene, Chagataev looks at the distant night sky, the endless, linear quality of which acts as a metaphor for the communist project: "The great dark night filled the sky and the earth—from the foothills of the grass to the end of the world. Only the sun had gone away, but all the stars opened up and the anxious, ploughed up Milky Way became visible, as if someone had just completed a trek without return there" (*Dzhan*, 358).

52. Stephen Hutchings, "Remembering of a Kind: Philosophy and Art, Miscegenation and Incest in Platonov's *Dzhan*," 57.

53. The writer's strategy in this instance is not unlike that employed by Pasternak during the same period. For, as Zholkovsky points out, Pasternak's poetry of the 1930s is marked by a naturalization of the symbolist/futurist distance-perspective manifested in the poet's preference for metonymy (i.e., closeness/contiguity) over metaphor (i.e., distance). As a result, the kinds of miracles only dreamt of by the earlier symbolist generation became a possibility in the poetic world of the late Pasternak. See A. Zholkovskii, "Dusha, dal' i tekhnologiia chuda," in *Andrei Platonov: Mir tvorchestva*, comps., N. V. Kornienko, E. D. Shubina (Moscow: sovremennyi pisatel', 1994), 390.

54. Andrei Platonov, *Dzhan*, 341.

55. Platonov's interest in the Eastern bazaar as a place of community/communion is highlighted in his notebooks for the year 1935. Anticipating his portrayal of the bazaar as a place of rebirth in the short story "The River Potudan'" and in the unfinished novel "Happy Moscow," he describes the familial atmosphere of the bazaar as

a "resurrection": "The bazaar is not only trading; it's community and friendship. The desert dweller comes to the bazaar from out of his solitude and mixes with other people beneath the sun, seeing the desolate mountains from a distance, the desert, the lonely place of his labor, of his sad industry. It is also at the bazaar that love is born. Here the women from the sand meet their future husbands; here friends feast—here there is resurrection" (Andrei Platonov, *Zapisnye knizhki*, 163).

56. Paul Hegarty, *Georges Bataille: Core Cultural Theorist*, 36. Seifrid, who is the first to have made the connection between Bataille's interest in the institution of the *potlatch* and Platonov's prose, links the *potlatch* emphasis on giving to the multiple images of entropy and energy expenditure throughout the writer's oeuvre (Thomas Seifrid, "Smradnye radosti marksizma," 56).

57. Cf. the following from the essay "About the First Socialist Tragedy" (*Andrei Platonov: Vospominaniia sovremennikov*, 320): "Nature holds itself closed. It is only able to function tit-for-tat."

58. Hans-Dieter Bahr, *Die Sprache des Gastes: eine Metaethik* (Leipzig: Reclam Verlag, 1994), 36.

59. Ibid.

60. Ibid., 35–36.

61. Anne Dufourmantelle and Jacques Derrida, *Of Hospitality*, tr. Rachel Bowlby (Stanford: Stanford University Press, 2000), 4.

62. The connection between feces and the sacred is not entirely far-fetched here. In a telling moment in the novella *Dzhan*, one of the minor characters named Old Van'ka throws a piece of dung at a sacred bird (a peacock) in a fit of rage. Yet the peacock simply swallows the dung as if it were food. Later the narrator notes that after being beaten for having attacked a sacred bird "Old Van'ka . . . loved afterwards to throw something "unclean" at birds that were flying or sitting" (Andrei Platonov, *Dzhan*, 404–5). Key in Platonov's description is the rather peculiar combination of "sacred" and "unclean." The confusion of food and feces/waste is something of a commonplace in Platonov's work of the period. Thus in his notebooks for the year 1934, Platonov notes that the Turkmen girl Dzhumal' (who bears the same name as the protagonist of the short story "Takyr'") lived for a time by eating the garbage thrown from passing trains. Most important, perhaps, is the fact that the Russian word for "garbage" or "waste products" (*otbrosy*) is distinctly reminiscent of the word for "waste products" (*otkhody*) that the author will use in structurally similar situations elsewhere: "The crows of the steppe sit atop the telegraph poles. After a train passes by they swoop down onto the track and eat the garbage. That's how they live in the open steppe. Dzhumal' lived that way for a while herself" (Andrei Platonov, *Zapisnye knizhki*, 146).

63. Thus the initial portrayal of "the guest" as the great theme of Asia ("The great theme of Asia is that of the guest [perhaps happy, and perhaps sad, perhaps some other kind]" [Andrei Platonov, *Zapisnye knizhki*, 148]) becomes the following: "An idea for a *p-l-a-y*/ Asia is the guest of Europe" (Ibid., 154).

64. N. V. Kornienko, in commentary to Andrei Platonov, *Zapisnye knizhki*, 375.

65. David M. Bethea, "Literature," in *The Cambridge Companion to Modern Russian Literature*, ed. Nicholas Rzhevsky (Cambridge: Cambridge University Press, 1998), 165.

66. Ibid. In this connection, it is worth noting that in his notebooks for the year 1934 Platonov describes Christ using the word *gospod'*, which is etymologically related to the word for "guest" (*gost'*). The writer mentions Christ twice and in both instances as a way out of the "blind-alley" or "trap" of history, and in this regard one cannot help wondering if it is not because Christ represents that which is dialogically opposed to humankind: "There's no way out even in thoughts, in hypotheses, in fantasy,—after a careful examination one invariably comes up with CHST. No matter what" (Andrei Platonov, *Zapisnye knizhki,* 147–48).

67. The distinction between "conquest" and "coexistence" is by R. Cockrell, "Conquest or Coexistence: The View of Nature in Early Platonov," (Unpublished paper delivered at BASEES Twentieth-Century Studies Conference, Mansfield College, Oxford, 15–16 September 1999).

68. The importance for Chagataev and Moscow of the temporal dimension is suggested by the numerous mentions throughout *Dzhan* of Chagataev's impatience to carry out his plan of reclaiming the Dzhan.

69. Andrei Platonov, *Dzhan*, 335, 419.

70. The picture echoes the very famous comments by Georges Bataille concerning humankind's obsessive dividing of existence into high and low: "The division of the universe into subterranean hell and perfectly pure heaven is an indelible conception, mud and darkness being the principles of evil as light and celestial space are the principles of good: with their feet in the mud but with their heads more or less in light, men obstinately imagine that a tide will permanently elevate them, never to return into pure space. Human life entails, in fact, the rage of seeing oneself as a back and forth movement from refuse to ideal, and from the ideal to refuse —a rage that is easily directed against an organ as base as the foot" (Quoted in Mary Russo, *The Female Grotesque: Risk, Excess and Modernity* [New York: Routledge, 1994], 144).

71. Here Platonov anticipates the argument made in *Happy Moscow* that disease is so much a part of the human organism that it cannot be banished without totally obliterating the body itself. Describing Sambikin as he operates to remove a tumor from a young boy's brain, the narrator writes: "It was clear to Sambikin the hot, defenseless body of the patient, which was opened up, with thousand of sliced blood-vessels, greedily took the streptococci into itself from everywhere: from the air, and particularly from the instrument, which it was impossible to sterilize completely" (*Happy Moscow*, 20).

72. Andrei Platonov, *Dzhan*, 343.

73. M. N. Zolotonosov, *Slovo i Telo: Seksual'nye aspekty, universalii, interpretatsii russkogo kul'turnogo teksta XIX-XX vekov* (Moscow: Ladomir, 1999), 486. Cf. Also Igor' Smirnov, *Psikhodiakhronologika: Istoriia russkoi literatury ot romantizma do nashikh dnei* (Moscow: Novoe literaturnoe obozrenie, 1994), 197.

74. M. N. Zolotonosov, *Slovo i telo*, 486.

75. Cf. The following from Platonov's notebooks for the year 1934: "The slime of Amu is more fruitful than black earth: it is the dust of the past. The washed out fabric of history is better raw material for the future than the freshness of virginal humus. Pessimism is the best ore for optimism. Strange, but true!" (Andrei Platonov, *Zapis-*

nye knizhki, 137). Moreover, as Marina Koch-Lubouchkine has demonstrated in connection with *Dzhan* (Marina Koch-Lubouchkine, "The Concept of Emptiness in Platonov's *Fourteen Little Red Huts* and *Dzhan*," in *Essays in Poetics: Journal of the British Neo-Formalist School* no. 26 [2001]: 91–94), Platonov portrays the desert (*pustynia*) as a place of entropy/death and as a place that gives life, just as the very word "pust–" from which the Russian term for "desert" is derived can connote emptiness/oblivion or freedom and openness.

76. Mikhail Epstein, "Charms of Entropy," in *Russian Postmodernism: New Perspectives on Post-Soviet Culture*, eds. Mikhail N. Epstein, Alexander A. Genis, Slobodanka M. Vladiv-Glover (New York: Berghahn Books, 1999), 430.

77. Mary Russo, *The Female Grotesque: Risk, Excess and Modernity*, 144.

78. In this sense, A. Kretinin's remark ("Moskva Chestnova i 'drugie': O nekotorykh elementakh struktury teksta romana," in *Strana filosofov Andreia Platonova: Problemy tvorchestva, vyp. 3*, 294) that "'uncleanliness' (filth, dirt, pus)" connotes closure and the absence of plenitude is simply too one-sided.

79. This sense seems to have been inspired by the author's observations of the local Turkmen people. As he writes in his notebooks: "The Turkmen girl, she doesn't pick her nose, she doesn't feel the snot, nor her own dirt. It's a different relationship to nature, a completely different sense of self than in Russia" (Andrei Platonov, *Zapisnye knizhki*, 143).

80. Andrei Platonov, *Dzhan*, 421. It bears noting that when we first see Khanom, she is leaning up against a garbage can—an image that anticipates analogous poses by various characters in *Happy Moscow*: "Next to the garbage box, leaning up against, stood a Turkmen girl" (Andrei Platonov, *Dzhan*, 420).

81. The same process of cleaning away filth is also associated with Aydym. At one point she is shown washing dishes and the narrator remarks: "Aydym was making noise with the new dishes, cleaning up all sorts of filth and leftovers" (Andrei Platonov, *Dzhan*, 411).

82. Thus Marina Koch-Lubouchkine notes that in *Dzhan*, just as in "all his works from the beginning of the twenties, ideal constructions collapse, utopia is crushed" (Marina Koch-Lubouchkine, "Platonov's Concept of Emptiness," 93).

83. Stephen Hutchings, "Remembering of a Kind: Philosophy and Art, Miscegenation and Incest in Platonov's *Dzhan*," 64–66.

84. Marina Koch-Lubouchkine, "Platonov's Concept of Emptiness," 92. As Koch-Lubouchkine notes, the original text ends with the dispersal of the Dzhan (utopia's collapse), while the added four chapters that constitute the "Socialist Realist" ending provide a happy end to Chagataev's tale of reclaiming his tribesmen.

85. Irina Gutkin, *The Cultural Origins of the Socialist Realist Aesthetic: 1890–1934* (Evanston: Northwestern University Press, 1999), 113. See also Hans Günther, "Arkhetipy sovetskoi kul'tury," in *Sotrealisticheskii kanon*, eds. Hans Günther and Evgenii Dobrenko (Sankt-Peterburg: Akademicheskii proekt, 2000), 777.

86. By contrast, Stalinist mythology placed the marriage of male and female attributes within a clear conceptual hierarchy. This is reflected in the fact (among others) that at the VSKhV a giant Stalin statue as well as Mechanization Square occupy the mythological center of the exhibit, while the statues and pavilions associated with

agriculture/fertility and the like are placed around these (Hans Günther, "Arkhetipy sovetskoi kul'tury," 777).

87. Keith Livers, "Scatology and Eschatology," 161.

88. Andrei Platonov, *Zapisnye Knizhki*, 162.

89. I. Spiridonova, "'Uznik': Obraz Sartoriusa," in *Strana filosofov Andreia Platonova: Problemy trorchestra*, vyp. 3, 310.

90. Eliot Borenstein, *Men Without Women*, 237, 232.

91. The importance for Platonov of the image of the mother as that which is inextricably tied to the very source of being is made clear in the following remarks, the first of which attempts to find a etymological basis for redefining maturity as the process of becoming like the mother. Note that the word Platonov uses is a neologism, formed from the adjective "materyi," meaning "mature" or "experienced": "Kak obmatereet (podrastet) rebenok." "[It] happens that a [father] son murders his old man father (there are m[any] Rus[sian] stories about that), but it doesn't happen that a son murders his mother," Andrei Platonov, *Zapisnye knizhki*, 166.

92. See Hans Günther, "Arkhetipy sovetskoi kul'tury," 764–69. Also Hans Günther, "'Broad is My Motherland': The Mother Archetype and Space in the Soviet Mass Song," in *The Landscape of Stalinism: The Art and Ideology of Soviet Space* (Seattle: University of Washington Press, 2003), 77–95.

93. Andrei Platonov, *Zapisnye knizhki*, 166.

94. Ibid., 166.

95. Stephen Hutchings, "Remembering of a Kind: Philosophy and Art, Miscegenation and Incest in Platonov's 'Dzhan,'" 61.

96. Eliot Borenstein, *Men without Women*, 245.

97. It should be noted that from the beginning of the story Semion fantasizes about being a mother: "While running Semion raised the hem of his shirt and looked at his stomach. It seemed to him that someone separate from him was living there" (Andrei Platonov, *Iamskaia sloboda* [Voronezh: Izd-vo im. E. A. Bolkhovitinova, 1999], 434, 442).

99. As Evgenii Iablokov notes ("Gorod platonovskikh polovinok: 'Pushkinskii' podtekst v kinostsenarii 'Otets-mat'," in *Strana filosofov Andreia Platonova: Problemy tvorchestva, vyp. 4, iubileinyi*, 701), quoting Platonov's screenplay: "'There have to be two—a father and a mother. A mother alone is only a half.'"

99. As Aleksandr Etkind points out (*Khlyst: Sekty, literatura i revoliutsiia* [Moscow: Novoe literaturnoe obozrenie, 1998], 97, 157, 167), for such figures as Dostoevsky, Solov'ev, Ivanov, Berdiaev, Bakhtin, and others the perfect human being of the future is conceived of as neither male nor female but as androgynous

100. The political component of this project is echoed in the screenplay's attempts to reconcile the perennial "little man" of Russian literature—in this case, not Pushkin's Evgenii but Evgeniia—with the two foremost cultural heroes of the Stalinist era, that is, Pushkin and Stalin (See Evgenii Iablokov, "Gorod platonovskikh polovinok," 702). Platonov will take up this same idea in his famous essay on Pushkin, "Pushkin is Our Comrade" (1937), in which he attempts to merge the images of state power and utopian striving (Peter the Great) with the private/procreative realm (Evgenii) in the image of Pushkin's poetry.

101. Andrei Platonov, *Iamskaia sloboda*, 452. A similar argument might well be made about the character of Nikita in the short story "The River Potudan'," where the narrator remarks that "in good time Nikita Firsov had a woman's coat made out of his Red Army greatcoat" (Andrei Platonov, *Iamskaia sloboda*, 403).

102. Igor' Smirnov, "Sotsrealism: Antropologicheskoe izmerenie," in *Sotsrealisticheskii kanon*, 20.

103. Katerina Clark, "Socialist Realism and the Sacralizing of Space," in *The Landscape of Stalinism: The Art and Ideology of Soviet Space*, eds. Evgeny Dobrenko and Eric Naiman (Seattle: University of Washington Press, 2003), 10.

104. A. Platonov, "O pervoi sotsialisticheskoi tragedii," 320.

105. Quoted in Eliot Borenstein, *Men without Women*, 214.

106. Keith Livers, "Scatology and Eschatology," 163. In an analogous vein, Hutchings remarks ("Remembering of a Kind: Philosophy, Art, Miscegenation and Incest in Platonov's *Dzhan*," 62) that in the relationship (in *Dzhan*) the need for biological intimacy is dialectically/dialogically entwined with the simultaneous rejection of biology as a model for intimacy. Thus, Chagataev rejects the possibility of an incestuous relationship with his mother (distance) at the same time that he engages in a quasi-incestuous relationship with Ksenia (closeness). In the first case, biology cannot serve as a model for intimacy—lest intimacy deteriorate into solipsism—and in the second physical intimacy is invoked as a means of overcoming the abstract, Fyodorovian idea of universal "brotherhood."

107. A. Platonov, *Schastlivaia Moskva*, 34.

108. Stalin quoted in commentary to Platonov, *Schastlivaia Moskva*, 64.

109. In the published version she is altogether orphaned.

110. As Mary Russo notes (*The Female Grotesque*, 44), "The representation of femininity as an effortless mobility implies enormous control, changeability, and strength. She is, in other words, 'an idol of perversity.'"

111. Ibid., 44.

112. Clint Walker, "*Happy Moscow* and *The Bronze Horseman*," in *Poetics: Journal of the British Neo-Formalist School* 26 (autumn 2001): 164.

113. N. Kornienko, "'Proletarskaia Moskva zhdet svoego khudozhnika': K tvorcheskoi istorii romana," in *Strana filosofov Andreia Platonova: problemy tvorchestva*, 360.

114. Katerina Clark, "Socialist Realism and the Sacralizing of Space," 10.

115. Ibid., 367.

116. Boris Groys, *Die Erfindug Rußlands* (München: Carl Hanser Verlag, 1995), 165.

117. Cf. Smirnov's remark (in "Sotsrealizm: Antropologicheskoe izmerenie, 20) that "man has no biological reverse side. He who claims the opposite in Socialist Realism is discredited."

118. Thus in the seminal essay "About the First Socialist Tragedy" ("O pervoi sotsialisticheskoi tragedii," 322), Platonov writes: "Ideology, by the way, is not located in the superstructure, not in the 'heights,' but inside, in the middle of society's public sense." In her commentary to the piece, Kornienko notes that Platonov had originally written "heart" rather than "middle" (the two words *serdtse* and *seredina* are related in Russian).

119. Natasha Drubek-Meier sees the image of the plummeting Moscow Chestnova as a kind of carnivalesque undermining of Stalinist culture's aerial aspirations ("Rossiia— 'pustota v kishkakh' mira," *Novoe literaturnoe obozrenie*, no. 9 [1994], 256).

120. Julia Kristeva, *The Kristeva Reader*, ed. Toril Moi (New York: Columbia University Press, 1986), 160–61. Similarly, in *The Pillar and the Affirmation of Truth*, Pavel Florenskii describes the Virgin as the "center of created life, the point of contact between heaven and earth." In addition, Florenskii notes, concerning the same image of the heart: "Thus the church mysticism is the mysticism of the heart. But the heart . . . has from ancient times been considered the center of the breast. If the breast is the central point of the body, then the heart is the central point of the breast. And it is at the heart that the attention of the church has always been directed" (Pavel Florenskii, *Stolp i utverzhdenie istiny: Opyt pravoslavnoi feoditsei v dvenadtsati pis'-makh* [Paris: YMCA-Press, 1989], 267). In this sense, it is probably no accident that Chestnova's movement through the novel combines all three elements: fire, earth, and water, as I. Matveeva notes ("Simvolika obraza glavnoi geroini," in *Strana filosofov Andreia Platonova: Problemy tvorchestva*, vyp. 3, 319).

121. J. Szymak-Reifer, "V poiskakh istochnikov platonovskoi prozy," *Novoe literaturnoe obozrenie*, 9 (1994): 269. See also I. Matveeva, "Simvolika obraza glavnoi geroini," in *Strana filosofov Andreia Platonova: problemy tvorchestva*, vyp. 3, 319.

122. Mary Russo, *The Female Grotesque*, 80.

123. V. Papernyi, *Kul'tura "Dva"* (Ann Arbor: Ardis, 1984), 72.

124. Here, Platonov polemicizes with the Stalinist call (in 1932) for a more "intrusive" approach toward all spheres of socialist construction: "'It's time to have finished with the putrid policy of not intruding into production. It's high time to establish a new policy, more appropriate to the current period: *to intrude in everything*'" (quoted in *Andrei Platonov: Vospominaniia sovremennikov: Materialy k biografii*, 323).

125. A. Platonov, *Happy Moscow*, 17. A further obvious parallel of this intrusive thrust (this time directed at the human body) is found in the image of Sambikin entering the body of the ailing boy on whom he is about to operate: "Sambikin took a keen and gleaming instrument and entered with it into what is the essence of all things—the human body" (*Happy Moscow*, 34). And more to the point, in an obvious allusion to Stalin's slogan the engineer Sartorius describes his own desire to re-engineer the human organism by saying: "Now we will intrude into the human being" (Quoted in I. Esaulov, "Vorota, dveri i okna v romane *Schastlivaia Moskva*," in *Strana filosofov Andreia Platonova: Problemy tvorchestva*, vyp. 3, 252).

126. A. Platonov, "O pervoi sotsialistichekoi tragedii," 322.

127. Here one cannot but disagree with R. Hodel's assessment of the image of the fence as segregating the two worlds of utopian striving from that of the everyday in the spirit of Platonov's early essays (R. Hodel, "Zabornost 'Schastlivoi Moskvy' i rastvorenie nesobstvenno-priamoi rechi," in *Strana filosofov Andreia Platonova: Problemy tvorchestva*, vyp. 3, 245).

128. Indeed, while the musician seems to perceive the activity of the institute as located in a kind of remote otherworld (i.e., "po tu storonu zabora," which suggests both the concrete "on the other side of the fence" and the more metaphysical "in the

other realm on the other side of the fence"), the narrative as a whole works to undercut this perception.

129. To a certain extent, this dilemma is the same as that experienced by the maturing child. As Igor' Smirnov remarks (I. Smirnov, *Psikhodiakhronologika: Psikhoistoriia russkoi literatury ot romantizma do nashikh dnei*, 89), describing the shape of the Oedipal dilemma in childhood: "The dialecticality of psychological maturation lies in the fact that the child can anthropomorphize that which is given in nature only by using the resources of its own body, that is, with reference to the very same nature."

130. Consider the following example from "The River Potudan'": "The father in the meantime—by the month of March—unhurriedly made a large dresser as a present for the young people, similar to the one that had been in Lyuba's apartment when her mother was still more or less Nikita's father's fiancée. The old carpenter watched life repeat itself, coming full circle for the second or third time. One could understand it, but it probably was not possible to change it, and sighing Nikita's father put the dresser on a sledge and took it to the apartment of his son's fiancee" (A. Platonov, *Vzyskanie pogibshikh* [Moscow: 1995], 435).

131. This shift is from what Hutchings calls ("Remembering of a Kind: Philosophy and Art, Miscegenation and Incest in Platonov's *Dzhan*," 61) the abstract principle of male kinship associated with Fyodorov to the principle of bodily contact and closeness in the repetition that occurs at the beginning and end of the story. At the beginning of the piece Nikita knocks on the window of the house of his father, who recognizes him and lets him in. At the end, Nikita knocks on the window of his and Lyuba's house and finally has to enter it by climbing over the gate.

132. Leon Trotsky, *Revolution Betrayed: What is the Soviet Union and Where Is It Going?* (New York: Pathfinder Press, 1972), 214.

133. A. Platonov, "O pervoi sotsialisticheskoi tragedii," 322.

134. Ibid.

135. As Eric Naiman notes, throughout NEP pleasure was identified as a "weapon of the bourgeoisie" and was infinitely more reprehensible than the sexual act itself, since it could be recuperated through sublimation—through productive channeling (Eric Naiman, *Sex in Public*, 138).

136. A. Platonov, "O pervoi sotsialisticheskoi tragedii." 320.

137. Ibid., 322.

138. A. Platonov, *Vzyskanie pogibshikh*, 446.

139. In *Happy Moscow* Sartorius dreams of creating a device that would pump nourishment into the body automatically: "He awoke satisfied, resolved to construct and bring to perfection a complete technological apparatus that would automatically pump the basic vital force of food out of nature and into the human body" (A. Platonov, *Happy Moscow*, 71).

140. Dietmar Neutatz, *Die Moskauer Metro: Von den ersten Plänen bis zur Grossbaustelle des Stalinismus (1897–1935)* (Köln: Böhlau Verlag, 2001), 601.

141. A. Kretinin, "Moscow Chestnova i 'drugie': O nekotorykh elementakh struktury teksta romana," 293–94.

142. As Kornienko notes ("Rossiia—'Pustota v kiskhakh' mira," 263), Moscow's new name is reminiscent of the Russian word *musor* or "garbage."

143. As I mentioned earlier, Sartorius's new name "Gruniakhin" (a derivative of "Grunia") would seem to support this.

144. A. Platonov, *Iamskaia sloboda*, 449.

145. Strangely, even the most recent wave of Platonov scholarship seems largely to have overlooked the author's clear desire to find a point of compromise between the ideal and the real. Thus the Russian critic Kretinin sees Sartorius's transformation into Gruniakhin at the end of *Happy Moscow* as simply signifying the protagonist's failure to achieve the self-transcendence he seeks (A. Kretinin, "Moskva Chestnova i 'drugie,'" 297).

146. This shift corresponds roughly to the transformation undergone by Grushen'ka following her meeting with Alyosha in the *Brothers Karamazov*. Repeatedly described as "carnivorous" by Rakitin, she ultimately does not seduce Alyosha, even though she had earlier fantasized about "eating him up." The shift is from carnivorous egoism to the overcoming of ego. Similarly, in *Happy Moscow* the meek Gruniakhin's final profession involves precisely not feeding off others but *feeding* them— a gesture that stands in obvious contrast to the quasicannibalistic quality Platonov sees as the core defect of human nature. Thus Sartorius notes that if human nature is not substantially changed then "nothing new would happen and every inhabitant would go off to live separately . . . in order to sink their teeth into each other once again in voluptuous despair" (*Happy Moscow*, 37). Such examples could be easily multiplied and point to a fundamental connection with such works as Dostoevsky's *Idiot* and *Brothers Karamazov*.

147. V. Iu Viugin, "Obshchee delo A. Platonova: motif voskresheniia v rasskazakh 30-kh—40-kh godov," in *Russian Literature XLVI* (1999): 272. See also E. Tolstaia-Segal, "Naturfilosofskie temy Platonova," *Slavica Hierosolymitana*, 1979, no. 4: 239.

148. As Natalia Poltavtseva notes ("Tema 'obydennogo soznaniia' i ego interpretatsii v tvorchestve Platonova," in *Strana filosofov Andreia Platonova*, vyp. 4, 275), Platonov's unusual project rhymes with the pathos of total synthesis character of the Russian cosmists—that is, such important philosophical figures as V. Solov'ev, N. Fedorov, S. Bulgakov, N. Berdiaev, and P. Florenskii.

149. A social correlative of this can be found in Platonov's unusual attention to the dregs or "ejecta" of society. As if admonishing the era not to forget its chthonic roots, he polemically characterizes society's "waste matter" as the driving force behind any revolution (*Zapisnye knizhki*, 147). In a similar vein, Eric Naiman notes that Platonov's heroes of the late 1930s are sooner inclined to idealize the "waste matter" (*otkhody* or *otbrosy*) of utopia than utopia itself ("Andrei Platonov mezhdu dvukh utopii," 242).

150. In a strikingly similar episode in *Happy Moscow*, Platonov's narrator says of Sartorius that "Chestnova Moscow gave him her shoes to carry. Without noticing, he sniffed them and even touched them with his tongue" (A. Platonov, *Happy Moscow*, 55).

151. A. Platonov, *Zapisnye knizhki*, 146.

152. The same idea is applied to the body of Dzhumal' in the short story "Takyr": (A. Platonov, *Iamskaia sloboda*, 356).

153. Zolotonosov refers to the "epidemic of stasis that is celebrated in the abundant statuary of the era" (*Slovoi i telo,* 612).

154. A. Platonov, *Zapisnye knizhki*, 149. This should be with Zolotonosov's claim that the ideal Soviet person, "like a statue, should always be the same; the potential for elusive transformations should be absent in him. History has ended, . . . and with it man, he has become petrified, 'frozen'" (*Slovo i telo*, 611).

155. Anat Vernitski, "Christian Motifs in Platonov," *ASEES*, Vol. 14, Nos. 1–2 (2000): 69.

156. The Russian word for "completely," comes from *chistyi*, which means "clean" or "pure."

157. The exchange of feces for food is quite clear in the following sentence: "Ego zhena vsegda pochti vsegda vylivala ostatki vcherashnikh miasnykh shchei v pomoinoe mesto, tak chto storozh vsegda mog kormit' kakogo-nibud' bednogo cheloveka za uborku otkhozhego mesta" (A. Platonov, *Vzyskanie pogibshikh*, 442).

158. Eric Naiman, "The Inadmissibility of Desire," *Russian Literature* 23 (1998): 352.

159. A. Platonov, *Zapisnye knizhki*, 147. Cf. this to Fyodorov's fetishization of "ancestral dust," which, as Naiman points out ("Lexical Heroes in *Happy Moscow*," 98) must be lovingly . . . preserved until the moment of scientific resurrection."

160. As M. N. Zolotonosov writes (*Slovo i telo,* 621), the popular sculptures of sportsmen and –women of the day functioned as "models of the people of the future."

161. Eric Naiman, "Lexical Heroes in *Happy Moscow*," 104).

162. This image stands in stark opposition to Platonov's later description of the youthful generation of Stalinist engineers and constructors, whom the republic had "dressed . . . with its finest goods" (*Happy Moscow*, 23). Likewise, Papernyi remarks on the pathos of re-dressing that supposedly lay at the heart of Stalinist culture's promotion not only of the body beautiful but of the costly fabrics that would be used to adorn it (*Kul'tura "Dva,"* 93).

163. Natasha Drubek-Meier, "Rossiia—'pustota v kishkakh' mira," 264n44.

164. Rolf Hellebust, *Flesh to Metal: Soviet Literature and the Alchemy of Revolution* (Ithaca, NY: Cornell University Press, 2003), 58–59.

165. Dennis Patrick Slattery, *The Wounded Body: Remembering the Markings of Flesh* (Albany: State University of New York Press, 2000), 121. Further, one might say that Platonov's strategy here seems to be aimed much more broadly at the dominant norms of beauty within Western culture. As Sergei Brel' notes ("Kul'turnye konteksty poetiki 'zhivogo—nezhivogo' A. Platonova," in *Strana filosofov Andreia Platonova: Problemy tvorchestva*, vyp. 4, 242), classical physics and classical architecture were largely informed by the idea of symmetry. Borrowing from antique models, classical architecture equated the aesthetically pleasing with the symmetrical. Platonov repeatedly undercuts this ideal, particularly in the case of his heroine Moscow Chestnova whose body will remain forever asymmetrical. As Brel' notes, Platonov's poetics of asymmetry seems to reflect a considerably older worldview.

166. Julia Kristeva, *The Powers of Horror: An Essay on Abjection*, 74. In his essay "Ulysses in the Russian Looking-Glass," Sergei Horuxy describes Platonov

(alongside Joyce) as a writer of the Eleusinian (as opposed to the Orphic) type, with his mythology returning to the Earth, "of pushing in and down." He goes on to note that unlike the symbolists with their "disparagement of the corporeal element as opposed to the spiritual," for artists like Platonov the "theme of corporeality, the life of the body, is most important . . . and were developed by them with keen attention" ("Ulysses in the Russian Looking-Glass," *Joyce Studies Annual: 1998*, ed. Thomas F. Stanley [Austin, 1998], 107).

167. Note that Platonov's use of the phrase "about her" (in Russian he uses *kasat'sia*, which means both "to touch" and "to concern") reprises the earlier gesture of Sartorius touching Moscow's shoes with his tongue.

168. In his *Filosofiia khoziaistva*, Bulgakov writes: "And I attribute all of the changes in the life of my body—both those of a normal and those of a pathological character—to the workings of the same self-identical force and energy—my corporeal organism, in which there arise, develop, and disappear all of these so varied, sometimes mutually contradictory and even seemingly mutually exclusive phenomena" (Sergei Bulgakov, *Sochineniia v dvukh tomakh*, v. v. 1 [Moscow: "Nauka," 1993], 119).

169. Recent studies demonstrate that Platonov's vision of the digestive tract/ anus connection as positive is not entirely novel. As Jeffrey Masten notes in his essay "Is the Fundament a Grave?" (in David Hillman and Carla Mazzio, eds., *The Body in Parts; Fantasies of Corporeality in Early Modern Europe*, 134) the culture of early Modern England visualizes, to a significant degree, the body as attached to or articulated around the anus. In particular, Masten emphasizes the extent to which—in contrast to the more familiar Bakhtinian hierarchy of high and low—the "fundament" or foundation acquires a distinctly positive valence in the culture under consideration. Indeed, for one author of the period, "the mouth and the fundament are equally salubrious sites of evacuation; like the mouth, the fundament produces health through purgation." And perhaps in this sense it is seen as more productive: what the fundament passes has been "tourned in to another fygure."

170. Lev Kassil', *Metro: Chudo pod Moskvoi* (Moscow: Gos. izd-vo "Khudozh. lit-ra," 1936), 17.

171. Clint Walker, "*Happy Moscow* and the *Bronze Horseman*," 138.

172. This is made clear in a scene where Moscow washes her hair after having been hospitalized: "For instance, every day she would wash her hair because she constantly felt there was dirt in it, and she would even cry from vexation that dirt just wouldn't go away" (*Happy Moscow*, 44).

173. Hallie White, "Sequence and Plot in Platonov's *Chevengur*," *Slavic and East European Journal* 42, no. 1 (Spring 1998): 104.

174. Hallie White, "*Happy Moscow* and the Unbearable Present," *Essays in Poetics: Journal of the British Formalist School*, 117. This development seems to mark the writer's move away from what I. Smirnov calls (*Psikhodiakhronologika*, 197) the earlier avant-garde's inclination to "exaggerate its autonomy in the temporal and spatial planes."

175. A. Platonov, *Dzhan*, 421.

176. As Svetlana Semenovna notes ("Voskreshennyi roman Andreia Platonova: Opyt prochteniia *Schastlivoi Moskvy*," *Novyi mir*, 1995, no. 9: 216), "Health and sickness have become so thoroughly intertwined in the human body, the pathological microbe had nested so deeply in the textures and fibers and liquids of the organism that it was inseparable from them, like light from dark, death from life."

177. Thus the ontological pus that Sartorius imagines will be released from the organism through socialism's intrusive manipulations (39) is shown to be an inalienable part of the that same organism (19).

178. A contemporary of Platonov's, S. Zalkind, writes that Mechnikov "indicated the exact spot where constantly, drop by drop, the poison intoxicating the body seeped every hour, every moment of its existence. This spot is the large intestine" (S. Zalkind, *Ilya Mechnikov: His Life and Work* [Moscow: Progress Publishers, 1959], 39).

179. S. Zalkind, *Ilya Mechnikov*, 140.

180. Ibid., 19.

181. Zolotonosov, for instance, draws the connection Kazakov's method of using lysates for therapeutical purposes (*Slovo i telo*, 760–61). Likewise, Sambikin's attempt to find a "mysterious substance" within the bodies of the recently deceased to prolong the life of the living (33) is reminiscent of Aleksei Zamkov's experiments with gravidan—a "miracle" drug derived from the urine of pregnant women (See Eric Naiman, "Diskurs, obrashchennyi v plot: A. Zamkov i voploshchenie sovetskoi sub"ektivnosti," in *Sotsrealisticheskii kanon*, 625–38.

182. E. Tolstaia-Segal, "Ideologicheskie konteksty Platonova," 56.

183. Similar thoughts are found among Platonov's jottings for the mid-'30s. In one set listed under the heading "Fairy-Tales," Platonov writes: "7. Reflecting with the intestines, digesting with the brain" (A. Platonov, *Zapisnye knizhki*, 262).

184. This is quite significant, since—as Eric Naiman remarks ("Lexical Heroes in *Happy Moscow*," 105–6), Platonov's punning play with the verb *sluchit'sia* in *Happy Moscow* (it can mean both "to happen" and "to mate") suggests a strong connection between events (*sobytie*, which literally means "co-being" in Russian) and copulation. Naiman's point is well-taken, since at one point in the novel Platonov openly merges the two ideas/words (i.e., *sovokuplenie* and *sobytie*): "He stayed awake in expectation, observing in the dark silence the gradual passage of the night's time, which was full of events. From behind the third door, counting from the sewage-pape, there began the orderly sounds of copulation. . . . In the other rooms of the corridor there were also events going on, minor, but constant and essential, so that night was as filled with life and activity as daytime" (*Happy Moscow*, 48).

185. Igor' Smirnov, *Psikhodiakhronologika*, 277.

186. Boris Groys, "Die gebaute Ideologie," in Peter Noever, ed. *Tyrannei des Schönen: Architektur der Stalin-Zeit* (München: 1994), 18.

187. Igor' Smirnov, *Psikhodiakhronologika*, 277.

188. Ibid., 279.

189. As Katerina Clark notes, this is surely a variant of those rites of passage in which the entry of the individual into a larger collective body is accompanied by some form of 'token mutilation'" (Katerina Clark, *The Soviet Novel: History as Ritual*, 178).

190. L. Kassil', *Metro* (Moscow, 1936), 13.

191. Katerina Clark, *The Soviet Novel: History as Ritual*, 180.

192. Alexander Zholkovsky, *"The Obverse of Stalinism,"* in *Self and Story in Russian History*, eds. Laura Engelstein and Stephanie Sandler (Ithaca: Cornell University Press, 2000), 63.

193. The difference between these two is that for Stalinist culture (physical) suffering is not so much a means toward greater consciousness as it is a token of the person's ideological and spiritual promotion. As Smirnov notes (*Psikhodiakhronologika*, 255), in Stalinist culture the sufferer knows only that "if there were no suffering, there would be no cultural superiority over the other characters."

194. A. Platonov, *Dzhan*, 343.

195. A. Platonov, *Zapisnye knizhki*, 172.

196. Ibid., 229.

197. Note that the Russian letter "Я" is the equivalent of the English "I."

198. Quoted in Eric Naiman, "Andrei Platonov mezhdu dvukh utopii," 246.

199. In this sense, I cannot entirely agree with Naiman's claim that the image simply connotes the high price (in physical) terms of entry into the Stalinist utopia (see "Andrei Platonov mezhdu dvukh utopii," 246).

200. This development might also be described as a shift from a subsuming gesture (the attempt to subsume the other within oneself) toward a gesture of incorporation. This is implicit, for instance, in Chagataev's relationship to the Dzhan at the end of the novella of the same title. Similarly, at the conclusion of "The River Potudan'" Nikita retreats from his momentary desire to subsume Lyuba within himself, preferring instead to share his heart's blood with "poor pleasure": "Nikita embraced Lyuba with the kind of force that attempts to put the other, beloved person inside one's needing soul; however, he soon came to his senses and felt ashamed" (A. Platonov, *Vzyskanie pogibshikh*, 446).

201. A. Platonov, *Iamskaia sloboda*, 349. Note that like Zarrin-Tadhz, Moscow Chestnova is also closely associated with the image of the tree (Ol'ga Kapel'nitskaia, "Mifologema 'Zhenshchina-gorod,'" 673).

202. A. Platonov, *Sochineniia v t-kh tomakh*, 3:302.

203. Ibid., 302.

204. John McCannon, "Tabula Rasa in the North," in *The Landscape of Stalinism: The Art and Ideology of Soviet Space*, eds. Evgeny Dobrenko and Eric Naiman (Seattle: University of Washington Press, 2003), 253.

205. This, too, represents a significant departure, since the more frequently quoted Pushkin verses of the Stalinist '30s were the upbeat, life-embracing "Bacchic Song" and the solemn "Exegi monumentum." Even a casual glance at *Literaturnaia gazeta* for the year 1937 (the year of the Pushkin centennial) will confirm this.

206. B. M. Gasparov, "Poeticheskii iazyk Pushkina kak fakt istorii russkogo literaturnogo iazyka," *Wiener Slawistischer Almanach* 27 (1992): 246.

207. Note that the letter "Я" in Russian means "I" and also possesses a slightly anthropomorphic look. The conflated image of self and letter is not accidentally accompanied by physical mutilation. As Jonathan Goldberg notes (*Writing Matter: From the Hands of the English Renaissance* [Stanford: Stanford University Press,

1990], 80), the passage from nature to culture implicit in the "civilizing" practice of writing is often represented in terms of violence and physical mutilation. Moreover, as Stephen Greenblatt remarks ("Mutilation and Meaning," 223), for medieval Christians the wounded flesh of Christ was seen as a kind of universal text: "For Christians God's flesh was itself a text written upon with universal characters, inscribed with a language that all men could understand since it was a language in and of the body itself, independent of any particular forms of speech."

208. I. Paperno, "Pushkin v zhizni cheloveka Serebriannogo veka," in Boris Gasparov, Robert P. Hughes, and Irina Paperno, eds., *Cultural Mythologies of Russian Modernism: From the Golden Age to the Silver Age* (Berkeley: University of California Press, 1992), 23.

209. A. Platonov, *Vospominaniia sovremennikov: Materialy k biografii*, 415.

210. The term is taken from Zholkovsky's essay of the same title.

211. Such images abound in Platonov's descriptions of his self-reformation. Thus in a meeting with various writers that took place in 1932, Platonov describes his path toward rehabilitation as predicated on "breaking his bones": "I began to break my bones, began to work" (A. Platonov, *Vospominaniia sovremennikov: Materialy k biografii*, 296).

212. Quoted in Vladimir Vasil'ev, *Andrei Platonov: Ocherk zhizni i tvorchestva* (Moscow: 1990), 259.

213. Thomas Seifrid, *Andrei Platonov: Uncertainties of Spirit*, 176, 183.

214. Eric Naiman, "Andrei Platonov mezhdu dvukh utopii," 248.

215. Julia Kristeva, *Powers of Horror*, 76–77.

216. Daniil Kharms, *Menia nazyvaiut Kaputsinom: Nekotorye proizvedeniia Daniila Ivanovicha Kharmsa* (Moscow: MP "Karavento": "Pikment," 1993), 224.

Chapter Two

Mikhail Zoshchenko: Engineering the Stalinist Body and Soul

> I'm going past the Winter Palace. I see a red flag on the palace. So, it's a new life. A new Russia. And I, too, am new, not like I used to be. Let it all be behind me now, my afflictions, nerves, my spleen, my bad heart.
>
> Mikhail Zoshchenko (*Before Sunrise*)

Andrei Platonov's vision of the communist utopia as it emerged from such works as *Dzhan* or *Happy Moscow* was one in which nothing, not even filth and bodily waste, were to be left behind. The writer's image of a genuinely "humanistic communism," which surely owes more to Vladimir Solov'ev's dream of "all-inclusiveness" than it does to political ideology,[1] sought to counter the strategies of ideological and physical purification that were the twin pillars of Stalinist transformationalism. Taking leave of the earlier radical tradition that viewed physiology in its unreconstructed form as a threat to the building of communism, the Platonov of the '30s and '40s sees the human body with its inherent refusal to distinguish between pure and impure—between filth and perfection—as a model of almost utopian inclusion.[2] This is manifested, among others, in the peculiar kind of narrative incontinence displayed by such works as *Happy Moscow*. It concerns not only the characters' physical disposition but more broadly the author's refusal to portray his characters' "desire for social coherence in a tightly cohesive form." Yet whether physiological or narrative, such incontinence clearly ran counter to the broader culture's increasing appetite for ideological closure.[3] By contrast, Mikhail Zoshchenko's fiction of the same period betrays nearly the opposite impulse. Indeed, beginning with his *Youth Restored* (1933) much of Zoshchenko's writing of the 1930s looks like an attempt to embody the very ideals that Platonov had professed in his essays of the early '20s but had since come to reject.[4] In many of Zoshchenko's stories, feuilletons, and longer

91

works from the '30s, body and body politic alike are increasingly subject to a regimen of painful but ultimately beneficial restraints. Thus in the commentary section of *Youth Restored*, Zoshchenko cites in a manner that is not entirely negative the example of the German philosopher Kant who managed to subject the vicissitudes of his body to "pure reason," turning his "bodily organism" into a machine.[5] Mirroring this push for corporeal continence, Zoshchenko's writing as a whole edges steadily—albeit ambivalently— toward greater narrative "resolution," from the "the back and forth of *Youth Restored*" and the "zigzag of *The Blue-Book*" to the "uncommon simplicity . . . and directness" of *Before Sunrise*.[6]

What would seem to be a rather unusual preoccupation with attaining ideological and corporeal self-mastery is far from atypical, however. Rather it reflects the extraordinary embeddedness (throughout the decade of the 1930s) of even the most microcosmic aspects of private and everyday existence in the broader narrative of socialist construction.[7] One need hardly repeat, for instance, that the epic accounts of Stalinist labor emphasized not only how individuals carried out Stalin's "second revolution," but the manner in which citizens themselves were formed and *transformed* through their participation in these grandiose undertakings.[8] A relatively late Socialist Realist novel—V. Popov's *Steel and Slag* (1948)—makes the point admirably. Its worker-protagonists are able to accomplish their goal of mastering new steel-tempering techniques only by overcoming ingrained ways of thinking. The immediate task of tempering steel, the author suggests, goes hand in hand with the greater goal of "forging" a new species of Homo sapiens.[9] And this extends to what is surely the most fundamental expression of individual/collective selfhood—that is, the body.[10] Throughout the previous decade the ritual of *perekovka* ("reforging") was envisioned in coldly futuristic terms that celebrated the transformation of flesh to metal, as was the case with Aleksei Gastev's "We Grow out of Iron" (1920), Vladimir Kirillov's poem "Iron Messiah" (1918), Serafimovich's novel *The Iron Flood* (1924), and numerous others. Meanwhile, the following decade brought about what might be described as the interiorization of the forging narrative. Unlike the Bolsheviks of Serafimovich's *Iron Flood*, who are "'as if forged out of black iron,'" Ostrovsky's Korchagin (the quintessential Socialist Realist hero of the '30s) is internally, metaphorically tempered, even as his physical body wastes away.[11] In an effort to produce positive heroes who were both life-like and utopian, Socialist Realism projected the process of transfiguration inside the body, turning not flesh to metal but rather metal to flesh. This despite the fact that "by the end of the 1930s the imagery of iron and steel had penetrated every aspect of Soviet society."[12] Yet the increasing anthropomorphization and interiorization of such metaphors during the Stalin era ultimately produced a reforging rhetoric that was at once more "natural" (i.e., amenable to traditional paradigms) and more insidious (because less obtrusive).[13]

Stalinist ideology's unprecedented push into the interior spaces of the body is mirrored in the abundance of autobiographical and autotherapeutic writing from this period. It is here that we truly enter what might be called the workshop of the Stalinist soul. As Jochen Hellbeck demonstrates, diaries in particular provided the Stalinist subject with a place where the profane self sought purification and ultimately spiritual rebirth.[14] The diaries of the Stalinist playwright Aleksandr Afinogenov provide an excellent case in point. Written at the height of the purges between 1936 and 1938, Afinogenov's diary entries provide the writer with a forum for intense introspection and self-reflection. At the same time, they allow him to engage in a ritual of self-purging that neatly mirrors the party leadership's call for a global cleansing of the body politic.[15] Likewise, many other Stalin-era diaries functioned as a "controlling, and regulating device," enabling their authors "to monitor the physiological and intellectual processes at work in them." Indeed, appeals to "control" and "rationalize" one's life, to illuminate unconscious feelings so as to be able to live one's life in a "'plan-like'" manner were not uncommon. The well-known writer Vera Inber goes so far as to advocate a process of "'technicizing the soul,' justifying the procedure by claiming that 'Man is a factory. And his mind is the director of this factory.'"[16] What, one might ask, is the common theme in such imagery? The answer lies in the pitched battle between the supernal realm of ideology and the benighted netherworld of (human) nature that was at the forefront of Stalinism's campaign to fashion a new world.[17] And as the case of Zoshchenko will shortly demonstrate, the issue of human psycho-physiology (in short, of the body) was at once a promising arena and an intractable dilemma within that campaign.

If the human body represented for Stalinism the "raw material" to be re-forged, the Word was the mythic Philosopher's stone that promised to make such a transformation possible. Such revolutionary alchemy, as Rolf Hellebust demonstrates, was entirely in the spirit of the era.[18] Thus Aleksei Zamkov's experiments with the "miracle drug" gravidan produced results that seemed to demonstrate the very real possibility of creating a socialist überworker. In the same vein, one of Zamkov's correspondents—a certain Ol'ga Sotnik—wrote that "We live in a time, when the fairy-tale is being transformed into life, dreams into reality."[19] And more to the point, at least one diarist—a *komsomol* activist named Anatolii Ul'ianov—seemed to believe that the discipline and heroicism of his narrative efforts would translate automatically into real-life discipline and heroicism. Like Stalinist culture itself, Ul'ianov proceeded from the assumption that there was no difference between "'writing like this' and

'living like this.'"[20] One cannot help but see in this the broader culture's uncommon preoccupation with the very act of writing. As Yury Murashov notes,
the written word achieved the same prominence in Stalinist culture as had oral
speech during the revolutionary decade of the '20s. Though it could easily de-
volve into a medium for double-dealing or deception, at the same time writing
held forth the promise of a "magical connection with the very center of
power."[21] One wonders if it is not for this reason (among others) that the figure of Nikolai Ostrovsky/Korchagin achieved such prominence in the Stalinist '30s. For the author's legendary biography was built precisely on the transformation of his prematurely mummified body into a heroic text—that is, on
the passing of flesh into Word.[22] For Zoshchenko, as for Ul'ianov and numerous others, this mythic sense of the written word's power would play a crucial
role in the author's strategy of self-healing.

As in Vera Inber's case, for Zoshchenko of the '30s the ideal of "technicizing the soul" acquires uncommon resonance. This is not to say that the writer
was as wholehearted in his embrace of Stalinist virtues as any of the figures
mentioned above. Indeed, the reality of Zoshchenko's relationship to the
regime had always been one of some ambivalence. And all indications are that
Zoshchenko saw in Soviet power both a bulwark of stability against an inherently unstable universe, as well as a troubling source of chaos and disorder.[23]
Nevertheless, it does not seem to be fortuitous that many of Zoshchenko's
short stories, feuilletons, and longer works of the '30s play out a scenario in
which the chaotic body and soul of various "preideological" subjects are reformed through their (oftentimes violent) contact with the rigors of Stalinist
order and "culture." In this regard they clearly anticipate Zoshchenko's most
famous attempt at ideological self-reform in *Before Sunrise*, where the writer
aspires to nothing less than becoming—à la the late Gogol—the ideal author
of the ideal book.[24] Finally, if the analogy between autobiographical/
diaristic texts and Zoshchenko's writing seems somewhat inappropriate, one
need only consider the significant extent to which his writing was, in fact, "autobiographical," artistically refracting in infinite variations the anxieties and
phobias that beset the writer in real life. Indeed, when seen through the prism
of his explicitly autobiographical *Before Sunrise*, Zoshchenko's oeuvre
seems—as Zholkovsky has so convincingly demonstrated—strongly reminiscent of Gogol's confession that his fiction represented an attempt to expose
and ultimately discredit his own internal "rubbish."[25]

There is no dearth of scholars, critics, and memoirists who have commented
on the sea change that occurred in Zoshchenko's writing during the 1930s. A
significant aspect of this change concerns the author's ambition to engineer
his own physical and artistic health—to exorcise his "internal rubbish"—as a
prelude to a future moment of mythical rebirth and resurrection.[26] As the

prominent literary critic, memoirist, and friend of Zoshchenko, Kornei Chukovsky, wrote in 1937: "a great man, but crazy. His madness is self-healing."[27] Indeed, Zoshchenko's near obsession with matters of sickness and health had played a prominent role in his fiction since the beginning of his career as a writer, reflecting a long-standing battle with melancholy and depression.[28] Among others, the author's quest for convalescence during the decade of the '30s is thematized in nearly autobiographical fashion in *Youth Restored*.[29] Like the diaristic writings mentioned above, this unusual work—part fiction and part nonfiction—blurs any clear distinction between private pathology and public ideology. The unusual convergence of these two is no accident, for as one contemporary scholar suggests, Stalinist subjects were inclined to localize the dysfunctions of the political sphere deep within the realm of private physiology. Ideology and physiology, it follows, often appeared as two sides of the same coin. Thus Aleksei Zamkov's patients sought to rehabilitate themselves as ideological subjects by taking doses of gravidan—the same "miracle drug" that was fabled to turn ordinary workers into Stakhanovites.[30] Similarly, in Zoshchenko's *Youth Restored*, the main protagonist Volosatov transforms his ailing and aging body in a manner that goes hand in hand with his ideological rehabilitation proclaimed (thought not entirely demonstrated) at the end of the work.[31] Likewise, in his diary from the year 1938, the Stalinist hack writer and head of the Writers' Union Vladimir Stavsky describes health and the struggle for communism as twin fronts within the same larger battle. Convincing himself to take up a physical fitness regime, he notes: "'You are a Communist, history has placed great tasks before you. Your health is also a front in the battle. You must struggle and triumph here as well.'"[32] And, in a short piece entitled "The Montage of Life" (written in 1935 for a newspaper of the Corrective Labor Camp of the Baikal—Amur line called *Putearmeets* or "The Soldier of the Tracks"), the Stalinist writer Vasily Azhaev unequivocally evokes the nexus between Stakhanovite production and psychophysiological reforging. At one point in the piece the fictional Aleksandr Medvedev (Azhaev's pseudonym) complains of having to construct sewer or water pipes instead of the great path to the future, only to be reminded by a comrade that assembling a machine is the same as constructing one's life: "There was a rather clever fellow standing next to me. 'What are you thinking,' he said. 'That you're just assembling a machine?' 'You're re-assembling your life, Medvedev."[33] Finally, Zoshchenko himself provides what is perhaps the best illustration of Stalinism's linking of individual bodies with public ideology. In 1935 he participated in the writing of the volume meant to commemorate the reforging triumphs of the Baltic-White Sea canal project. Zoshchenko's contribution to the volume was a short story entitled "Story of a Reforging." The piece recounts the life of a career criminal named Abraham

Rottenburg who was supposedly rehabilitated through hard labor. Zoshchenko published the story under the title "Youth Restored" in *Literary Leningrad* in 1933—only half a year before the longer work of the same title would begin appearing in serialized form in *Zvezda*.[34] And it is obvious from this that Zoshchenko wrote the piece not simply to curry favor with the authorities but for reasons that "went beyond simple duty."[35] The connection between the reforging of the criminal Rottenburg and Zoshchenko's later fictional quest for "youth restored" is only too clear. By internalizing the Stalinist myth of reforging—in a sense, introjecting the public myth into his "private parts"—the author hoped to remake himself (both physically and emotionally) as the New Man triumphantly projected by Stalinist mythology.

While Zoshchenko scholars have traditionally divided the writer's work into two distinct periods, segregating the later, supposedly "serious," works from the author's earlier comic writing, recent criticism has stressed the extraordinary uniformity of Zoshchenko's worldview and of the (non)fiction it produced.[36] It now seems entirely possible to read much of what Zoshchenko wrote not only for its satirical, comic, or didactic pathos, but as an intricate literary edifice erected atop a myriad of authorial inner demons. Using the autobiographical and autotherapeutic *Before Sunrise* as his point of departure, Alexander Zholkovsky lays out a veritable labyrinth of phobias and fears, which when taken together map out Zoshchenko's career-long search for stability and order in an inherently unstable cosmos. There can be no doubt as to the value and attractiveness of such an approach. What still remains to be elucidated, however, is the manner in which Zoshchenko's attempts to liberate himself from long-standing fears was, in fact, molded by broader cultural and ideological trends. How, in other words, does the writer's legendary quest for self-healing mesh with Stalinist culture's program of social hygiene and ideological purification? At least a partial answer can be gleaned from the Zoshchenkovian narrative of reforging mentioned above. For here one is hard-pressed to distinguish between the "thief and swindler" Rottenburg (like Zoshchenko a product the discredited past), whose voice the author assumes and whose reeducation he eagerly chronicles, and the ideologically suspect author himself. It does not seem a stretch, in other words, to believe one of the writer's shipmates on the trip, who speaks of Zoshchenko's genuine desire to believe in the successes of the Belomor reforging story, despite their obviously having been staged.[37] Not unlike Aleksei Zamkov, whose miracle drug provides a medicinal counterpart to the reeducation narrative, Zoshchenko's battle to exorcise his emotional and physical demons was surely as much a reflection of public myths as it was the result of the author's purely private struggle with depression. By the same token, Zoshchenko's struggle with such "phobic objects" as water, women, sex, or the arm must ultimately be understood not only as the writer's "internal rubbish" but in terms of the most potent cultural myths and stereotypes of the time.

One of the most important of these, according to Katerina Clark, was the so-called struggle with nature.[38] And as Clark notes, the theme of struggle with nature in the culture of the '30s had as much to do with a kind of Nietzschean self-overcoming (i.e., the overturning of human nature) as it did with over-coming nature per se. "Soviet man," writes Clark, "proved himself superior to all men who had existed before by combatting the natural phenomena of the greatest symbolic resonance in Russian oral and written literature: water and ice (floods, disasters as the ice breaks up, snowstorms, etc.)."[39] At the same time, humankind's inevitable triumph over the elements was variously attrib-uted to sheer willpower,[40] or to rational self-control.[41] In this manner, the Stal-inist subject acquired a powerful (if overly simplistic) symbolic vocabulary by means of which he could aspire to master the most far-flung and hostile reaches of the cosmos. Moreover, it is hardly surprising that in the case of Afinogenov and the other diarists mentioned above, the hostile territory to be mastered proved to be nothing less than the individual's own flawed psycho-physiology. Zoshchenko's writing of this period reveals a similar pathos. In *Youth Restored*, *The Sky-Blue Book*, and *Before Sunrise*, as well as other shorter works, the author echoes the Stalinist campaign against "the natural" in his own struggle to exorcise such phobic objects as water, food, the arm, etc. Indeed, the writer's attempts to master his "internal" chaos using various kinds of mind-control techniques—though grounded in sources as diverse as Stefan Zweig, Mary Baker Eddy, and Freud[42]—is suspiciously reminiscent of a drama that is tirelessly played out within the culture at large. That drama con-cerns the rechanneling of "spontaneousness" into "consciousness." The Stal-inist subject, according to one critic, inhabited a world that modulated cease-lessly between the extremes of Dionysian energy and Apollinian order.[43] Stakhanovites, for instance, could carry out their feats of labor only by draw-ing on their bodies' hidden reserves. Likewise, the famous fliers of the '30s, who represented the very essence of the culture's desire to produce a race of socialist superhumans, seemed to have been endowed with a special kind of cosmic energy.[44] Thus the Stalinist hero's Dionysian underground was never without its Apollonian guardian and twin. The culture's praise of enthusiasm was invariably accompanied by the caveat that it should be made subordinate to rational control and "iron will."[45]

Arguably the most potent of Zoshchenko's phobic objects is the arm or hand. Paradoxically, it is this very image that will later provide the writer (in such major works as *Youth Restored* and *Before Sunrise*) with a powerful symbolic means of dislodging this very phobia. Particularly in *Before Sunrise*, the author's fear of the father's unjustly punishing arm is sublimated in the chastening arm of Stalinist ideology, which securely binds and masters the unruly subject. And as the writer Vasily Azhaev (alias Aleksandr Medvedev) demonstrates, Stalinism's "montage of life" must ultimately be understood in the most literal, biological terms, as the reforging of the human body—right down to the movements of the hands and arms: "Stakhanov has put the emphasis on the mechanism. Our principal mechanism is the hands. Which is to say that one has to organize the hands."[46]

As Zholkovsky and Masing-Delic have argued, the image of the arm in Zoshchenko's work serves as a potent and enduring reminder of the writer's inability to resolve a lingering Oedipal crisis.[47] While Zoshchenko himself goes to elaborate lengths (in *Before Sunrise*) to deny this,[48] the writer's authorial hand tells a rather different tale. Zoshchenko's denials aside, the recurring theme of hostile arms/hands can easily be traced back to the "irrational" and arbitrarily punishing hand of the Father. And if Zoshchenko's own account of his childhood in *Before Sunrise* is any indication, it is not only the mother's but the *father's* hand which denies the nursing infant access to the maternal breast, in essence punishing the child for his most fundamental desires.[49] Later, (as recounted in *Before Sunrise*) this same paternal hand will complicate the young Zoshchenko's bid for his mother's affections, causing the boy to fantasize about the day when he will become a man and have power to determine the way the adult world functions.[50] In the meantime, the young Zoshchenko views the cosmos as governed by irrational, chaotic, and oftentimes despotic forces. No doubt the most despotic of these is God himself. As with Dostoevsky's Ivan Karamazov, for Zoshchenko, too, it is God the Father who unjustly punishes his children by permitting them to suffer the reality of death.[51]

Similarly oppressive and unjust authority figures abound in the vignettes recounted throughout *Before Sunrise*. Among others, they symbolize the inherently corrupt nature of the prerevolutionary world, and the flawed inheritance it threatens to pass on to its sons. Thus in one of the first story-vignettes of *Before Sunrise*, a teenaged Zoshchenko travels to Kislovodsk to take up a summer job. Full of youthful idealism about finally entering the adult world, he is soon confronted with the sobering reality of rampant corruption and cronyism. As if to confirm the narrator's worst fears of authority, the old world literally looms over Zoshchenko in the form of an enormous tsarist gendarme. And like every other oppressive "patriarch" evoked in *Before Sunrise*, the gendarme appears as monumental and motionless as the ossified ancien régime he exemplifies: "Kislovodsk. I walk out onto the platform. Near the station doors stands an enormous gendarme, with medals on his chest. He is frozen, like a monument."[52] There is no shortage of such figures in

Zoshchenko's autobiographical work. The thematic equivalent of the father's oppressive and punishing arm, they symbolize the moribund immobility of the prerevolutionary status quo. By contrast, the Bolshevik Revolution, with its promise of violent overthrow and global cleansing, clearly embodies Zoshchenko's own "Oedipal" wish to make a clean break with the tyranny of the past. This is most obvious in the first part of *Before Sunrise*, where the narrator-author identifies himself with the revolution on the most basic of levels—that of physiology. For Zoshchenko October holds forth the promise not only of social and political renewal, but of a global psychophysiological rebirth. Describing the days that followed the revolution in a vignette entitled "I Don't Understand," he writes: "So, it's a new life. A new Russia. And I'm new, not the way I was. Let everything be behind me, my afflictions, my nerves, my spleen, my sick heart."[53]

Still, the reality of October frequently falls short of the myth. In *Before Sunrise* the revolution's early promise of "a new life" is often overshadowed by the sheer tenacity of the old world. Thus in the same vignette mentioned above, Zoshchenko writes: "For about two days I feel wonderful. By the third day my spleen is back. Again the heart palpitations, gloom and melancholy."[54] Likewise, in the short story entitled "Thy Neighbor's Hand" (1927) the writer describes a scenario in which the democratic pathos of the revolution (symbolized by the gesture of shaking hands) is undercut by the sudden realization that the hand of one's fellow man conceals unknown perils. In the story Zoshchenko recounts his encounter with a peasant in 1919. Unaware that the peasant is from a nearby leper colony, the young Red Army officer insists on displaying his democratic principles by shaking the man's hand. Yet when he discovers the truth he immediately goes outside to wash his hands with snow. And in the last line of the piece the writer exclaims: "It's a pity to extend such hands to one's fellow man."[55] Here the revolution's promise of a cosmic cleansing of the body politic,[56] one that would remove the ulcers of the past (both social and physiological), is offset by the unchanging reality of the unclean body itself.

More importantly, the revolution's punishing arm can itself come to embody the very irrational and chaotic force it originally aspired to overthrow. This is true of a number of short stories from the '20s, where Soviet power is identified with an aggressive or destructive hand.[57] The dilemma sketched above surely mirrors the deeper structure of the Oedipal crisis itself. For the Oedipal subject can choose between only two extremes: submit to an arbitrarily punishing authority figure or take up the reins of power oneself. Either way the flawed legacy of the old world remains locked in place. And this is repeatedly demonstrated in those vignettes throughout *Before Sunrise* where Zoshchenko occupies the place of the father with less-than-happy results.[58]

As Masing-Delic writes, this no-win situation consistently presents the writer with a choice between "self-effacement and bullying, fear and brutality, pain or "zoological normality."[59] Is it any accident, then, that *Before Sunrise* contains clear echoes of both Pushkin's "Bronze Horseman" and Belyi's *Petersburg*?[60] Perhaps more than any other two works of the Petersburg tradition, these two embody the destructive cycle of Oedipal violence that characterizes the relationship between Russia's literary fathers and sons. The solution to Zoshchenko's dilemma, to the multiple fears, phobias, and anxieties that he undertakes to exorcise in his later work, lies not in the first revolution of 1917 but—I would argue—in the "second," Stalinist revolution of the 1930s. It is here, in Stalinism's optimistic projection of a totally unified and transfigured body (politic), that the perennial standoff between father and son is finally resolved for Zoshchenko.

As Platonov's *Happy Moscow* demonstrates only too well, the body of the Stalinist subject arose out of a violent separation of the self from its biological point of origin. The ritual passage from primordial nature to Bolshevik culture and technology is incessantly played out throughout Stalinism's *Gesamtkunstwerk*, from the bowels of the Moscow underground to those of the writer Mikhail Zoshchenko himself. A number of his stories and longer works from the period are nothing if not allegories of the progressive rationalization of the author's body and soul. A significant role in this process is played by the same image of the arm/hand that stands at the heart of Zoshchenko's lifelong trauma. In such works as *Youth Restored, The Sky-Blue Book*, and, most importantly, *Before Sunrise*, it is the authorial hand that underwrites the process of bodily control. As Zholkovsky notes, in these and similar works Zoshchenko resolves the dilemma of the punishing hand or arm by sublimating its inherent aggression in the image of the author's masterfully writing hand, guided as it is by all-encompassing Reason.[61] Yet what this critic and others fail to mention is the extraordinary degree to which Zoshchenko's scriptive strategy is implicated in the ideology and cultural mythology of the Stalinist '30s. As Jonathan Goldberg notes, it is precisely in the gesture of the writing hand (i.e., in the violent act of dislodging humanity from the natural and resettling it "within domains of scriptive instrumentality") that Homo sapiens is born.[62] Not surprisingly, Stalinism, with its heavily mythologized struggle against nature, privileges not the spoken but the *written* word. Thus representations of Lenin invariably emphasize the aspect of orality, while Stalin is usually shown surrounded by the attributes of writing.[63]

This crucial nuance seems not to have been lost on such authors as Afinogenov or Zoshchenko, who saw in the written word nothing less than the keys to their own happiness. Here was a chance to rewrite oneself in the image of the premier author of the Soviet land. By the same token, Zoshchenko's sublimation of the aggressive hand in the "civilized" authorial pen in such works as *Before Sunrise* is not so much a resolution of the earlier Oedipal dilemma as it is a *continuation* of it. The throng of unjust and oppressive authority figures from the author's past, rather than being overthrown, are simply superseded by a single Grand Inquisitor-like benefactor in the guise of Stalinist ideology and, ultimately, Stalin himself. As in the case of Dostoevsky's Grand Inquisitor — who takes upon himself the burden of collective doubt and uncertainty — for Zoshchenko the anguish of life and literature is dissolved in an all-encompassing "inquisitorial" ideology. Not unlike Afinogenov, whose anguished attempts at self-purification led him to proclaim in his diary 1937 as the "'year of [his] birth,'"[64] Zoshchenko's *Before Sunrise* carries out a purge of the author's past as a prelude to the author's reemergence in the guise of an ideologically and spiritually pure subject. Yet every rebirth presupposes a prior death. Thus Afinogenov's claim to have been "born" in 1937 goes hand in hand with an acute awareness of the death(s) that accompanied it. "Writing that 1937 was the 'year of [his] birth,' Afinogenov undoubtedly also had in mind many other Party members and writer colleagues for whom this year had brought destruction and death (12/30/37)."[65] Likewise, Zoshchenko begins his *Before Sunrise* with the rather macabre pronouncement that speaking about his past is tantamount to speaking about a dead person.[66] Here, too, death and rebirth appear as two sides of the same coin. It is undoubtedly for this reason that Zoshchenko's repeated claims in *Before Sunrise* and elsewhere to have finally cured himself ring hollow. As Platonov's *Happy Moscow* makes only too clear, the chaos of human nature, which Stalinism aspired to banish entirely from the bowels of the body politic, could be purged only at the cost of destroying that very body.

Yet the tale that culminates in *Before Sunrise* begins much earlier, in the works (both long and short) of the '30s, where Zoshchenko undertakes what appears to be a progressive rationalization of the human organism. In these "accomodationist" works, the body along with its atavistic instincts is subjected to a regime of often violent but ultimately beneficial constraints. The necessity of such restraints reflects a lingering sense that the realm of desire itself threatens the proper functioning of the individual in society. This is hardly surprising if one considers the Oedipal conflict that stands squarely at the center of Zoshchenko's *Before Sunrise*. One such work is a minor masterpiece entitled "The Sufferings of the Young Verter."[67] Adduced by memoirists and critics (along with such stories as "The Lights of the Big City," 1935) as evidence of a sea change in Zoshchenko's style during the 1930s, "The Sufferings" mirrors the author's ambivalent embrace of Soviet power. Ambivalent because while the story as a whole conjures up a naïve vision of society in which state and individual function in complete harmony, the reader has every reason to distrust the glib conclusions of Zoshchenko's narrator—a hapless enthusiast bent on viewing the world through rose-colored glasses. Indeed, the final lines of the piece, which paint a picture of the future Soviet society as one in which policemen pass out flowers to hooligans, seem less than wholly convincing. Still, a more profound and fundamental ambivalence concerns the broader sense that the author's worldview itself is caught squarely in the vice of conflicting desires. Here the volatile realm of individual desire abuts against the no less violent domain of public restraint. Instinctively drawn to the notion of an ideal (pre-Oedipal?) society in which human beings would exist in a state of "unconditional," unmediated being, the writer nevertheless remains painfully aware that such unfettered, pure being cannot be experienced except perhaps "beyond the limits of life itself."[68] What emerges from Zoshchenko's "Sorrows" is thus an apology of benevolent, rational restraints. The author's notorious ambivalence notwithstanding, the openly masochistic overtones of "The Sufferings" echoes the masochism that lay at the very core of Stalinist anthropology. And is this really surprising? Written at the outset of the Stalinist era, the piece merely echoes what the public sphere never tired of intoning: the Dionysian energy and enthusiasm of the Stalinist body (politic) must be *tempered* by rational, Apollinian control.[69]

The plot is deceptively simple, describing the narrator's fantasies (during a bicycle ride) about the idyllic society of the near future. Oblivious to his surroundings, the dreamer mistakenly rides into an area closed to bicycles, where he is intercepted by an angry guard and his assistant. The guard initially proposes arresting the man but later relents, allowing him to depart with nothing more than a ticket. At first the narrator is indignant about his treatment, but he soon resumes his ride and his fantasies about the more humane society of the future, announcing: "We're building a new life. We've won. We've gone through enormous difficulties, so let's try to respect each other."[70]

Thematically, Zoshchenko's "Sufferings" modulates between the ideal state of "pure" or unfettered being associated with the narrator's bicycle ride and its violent interruption by the arresting motion of the authorities. The fact that Zoshchenko uses the image of the bicycle to symbolize the narrator's dream state is quite significant. Associated in both the nineteenth and early-twentieth centuries with freedom, lack of inhibition, and even sexual liberation,[71] the bicycle symbolizes not only unrestricted movement but the author's longtime fascination with the machine as an icon of the harmonious functioning of individual parts within a greater whole.[72] Moreover, given Zoshchenko's frequent allusions to Chekhov elsewhere in his writing,[73] it might not be going too far to suggest a connection with Chekhov's short story

"Man in a Case." Chekhov's story, too, wavers between images of unrestricted movement (i.e., the boisterous Varen'ka, who like Zoshchenko is Ukrainian), and its antipode in the teacher Belikov's fearful love of order.[74] Zoshchenko's "Sufferings" comprises both of these extremes, combining the freewheeling enthusiasm of the narrator with the anxious desire for stasis and restraint embodied by the sadistic guard.

More than a simple icon of individual freedom, the bicycle in Zoshchenko's "Sufferings" symbolizes the dark, unregulated realm of human desire. The quasi-ontological resonance of the image follows from Zoshchenko's peculiar repetition of "turning" and "twisting" verbs (*vert-* and *vorot-* in Russian).[75] By projecting the circular motion of these verbs not only onto the surrounding landscape but into the very soul of the narrator himself,[76] Zoshchenko creates a sense of the unreconstructed, "cyclical" trajectory of human desire. The suggestion (echoed elsewhere in the author's writing) seems to be that the inherently circular, chaotic shape of human nature precludes any possibility of linear, historical progress. Thus in the commentaries to the "love" section of his *Sky-Blue Book* Zoshchenko tells the story of the Roman emperor Servius Tullius who is killed by his daughter's lover. What Zoshchenko chooses to emphasize, however, is the perverse behavior of the daughter, who in her headlong rush to greet the new emperor rides over her dead father with the *wheels* of her chariot. Amorous passion, Zoshchenko suggests, is a part of a dangerous *cycle* that blinds the subject to her or his conscious obligations.[77] At the same time it can be argued that the shape of the Oedipal dilemma, which sets the violent desires of the sons against those of the fathers in a potentially open-ended conflict, is precisely that of the circle. Indeed, in *Before Sunrise*, the threat of an endless recycling of the conflict between fathers and sons is averted only through the timely intercession of a "rational" higher power—that is, Stalinist ideology.

Zoshchenko's "Sufferings" suggest an analogous if slightly more ambiguous scenario. This follows from the Goethian subtext of the piece. The reader will recall that Goethe's "Sorrows" depict the Oedipal tête-à-tête (precipitated by a woman) between the romantic Werther and the establishment, which eventually leads to the former's suicide. All of these elements are present in one form or another in Zoshchenko's "Sufferings," with its unbroken modulation between the dreamy, emotionally unbalanced posture of the narrator and the body-as-machine ideal symbolized by Goethe himself.[78] A clear allegory of the author's personal desire to exorcise his own internal "instability" via a regimen of rational restraints, Zoshchenko's "Sorrows" must at the same time be seen in the context of the broader narrative of Stalinist transformationalism.[79] Here the human subject is both the instrument by means of which socialist construction is carried out, as well as the construction site itself. Indeed,

how else are we to understand Vasily Azhaev's enthusiastic equation of assembling sewage pipes with the heady pathos of socialist life-creation? "When
I try to explain it to my guys, I talk about the montage of life. 'You are assembling a sewer? Just a sewer and that's it? No, that's not all of it. It's life that
you are assembling.'"[80] Likewise, desire in Stalinist culture is significant only
as energy to be productively rechanneled into love of the party and Stalin.[81]
Zoshchenko's "Sufferings" reproduce this model, even as they ultimately re-
sist any suggestion that the dichotomy of excess and restraint can be fully,
completely resolved. Thus the story begins with a rush of romantic elan directly tied to the circular motion of the cyclist's pedalling. Indeed, it is this
imaginative "romantic excess" that temporarily blinds the narrator, causing
him to run afoul of the law. And the hero's vision of a future society in which
the gulf between individual desire and public order is reduced to a bare minimum (i.e., "pure being") is not simply premature from Zoshchenko's standpoint. It is subversive, as the narrator's overly optimistic announcement "Soon
we'll be living like the Von Barons" (which is to say, like capitalists) would
appear to indicate.[82] Like many a Zoshchenkovian protagonist who—given the
proper circumstances—sheds his or her politically correct garments only to reveal a nature as yet unclaimed by Bolshevik ideology,[83] Zoshchenko's Soviet
Verter is the embodiment of desire's excess. His externally quiet, law-abiding
demeanor notwithstanding, the narrator of "Sufferings" exemplifies the problem of *natural* desire unchecked by *cultural* restraint ("In the future, . . . we
won't hear those sharp whistles, reminding us of misdemeanors, fines and in-
fringements of the law").[84] As such, his obvious and logical counterpart is
someone capable of redirecting or—at the very least—curtailing his movement and thus taming the swell of the hero's Dionysian energy.[85]

As Katerina Clark has shown, one of the founding myths of Stalinist culture concerns the ritual inauguration of an immature youth into political consciousness by a more experienced mentor figure. If Zoshchenko's "Sufferings" seem at first glance a somewhat unlikely arena for the unfolding of this
myth, closer inspection reveals some distinct similarities. Thus, one might argue that the role of the politically "conscious" elder in "Sufferings" is taken
up by a constant in Zoshchenko's fictional universe—the guard—while the
part of the ebullient but inexperienced youth is played by the narrator himself. The apparent contradiction of assigning Zoshchenko's coarse guard the
role of a conscious mentor disappears if one recognizes that the core dichotomy in Clark's paradigm is that of spontaneous excess and conscious restraint.[86] In other words, the guard figure need not be politically or otherwise
"conscious" in order to be effective as a bulwark against excess. All he needs
is a strong arm. A simple illustration of this can be found in "How Much Does
a Person Need"—a short story that Zoshchenko rewrote for his *Sky-Blue*

Book. Originally published in 1923,[87] the later expanded and reworked version of the story includes an aggressive guard who symbolizes the violent, even sadistic constraints necessary to curb the natural exuberance of the Stalinist body (politic).[88] Like its 1920s predecessor, "How Much Does a Person Need" reflects on the impossibility of creating a truly socialist (which is to say, moneyless) economy. The author muses that if, for instance, street cars were to become free people would simply ride them nonstop, even going in *circles* just for the fun of it. As in "The Sufferings," here, too, Zoshchenko uses the image of the circle to symbolize the inexhaustible circuit of human desire: "And if the streetcar were circular, then he [the patron], I'll bet, would ride the whole circle rather than getting off voluntarily at his stop. That's what kind of people there are. Some folks would even circle around three times."[89] Socialism cannot be achieved, Zoshchenko argues, without a radical overhaul of human nature. What's more, such an overhaul would not exclude the author himself, for Zoshchenko ultimately proves no less susceptible to the chaos of desire than the characters he creates: "Just the other day, I myself, having not yet re-made my psyche, ate about ten scoops ("circles" or *кружки* in Russian) or so of ice-cream at a single banquet" (III: 190).[90] For two weeks after, the writer notes, he was unable to "straighten out his body." Meanwhile Zoshchenko concludes with the tale of a man who rode a free carousel even to the point of becoming physically ill and vomiting.[91] And here, too, desire's vicious circle is equated with physical illness. Finally, as in "The Sufferings," here, too, the relationship between desire/appetite and circularity is crucial. Zoshchenko describes the motion of the carousel using the same verb ("to spin" or *кружиться* in Russian) that he had used to evoke the spinning pedals in his "Sufferings" (published only one year earlier). In both instances there is no logical end to what appears to be a vicious cycle. Indeed, only the guard's sadistic intervention seems capable of bringing the man to his senses and thus lending closure to the tale. Zoshchenko's point—quite simply—seems to be that human nature is perhaps best reformed with the help of a right hook: "At this point he had to get off—whether he wanted to or not. . . . But at that point a guard pulled him down, and, it seems, even gave him one in the chops for such scandalous behavior" (III: 190).

Likewise, the guard in Zoshchenko's "Sufferings" recalls the rationalist, disciplinary strain of Stalinist ideology that serves to rechannel the body's excess or, at the very least, to hold it in check.[92] In this regard, it is worth noting that the story as a whole modulates carefully between images of the protagonist's strangely unchecked movement ["In the meantime, there's a sign. And like an abnormal person he's riding. I whistle at him and he's spinning with his legs" (III: 366)] and the clearly sadistic measures employed by the guard to arrest it. Indeed, verbs denoting grabbing or holding appear no fewer

than eight times in the narrator's description of the arrest. To the extent that
the arm or hand frequently symbolizes for Zoshchenko desire or aggression
in their primordial form,[93] it is precisely this limb that is targeted for narrative reforging. Thus the guard's assistant, Lyoshka, hopes to break the inertia
of the narrator's moving body by breaking his arm: "I wanted to break his
arm, the slime, so that he wouldn't be able to ride" (III: 366). Curiously, from
our perspective, the narrator's response quickly turns from one of outraged
protest to an apology of the guard's sadistic measures. And it is here that the
protagonist-cum-masochist's true colors are revealed, for Lyoshka's sadistic
"claw" is now shown to perform a beneficial rather than a destructive function. The authoritarian arm, Zoshchenko seems to believe, is necessary in order to curtail the riot of human desires, desires that threaten to lead the subject back into the mire of capitalism: "Well, what's the big deal. You'd think
I was a Von Baron or something. Can't have my hands twisted" (III: 367). The
resulting image is a curious corporeal hybrid that fuses the hand of the protagonist with the "claw" of authoritarian rule in such a manner that neither
can be disengaged from the other.[94]

The narrator's unusual reaction reflects the curious imbrication of
Zoshchenko's biography with the ideological and mythological currents of
the time. On the one hand, there is the sense which runs throughout
Zoshchenko's writing of the '20s and '30s that the victim is always to
blame—that is, the tendency to situate blame not within the social or public
realm but in the subject her- or himself.[95] This in turn mirrors the author's
profound sense of the self as indelibly marked by original or inherited sin.[96]
In *Before Sunrise*, for instance, the child-narrator frequently complains about
being punished by his father despite the fact that he is not to blame.[97] Likewise, the culture of Stalinism defines the subject as worthy a priori of blame
and therefore punishment, in effect creating what one might call a society of
professional masochists. "In a masochistic social structure," Igor' Smirnov
writes, "blame lies with all. . . . Under conditions of mass terror all become
bearers of sin, i.e., masochists."[98] The narrator's odd pedalling back and forth
between protest against his punishment and acceptance of its necessity—
between asserting freedom from blame or his own culpability—is reflected in
Zoshchenko's curious use of the verb "to twist/turn" (*вертеть* in Russian).
At the end of the story, for instance, the narrator describes himself riding his
bicycle and "twisting his legs" ("верчу ногами") (III: 367). In this case, the
verb connotes freedom of motion. Earlier in the story, however, the same verb
had been used to describe the painful twisting of the narrator's arms. In both
instances, the author's use of "вертеть'" represents a grammatical stretch,
leading one to suspect that Zoshchenko's catachresis is intentional.[99]
Zoshchenko's openly paradoxical use of one and the same verb to designate

semantically incompatible states raises an important philosophical question. If the cyclist-narrator's twisting of the pedals in "Sufferings" is structurally parallel to the harsh twisting of the narrator's arms, what is the difference between individual excess and public restraint? To a large extent, the answer to this question lies in the anguished existential back and forth of the writer himself. For Zoshchenko's entire oeuvre is, in essence, fueled by the author's inability to reconcile his desire for unfettered "pure" being with his longing for an overarching Order.

More broadly, we can see in this an echo of the same issues that haunted such contemporaries of Zoshchenko as Isaac Babel or Andrei Platonov. For if the violence of Stalinist transformationalism mimics the chaos of unreconstructed nature, how are we to distinguish between the new world and its flawed predecessor? This is the gist of the argument put forth by Gedali in Babel's *Red Cavalry*. As Babel's homespun philosopher makes clear, the antinomy of revolution and counter-revolution is such that the Bolshevik claim to historical novelty no longer holds true: "'But the Pole shot, my dear Sir, because he was the counter-revolution. You are shooting because you are the revolution. . . . Who will tell Gedali where is revolution and where is counter-revolution?'"[100] The dilemma implied by Babel's "Gedali" or Zoshchenko's "Sufferings" is essentially that of many Russian writers and intellectuals of the time. Genuinely drawn to the professed ideals of the revolution, they were unsettled by its violent methods, which more often than not effaced any distinction between the execrable past and the heroic present, between revolution and counterrevolution. And for Zoshchenko, as for Babel or Platonov, it is not only the ideological but the ontological dimension of the question which occupies the foreground. In Andrei Platonov's *Happy Moscow* (1933–1936), for instance, the heroism of revolution quickly devolves into egoism and self-satisfied revelry. In a key scene in the novel a spinning spherical restaurant filled with drunken revellers comes to symbolize the closed circuit not merely of desire but of history itself. Here the triumphant telos of revolution has given way to "self-indulgent spinning—repetition without progress."[101] In the same manner Zoshchenko's "Sufferings" seems to ask whether the revolution is genuinely capable of altering human nature or whether, as one of the characters in *The Sky-Blue Book* puts it, "people are people . . . even here the shoe will wear down to fit the foot."[102] In other words, will the sadistic strong-arm tactics of the revolution become nothing more than a variant of the protagonist's own excess? The inability of the story to resolve this conundrum is encoded in its very title, "The Sufferings of the Young Verter." For Verter ("one who spins") is literally a person who turns or goes in a circle. His trials are those of one condemned to move back and forth between the inexorably joined states of freedom and bondage—between individual excess and public restraint.

If there is any answer at all to this dilemma it is to be found in the purely imaginary scene of rapprochement between protagonist and powers-that-be with which the story ends. The erotically tinged scene where a more humane guard hands the protagonist a flower for taking the wrong turn instead of brutally twisting his arms recalls the romantic subtext of Zoshchenko's "Sufferings." Yet in contrast to Goethe's "Sorrows," here the erotic object that causes the hero to run afoul of the establishment and ultimately to commit suicide is conspicuously absent. *Her* absence is all the more striking, since the Oedipal contest between son and father for the affections and interest of the mother (figure) is broadly thematized throughout Zoshchenko's work. The answer lies (once again) in the almost uncanny merging of the author's private myths with the ideology of Stalinism—which is to say, in the fusing of the authoritarian and the authorial hands. In *Before Sunrise*, Zoshchenko relates a story from the past that provides a link between his own biography and the tragic tale of Goethe's Werther. In a vignette entitled "Nonsense," the narrator-author recounts his sense of humiliation at receiving a poor grade for a school composition about Turgenev's Liza Kalitina—a disappointment that causes him to attempt suicide. As in the case of Werther, the young Zoshchenko's conflict with a paternal authority figure (in this case, his teacher) as well as his attempted suicide are caused by nothing less than Woman herself.[103] More interesting is the narrator-author's unspoken desire to rid himself of the female figure who precipitates the crisis: "Liza Kalitina. What do I care about her?" (III: 467), Zoshchenko writes. The author's unconscious fantasy of circumventing the conflict by subtracting woman from the equation is, in a sense, realized in the final lines of his "Sufferings." Here the root cause of Werther's conflict with the establishment, as well as Zoshchenko's feuding with a long line of "father figures," disappears, allowing the two male figures to reenter a state of primordial harmony.

Zoshchenko's attempt to resolve this conflict in such works as "Sufferings" cannot—I would argue—be seen separately from a strong homoerotic strain within the broader context of Stalinist ideology. Thus Zolotonosov argues that the obligatory relationship of dominance and subordination that encompasses all Stalinist subjects invariably takes on erotic overtones, resulting in "the 'feminine' adoration of the male Leader or *Vozhd'*."[104] Likewise, the relationship between the excessive subject (Verter) and the more humane guard at the end of Zoshchenko's "Sufferings" contains obvious romantic overtones. The image of a forget-me-not lovingly passed from one man to another requires no further explication. The argument becomes that much more inviting when we consider that Stalin (i.e., the leader par excellence) was often portrayed in the iconography of the period as a sentinel or guard.[105] Most importantly, the erotic tension that traditionally accompanies the Oedipal triangle is resolved in the idealized image of rapprochement between "father" and "son" that concludes the story—in the love of the Stalinist subject for her or his creator, to borrow Groys's apt phrase.[106] We would no doubt be remiss if we did not see in this scenario more than a trace of authorial wish-fulfillment. For by projecting his own desire onto the relationship, Zoshchenko as author seems to bring about the very reconciliation of individual anarchy and state power loudly trumpeted by Stalinist culture itself. Instead of twisting the protagonist's arms, the imaginary humane guard passes him a flower: "'Now where are you going, little buddy? What were you thinking taking that wrong turn? What a scatter-brain you are, dearie. OK., back you go, or else I'll fine you. I won't give you the flower.' Now, quietly smiling, he hands me the forget-me-not. Admiring each other, we part" (III: 367). Not surprisingly, given Zoshchenko's reputation for "back pedalling," even in this romantic idyll the basic tension of the story remains intact. This is made clear in Zoshchenko's curious repetition of the verb "вертеть" to describe both the narrator's continued pedalling and the humane guard's twirling of the flower. A structural echo of the earlier collision between the two protagonists, it seems to suggest that even the more perfect world of the narrator's fantasy cannot fully resolve the ontological tension that constitutes the core of "The Sufferings." And here we have a microcosm of the tension of Zoshchenko's oeuvre as a whole, with its anxious oscillation between order and chaos, stability and instability. As the slightly perplexed narrator of Zoshchenko's "Incident on the Volga" (rewritten by him in 1933 and included in the same section of *The Sky-Blue Book* as "The Sufferings") puts it: "On the one hand, it's sometimes advantageous for us to be not-alive. At the same time, being alive is also, in this sense, relatively disadvantageous" (III: 360).

What Lezhnev described as the shift from the love triangle of the classical Russian novel to a contest between a pair of juxtaposed forces is clearly echoed in another of Zoshchenko's short stories from the period. This piece is entitled "The Story of the Student and the Diver." As in the "Sufferings," here, too, the troublesome female figure who represents the bone of contention in the relationship between the story's two protagonists is less important than the final contest between student and diver. Indeed, one might even say (following Irigaray) that in this instance the woman "exists only to facilitate relationships among men."[107] Yet if Zoshchenko's "Sufferings" resolves the dichotomy of excess and restraint through a "marriage" of the two male protagonists, "The Story of the Student and the Diver" attains the same goal by allowing the mythological forces of chaos (here represented by the diver) to be vanquished and tamed by a student who embodies the very essence of Stalinist culture's mind-over-matter philosophy.[108] Originally published in 1929 under the title "Serenade,"[109] the piece was later included in the "Amazing Events" section of

Zoshchenko's *Sky-Blue Book*. The story recounts the curious rivalry of a student and a diver over a young woman named Shurochka. Initially the girlfriend of the diver, Shurochka takes an unexpected liking to a student named Malashkin, precipitating the violent rivalry between the two male figures. The physically unimpressive student is repeatedly pummelled by his stronger rival, but keeps coming back until the diver finally gives up and lets him have the girl. The two men go their separate ways, and Malashkin eventually breaks up with Shurochka.

That the story represents a variant of the Oedipal conflict already discussed seems fairly clear. The frail intellectual's fantasy of besting a physically superior opponent in order to "get the girl" is suspiciously reminiscent of an episode recounted in *Before Sunrise*. There the young Zoshchenko had imagined the day when he would become an adult and would thus be able to compete successfully against his father for the affections of his mother. More importantly, the victory of the student over the diver faultlessly enacts the triumph of civilization and culture over the realm of brute force or nature mandated within Stalinist ideology.[110] Through sheer force of will the student takes on an opponent who is nothing if not the quintessence of unreconstructed physicality. But what exactly is meant by his "unreconstructed physicality"? As we know, the image of arm/hand was a loaded one for Zoshchenko, figuring repeatedly throughout the author's prose as an emblem of animalistic aggression and desire. To confirm this one need only cast a cursory glance at the vignette entitled "Beasts" in Zoshchenko's *Before Sunrise*. In the vignette a bear cub has its paw ripped off by two older bears who after maiming the cub immediately begin mating. Here sexual desire, violence, and the paw-as-hand are all brought together in a composite image of primordial bestiality that could not but have confirmed the author's worst suspicions about the natural kingdom. In Zoshchenko's "Story About a Student and a Diver," the animalistic paw or arm is simply reconfigured in the threat of the diver's powerful fists. Equally important is the fact that the image of the diver recalls not only the writer's life-long aversion to water but more broadly the common mythological perception of water as embodying originary chaos.[111] Finally, the near-mythological dimensions of the contest between the forces of order and chaos in the story are suggested by the author's curious use of folk-tale-like repetitions, as for instance in the phrases "two people grappled" or "two people got into a fight." To be sure, this image could be interpreted solely in the context of the author's own biography. Yet the complete picture emerges only when we bring together the turbulent world of the author's private psychology with the no less volatile battleground of the collective "Stalinist" psyche.

The antipode of the "chaotic" diver in Zoshchenko's tale is the "cultured" Malashkin. A sort of alter ego of the writer himself—Sergei Malashkin was, like Zoshchenko, a writer—the student manages to overcome his opponent not with brute strength but through a masochistic feat of willpower. Describing the student's unprecedented triumph, Zoshchenko's narrator exclaims: "It's just unbelievable. That is, how a weak guy can break all the basic physical and chemical laws? It's just that his personality prevailed. Or better yet, courage" (III: 429). In this regard, Malashkin recalls the archetypal Stalinist hero who vanquishes his or her opponent "partly by native intelligence . . . and, above all, by willpower."[112] In the foreground of the culture's portrayal of the Bolshevik hero stood, according to Hans Günther, "iron will" and a "consciousness of steel."[113] And it is precisely in the hero(ine)'s ability to miraculously raise her- or himself up above the laws of the physical world that the Bolshevik's "iron will" is most clearly revealed.[114] According to the popular song, the true mark of Stalin's heroes lay in their ability to "make the fairy tale come true." One can imagine that for Zoshchenko the frail student's victory over a pugnacious strongman is just such a fairy tale made flesh. Yet ultimately Malashkin's feat is not so much the victory of one person over another as it is yet another success story within the Stalinist narrative of tempering and reforging. For as in the case of Ostrovsky's Korchagin, here, too, the hero's conquest of the elements merely externalizes the triumph over one's own nature that is the Stalinist hero's crowning achievement. For Zoshchenko Malashkin's win is thus important primarily in terms of its symbolic resonance: this Stalinist fairy-tale-come-true prefigures the lofty vision of bodily and spiritual control that Zoshchenko will project in such later works as *Youth Restored* and *Before Sunrise*. In both of these the image of the aggressive arm or hand is sublimated in punning references to the Russian verb for "to manage" or "to control" (in this case, *руководствовать*, which literally means "to lead with the hand").[115] Likewise, the ending of Zoshchenko's "Story About a Student and a Diver" inscribes the aggressor's arm in a taming gesture (*дойти до ручки*) that promises nothing less than the "castration" of the symbolic father figure by a newly ascendant son. Exhausted after his final bout with the student, the diver finally gives up, saying: "I, he says, am completely worn out 'cuz of you, comrade Kostia. I'm just at the end of my rope" ("дошел до ручки") [III: 431].

Like Stalinist culture as a whole, Zoshchenko views the body with suspicion and distrust. The human organism, its products and by-products, are seen as the unscientific, unregulated work of a fundamentally flawed natural order. In such works as *Youth Restored*, *The Sky-Blue Book*, *Before Sunrise*, and others, the author looks optimistically forward to the creation of a new, more "rational" body politic—one in which the very foundations of human psychophysiology would have been scientifically improved. In this regard, Zoshchenko's quest for health during the '30s and '40s is more than slightly

reminiscent of the fantastic plans for prolonging life envisioned by one of the
protagonists of Andrei Platonov's unfinished novel *Happy Moscow*. And the
surgeon Sambikin's project of using the bodies of the recently deceased as a
means to prolong the life of the living is in turn not far removed from actual
experiments undertaken by Soviet scientists at the time. Consider the case of
a certain I. N. Kazakov, who attempted to use the the organs of freshly killed
animals as a means of curing human ailments and diseases.[116] Likewise, Soviet scientists of the time claimed that the urine of pregnant women could be
used to produce a drug that would heighten the energy levels of the entire
body politic.[117] For the surgeon Sambikin in *Happy Moscow* the future triumph of socialism appears in similarly medicalized form. Its ability to improve the species (to purge the ontological filth that has infested human nature since its primordial beginnings) depends on socialism being able to
"reach into the last hiding-place of a man's insides" so as to "clean out the
pus that had accumulated there drop by drop over the centuries" (*Happy
Moscow*, 39). Yet it goes without saying that the process which produced this
"superior breed" was an extraordinarily violent one. Indeed, everything
seems to suggest that the (fictionalized) creation of a collective body politic
exacted an unusually high price from individual organisms. Witness the high
frequency of mutilations, amputations, and the like that distinguishes the literature of Socialist Realism.[118] Such woundings function, as Katerina Clark
notes, as emblems of the psychophysiological death and rebirth that enables
the Stalinist subject's incorporation into a higher order of being.[119] The fact
that death represents an essential component of this process is as clear from
the macabre fantasies of a Sambikin as it is from the real-life experiments of
Kazakov. Zoshchenko, too, breaks the ground for the New Adam by evoking
the death of the old. It is no accident, for instance, that *Before Sunrise* opens
with the pronouncement that the old Zoshchenko is no more. Just as often
what marks the New (Wo)Man is the death not of the whole body but some
essential part. Thus in the initial scenes of his novella *Mishel' Siniagin* (1930),
Zoshchenko relates a curious story about a species of African lizard that can
eject part of its internal organs when threatened by a predator. One can easily
imagine that Zoshchenko's interest in the lizard's unusual physiology is fueled by the author's own lifelong ambivalence about food and eating. More
importantly, the image of the lizard ejecting its internal organs prefigures the
violent self-transformation envisioned both in Zoshchenko's project of personal reform as well as in the broader Stalinist narrative of reforging.

The violence implicit in the creation and maintenance of Stalinist subjectivity represents the (unconscious) subject of a short story entitled "The
Lower Depths" (1935). According to Jochen Hellbeck, the Stalinist purges of
the mid-to-late '30s were significant not only for the profound effects they

had in the political sphere, but for their ability to provide a compelling model for "specifically Soviet modes of self-constitution."[120] A natural and perhaps inevitable corollary of Stalinism's focus on the purgation of the body politic was a shift in the idea of criminality away from the social sphere toward the interior realm, that is, toward the individual body.[121] Zoshchenko's "Lower Depths" mirrors this development by portraying the Stalinist subject as one who is in essence tainted by the original sin of his or her own *nature*. And if the body represents a kind of terra incognita of untamed desires and impulses, violent reforging offers the sole means of bringing it in line with the culture's civilizing mission.[122] Curiously, the aggressive hand-arm combination that elsewhere in Zoshchenko's oeuvre had proved a potent reminder of the "chaos of the natural" is here positively reconfigured through its contiguity with Soviet ideology. Through a conceptual sleight of hand Zoshchenko allows the sadistic fist of the criminal to become the justly punishing arm of the law.[123] What better illustration could one find of the Marxist dialectic which in Stalinist hands enabled any negative phenomenon to be deftly retooled as positive? Just as in his "Stern Youth" (1934) Olesha had proclaimed that beauty was a dialectic concept—all it requires for an ugly person to become beautiful is for someone else to perceive him as such—here the animalistic claw morphs into a civilized hand.

The shift away from criminal elements toward the element of criminality latent in each individual is made clear at the outset of the story. The narrator of "The Lower Depths" attributes a drop in crime to the fact that many thieves have managed to reform themselves, as well as to the increased prestige and efficiency of the militia. Indeed, the real criminal in the story is no Raskolnikov but rather a completely ordinary, respectable citizen. A father and "a wonderful worker in the building sector" (II: 253), his only crime lies in having had bit too much to drink. Notably, the expression Zoshchenko uses to refer to the man's excessive drinking ("перелить через край" in Russian) has not so much to do with getting drunk as it does with excessive behavior as such. It is presumably for this reason that the narrator leaves unclear whether the man has became intoxicated from drinking too much or simply from overeating. For Zoshchenko one is as bad as the other, since both point toward the fragile economy of excess and restraint—of Dionysian excess and Apollonian order—that constitutes the body of the Stalinist subject.

After having been joined at his table by a pair of bandits whose false joviality causes him to drink even more, the man is taken outside the restaurant, where he is beaten and robbed. A conscious gesture on Zoshchenko's part reveals a human nature literally *divested* of its thin veneer of civilization. Once the bandits steal his clothing, the father and "wonderful worker in the building sector" is left literally and figuratively exposed. A similar anxiety about losing one's clothes (and with it one's ideological integrity) plays itself out in Zoshchenko's "A Tale About Bathhouses and Their Patrons" (1935), a story that was included in *The Sky-Blue Book*. As in the piece above, here, too, the loss of clothing precipitates the subject's reversion to his "lower depths." Thus a visitor to a bathhouse whose clothes are stolen suddenly begins speaking in the stilted, politically suspect manner of a member of the ancien régime.[124] Likewise, in "The Lower Depths" there is a clear juxtaposition of the "cultured" or "civilized" domain of the Stalinist metropolis and the chaotic "natural" realm identified with the drunken protagonist's body. Moreover, it is hardly accidental that Zoshchenko associates his naked protagonist with a bathhouse. In the writer's first bathhouse story (1925) the Soviet *bania* similarly causes a reversion to capitalist ways, suggesting the failure of socialism's program of social cleansing. Indeed, throughout Zoshchenko's writing the image of water functions not only as a phobic object but as the emblem par excellence of originary chaos.[125] The fact that Zoshchenko's near-naked hero is compared to a person walking around a bathhouse dressing-room signals his temporary descent into the realm of "anticulture":[126] "And it really was uncomfortable, embarrassing. Maybe it was already morning. The birds went chirp-chirp. And then, too, a *cultured, model city*. Everywhere it's clean and ship-shape. And then, all of the sudden, this mug comes walking along, like he's in the *dressing-room of a bathhouse*" (II: 253; my emphasis).

Perhaps the most unsettling aspect of the story concerns the manner in which Zoshchenko transforms the drunken protagonist from a victim into a criminal. Toward the end of the story the police remark that while they have captured both thieves and recovered the stolen clothes, they cannot locate the victim. "Criminals are relatively easy to get," they say. "We have the most trouble finding the victims. . . . It seems to us . . . that the victim is covering his tracks. . . . They really don't like to be found" (II: 254). If in "The Lower Depths" the victim is somehow more elusive, more crafty, than the criminal her- or himself, it is surely because the writer had always seen the self as fundamentally culpable. Yet to view this twist in the story's logic exclusively in terms of Zoshchenko's private psychopathology is to lose sight of its larger ideological and cultural resonance. The Stalinist culture of the 1930s saw in both the broader body politic and the individual organism an arena in which a mythological contest between good and evil was being waged. As Lars T. Lih writes, by the mid-'30s the "main struggle to establish socialism in the Soviet Union was over, and the power of the opposing classes—*kulaks*, hostile specialists, nepmen—had been broken in open battle."[127] By the same token, the battle against evil shifted deep into the body of Stalinist society, where the remaining class enemies were now hidden, having donned "the mask of 'workers' and 'peasants.'"[128] In order for virtue to triumph, the evil within had to be continuously, ritually exorcised and purged. One can easily imagine, then, that internal enemy or saboteur proved to be as urgent a matter as the traditional career criminal. Likewise, for Zoshchenko writing on the eve of these same purges, the criminal is located not so much in the public sphere as he or she is found *inside*, lurking in the "lower depths" of even the most respectable folk, whether it be a family man and excellent worker or the renegade writer himself.

Zoshchenko's model family man and worker is rehabilitated—not unlike the overly enthusiastic carousel rider in "How Much Does a Person Need?"—with the help of a strong arm. Yet unlike the fearful arm encountered throughout Zoshchenko's oeuvre, this one is easily recuperated through its participation in the Stalinist project of reforging. Thus, individual excess is redeemed by an act of "civilizing" violence, one that allows the wayward protagonist to reenter the ideological community. Is it any accident, then, that it is precisely the physical trace of the thief's hand on the hero's face that ultimately leads to his confession and rehabilitation? Most likely not. Zoshchenko's notorious angst about the instability of existence was overpowering enough that he repeatedly rationalized even the most sadistic measures to calm it (though these, too, produced their own brand of anxiety). This in turn made him if not the ideal then at least a compelling apologist for Stalinism's fabled strong-arm tactics.

The writer's apology of "civilizing violence" is apparent in his unusual description of the thief's handprint. Employing one of his trademark solecisms, Zoshchenko has the thief refer to his handprint as a "note" (*заметка* in Russian) instead of the expected "imprint" or "trace" (*отпечаток* or *след* in Russian). This tactic prefigures the strategy to be used in such later works as *Before Sunrise*, where the writing or "civilized" hand—duly armed with Stalinist Reason—will finally put to rest the discontents of the body. In "The Lower Depths," too, "culture" is forcibly written onto the body of the victim-as-criminal in the form of a *note*—a strategy that echoes not only Stalinism's fetishistic attachment to the written Word but the very history of writing as a phenomenon.[129] More to the point, the *print* of the criminal's hand signals the passage of the hero from the "antiworld" of nature to the superior realm of Stalinist civilization: "The thieves were brought in to identify their victim. One of the thieves says: 'That's him for sure. I recognize him by the cheek. Here's where the mark from my hand is.' At this point, the victim lowers his eyes and says: 'In that case, I confess. It was me'" (II: 254). Not accidentally, the hero's confession coincides with the narrative's reaffirmation of "culture" and "consciousness"—the ideological telos of any proper Socialist Realist narrative. Admonishing the hero not to forget himself in the future, the militiaman says: "Next time eat and drink but don't lose your head ["consciousness," or *сознание* in Russian]" (II: 255).

One of the most well-known of Zoshchenko's accomodationist pieces is the short story "Lights of the Big City" (1936). If the preceding tale presents the hand/arm as an instrument of "civilizing violence," in "Lights of the Big City" violence is sublimated via the image of a civilized, authoritarian hand. Here it is no longer the thief's fist (under the auspices of the militia) but the hand of the militiaman itself that models the rehabilitation of unruly subjects. In a sense, this represents the fulfillment of the author's long-standing vision of a scientifically organized, ontologically sanitized body politic. Thus in the earlier piece "The Hand of Thy Fellow Man" (1927) the author had imagined a future time when people would no longer indulge in the unsanitary custom of shaking hands but would simply greet one another like the ancient Romans—with a raised arm. The underlying image is of a social body so rationalized and cleansed that it no longer seeks crude physical contact. A hint of this future can be glimpsed, according to Zoshchenko, in the greeting of the contemporary Young Pioneers. The logical next step is the militiaman's salute. The representative par excellence of Soviet power's civilizing mission for Zoshchenko,[130] the miltiaman embodies the regime's ambition to ideologically improve its wayward subjects. Yet where "The Hand of Thy Fellow Man" could only speculate about a distant future, "Lights of the Big City" realizes it in a variant of the coming-to-consciousness myth that was the crux of Stalinism's master narrative.

The simple plot of the story concerns a quarrelsome, physically boisterous old man from the country who comes to Leningrad to visit his son and is reformed through a chance encounter with a militiaman. Fearing that he might die, the hypochondriac son (a variant of the health-obsessed author himself) invites his parent to come stay with him. While he expects to find in him a meek and pious old man, it turns out that his father is a bastion of physical health and ideological backwardness. The opposition of frail son and coarse father here echoes Zoshchenko's ambivalent attraction to the figure of the "strong simpleton."[131] Drawn throughout his career as a writer to the unassailable health and vigor of the vulgarian, the civilized author was at the same time repulsed by the latter's crude aggressiveness. Zoshchenko resolves this dilemma in "Lights of the Big City" by appealing openly to the Stalinist myth of reforging. Deviants and miscreants, it was believed, could be remolded through hard labor into productive members of Soviet society.[132] And as we know, Zoshchenko himself helped to chronicle the putative successes of such reforging efforts (in his contribution to the White Sea Canal commemorative volume), where the secret police were said to have played a key role.[133] Likewise, in "Lights" it is the militiaman who becomes the instrument of the father's miraculous volte-face.

Mocked by his son's neighbors for his backwardness, the old man gets drunk and nearly causes a brawl in a local pub. On his way home he loses his way—an obvious metaphor for the loss of self-control occasioned by excess. Yet the situation is miraculously reversed when he asks a militiaman for directions and is greeted by the latter with a salute. Superficially, this gesture of respect serves to offset the abuse the old man had endured at the hands of his son's neighbors. This, in any case, is the moral of the story as summed up by Zoshchenko himself.[134] However, the deeper significance of the tale mirrors the processes of bodily and social reengineering that were the stock-in-trade of Stalinist myth. Thus the excess and aggressiveness that marred of the old man's behavior before his conversion are now rechanneled into a posture of rigid, military-style discipline and self-control. By the same token, the fear of physical contact implicit in the earlier "Hand of Thy Fellow Man" is defused in the present scenario, where the violent hand is divested of its animalistic nature. "The old man," Zoshchenko writes, "returned home restrained in the highest degree and, walking past the *dvornik*, didn't enter into the usual squabbles with him but silently saluted and proceeded to his room" (II: 280).

For Zoshchenko the emblem of this reforging is none other than the authoritarian hand. For just as the natural aggression of the bare arm is sublimated in the image of the militiaman's gloved and saluting hand, so the old man's surplus vigor is finally clothed in the military posture of the exemplary Stalinist subject. Likewise, in both *Youth Restored* and *Before Sunrise* the civilizing authorial hand rewrites the chaos of various unstable subjects in order to produce physical and ideological health. Consider the following example taken from the beginning of *Youth Restored*. In this vignette Zoshchenko relates the tale of a man who loses at billiards and succumbs to a hysterical fit. The natural economy of the body, Zoshchenko suggests, is governed by dark, irrational forces—by a kind of feminine excessiveness. Symptomatically, Zoshchenko links the body's squandering of energy with the image of flailing *arms*: "His arms wouldn't obey him. He yelled like a woman. . . . The enormous energy that arises in the process seems to be wasted on nothing. Instead, it is spent on the devil knows what—on outcries, fussing and even, as we saw, lifting tables and heavy furniture" (III: 18, 19). Zoshchenko's solution is quite simply to substitute his own enlightened and writing hands for the uncontrolled limbs of his benighted protagonists.[135] This is hardly surprising, for the mind-over-matter philosophy preached by Zoshchenko and Stalinist culture alike requires that the body's natural energy not be spent in vain (i.e., in hysterical fits or by picking up tables) but rather that it be channeled into the larger project of socialist construction.[136]

Zoshchenko's strategy in such works as *Youth Restored* (this is especially evident in the commentaries section) echoes this, providing the reader with a comprehensive blueprint for corporeal management. And as is obvious from the quote above, the author does not shy away from the juxtaposition of "feminine" nature with "masculine" reason and self-control typical for Soviet culture as a whole.[137] Hence the opposition of the hysterical protagonist's uncontrollable arms (*руки* in Russian) at the beginning of *Youth Restored* with the verb that Zoshchenko uses to designate the "masculine" regime of bodily self-control at the end of the work (*руководствовать* or "to be guided by").[138]

Zoshchenko's vision of the scientifically reengineered body is particularly well outlined in a feuilleton entitled "Outside" (1940). Like many of Zoshchenko's short stories and longer works of the '30s, this seemingly innocuous feuilleton echoes the juxtaposition of natural and machine-body that was implicit in the Stalinist project of reforging. The feuilleton contrasts the traditional practice of using fire hydrants and long hoses to wash down the streets with more contemporary methods that rely on water trucks. Yet Zoshchenko's unusually evocative descriptions of the equipment itself make it clear that more is at stake than simply determining the most efficient way to clean city streets. Particularly revealing is the writer's use of the word "hose" (*кишка* means both "intestine" and "hose" in Russian). The implicit equation of hose and intestine spotlights one of the core dilemmas of the author's private mythology, since food, as Zholkovsky notes, represents one of the author's most potent phobic objects.[139] In particular, one might recall Zoshchenko's lifelong struggle to neutralize his anxiety surrounding this most basic of human needs—in essence, to discover a kind of scientific method of alimentation. Here again the cultural context is all important. For the previous decade had witnessed more than one attempt to carry out an such reforms. One need only recall Zamyatin's evocations of scientific foodstuffs and methods of eating (as well as their subversive counterparts in the novel *We* [1920–1921]). Likewise, the popular (throughout the '20s) utopian notion of communal kitchens points toward a similar desire to reform the most basic patterns of human biology. Consider Andrei Babichev, who, as Brett Cooke points out, threatens to bring about the "'industrialization of the kitchens.'"[140] More to the point, the image of Babichev's prodigious gut or *кишечник* underscores not only Babichev's epic appetite, but the hero's grandiose ambition to produce in sausage-like fashion a new species of Soviet Homo sapiens by digesting and processing the representatives of the old world.[141] Finally, Andrei Platonov's *Happy Moscow* places the alimentary canal at the very center of his characters' quest to build a new world. For them the large intestine serves as an icon of that which must be remade in order for the new world to come about. This, too, was very much in the spirit of the times, for the famous early-twentieth-century zoologist and microbiologist Ilya Mechnikov (whose work was well known to such authors as Platonov, Bulgakov, Zoshchenko, Kharms, and others) theorized that life could be considerably prolonged by shortening the large intestine. For Zoshchenko, too, the stomach and intestines stand in the foreground, symbolizing the body in its "prescientific," or natural state.[142] Hence, the narrator's curious reflections on the incompatibility of the intestine-like *kishka* with modern life:[143]

> Up until recently the streets were watered in our country using a hose. A *dvornik* would be standing there, holding a hose and watering. What's that supposed to be? And a hose was hooked right up to the hydrant. Well, it's ugly. Unnatural. It doesn't fit the spirit of the times. Of course, scientific thought couldn't reconcile itself to this method of watering the streets.[144]

Zoshchenko's alternative scientifically remakes the body by joining man to machine. The earlier hydrant/hose combination is both "ugly" and "unnatural," according to Zoshchenko, presumably because by recalling both the large intestine it reveals the organism's closeness to nature. By contrast, the water truck, with its metal torso, erases any trace of the body's origin, at the same time that it "scientifically" regulates the flow of water leaving the tank. Implicit in this is the author's fantasy of a situation in which the irrational inertia of the body (i.e., water) would be channeled through the controlling offices of the mind. Likewise, in the commentaries section to *Youth Restored*, Zoshchenko writes that "it is necessary to manage one's inertia, it is necessary for a person to control his/her machine" (III: 125). For Zoshchenko the scientific body is one in which a kind of ideal economy or "exchange of substances" is established to replace the irrational, uncontrolled flood of nature.[145] This, as we shall see presently, was not entirely unprecedented. Contemporary representations of the Moscow metro, to cite only one example, portrayed the constant battle against the abundant groundwater in the fledgling Moscow metro as a contest between technology and incontinent Mother Earth. Likewise, the narrator of Zoshchenko's *Before Sunrise* remarks on the importance for health of a proper exchange of fluids between the body and the outside world. And the author is supposedly cured, as Masing-Delic remarks, when a "balance between 'storage' and 'outlet' has been found."[146] Not surpisingly, then, in Zoshchenko's feuilleton "Outside," the ideal organism is symbolized by the metal torso of a water truck, for here the flow of liquid between inside and outside is scientifically controlled by the driver sitting inside the cabin:

> And so the water trucks have appeared. It's like a tank on wheels, and little tubes come out of it, where the water spurts out. The truck goes by, and the

street's perfectly watered. Evenly, economically, and even scientifically, since
a man sitting next to the driver controls the water.[147]

Still, the relative perfection of the machine vis-à-vis its predecessor does
not exclude the possibility of individual passersby being splashed with water.
Quite the opposite, in fact. The grand project of rationalizing life seems to
presuppose that some must be victimized. After all, Zoshchenko remarks, the
water regulator cannot take into account every pedestrian who walks by: "It's
doubtful that he'll take into account two individual people. It can't be, I'm
thinking to myself, that he'd turn down the stream. That would be too
grandiose—to see such respect in such a small, everyday dimension."[148] At
least one pedestrian ignores the truck and is splashed, causing him to curse at
the water regulator in a manner that recalls seventeenth-century Russia rather
than the contemporary Soviet Union. Yet the potential disturbance is quickly
defused by none other than a passing militiaman. Not unlike the saluting militiaman of "The Lights of the Big City," he resolves the conflict by invoking
the scientific principles that underwrite Stalinism's rationalist project. Thus
the physical fact of the passersby being soaked with water is offset by the objective, scientific laws that govern the cosmos. The symbolic significance of
this for Zoshchenko is quite clear: the underlying order or rationality of the
Soviet worldview serves to dissipate the chaos of the natural world[149]—just
as water must invariably give way before the drying effects of the sun.[150]

A militiaman walks up to the outcry. Having found out what happened and
looked the soaked man over he says: "That is I don't see any traces of your having been soaked. Your trousers and shirt are dry. What are you getting worked
up about?" The soaked man slaps himself on his trousers and shirt. "It's true, dry
as a bone. Of course, heat, sun, and a breeze blowing. You can be dry in three
minutes."[151]

A similar reenactment of culture's victory over chaos is played out in the
story "Anna around the Neck," written in 1934 and published in the satirical
magazine *The Crocodile*. Like the stories discussed above, this piece, too,
borrows liberally from the repertoire of Stalinist myths in order to resolve the
psychological traumas that troubled the author. Only superficially reminiscent of the Chekhov story that lends it its name, [152] the piece concerns a militiaman who saves a hysterical young woman from drowning in the Neva
river. And in many ways the story is not unlike the numerous contemporary
accounts of the heroic Soviet fliers who rescued the Cheliuskin expedition in
1934. Such narratives invariably emphasized the triumph of such cardinal
Stalinist values as bravery, daring intelligence, and willpower over the natural elements. These were most often symbolized by floods, ice, storms, and

the like.[153] At the same time, repeated allusions to "psychology" invite us to read the piece in a more intimate, biographical key. For unlike the typical Socialist Realist narrative, in which the forces of chaos and disorder would be divided between juxtaposed characters, in the present story the author-as-character is simultaneously present in both extremes. The courageous and high-spirited militiaman (whose name is not accidentally Mikhail) is like Zoshchenko himself linked to Russia's imperial past. He admires the "monumental" architecture of the capital, even keeping watch over it. And the building he is most closely associated with (i.e., the zoological museum) reflects the author's long-standing fear of the natural world, even as it conveniently neutralizes the object of Zoshchenko's anxiety. Finally, like the author himself, the militiaman is intrigued by water. The most telling difference only confirms the character's status as authorial alter ego. A veteran of World War I, Zoshchenko suffered a lifetime of poor health as a result of his war wounds. By contrast, the fictional militiaman was, as the narrator remarks, "never in the war and his health was quite perfect" (II: 248).

The militiaman's antipode is quite predictably a woman—one who perfectly embodies the author's neurotic instability. Her gait, as the narrator notes, is "mincing and unstable."[154] Meanwhile, the woman's decision to drown herself in the Neva is nothing if not a reflection of the author's own subconscious fears and desires. For if the writer-cum-militiaman is associated with the Neva in its "stately flow,"[155] his female counterpart mirrors the author's hysterical, "feminine" side. Zoshchenko's subconscious desire to be folded back into the primordial chaos of the natural—his death wish, in other words—is evident in the image of the woman "hopping down into those waters, from whence there is no returning" (II: 249). Next to the psychological incontinence of Woman, the militia*man* serves not only to embody the author's longing for stability, but as an emblem of Stalinist culture's preoccupation with statuary bodies. "The ideal Soviet person," Zolotonosov writes, "should . . . always be the same; the potential for elusive changes should be absent in him."[156] The quintessential expression of this brand of subjectivity is found in the figure of the border guard or sentinel—a type which, judging from the wealth of sculptural and literary representations, occupied a dominant position in the cultural imagination of the period. Charged with the task of preserving cultural and ideological boundaries, the border guard served to bring the body politic into conformity with the statuary ideal it itself symbolized. Zoshchenko's militiaman fulfills a similar function. Posted on the boundary separating water from dry land, the militiaman guards the flood-prone city of St. Petersburg from the everpresent danger of encroaching water. Presumably, it is as a representative of that same statuary body politic that the militia*man* jumps into the Neva to save the *woman* from drowning, in essence saving her from herself.

Viewed biographically, the episode clearly prefigures Zoshchenko's attempts to come to terms with the troubled waters of his own unconscious in *Before Sunrise*. The sense of an almost epic contest between the opposed forces of chaos and order follows from Zoshchenko's dramatic exposition of the militiaman's contest with the Neva. The protagonist is not so much swimming through the water as doing battle with it. Thus Zoshchenko writes that "he quickly breaks the waves that crash on top of him" or "Our hero spiritedly breaks through the water with his arms" (II: 250).[157] Notably, the drowning woman's return to the realm of "culture" is tied to a prototypical feature of the Stalinist landscape—that is, the airplane. As numerous critics have noted, pilots were arguably the most high-profile of Stalinism's Promethean heroes. Alongside the Stakhanovites and others, they pushed the envelope of physical law and human endurance. Here, as well, the sudden appearance of a plane marks the mythological triumph of civilization over chaos implicit in the militiaman's feat: "Somewhere an airplane is flying with its buzzing. And in that flight you see people's unheard-of bravery and their desire to live excellently" (II: 250).

The conclusion of the story makes explicit the deeper, psychological significance of the militiaman's "unheard-of bravery." His task, which began with physically saving the drowning woman, now involves helping her to recuperate emotionally. If earlier she had been described as "slightly hysterical and a bit distanced from life," now the narrator remarks that the militiaman visits her in the hospital with the intention of "bringing her closer to life" (II: 251). Accordingly, her release from the hospital is cast (through a Freudian slip on the narrator's part) in terms of the same juxtaposition of water and dry land that informs the story as a whole: "And then they discharged her so she could return to dry land—I mean—home" (II: 251). Presumably it is this same desire to rehabilitate the hysterical woman that justifies the otherwise puzzling marriage between polar opposites. And the difficult nature of the militiaman's task is implicit in the very title of the story. "Anna around the Neck" suggests both the tsarist medal given to the hero for his heroism and the burden of trying to rehabilitate an unstable female. Interpreted figuratively, Zoshchenko's "marriage" of the militiaman and the hysterical woman looks forward to the more difficult task of bringing himself closer to life that the author will undertake in *Before Sunrise*.

An analogous desire underpins Zoshchenko's *Youth Restored*. Here the author emerges as the spiritual antipode of his prominent contemporary, Andrei Platonov. While the latter's *Happy Moscow* depicted Stalinism's efforts to purify the body (politic) as nothing less than a disaster-in-progress, *Youth Restored* paints a considerably more optimistic scenario. Literalizing, in a sense, Stalin's call for writers to become engineers of human souls, Zoshchenko suggests that the task of creating the ideal body (politic) is not merely a problem for the physiologist or the physician. Far from it, in fact. As in the case of his unfortunate spiritual predecessor, Nikolai Gogol, it is the task of the Word. And if Aleksei Zamkov's experiments with the miracle drug gravidan had seemed to "raise medicine to the level of an art,"[158] Zoshchenko's *Youth Restored* betrays a similar logic by attempting to make art into the ultimate miracle drug. My mention of Gogol here is not accidental. There is every indication that the Zoshchenko of *Youth Restored* and *Before Sunrise* saw the success of his own project of self-reform as a rewriting of Gogol's tragic legacy. The success of this undertaking depended, according to Masing-Delic, on Zoshchenko's being able to exorcise the morbid influence of Gogol (i.e., irony) from his own life and replace it with the life-affirming spirit of Pushkin. In *Youth Restored*, the critic writes, "Zoshchenko made the transition from 'psychology'—that is, the complex 'laughter through tears' connected with 'introspection' and 'eccentricity'—to simple laughter . . . and to the principle of *mens sana in corpore sano*. . ."[159] Moreover, if the author's short story "The Sixth Tale of Belkin" (written four years after *Youth Restored* in 1937) is any indication, this period of Zoshchenko's career is marked by the desire to exchange the hysterical, "feminine" mysticism of Gogol for the harmonious, "manly" personality of Pushkin.

Zoshchenko's renunciation of Gogol in favor of Pushkin mirrors a broader ambivalence within Stalinist culture surrounding the anguished creator of *Dead Souls*. Perhaps the most eloquent expression of this was the decision taken in 1936 to replace the old Andreev sculpture, which supposedly "distorted the image of the writer, treating him as a mystic and a pessimist," with a statue more consonant with the spirit of the times.[160] In stark contrast to the pessimistic Gogol, the lucid and life-affirming Pushkin assumed a position within the literary hierarchy equivalent to that of Stalin—witness the statue of Stalin created by S. D. Merkurov for the centenary of Pushkin's death. Based as it was on the famous Opekushin statue of Pushkin (1880), its message was clear: Stalin is the Pushkin of today.[161] Like Zoshchenko, Andrei Platonov, too, attempted to distance himself from Gogol, all the while stressing his Pushkinian credentials. In his 1937 essay on Pushkin and Gorky, Platonov describes Gogol as little more than a gifted student of the great nineteenth-century poet. Gogol's *Dead Souls*, the writer argues, had succeeded in presenting only one facet of Pushkin's great idea, leaving the more pressing matter of *resurrection* unresolved.[162] Yet Gogol's failure ultimately becomes Platonov's success. By taking up the banner of resurrection abandoned by the latter, the writer demonstrates his affinity not only for Pushkin but for the larger project of redeeming human souls. Still, for Platonov the idea of "resurrection" could be achieved only in the context of humanity's enduring connection to the biological cycle.[163] Certainly, this is the lesson to be learned from *Happy Moscow*. By contrast, Zoshchenko's approach is at once more ambitious and more literal. In *Youth Restored* and other works, the author seeks nothing less than to *rewrite* the flawed biography of Gogol, and thereby magically undo the consequences of his own unhappy past.[164] Thus in a letter to Chukovsky written as early as 1927, Zoshchenko announced that he had studied Gogol's biography and now understood "what I need to do in order to make myself a writer of optimistic, positive works."[165] What makes Zoshchenko's undertaking appear to succeed (where Gogol's had failed) is not simply the advent of the October Revolution,[166] but that of the Stalinist "second revolution," with its avowed goal of a total transformation of the body politic. Endowed with good health and *armed* with the proper ideology, Zoshchenko could now aspire to become the writer that Gogol never was, and thus to compose the positive sequel to *Dead Souls* that his benighted predecessor had not.[167]

The centerpiece of the Zoshchenkovian project was the idea of overcoming suffering, which Zoshchenko had vowed at Gorky's behest to "mock" in a future work. This idea was not Gorky's alone. For the mythology of Stalinism was such that physical pain (i.e., suffering) was viewed as a kind of lower-order reality which could be overturned by means of a highly developed consciousness. Pain, it was reasoned, was nothing more than a symptom of the mind's own weakness. And from here it was only a small step to eliminating the same phenomenon that Dostoevsky had defined as the very root of consciousness.[168] Thus in the commentaries section of his *Youth Restored* Zoshchenko envisions a scenario in which the power of the brain could be used to control the body's natural entropy, the most potent expression of which was death itself. Combining the writer's reflections on the effectiveness of a mind-over-matter philosophy with historical anecdotes taken from various periods, the commentaries section of *Youth Restored* provides a colorful gallery of historical and cultural figures, many of whom had proven successful (or singularly unsuccessful, as in the case of Gogol) in remaking their flawed bodies and, thus, challenging death's ancient reign. Among the most important of these are those who, like Seneca, Goethe, or Tolstoy, are associated with the written word.

The Word, according to Evgeny Dobrenko, represents the central category of Stalinist mythology, since it is in the discursive rather than the empirical realm that the culture's fairy-tale-come-true ethos is most completely realized.[169] Thus even projects that appear fundamentally technological by nature are at the highest levels viewed as part of a specifically verbal tableau. In nearly every representation of the Moscow metro, for instance, engineers and other technocrats are roundly reproached for their blind allegiance to empirical fact. On the other hand, party leaders such as Kaganovich, who can claim direct access to the narrative of socialist construction, invariably prove more capable than their technical staff in solving the most vexing problems. For Zoshchenko, as well, it is the Word—understood not as slavish mimesis but as a means of mastering reality—that captures the imagination. And it is no accident that among the people most likely to live long lives and enjoy good health, according to the writer, are "all sorts of philosphers, naturalists, chemists . . . and all manner of professors and wise men" (III: 12). Near the top of Zoshchenko's list of most-admired is the philosopher Seneca, who like the author himself was sickly in his younger years but managed through a colossal feat of willpower to "reforge his psyche" and regain health later in life. Likewise, Tolstoy's success in curing himself of neurasthenia is attributed to the author's rejection of belles lettres in favor of the more "orderly" discipline of philosophy. The most dramatic biography is surely that of the poet Goethe. For it was the latter's mind-over-matter philosophy, according to Zoshchenko, that allowed the poet to "create" his own health and finally achieve something resembling immortality. Even after his death at the age of 82, Zoshchenko remarks, he was "young, fresh and even beautiful" (III: 100).

By contrast, in his treatment of those historical and literary figures whose timid efforts at self-healing fall short of total transformation, Zoshchenko offers us a cautionary tale. All of these share one thing in common. Instead of harnessing the power of the mind to rechannel the body's natural inertia they rely on purely physiological remedies, such as pills, baths, electric shocks, and the like. Yet these traditional cures invariably involve the very element which for Zoshchenko is most emblematic of the body's indebtedness to the chaotic realm of nature: that is, water.[170] Thus the protagonist of *Youth Restored*, an aging professor of astronomy named Volosatov, initially turns to medical doctors in hopes of regaining his health, but is treated to a combination of wet blankets, baths, and enemas. A clear allusion to Zoshchenko's own traumatic experiences with hydrotherapy! Likewise, Karetnikov, whom the narrator refers to as "a neurasthenic and a psychopath" (III: 37), sits in a tub filled with snow during winter and in a tub up to his waist in water during the spring as a means of curing his illness. At the top of the list is Gogol himself, who—as Zoshchenko notes—attempted to cure his ailments by wrapping himself in wet towels every morning and drinking large quantities of water before lunch. Ultimately the writer's argument with traditional medicine concerns more than just hydrotherapy, however. Rather, it is part of a larger attempt to redefine the very relationship between body and brain. As I have already mentioned, within Stalinism's voluntarist worldview it was understood that the human body is governed not by base instinct but by the higher realm of consciousness.[171] The more developed a person's conscious mind, the less likely it was that she or he would experience lower-order sensations such as physical pain.[172] Zoshchenko's *Youth Restored* takes this idea to its logical end. Suicide, disease, even death most often result from the individual's inability to regulate the "inertia" of the body using mind control, according to the author. Thus all that is required to eliminate such "accidents" is an adequate knowledge of how to "manage one's body."

The fictional part of *Youth Restored* provides at least a partial illustration of Zoshchenko's reforging agenda. Notably, the same juxtaposition of scientific and unscientific healing techniques characteristic of the commentaries section carries over into the opposition of the protagonist Volosatov with his counterpart Karetnikov, both of whom are equally preoccupied with the task of restoring their own health. And of these two it is Volosatov who wins out. The professor's successes are initially muted by the fact that in shedding the burdens of old age Volosatov acquires many of the negative traits he had earlier despised in the young and healthy. Here we see the dilemma of many a Zoshchenkovian hero. The fantasy of conquering sickness can be realized only at the cost of falling into the opposite extreme. In other words, frailty is replaced with animalistic strength. Thus at the outset of his transformation Zoshchenko's narrator notes that the professor began "to notice in himself a sort of cruelty of youth and at times, perhaps, a meanness which he did not at all wish to have" (III: 54). And even after he finally decides to return to his wife at the end of the book Volosatov still looks longingly back at Tulia's window (the same Tulia who is the very embodiment of the capitalist past).[173] Moreover, Zoshchenko's narrator notes that while Volosatov now addresses his wife using the diminutive "mamulia," the word itself frequently "reminded him of the sunny name Tulia" (III:7).

How, then, are we to understand Volosatov's "rehabilitation?" To be sure, almost no rehabilitation in Zoshchenko's oeuvre is ever complete. Witness the case of the criminal Rottenburg, about whom Zoshchenko wrote his contribution to the White Sea Canal volume entitled "Youth Restored." In typically Zoshchenkovian form, the author suggests three possibilities for reform and then chooses the most ambivalent: (1) Rottenburg really was reforged; (2) he simply engaged in a "new speculation"; and (3) "'being not a dumb person, and having realized that the criminal world was really coming to an end and now a thief needed to restrain himself.'"[174] Something similar occurs in Volosatov's case, though here the transformation reflects more the workings of myth (both public and private) than any rational decision on the part of the protagonist. Let us recall that in the realm of Zoshchenko's personal mythology excess frequently leads to punishment or retribution of some sort.[175] Meanwhile, in the mythology of Socialist Realism the excessive, Dionysian hero is most often transformed through a process of physical wounding or symbolic castration, as a result of which he or she is spiritually tempered or steeled (à la Ostrovsky's Korchagin). This wounding marks the moment when the hero parts with his or her individualistic self in order to be reintegrated into the socialist collective.[176] Likewise, in *Youth Restored* it is Volosatov's "wounding" that precipitates his entry into what one might call the ideological community. Because the hero's punishment comes in the form of a stroke (*удар* in Russian), one cannot help but wonder if this is not a variant of the same stroke of the hand/arm that the hero of "The Lower Depths" had received as punishment for his excessive behavior. Likewise, in Zoshchenko's "Sixth Belkin Tale," the mysterious Lieutenant B.'s passage from one whose life is governed by mystical, irrational forces to an "enlightened," "conscious" hero in control of his fate coincides with the wounding of his hands. Such instances of ritual mutilation are, as Smirnov notes, commonplace in the literature of Socialist Realism,[177] marking the passage in stark corporeal terms of the subject from "spontaneity" to "consciousness." Zoshchenko's narrative makes this connection explicit by his punning reference to the physically and ideologically convalescent Volosatov's having joined a brigade of shockworkers. For the very term "shockworker" (*ударник*) seems to derive from the work for "stroke" (*удар*). In other words, the ideal Stalinist subject is necessarily one who has been punished or stricken.

Volosatov's recovery and rehabilitation are that much more dramatic when viewed against the backdrop of his alter ego Karetnikov's death of a heart attack. In a deft use of counterpoint Zoshchenko sets the success story of the "enlightened" and "conscious" Volosatov in relief against the failed cure of the irrational Karetnikov. Reworking material culled from his own biography, Zoshchenko has Karetnikov die of a heart attack caused by a lightning bolt. The lightning bolt is reminiscent of the ones that terrified Zoshchenko as a child,[178] while Karetnikov's sudden death of a heart attack (*разрыв сердца* in Russian) calls to mind a vignette in *Before Sunrise* that describes the death of Zoshchenko's father from the same cause. And if the funeral described in the vignette "At the Cemetery" underscores the boy's liberation from the father's flawed physiology (i.e., his "closed heart"), here Karetnikov's death serves to highlight the triumph of Volosatov. One might go even further and suggest that it is precisely by means of this death that Zoshchenko as author manages to distance himself from the failed ("unscientific") attempts at self-healing undertaken by Gogol. In this manner the author appears to pave the way for his own future success story. Just as the rational Volosatov triumphs over his irrational alter ego, so will the enlightened Zoshchenko succeed where the mystic Gogol had not. As was the case with Afinogenov, who remade himself by jettisoning the ballast of his ideologically flawed past, here, too, the re-birth of the hero goes hand in hand with the demise of the antihero.

Still, Zoshchenko's allegory of psychophysiological and ideological reform ends on a rather ambiguous note.[179] Such ambiguity is probably not so much an attempt to polemicize with Socialist Realism as it is a reflection of the unresolvable ambivalence surrounding the very project of reforging that Zoshchenko generally appears to support. This in turn mirrors the anguished modulation between enlightenment optimism and deep-rooted pessimism characteristic of Zoshchenko's oeuvre as a whole. For this reason Volosatov's rejuvenation/rehabilitation at the end of *Youth Restored* can neither be written off as mere window dressing nor can it be embraced without reservation. Witness the remark that the convalescent Volosatov makes to his daughter after partially recovering from his stroke. Volosatov's suggestion that his basic idea was right reads as an authorial endorsement of the protagonist's undertaking: "Thah' wah' mahstakes, but the general line wahs right" (III: 76).[180] Yet in the same breath Zoshchenko makes clear that even the most enlightened order remains vulnerable to the forces of entropy. The possibility of a violent incursion of chaos and death—even amid the final scenario of relative happiness— remains for Zoshchenko's hero, as it does for the writer himself. Hinting at the precariousness of Volosatov's recovery, the narrator notes: "One can assume that in two years or so he'll be bending horseshoes with his left hand, *if for some reason he doesn't die by accident*" (III: 79; my emphasis).

Without a doubt the most dramatic piece of narrative reforging is to be found in Zoshchenko's psychotherapeutic tour de force *Before Sunrise*. And here it is not so much the body as the psyche that the writer has in his sights. Without taking up the issue of the body as such, Zoshchenko represents ideological and psychophysiological well-being as two sides of the same coin. Even more than this, great art and health are shown to be intimately interconnected. "'Absolute health,'" Zoshchenko writes in *Before Sunrise*, "'that is the ideal for art. Only then can it be truly worthy.'"[181] While Zoshchenko only began writing *Before Sunrise* in 1942–1943, he had started collecting and mulling over materials as early as 1933. Using the hybrid form of such earlier works as *Youth Restored* and *The Sky-Blue Book*, which combine the short-story form with an explanatory and/or historical apparatus, *Before Sunrise* presents the reader with a series of vignette-like "snapshots" taken from various periods in the narrator-author's life. These are manipulated in such a manner as to expose and, presumably, exorcise the author's long-standing phobias. The purpose of the work, as Linda Hart Scatton remarks, is to articulate the cause and cure for Zoshchenko's lifelong battle with depression.[182] If Zoshchenko's own textual pronouncements are to be believed, the cure for (his) depression lay in filtering the chaos of the individual psyche through the enlightening offices of reason. That the writer is ultimately less than successful in his quasi-literary exorcism should not surprise us. As numerous critics have remarked, there is a profound gulf separating the raw material of *Before Sunrise* (i.e., its richly evocative vignettes) and the author's impoverished attempts to make sense of them.[183] Zoshchenko's tragedy lies in attempting to understand his own story by forcibly viewing it through the lens of Stalinist ideology and myth. In contrast to earlier works in which the author's desire for (self)-reform is offset by lingering fears concerning the steep cost of carrying it out,[184] here such ambivalence has been all but banished from the field of play.[185]

The phobias and anxieties that permeate Zoshchenko's vignettes in *Before Sunrise* are the same as those described earlier. Water, women, food, arbitrary and intrusive paternal authority, invariably configured as the predations of a rapacious hand or arm—all of these come together to produce the history of the writer's melancholic, perennially anxious relationship to the world around him. Cast in the role of analyst, Zoshchenko maps out the etiology of his phobias using Pavlov's theory of conditioned response, all the while rejecting any suggestion that an unresolved Oedipal dilemma (à la Freud) might lie at the root of his problems.[186] Here the author shares wholeheartedly the anti-Freudian bias of the surrounding culture. For as Boris Groys notes, Stalinist culture expressed a keen interest in the various models explaining the formation of the unconscious, while remaining profoundly indifferent to the concrete mechanisms of its functioning. The culture, Groys writes, "was oriented not toward the de-automation of consciousness but toward its automation, toward its systematic formation in the necessary direction by means of controlling its environment, its base and its unconscious."[187] Zoshchenko's attempt to represent his anxieties as mere "conditioned responses" mirrors this larger, culture-wide push toward the automation of consciousness. As one might imagine, the real story behind Zoshchenko's repertoire of phobias is significantly more complex, reflecting the aftershocks of an Oedipal crisis, as well as the broader landscape of cultural and mythological stereotypes. His ambivalence about women, to choose just one example, seems firmly anchored in the mother-father-son triangle of early childhood, at the same time echoing the culture-wide stereotyping of women as oversexed, materialistic, and ideologically retrograde. In this regard, one need only recall the heroine of Zoshchenko's "Aristocrat Lady" (1923) or Tulia in *Youth Restored*. Particularly the former threatens the hapless protagonist not only with her overt sexuality, but with a resurgence of capitalist values in the socialist present: "I was overcome by a kind of bourgeois bashfulness. A bachelor, I'm thinking, and with no money" (I: 172). Roughly the same can be said of Zoshchenko's attempt to defuse his arm-phobia by placing it in a Pavlovian procrustean bed. If the writer himself is to be believed, this anxiety stems from his having been violently weaned from his mother's breast as a child (III: 614). Yet the stories within *Before Sunrise* that deal with this theme suggest not so much a pattern of conditioned response as they do a deeper dilemma, based on the author's conflict with paternal and other authority figures.[188]

As Jochen Hellbeck notes, the struggle of many Soviet citizens to turn themselves into exemplary Stalinist subjects involved a pitched battle between such pairs of opposites as mind/body or ideology/psychology, where the former terms invariably gained ascendancy over the latter.[189] Like these, Zoshchenko seeks salvation in a process of psychophysiological reforging that subordinates the vagaries of "body" and "psychology" to the rigors of ideology. Needless to say, the image of the arm/hand so prominent throughout Zoshchenko's writing plays a vital role here, as well. To be sure, in such works as *Youth Restored* or *Before Sunrise* Zoshchenko employs the image of the writing or *authorial* hand as a means of sublimating the violence associated with this same limb elsewhere in his work. And a full regeneration of the "authorial hand" is ultimately possible only in concert with Reason, as Zholkovsky demonstrates.[190] Still, the author's fascination with writing as the product of a "firm hand" (*твердая рука* in Russian) suggests further possibilities. Indeed, as much as it might point toward a generalized enlightenment posture on Zoshchenko's part, this image also suggests the author's desire to embody the characteristics of totalizing self-mastery and control that were the very hallmarks of Stalinist subjectivity. Zoshchenko's remark at the end of *Before Sunrise* that "my hand had become harder" surely has less to do with achieving enlightenment than with acquiring the legendary quality of strong or "iron-handedness" that was associated with Stalin himself. The bitter irony is that Zoshchenko's fantasy only substitutes one oppressive hand for another. Thus the unjustly punishing hand of the writer's biological father, which had prompted the young Zoshchenko to muse that he would one day "grow up and find out why people are guilty who are not the slightest bit guilty (III: 539) becomes the wisely chastening, firm hand of the writer's ideological father (i.e., Stalin).

Zoshchenko's mythologization of the authorial hand is evident from the first pages of *Before Sunrise*. Among others, it is mirrored in the writer's near-Bulgakovian faith in the power of his manuscript to survive even the perils of world war. In the preface to *Before Sunrise*, Zoshchenko recounts his evacuation from Leningrad to Central Asia at the beginning of the blockade. Describing the beleaguered manuscripts that would one day become the finished version of *Before Sunrise*, he notes: "The fire's flame was already licking them. And I am amazed that they remained intact" (III: 448). An equally mystical faith in the power of the word inheres in Zoshchenko's characterization of the book as a whole as a "cure" for the irrational, destructive philosophy of fascism—even if we make allowances for the author's obvious political calculation.

This extraordinary belief in the power of writing, coupled with skepticism toward writing guided by an unstable hand, provides the subject of an early vignette entitled "Elvira." In it the young writer encounters a circus performer named Elvira, who comes to the town where Zoshchenko is staying in order to find a general with whom she had a brief affair. Illiterate, she asks Zoshchenko to compose a letter to the general asking for financial compensation. The narrator consents to the ruse, hoping ultimately to get rid of her. Yet the plan backfires when Elvira receives the money and decides to remain with her new "benefactor." Here writing initially holds forth the promise of salvation from the grotesque Elvira, whose arms—not accidentally—are strong enough to have held up three men during a circus routine (III: 471). And if the illiterate, hysterical strongwoman represents the very quintessence of feminine chaos for Zoshchenko, his civilized, writing hand seems to embody the distant hope of a transcendent cultural *order*. Yet in this instance the redemptive power of the Word is corrupted by its questionable source. Zoshchenko's fledging attempt to liberate himself from Woman—metaphorically speaking this is precisely what the tale encapsulates—backfires because it is *she* who controls the movements of *his* pen. Elvira's letter, after all, is referred to as "the cry of a woman's soul" (III: 472). Indeed, it is only much later, in the überoptimistic conclusion to *Before Sunrise* where the author's pen is guided by none other than Stalinist ideology, that chaos is definitively exorcised from Zoshchenko's world.

Zoshchenko's problems with women as portrayed in *Before Sunrise* are matched only by his ambivalence toward a host of paternal and authority figures. These represent not only the reality of unjust punishment (the castigating arm or hand), but symbolize more broadly a cosmos governed by an unchanging, oppressive patriarchal order—one that consistently denies its sons any sense of agency. The adult writer will attempt to overturn this reality by appealing to the "scientific" order governing the new Soviet world,[191] yet to the adolescent Zoshchenko the universe still appears monolithic and unchanging. The touchy issue of fathers and sons is revisited in two key vignettes, respectively entitled "No Yelling Allowed" and "Heart Attack." Here, too, the stories' thematics suggests the son's revolt against the father's imposing rule. The second vignette in particular cements this idea by describing Zoshchenko's father as a kind of immobile Peter the Great figure. And the implicit allusions throughout *Before Sunrise* to such masterpieces as Pushkin's *Bronze Horseman* or Belyi's *Petersburg* link it to a long line of works that chronicles the complex relationship between fathers and sons within Russian literature.[192] Zoshchenko's *Before Sunrise* adds yet another chapter to that saga. Thus in the first vignette ("No Yelling Allowed"), the young Zoshchenko is sent home by his teacher for yelling the word "revolt" at the same time that social unrest has taken over the streets. Zoshchenko's father jokingly suggests that as punishment he could be sent to prison. This is only one of the many examples of "unjust punishment" that punctuate the work. As if building on this idea, in the following vignette (entitled "Heart Attack") the young Zoshchenko describes his father as if he were a latter-day incarnation of Peter the Great, the prototype of the oppressive patriarch in Russian literature: "Today he's standing *motionlessly* next to the window. . . . He looks like Peter the Great. Only with a beard" (III: 545; my emphasis).[193] Yet in contrast to the literary myth embodied in Pushkin's *Bronze Horseman*, it is not the son who perishes but rather the patriarchal figure himself. Zoshchenko's father dies of a heart attack after drinking a glass of water.

For the young Zoshchenko the cause of his father's death lies in his mysteriously defective heart. The symbolic connotations of this flaw, which the boy's mother casually ascribes to father and son alike, are even more important than the physiological problem itself. For Zoshchenko's father, who is described as having a "closed heart," seems to embody the very "closed circuit" of history itself. This is all the more unsettling because of its implications for the son. Accused by his mother of having the same "closed heart," Zoshchenko interprets his inability to cry over his father's death as a mechanical repetition of the paternal flaw. The sins of the father, he fears, have been visited upon the son: "I stand next to the door and watch this terrible sorrow. No, I just couldn't cry. Probably, I have a closed heart" (III: 546). Zoshchenko's sense of inhabiting a closed circuit (where death represents the ultimate expression of history's finality) is echoed in his description of his father's funeral. At the cemetery the dead bodies are described as "immobile, like wax puppets." The child-narrator reacts to this by intentionally leaving the enclosed space where the corpses are laid out. In a moment of high symbolism, the young Zoshchenko runs out of the church (God the Father's house) where the bodies lie in state: "With bated breath, I approach. I just barely touch his dead hand with my lips. I run out of the church" (III: 547).[194] Here the writer underscores his own desire to escape the unchanging, moribund realm of the past. Is it any surprise, then, that the young Zoshchenko experiences not so much grief as relief when his dead father is finally put to rest? Despite the narrator's warm feelings for his father (he remarks in passing that his father was satisfied with a small fir tree Zoshchenko had painted on one of his canvases), the death of the parent symbolizes for Zoshchenko an overcoming not only of the father's flawed physiology but—more broadly—the young boy's liberation from the prison house of temporal closure. With the passing of the father's closed heart the son is able to move from a flawed past into the future: "The pit is filled up. It's all over. The closed heart no longer exists. But I exist" (III: 547).

Zoshchenko's unconscious desire to overturn the "closed circuit" of biology/history provides the subject matter for another vignette, this one entitled

"Somebody Drowned." Perhaps recalling Nikolai Fyodorov, whose *Philosophy of the Common Cause* (1903) laid out an ambitious blueprint for reversing the biological cycle by overcoming death,[195] the narrator fantasizes about bringing a drowned boy back to life. The implications of this are that much more dramatic if we place the boy's accidental death in the context of Zoshchenko's own lifelong fear of water. Lying on the ground with his arms outstretched and his mother kneeling beside him, the drowned youth seems to recall a crucified Christ awaiting resurrection. Moreover, it is no less than Zoshchenko himself who aspires to the role of God in the piece. Yet unlike the punishing God of "At the Cemetery," this one promises liberation from the injustice of death. This motif will become particularly important for the adult Zoshchenko, who in such works as *Youth Restored* attempts (entirely in the spirit of the times) to scientifically overcome the "accident" of death using the power of the mind.[196] The obverse of "immobility," of closure and death, is evident in the narrator's fantasy of resurrecting the boy. The young Zoshchenko fantasizes about the drowned youth beginning to move: "I look askance at the drowned man. I want him to *begin moving*" (III: 533; my emphasis). Yet the sobering conclusion of the vignette negates the narrator's fantasy, reaffirming the very "immobility" that the young Zoshchenko had sought to undo. This in turn provokes a flight response in the boy not unlike the one that caused him to flee his father's funeral: "But he lies *immobile*. I am so scared that I close my eyes" (III: 533; my emphasis).

The child's fantasy of overturning a flawed natural order is best illustrated by several vignettes that describe the boy's desire to grow up and repair the injustices of the adult world. In one piece entitled "Terrible World," the child-narrator comes to the conclusion that the world is unjustly, irrationally organized, since it punishes people for expressing their most basic needs. In the given instance, it is the need for money, which—according to Zoshchenko's mother—leads people to steal and subsequently to be put in prison. Echoing in displaced form the young Zoshchenko's indignation at having himself been punished for his infantile needs (e.g., the need to feed), the vignette projects resolution onto an imagined future moment when the confused child will become a rational, knowledgeable adult in control of his own destiny. Only then, Zoshchenko imagines, will he be able to repair the fatally flawed adult world that unjustly "castrates" desire: "I am silent. I'll grow up and then I'll find out myself, what's going on in the world. It must be that adults have gotten things into a mess and don't want to tell children about it" (III: 532).[197]

Paradoxically, the vignettes that portray Zoshchenko's attempts to take the reins of power into his own *hands* more often than not reflect not confidence but a keen ambivalence on the part of the ascendant hero.[198] Such unease arises (presumably) because in taking up the mantle of patriarchal power one has the potential to become the same oppressive or "castrating" figure that had earlier been abhorred.[199] And faced with the choice between being either the oppressor or the oppressed, the narrator frequently abandons the arena in which he might act as a strong, charismatic "father" figure. The vignette "The Thief" provides a compelling illustration of this. In it Zoshchenko appears as a batallion commander concerned with flagging discipline among his subordinates. When one of the soldiers tries to steal Zoshchenko's razor—what more potent symbol of the "father's" ability to punish the son can one imagine?—the narrator is suddenly forced to assert his authority. Zoshchenko's god-like wrath is buttressed by the fact that he now holds in his own hands the ultimate symbol of authority—that is, a pistol: "I run after him with a pistol in my hand. I am enraged as never before" (III: 484). Yet faced with the image of the young soldier standing submissively before him, the narrator hesitates to use his weapon. Paradoxically, it is now Zoshchenko-as-father who threatens unjust punishment on a frightened son. After all, the young soldier's only fault lay in stealing a razor in order to buy tobacco. Although Zoshchenko takes back his razor (leaving the case to the soldier), he decides not to punish the young recruit and leaves the scene in disgust—having found in himself the same "punishing arm" that he resented in his father: "Taking out the razor, I give him the box. And I leave, irritated at myself" (III: 484).[200]

Symptomatically, it is in the vignettes that deal with the issue of writing that Zoshchenko proves best able to negotiate the transition from the stifling order of the fathers to the new world. Yet, as I have already mentioned, it is not writing per se that enables the transition. Rather it is the highly fetishized, quasimagical Word of Stalinist ideolgy that underwrites the process of transforming the Old Adam into the New. This is prefigured in the vignette "Nonsense Again," where Zoshchenko defends his status as a proletarian writer against a conservative editor who suggests that Zoshchenko write in a more traditional style. In contrast to the earlier vignette "Nonsense," in which Zoshchenko's composition on a classical text (Turgenev's *Liza Kalitina*) had been rejected by a dim-witted schoolmaster, now it is the writer himself who leaves in triumph. Moreover, Zoshchenko notes that despite being rejected he no longer feels "vexed"—an emotion that elsewhere in *Before Sunrise* signals the narrator's unsuccessful attempts to enter the adult world: "I leave the editor's office. I no longer have the same feelings that I experienced at school. I don't even feel vexed. I'm not distressed. I know that I'm right" (III: 507).

Much more important is Zoshchenko's symbolically charged portrayal of his connection to Gorky in the vignette entitled "At Gorky's Place." Here the encounter between literary "father" and "son" (between the energetic dean of Soviet letters and his ailing protégé) signals the possibility of a genuine transformation of the prerevolutionary body and soul into that of a healthy Stalinist subject. And why not? As Masing-Delic notes, for Zoshchenko Gorky represented the epitome of "manliness" and "personal harmony." Not merely the optimistic "Pushkin of today,"[201] he was the embodiment of Promethean rebellion against personal hardship as well as against the "historical fate" of an entire nation.[202] Zoshchenko's apprenticeship to Gorky provided him with a potent symbolic tool in his struggle to overcome the demons of his past. This becomes the subject of the vignette "At Gorky's Place," where the writer's membership in the "healthy" Soviet present enables him to purge his connection to a corrupt, prerevolutionary past. The strategic juxtaposition of the vignette "The House of the Arts" with "At Gorky's Place" makes the opposition of healthy present and ailing past explicit. Thus in the first story, Zoshchenko meets Aleksandr Blok, who is not accidentally described as "limp," "lifeless," and standing "amazingly motionlessly." More importantly, in his "motionlessness" Blok resembles numerous other "immobile" figures scattered throughout *Before Sunrise*, each of whom embodies the closed circuit of history. More than this, Blok seems to represent the legacy of a flawed psychophysiology that the old world—in this case, the ailing literary "fathers"—will invariably pass on to its sons: "He's standing there amazingly *motionless*, looking at the lights of Nevsky Prospect. . . . Once again I walk about the corridor. Some sort of agitation suffocates me. Now I almost see my fate. I see the finale of my life. I see the melancholy that will certainly smother me" (III:502–3; my emphasis).

The writer's meeting with Gorky provides the literary and spiritual antidote to this somber vignette. In a manner that is clearly meant to negate the earlier imagined connection between himself and Blok, Zoshchenko describes Gorky as lightly touching his shoulder and telling him that he should "undergo a treatment." The association of Gorky and health is no accident, for it is none other than Gorky who urged Zoshchenko (in a letter written in March of 1936) to write a book "'ridiculing suffering,'" which was the "'shame of the world.'"[203] The final lines of "At Gorky's" are most indicative of the almost magical power that Zoshchenko attributes not only to his encounter with Gorky but to the entire Stalinist project of psychophysiological reform. At the end of the vignette Zoshchenko and the other writers are shown walking out of the apartment. The street they walk out into is not Leningrad's former Kronverskii but the new *Gorky* Prospect. Renamed in 1932 in honor of the great Soviet writer, it recalls the fate of its Moscow counterpart: the famous Tverskaya. Also renamed in 1932, Tverskaya was the first thoroughfare to be transformed by the massive reconstruction of Moscow undertaken by Kaganovich and others in 1935. Zoshchenko's allusion to this in 1942–1943 has the effect of reminding the reader once again of the writer's firm resolve to make his own body and soul a part of that same project of socialist reconstruction.

One need hardly point out that the "cure" undertaken by Zoshchenko in *Before Sunrise* falls short of genuine analysis. To be sure, the richly evocative vignettes included in the first half of the book point in this direction. Yet Zoshchenko's own interpretation of them ultimately leaves the reader with the impression of brutal self-censorship rather than Freudian self-exploration.[204] Thus the potentially liberating process of storytelling must ultimately be weighed against the ultradidactic tract on the virtues of reason and self-control with which Zoshchenko concludes his *Before Sunrise*. Here the Word is significant not so much for its therapeutic or artistic potential as for its ability to construct a viable narrative of conversion. Rejecting in the manner of the late Tolstoy art that does lead to salvation, Zoshchenko denounces the "decadent" verse of various (minor) fin de siècle poets. Such art cannot be healthy, Zoshchenko opines, since it is the product of "trembling hands." Here one is reminded of the vignette "Elvira," in which the redeeming power of the written word is poisoned by its source. For the emotional missive that Zoshchenko composes is in fact the irrational cri de coeur of a hysterical woman. The logical antipode to this is the masterful engineer of human souls who appears at the end of *Before Sunrise*. Now that he is armed with the "iron formulas" of Stalinist Reason Zoshchenko is finally able to overcome the chaos of his own stories. Denying that this artistic lobotomy has affected his craft, the author writes: "Isn't it possible that along with my enemies victorious reason banished what was most dear to me: i.e., art? No. Quite the opposite. My hand has become more firm. And my voice more resonant. And my songs more joyful" (III: 689).

Likewise, the part of Zoshchenko's *Before Sunrise* that deals directly with the author's putative rehabilitation reflects not so much genuine enlightenment as it does the power of Stalinist myth making. And here Zoshchenko is little different from those of his contemporaries who employed equally questionable means toward their own self-reform. Witness the overwhelming success of Zamkov's experiments with gravidan. Hundreds of letters preserved in the institute archives suggest that the anesthetizing drug helped many of his patients overcome the dire consequences of trying to live out the "Stalinist dream."[205] Yet the tragedy of Zamkov's work, as Eric Naiman notes, lay in the fact that in order to live out that dream the patient was forced to pharmaceutically "amputate" a host of unpleasant memories associated with living in the same Stalinist utopia.[206] Zoshchenko's approach in *Before Sunrise* is unsettlingly close. Even more than the previous revolutionary decade, the Stalinist '30s saw Soviet society setting out to create a "new life"—one that could be forged only through a robust purging of the old. Perhaps even more insidious than the purges themselves was that fact that these invariably impinged upon the deepest levels of self-constitution. For the ritual of self-purification undertaken by many a Stalinist subject presupposed a dramatic separation between the former self (the Old Adam) and the reformed *Homo novus* of the present. Recalling the ritual of rebirth in Christian theology, self-transformation occurred as a sloughing off the sinful, flawed person still tethered to the past and her or his triumphant reemergence into the world in the form of a new and pure being."[207] Likewise, at the beginning of his *Before Sunrise* Zoshchenko comfortably likens his flawed former incarnation to a dead man: "I am consoled by the fact that I will be talking about my youth. It's the same as talking about a dead person" (III: 452).

A no less compelling subtext for Zoshchenko's transfiguration at the end of *Before Sunrise* is to be found in the mythologically charged figure of Pushkin—and more specifically, in the image of death and rebirth described in his famous "Prophet."[208] Not unlike Platonov in his 1937 essay "Pushkin and Gorky," Zoshchenko offers a subtle allusion to the poem in order to evoke the near-mythic transformation of the poet's/prophet's body in a ritualistic act of "sacred wounding." Yet in the case of Zoshchenko the metamorphosis affects not the poet's heart and chest but his stomach. This mirrors Zoshchenko's long-standing desire to resolve his anxieties about food, at the same time that it points toward the thematics of psychophysiological reforming that shaped his prose throughout the '30s.[209] In Pushkin's "The Prophet," the passage from profane to sacred self betokens a transfiguring of the poet's Word. Likewise, for many artists and cultural figures of the Stalin era the path to immortality lay in "the ascetic renunciation of everything bodily."[210] Witness Ostrovsky's Korchagin, who mortifies flesh in order to be able to write the ultimate Book. For Zoshchenko, too, a violent restructuring of the body is the price the writer must pay in order to take pen in hand and inflame the hearts of his fellow men: "With my belly ripped open I lolled about in bed. My weapon—paper and pencil—lay next to me. And at times I did not have the strength to lift my hand to take them up again. . . . I was killed, torn to pieces, cut up only to emerge once again from the dust" (III: 626).

Zoshchenko's account of his recovery in the final pages of *Before Sunrise* is no less a rhetorical and ideological construct. Among the staples of Socialist Realist rhetoric was the image of the "light of knowledge," according to Smirnov.[211] Zoshchenko picks up this cliché, using it to portray his internal struggle as an epic contest between the sunlight of reason and the murky darkness of one's irrational, subconscious fears. It is presumably by means of this light—"the light of logic, of high consciousness" (III: 575)—that the author will finally cast out his inner demons. Yet to gain victory over an enemy as potent as the unconscious requires more than mere sunlight. A key figure within Stalinism's cultural imaginary (as well as in Zoshchenko's own prose!) was the guardian or sentinel.[212] In the second half of *Before Sunrise*, Zoshchenko repeatedly invokes not only light but the guardian as a means of corralling the atavistic impulses of the human unconscious: "At night the doors of the lower floor open up. The sentinels of my consciousness fall asleep. And then the shades of the past, languishing in the underground, appear in dreams" (III: 575). The epilogue of *Before Sunrise* takes this image to its logical conclusion, explicitly evoking the culture's paranoid fears of ubiquitous hidden enemies and saboteurs. Here, too, the writer's imagery betrays a strict logic. For within Stalinism the villain acts as the hero's ontological twin, providing the curtain of darkness against which society's virtuous emerge purified and reborn. An analogous pageant is played out within the authorial soul. Here benighted consciousness, with its host of irrational fears, plays the part of the "enemy," while consciousness becomes the conquering hero:

> I undertook an attack against these *enemies*, which I discovered by means of criminal investigation. There were a great many of these *enemies*. . . . Others of my *enemies* surrendered to the mercy of the victor." (my emphasis)[213]

The final chord in Zoshchenko's paean to reason and civilization comes in the form of a rewritten poem included in the afterword to *Before Sunrise*. As if to complete the impression of a fairy tale finally come true, the writer remarks that he is penning the last lines of his book on the tenth floor of the Hotel Moskva—one of the most prominent architectural and visual landmarks of the newly reconstructed Stalinist Moscow. Zoshchenko's seemingly innocuous rewriting of a farewell poem by an anonymous Greek poet is significant because it echoes the passage of the subject from nature to culture envisioned throughout his writing of the '30s and '40s. Thus a poem about parting with life's simple pleasures becomes (in Zoshchenko's hands) nothing less than a short course in Stalinist ontology. In this new world the natural is duly subordinated to those "cultural" elements that occupy the highest rungs on the ladder of being. Not so in the Greek original. Here apples, melons, and pears continue to exist on a par with sunlight and stars: "Here is what is most splendid of what I have left behind in the world:/ The first is sunlight, the second are the calm stars/ And the moon, the third are apples and ripe melons and pears" (III: 692). Zoshchenko's recast version exalts not romantic moonlight or stars but the sun, at once recalling Stalinism's enlightenment pathos, as well as the enlightened architect of the Soviet project himself (i.e., Stalin).[214] As for ripe pears, water- and other melons, these Zoshchenko leaves out of the poem altogether. It is not difficult to see in this miraculous transfiguring of simple foodstuffs into "reason and art" (i.e., the third line in the Greek original becomes the second line in the reworked version) a nod to

Zoshchenko's perennial anxiety surrounding food. More broadly, however, the author's "reforged" variant of the poem encapsulates the very project of psychophysiological restructuring with which he had been most preoccupied in such works as *Youth Restored* or *Before Sunrise*. Thus with only a few pen-strokes Zoshchenko transforms the troublesome world of biology into an encomium to sunlight, reason, and art:

> Incidentally, I'm indifferent to the moon and the stars. I'll replace the stars and the moon with something more attractive to me. These verses I would pronounce as follows: "Here is what is most splendid of what I have left behind in the world:/ The first is sunlight, the second art and reason. . . ." And in third place one could mention something from the fruit category—ripe pears, watermelons and melons . . . (III: 692–93)

Of all his literary predecessors Zoshchenko seems to have identified most closely with Nikolai Gogol. As early as 1927 Zoshchenko wrote in a letter to Kornei Chukovskii that he had made a thorough study of Gogol's biography and come to understand why Russia's greatest comic writer lost his mind.[215] Zoshchenko attributes his literary and spiritual forefather's breakdown to a "certain hereditary defect, a kind of weakness of the mechanism built into the central parts of the nervous system . . ."[216] Not surprisingly, in *Before Sunrise* the greatest comic writer of the Soviet era describes the symptoms of his own malaise as nearly identical to those of Gogol.[217] Increasingly preoccupied throughout the 1930s and '40s with his own physical and spiritual rehabilitation, Zoshchenko sees Gogol's earlier failures in the perilous realm of self-healing as providing the keys to his own happiness.[218] As if prefiguring his own eventual triumph, Zoshchenko diagnoses the famously ailing nineteenth-century writer with a "psychoneurosis that could probably be removed by means of a thorough psychoanalysis and re-education of character."[219] More than a moment of simple Hippocratic hubris on Zoshchenko's part, this comment demonstrates the writer's unusual faith in the power of literature to cure what ailed humankind most. And in this regard Zoshchenko proved to be entirely in step with the era. The "hereditary defect" that had prevented the mystically inclined Gogol from completing his vaunted trilogy would now be "scientifically" overcome by his more enlightened, Soviet counterpart. Armed with the tools of Stalinist reason and self-control, the literary "son" would now complete the "father's" task by authoring a genuinely "life-embracing, positive book."[220] Likewise, if the young Zoshchenko could only fantasize about escaping the fate of his father's "closed heart," the author of *Before Sunrise* aspires to nothing less than a broad rewriting of the book of nature and with it his own biography. Here, if nowhere else, Zoshchenko really was a Soviet writer—which is to say, an "engineer of human souls."

NOTES

1. See Eric Naiman, "Lexical Heroes, 101.
2. Keith Livers, "Scatology and Eschatology," 170–72.
3. Ibid., 99.
4. N. Kornienko, "Zoshchenko i Platonov: Vstrechi v literature," *Literaturnoe obozrenie* 1, (249) (1995): 50.
5. Mikhail Zoshchenko, *Sobranie soch.*, vol. 3 (Leningrad: Khudozhestvennaia literatura, 1985), 98.
6. Gregory Carleton, *The Politics of Reception: Cultural Constructions of Mikhail Zoshchenko* (Evanston: Northwestern University Press, 1998), 146. Similarly, Aleksandr Zholkovskii (Mikhail Zoshchenko: poetika nedoveriia [Moskva: Shkola iazyki russkoi kul'tury," 1999], 310) on Zoshchenko's quest (along with such other authors as Akhmatova and Pasternak) for "existential, physical and stylistic simplicity." See also Linda Hart Scatton, *Mikhail Zoshchenko: Evolution of a Writer* (Cambridge: Cambridge University Press, 1993), 249.
7. Jochen Hellbeck, "Stalin-Era Autobiographical Texts: Working: Struggling: Becoming," *The Russian Review*, vol. 60/no. 3 (July 2001): 347.
8. Ibid., 343.
9. Rolf Hellebust, *Flesh to Metal: Soviet Literature & The Alchemy of Revolution* (Ithaca, NY: Cornell University Press, 2003), 80.
10. See Eric Naiman's "Diskurs, obrashchennyi v plot'," 625–38.
11. Rolf Hellebust, *Flesh to Metal*, 79.
12. Ibid., 89.
13. Hellebust notes, describing the difference between Socialist Realism and the previous decade in terms of the metal myth, that "Socialist Realism is highly sensitive to the dehumanizing aspect of such imagery. . . . The application of metal epithets to positive characters is kept on the abstract plane, as far as possible from the places where we are shown living, physical bodies" (Rolf Hellebust, *Flesh to Metal*, 108).
14. Jochen Hellbeck, "Writing the Self, 78.
15. Ibid., 74.
16. Jochen Hellbeck, "Stalin-Era Autobiographical Texts," 352.
17. Ibid.
18. See Rolf Hellebust, *Flesh to Metal*.
19. Eric Naiman, "Diskurs, obrashchennyi v plot'," 632.
20. Ibid., 349.
21. Iurii Murashov, "Pis'mo i ustnaia rech' v diskursakh o iazyke 1930-kh godov: N. Marr," *Sotsrealisticheskii kanon* (Sankt-Peterburg: Akademicheskii proekt, 2000), 600.
22. Lilya Kaganovsky, *Bodily Remains: The "Positive" Hero in Stalinist Fiction*, Ph.D. dissertation, 2000, 114.
23. Aleksandr Zholkovskii, *Mikhail Zoshchenko: poetika nedoveriia*, 164–70.
24. The analogy with Gogol is slightly complicated by the fact that Zoshchenko saw himself as a reformed version of the nineteenth-century writer.
25. Aleksandr Zholkovskii, *Mikhail Zoshchenko: poetika nedoveriia*, 308.

26. Cf. E. Zhurbina, "Puti istseleniia," in *Vospominaniia o Mikhaile Zoshchenko* (Sankt-Peterburg: Khudozhestvennaia literatura, 1995), 165.

27. K. Chukovskii, *Dnevnik 1930–1969* (Moskva: Sovremennyi pisatel', 1994), 154.

28. Gregory Carleton, *The Politics of Reception*, 85.

29. Linda Hart Scatton's characterization of *Youth Restored* suggests a certain autobiographical quality (*Mikhail Zoshchenko: Evolution of a Writer*, 170). Similarly, Carleton rejects the idea that the primary narrative and commentaries can function autonomously, characterizing the interaction between the two as marked by "seepage" and "contamination," which culminates in the appearance of the author (Zoshchenko) in the same frame of reference as the vulgar Kashkin (*The Politics of Reception*, 98).

30. Eric Naiman, "Diskurs, obrashchennyi v plot'," 629.

31. Ibid., 166.

32. *Intimacy and Terror: Soviet Diaries of the 1930s*, eds. Veronique Garros, Natalia Korenesvskaya, and Thomas Lahusen (New York: The New Press, 1995), 211.

33. Thomas Lahusen, *How Life Writes the Book: Real Socialism and Socialist Realism in Stalin's Russia* (Ithaca: Cornell University Press, 1997), 46.

34. Cynthia A. Ruder, *Making History for Stalin: The Story of the Belomor Canal* (Gainesville: University Press of Florida, 1998), 82–83.

35. Ibid.

36. The most dramatic example is provided by Aleksandr Zholkovskii's monograph *Mikhail Zoshchenko: Poetika nedoveriia*.

37. Cynthia A. Ruder, *Making History for Stalin*, 81.

38. Katerina Clark, *The Soviet Novel*, 100.

39. Ibid., 101.

40. Ibid., 102.

41. Bernice Rosenthal, "Sotsrealizm i Nitssheanstvo," 62.

42. Linda Hart Scatton, *Mikhail Zoshchenko*, 166.

43. Bernice Rosenthal, "Sotsrealizm i Nitssheanstvo," 62.

44. Ibid.

45. Ibid.

46. Thomas Lahusen, *How Life Writes the Book*, 46.

47. See Aleksandr Zholkovskii, *Mikhail Zoshchenko: poetika nedoveriia*, 111.

48. See Mikhail Zoshchenko, *Sobranie soch.*, v. 3, 624.

49. Aleksandr Zholkovskii, *Mikhail Zoshchenko: poetika nedoveriia*, 111.

50. See the story "U kalitki," *Sobranie soch.*, v. 3, 539–40.

51. Irene Masing-Delic, "Biology, Reason and Literature in Zoshchenko's *Pered voschodom solnca*," *Russian Literature* 8 (1980): 89.

52. Mikhail Zoshchenko, *Sobranie soch.*, vol. 3, 470.

53. Ibid., 486.

54. Mikhail Zoshchenko, *Sobranie soch.*, vol. 3, 487.

55. Mikhail Zoshchenko, *Sobranie soch.*, vol. 1, 385.

56. As Julie A. Cassiday says of Mayakovsky's long poem *About That* ("Flash Floods, Bedbugs, and Saunas," in *Against the Grain: Parody, Satire, and Intertextuality in Russian Literature* [Bloomington: Slavic, 2002], 135): "The flood of Revolution surges from country to country, east and west, north and south, until it encompasses the

world-wide proletariat. The deluge washes away the bourgeoisie and all its evils to leave the world cleansed of capitalism and purified for the building of communism."

57. Aleksandr Zholkovskii, *Mikhail Zoshchenko: poetika nedoveriia*, 62.

58. One vignette in *Before Sunrise* (entitled "The Thief") provides an eloquent illustration. In it the now adult Zoshchenko appears as a battalion commander in the tsarist army. After a young soldier steals his razor (in order to sell it and buy tobacco), the writer-cum-authority figure is placed in the unenviable position of having to punish a subordinate for expressing his all-too-human desires. Yet when confronted with the image of the soldier's childishly outstretched and trembling hands, Zoshchenko forgoes the posture of oppressive authority figure, circumventing the dilemma by means of a less-than-ideal compromise: "I feel disgusted that I chased after him. Taking out the razor, I hand him the box. I leave, irritated at myself" (*Sobranie soch.*, v. 3, 484).

59. Irene Masing-Delic, "Biology," 82.

60. Masing-Delic points, among others, to the similarity between Pushkin's Evgenii, who is punished by the tyrant father Peter the Great (also associated with an outstretched hand), and the reincarnation of the figure of poor Evgenii as Dudkin in Belyi's *Petersburg* ("Biology," 92–93).

61. Aleksandr Zholkovskii, *Mikhail Zoshchenko: poetika nedoveriia*, 129–30.

62. Jonathan Goldberg, *Writing Matter: From the Hands of the English Renaissance* (Stanford: Stanford University Press, 1990), 80.

63. Ibid.

64. Jochen Hellbeck, "Writing the Self," 92.

65. Ibid.

66. Mikhail Zoshchenko, *Sobranie soch.*, vol. 3, 452.

67. "The Sorrows of the Young Verter" was first published in the satirical magazine *Krokodil* in 1933 (no. 1).

68. Ibid. Cf. in this regard Zholkovsky's characterization of Zoshchenko's worldview as modulating among "'fear of life's instability,' 'the desire for peace and order,' and 'the uncertain search for protection from dangers'" (*Mikhail Zoshchenko: poetika nedoveriia*, 60). An extraordinarly telling example of this modulation is contained one of the final stories in Zoshchenko's *Sky-Blue Book* entitled "Incident on the Volga." Originally published in the magazine *Begemot* (1927: no. 33), the story relates the narrator's misadventures while traveling down the Volga river on a boat, the name of which is constantly being changed—presumably to reflect the precipitously changing political realities of the times. While both versions of the story contain the same basic plot, it seems telling that the later version includes several changes that reflect the ideological priorities of a later time. Thus while the original version merely remarks that the change of name from "Storm" to "Korolenko" is appropriate because "Storm" is less in keeping with the times, in the second "Incident" the narrator remarks: "And as concerns 'The Storm,' that was a less relevant name. It was partially unprincipled. It's a phenomenon of nature. And that gives nothing to the mind or heart" (*Sobranie soch.*, vol. 3: 360). The latter description seems to appeal more directly to the "nature versus culture" dichotomy described by Clark as a core aspect of Stalinist cultural mythology. More importantly, however, the later "Incident" mirrors

the narrator/author's embrace of stasis or death as the only possible resolution to life's inherent instability. Having said this, one must immediately point out that this "embrace" is an extraordinarily ambivalent one, since the writer is quick to mention the relative advantages of living over death. Nonetheless, it seems—at least to this reader—to be no accident that Zoshchenko's overall interest in the passage in stasis/death occurs precisely in the context of Stalinist culture's active promotion of a statuary or static corporeal ideal (see Zolotonosov, *Slovo i telo*, 611)—an ideal that is not accidentally mirrored in the writer's increasing attraction during the 1930s to monologism in art (see Carleton, *The Politics of Reception*, 159; Rachel May, "Superego as Literary Subtext," 120–21; N. V. Kornienko, "Zoshchenko i Platonov," 50): "To sum things up, we arrived safely in Astrakhan. And from there we set off on dry land. So the fate of the steamer after that point is unknown. But one can doubt whether it retained that name. For all times. All the more so since Korolenko died. And Penkin was alive, which was the fundamental failure leading to his being renamed. So that in this case the failure consists rather in the fact that people are, so to speak, alive. No, here it's even impossible to understand what the essence of the failure is. On the one hand, it's sometimes advantageous for us to be not-alive. On the other hand, so to speak, thanks but no thanks. A dubious advantage. Better not, after all. At the same time being alive is also, in this sense, relatively disadvantageous."

69. Bernice Rosenthal, "Sotsrealizm i Nitssheanstvo," 62

70. Mikhail Zoshchenko, *Sobranie soch.*, vol. 3, 67.

71. Aleksandr Zholkovskii, *Mikhail Zoshchenko: poetika nedoveriia*, 222.

72. Ibid., 222–23.

73. See chapter 9 of Zholkovskii's *Mikhail Zoshchenko: poetika nedoveriia*.

74. Thus Belikov becomes visibly agitated when he sees Varen'ka and her brother riding a bicycle.

75. In this regard, one must take issue with Zholkovskii's one-sided characterization of the intentionally etymologized name of the hero, according to which the *vert*– in Verter suggests the circular motion of the pedals and therefore the cyclist as machine (*Mikhail Zoshchenko: poetika nedoveriia*, 232).

76. Aleksandr Zholkovskii, *Mikhail Zoshchenko: poetika nedoveriia*, 229.

77. Mikhail Zoshchenko, *Sobranie soch.*, vol. 3, 235.

78. Aleksandr Zholkovskii, *Mikhail Zoshchenko: poetika nedoveriia*, 232.

79. Zholkovsky treats this topic too perfunctorily, commenting simply on the "obvious analogy with voluntary-obligatory self-remaking in totalitarian conditions" (*Mikhail Zoshchenko: poetika nedoveriia*, 227).

80. Thomas Lahusen, *How Life Writes the Book*, 46.

81. Mikhail Zolotonosov, *Slovo i telo*, 577.

82. Ibid., 365.

83. This is quite literally the subject of Zoshchenko's short story "A Story About Baths and Their Patrons" (1935), in which a man loses both his clothing and his ideological vestments in a bathhouse.

84. Mikhail Zoshchenko, *Sobranie soch.*, vol. 3, 365.

85. This equation—between desire or excess and criminality—is hardly isolated in the later Zoshchenko. Thus in one of the autobiographical Liolia/Min'ka stories entitled

"Galoshes and Ice-Cream," the adult Zoshchenko enjoins his young readers to consider whether such innocent pleasures as eating ice cream are not the result of some prior misdeed: "And even now, children, when I have become an adult and even a little old, even now I sometimes feel a kind of tightening and awkwardness when eating ice-cream. And every time I do it, according to my old childish habit I think to myself: 'Have I really earned this dessert, have I perhaps lied or cheated someone?'" (Mikhail Zoshchenko, *Izbrannye proizvedeniia v 2-kh t-kh*, vol. 1 [Leningrad: "Khudozhestvennaia Literatura," 1968], 221).

86. Moreover, as Clark suggests in her essay "Socialist Realism with Shores" (in *Socialist Realism without Shores*, eds. Thomas Lahusen and Evgeny Dobrenko [Durham: Duke University Press, 1997], 45), the degree of "consciousness" associated with a mentor character in a Socialist Realist novel is fluid and relative. Thus in a novel about children or adolescents an older boy may occupy a position with respect to his younger friends that is structurally analogous to that of a party official vis-à-vis a "spontaneous" son figure elsewhere. The distribution of roles in Zoshchenko's "Sufferings" is similarly relative, since the guard would not normally appear to symbolize political consciousness.

87. It was originally published under the title "Carousel" in *Drezina*, 1923 (May), no. 1.

88. Note that the original version of the story does not contain this figure and is considerably less violent.

89. Mikhail Zoshchenko, *Sobranie soch.*, vol. 3, 189.

90. Cf. the image of the narrator eating ice cream and the same Zoshchenko in the Liolia/Min'ka story "Galoshes and Ice-Cream," where ice cream also figures as a symbol of "criminal" appetites or desires.

91. Note, by the way, that after having vomited or "gone to Riga," according to the Russian idiom, the man lies precisely on his *stomach* in order to recover. This is symptomatic. For it may well be argued that for Zoshchenko the stomach represents the locus par excellence of human appetite and is therefore an essential component of desire's destructive reign.

92. Cf. in this regard one of the introductory vignettes to Zoshchenko's *Youth Restored*. In this piece entitled "A Nursing Woman's Baby Died," Zoshchenko relates the story of a woman whose husband develops a taste for her milk. The wife, who becomes a kind of milk cow, is finally cured of her ailment by a doctor who ties up her breast with a bandage in order to stem the flow of milk. Although the husband has in the meantime become dependent on his wife's milk (it is described as a "free drink"), he ultimately accepts the operation and even praises nature for her economy; he notices that his wife has begun to eat less and so he spends less money on food. Particularly significant is the characterization of nature (i.e., the female body) as subject to a particular kind of inertia that can be controlled only through the intrusion of science and technology, symbolized in this case by the doctor. Another obvious precursor can be found in the 1930 *povest'* "The Lilacs Are Blooming." In the following episode Zoshchenko's alter ego provides the following justification for preferring certain nontraditional (violent) remedies over those used by professional doctors (*Sobranie soch.*, vol. 2, 172): "He said that the whole picture of the disease was only too clear to him.

That it was the improper movement of the organism. And that it was necessary to interrupt that movement. All the more so, since the organism has, so to speak, its own inertia and as soon as it gets stuck on one thing, then there's nothing for it. That's what almost all our ailments and diseases come from, I says. And it's necessary, I says, to heal energetically, by giving it a good shaking up and turning the organism in the opposite direction, because it has a tendency, I says, to work blindly, without looking which way its wheels are spinning."

93. As, for instance, in the short story "Lights of the Big City."

94. Zholkovskii speaks of the superimposition of the claw onto the hand, *Mikhail Zoshchenko: Poetika nedoveriia*, 62.

95. Aleksandr Zholkovskii, *Mikhail Zoshchenko: poetika nedoveriia*, 33.

96. Irene Masing-Delic, "Biology," 89.

97. See Mikhail Zoshchenko, *Sobranie soch.*, vol. 3, 539.

98. Igor' Smirnov, *Psikhodiakhronologika*, 278.

99. Aleksandr Zholkovskii, *Mikhail Zoshchenko: poetika nedoveriia*, 229.

100. Isaak Babel', *Sobranie soch. v 2-kh t-kh* (Moskva: Khudozhestvennaia literatura, 1990),

101. Eric Naiman, "Lexical Heroes," 100.

102. Quoted in Aleksandr Zholkovskii, *Mikhail Zoshchenko: poetika nedoveriia*, 70.

103. Ibid., 28.

104. Mikhail Zolotonosov, *Slovo i telo*, 636.

105. Ibid., 649. Likewise, in *Happy Moscow* (*Novyi mir*, no. 9 [1991]: 53) Platonov writes: "The modest Stalin stood guard on the squares and streets."

106. Boris Groys, *Utopiia i obmen*, 66. In this one can see a clear echo of what A. Lezhnev once characterized as the fate of the Russian novel in the 1930s—that is, the breakdown of the love triangle that formed the core of the classical Russian novel into a *pair* of juxtaposed forces (A. Lezhnev, *Ob iskusstve* [Moskva: Gos-izd-vo "Khudozhestvennaia literature," 1936], 130–32).

107. Eliot Borenstein, *Men without Women*, 19.

108. See Katerina Clark, *The Soviet Novel*, 102.

109. *Chudak*, 1929, no. 4.

110. In a variation of this idea Igor' Smirnov characterizes Zoshchenko's story as symptomatic of the masochistic tenor of Stalinist culture. If the Stalinist subject is one who masters the violent chaos within through rituals of self-castigation and punishment, then Malashkin represents the ideal of Stalinist manhood and the logical favorite in the contest (*Psikhodiakhronologika*, 260)

111. See Mikhail Zoshchenko, *Sobranie soch.*, vol. 3, 584–85. I am not suggesting, of course, that the deep-sea diver is a symbol a priori of chaos, yet in the context of the story he becomes the chaotic Other to be subdued by Bolshevik will and discipline.

112. Katerina Clark, *The Soviet Novel*, 102.

113. Hans Günther, "Arkhetipy sovetskoi kul'tury," 749.

114. In this regard, it seems to me that Zholkovsky's identification of "the miraculous" as an invariant motif in Zoshchenko (see *Mikhail Zoshchenko: poetika nedoveriia*, 205) is insufficient.

115. Aleksandr Zholkovskii, *Mikhail Zoshchenko: poetika nedoveriia*, 129.

116. Mikhail Zolotonosov, *Slovo i telo*, 760–61,

117. Ibid., 763.

118. Igor' Smirnov, *Psikhodiakhronologika*, 253.

119. Katerina Clark, *The Soviet Novel*, 180.

120. Jochen Hellbeck, "Writing the Self," 71.

121. Vladimir Papernyi, *Kul'tura "Dva,"* 157. See also Eric Naiman, "Diskurs, obrashchennyi v plot'," 631.

122. Cf. Smirnov's remark than within a masochistic social structure such as that of Stalinism "fault lies with everyone" (*Psikhodiakhronologika*, 278).

123. An even more obvious example can be found in the story entitled "New Times" (originally published in *Krokodil*, 1938, no. 28/29. In this piece, the punitive/castrating/rehabilitating function of the justly punishing arm is associated with a woman. Zoshchenko describes an incident in which a young woman is verbally assaulted by several hooligans who have had a bit too much to drink in a local bar. When they try to do the same to a young female engineer named Liza B., she hits one of them so hard that he can hardly stand on his legs. When Zoshchenko hears about the incident he goes to visit the girl who explains her behavior as follows (II: 445): "'Of course, I understand it's not good to beat a person up. But I had no other choice. His behavior was so un-Soviet that I couldn't restrain myself. I beat him up as an enemy of Soviet power, not as a man."

124. "Our technician, having his wits confused, begins to speak in the Tsarist manner, using the word 'sirs.' It's obviously as a result of being so agitated that he lost certain traits of his new personality" (*Sobranie soch.*, vol. 3, 361).

125. Cf. Masing-Delic's comments on *Before Sunrise* ("Biology," 80).

126. The mythological notion of the bathhouse in Russian culture as an "unclean" place—as a kind of antiworld—is well documented.

127. Lars T. Lih, "Melodrama and the Myth of the Soviet Union," in *Imitations of Life: Two Centuries of Melodrama in Russia*, eds. Louise McReynolds and Joan Neuberger (Durham: Duke University Press, 2002), 191.

128. Ibid.

129. The practice of writing, as Jonathan Goldberg notes (*Writing Matter*, 80), is founded upon multiple levels of imagined violence. Indeed, a kind of originary violence is implicated not only in the mythological passage from nature to culture undergone by the plume or *penna* (Latin for "feather"), but in the "civilizing" structures of writing that retract the hand from the realm of nature in order to found the human.

130. Aleksandr Zholkovskii, *Mikhail Zoshchenko: poetika nedoveriia*, 121.

131. Aleksandr Zholkovskii, *Mikhail Zoshchenko: poetika nedoveriia*, 121.

132. Cynthia A. Ruder, *Making History for Stalin*, 146–47.

133. For a discussion of the role of the secret police in the reforging process see Cynthia A. Ruder, *Making History for Stalin*, 145.

134. At the end of the piece (*Sobranie soch.*, vol. 2, 280), one of the characters remarks: "I always maintained the point of view that respect for others, praise and esteem produce exclusive results. And many people's characters literally open up like roses at dawn."

135. Aleksandr Zholkovskii, *Mikhail Zoshchenko: poetika nedoveriia*, 129–30.

136. Mikhail Zolotonosov, *Slovo i telo*, 578–80.

137. See Katerina Clark, *The Soviet Novel*, 105.

138. Zholkovskii is the first to have remarked on the transformation of the aggressive *ruka* into the verb *rukovodstvovat'* (*Mikhail Zoshchenko: poetika nedoveriia*, 129).

139. Aleksandr Zholkovskii, *Mikhail Zoshchenko: poetika nedoveriia*, 234, 238.

140. Brett Cooke, *Human Nature in Utopia: Zamyatin's* We (Evanston: North-western University Press, 2002), 38.

141. Ronald LeBlanc, "Gluttony and Power in Olesha's *Envy*," *The Russian Review* 60 (April 2001): 231.

142. It should be noted, however, that in *Youth Restored* Zoshchenko polemicizes with Mechnikov's insufficiently radical idea of prolonging life through diet regulation (specifically, by eating yogurt). For Zoshchenko, whose preoccupation was using the mind to control the body, the idea that such base organs as the stomach or intestines could be involved in prolonging life would surely have been unacceptable. Moreover, given the author's fears/phobias about the breast, the idea that eating yogurt could prolong life would have seemed suspect. Thus at the beginning of *Youth Restored* the author writes (III: 13):

> Certain individuals, descending from the lofty heights and without pronouncing magnificent words about the soul, recommended monitoring the small, natural characteristics of the body. At the same time, they recommended eating *prostokvasha* [a yogurt-like product], calculating wholeheartedly that this vegetarian dish would produce particularly long life, by not allowing microbes to collect uselessly in our intestines and in the vulgar back alleys of our organism, which by nature possess a lower and secondary significance.

143. Whether the image suggests the large intestine or the penis is not particularly important, since both serve to mediate between the body and outside world.

144. Mikhail Zoshchenko, *Iz arkhiva pechati: Mikhail Zoshchenko*, ed. M. Z. Dolinskii (Moskva: Izd-vo "Knizhnaia palata," 1991), 491.

145. See Mikhail Zoshchenko, *Sobranie soch.*, vol. 3, 112.

146. Irene Masing-Delic, "Biology," 81.

147. Mikhail Zoshchenko, *Iz arkhiva pechati*, 492.

148. Ibid.

149. In this regard, one cannot but disagree with Zholkovskii's reading of the story as "anti-Soviet" in spirit. The critic notes that in the above story Soviet power undermines its usual function as the guarantor of order by sadistically splashing its own subjects (*Mikhail Zoshchenko: poetika nedoveriia*, 62). Yet such sadistic practices represent precisely the price that the individual must pay in order to enter into utopia.

150. It should be noted that despite Zoshchenko's keen interest in the scientifically reengineered body politic it is clear that the author remained ambivalent about a situation in which science would completely transform the natural world. In a feuilleton entitled "The Fairy-Tale Life" (published in *Krokodil*, 1935, no. 35/36) Zoshchenko seems to polemicize with this same idea of a completely "rationalized" life. Arguing the virtues of a particular kind of noiseless streetcar, Zoshchenko writes that while technology may have produced a completely silent streetcar, the people inside (the

narrator refers to them as "the minuses of nature") will still make noise. The only way to prevent such noise, he argues, is to "issue candies to stop up the passengers' mouths with, or some sort of wire tricks or interesting intellectual games to distract their attention" (II: 394). Only then, he suggests, will "complete silence reign in the middle of our street-car" (Ibid.). Zoshchenko then goes on to note that since a streetcar is made up of various parts, it cannot but make a certain amount of noise: "Since there are wheels, after all, rails and something is always turning in the motor, it's clear that you can't get by without noise. Then, too, it's probably better that way." One can easily imagine that here Zoshchenko is skeptical about the ultimate feasibility of transforming life into a "fairy tale."

151. Ibid.

152. As Zholkovskii points out, Zoshchenko was "fond of giving his works classical names that were only associated with their *suzhets* in a conventional, satirical manner" (*Mikhail Zoshchenko: poetika nedoveriia*, 225), and here the connection to Chekhov is limited to the common theme of medals and wives supported by their husbands.

153. Katerina Clark, *The Soviet Novel*, 100.

154. For a full discussion of the significance of the term "unstable" see Aleksandr Zholkovskii, *Mikhail Zoshchenko: poetika nedoveriia*, 146–47.

155. The adjective *derzhavnyi* here should be understood literally, as indicating the hero's affiliation with the orderliness of state power.

156. Ibid., 611.

157. Note that in this instance Zoshchenko reprises the image, used elsewhere, of the strong hand/arm of authority disciplining that which is excessive.

158. Eric Naiman, "Diskurs, obrashchennyi v plot'," 635.

159. Irene Masing-Delic, "Gorky's Tutorship and Zoshchenko's 'Metamorphosis,'" *Russian Studies in Literature* 33, no. 2 (spring 1997): 50.

160. Vladimir Papernyi, *Kul'tura "Dva,"* 137.

161. Mikhail Zolotonosov, *Slovo i telo*, 711. Likewise, Leonid Geller suggests that by the mid-to-late-'30s the figure of Pushkin became a weapon to be used against other less desirable writers (such as Dostoevsky), while at the same time being used as a means of creating a hierarchy in literature equivalent to the political hierarchy of Soviet society (*Andrei Platonov v poiskhakh schast'ia* [Paris: YMCA-Press, 1982], 373). Cf. also Platonov's explicit linking of Pushkin and the spirit of Stalinist construction in the essay "Pushkin is Our Comrade."

162. Andrei Platonov, "Pushkin—nash tovarishch," 308.

163. See chapter 1.

164. Gregory Carleton, *The Politics of Reception*, 155.

165. Ibid.

166. Ibid., 156.

167. Tat'iana Kadash, "Gogol' v tvorcheskoi refleksii Zoshchenko," in *Litso i maska Mikhaila Zoshchenko* (Moskva: Olimp/PPP, 1994), 308.

168. Igor' Smirnov, *Psikhodiakhronologika*, 256. It should be pointed out that Smirnov's claim here that suffering is negative for Dostoevsky is somewhat less than accurate. Even the most casual glance at *Crime and Punishment* or *The Brothers Karamazov* will demonstrate as much.

169. Evgenii Dobrenko, "Iskusstvo sotsial'noi navigatsii: ocherki kul'turnoi topografii stalinskoi epokhi," *Wiener Slawistischer Almanach*, bd. 45 (2000), 128. See also Vladimir Papernyi, *Kul'tura "Dva,"* 173.

170. Quoted in Aleksandr Zholkovskii, *Mikhail Zoshchenko: poetika nedoveriia*, 155.

171. A commonplace of Socialist Realist fiction, writes Igor' Smirnov, is the motif of "healing without medicine." In Pavlenko's novel *Happiness* (1949), for instance, a doctor treats his patients by giving them the following advice: "Do you feel like lying around senselessly in bed? Do the opposite. Do you feel like coughing? Hold it in. Is your head spinning? Overcome it with an effort of will. . . . The strongest medicine against tuberculosis, which has never failed any doctor yet, is willpower" (Igor' Smirnov, *Psikhodiakhronologika*, 256).

172. Ibid.

173. M. Keith Booker and Dubravka Juraga, *Bakhtin, Stalin, and Modern Russian Fiction: Carnival, Dialogism, and History* (Westport, CT: Greenwood Press, 1995), 91.

174. Cynthia A. Ruder, *Making History for Stalin*, 83.

175. Aleksandr Zholkovskii, *Mikhail Zoshchenko: poetika nedoveriia*, 238.

176. Katerina Clark, *The Soviet Novel*, 178.

177. Igor' Smirnov, *Psikhodiakhronologika*, 253.

178. See Mikhail Zoshchenko, *Sobranie soch.*, vol. 3, 78.

179. This is not the same thing as a polemic with Socialist Realism, as M. Keith Booker and Dubravka Juraga suggest (*Bakhtin, Stalin, and Modern Russian Fiction*, 91).

180. Here I agree with Linda Hart Scatton, who notes (*Mikhail Zoshchenko: Evolution of a Writer*, 179) that while Zoshchenko may "satirize the personal weakness of professor Volosatov for the attractive but worthless Tulya, . . . he is very serious when he has Volosatov utter with difficulty, upon partially recovering from his stroke."

181. Gregory Carleton, *The Politics of Reception*, 155.

182. Linda Hart Scatton, *Mikhail Zoshcheko: Evolution of a Writer*, 211.

183. Thus Gregory Carleton analyzes Zoshchenko's near-fantatical will to control the interpretation of his text—at the expense of the material to be interpreted (Gregory Carleton, *The Politics of Reception*, 152). Likewise, Rachel May emphasizes the extent to which *Before Sunrise* represents an exercise in violent self-censorship. Here, the critic suggests, Stalinist society's totalizing censorship of reality is reproduced on the narrative level as a catastrophic split between Zoshchenko's richly suggestive stories and the narrator-analysand's impoverished attempts to make sense of them (Rachel May, "Superego as Literary Subtext," 121).

184. Aleksandr Zholkovskii, *Mikhail Zoshchenko: poetika nedoveriia*, 187.

185. Richard B. Grose, "Zoshchenko and Nietzsche's Philosophy: Lessons in Misogyny, Sex and Self-Overcoming," *Russian Review* 54 (July 1995): 354.

186. See Mikhail Zoshchenko, *Sobranie soch.*, vol. 3, 624.

187. Boris Groys, *Utopiia i obmen*, 44–45.

188. Thus Zoshchenko overlooks the fairly obvious implications of the oft-repeated situation in which his (or other people's) love affairs with other women threaten to bring on retribution at the hands of an angry older man. Here the "punishing hand"

would seem to be a reflection of the father's hand that punishes the child for his desires toward the mother. Yet Zoshchenko treats it as a generalized version of the mother's hand, which punishes the child by weaning it from the breast (see *Sobranie soch.*, vol. 3, 614–15).

189. Jochen Hellbeck, "Stalin-era Autobiographical Texts," 352.

190. Aleksandr Zholkovskii, *Mikhail Zoshchenko: poetika nedoveriia*, 129.

191. Ibid., 82.

192. For a discussion of the similarities between *Before Sunrise* and the works mentioned above see Irene Masing-Delic, "Biology," 92.

193. It should be noted that Zoshchenko's grandfather is no less of a stern, unforgiving, and "motionless" authority figure; one, moreover, who attempts to negate the very existence of the young Zoshchenko: "A stern tall person arrived. . . . And I was even more surprised that we have a grandfather who was dissatisfied by the fact that mom has children, among whom I am one. . . . He sits in the chair and doesn't do anything. He looks motionlessly at the wall and smokes a long pipe" (*Sobranie soch.*, vol. 3, 543).

194. Likewise, in the previous vignette entitled "Yes, He's Dead," the young Zoshchenko leaves the room where his dead father is lying.

195. See Irene Masing-Delic, *Abolishing Death: A Salvation Myth of Twentieth Century Russian Literature* (Stanford: Stanford University Press, 1992), 87.

196. In this sense, I disagree with Masing-Delic, who sees Zoshchenko's rationalist/enlightenment philosophy as a means of conquering death by making oneself "ready" for it, by consciously accepting it ("Biology," 90). Rather, I would argue, Zoshchenko's idea in such works as *Youth Restored* or *Before Sunrise* concerns more the literal overcoming of the phenomenon of death.

197. The Oedipal dimensions of this same scenario are played out in a vignette entitled "At the Gate." Here the young Zoshchenko is temporarily separated from his mother, who goes to town. When she returns she is wearing a suggestive boa (the same boa that in an earlier vignette entitled "Mom is Crying" would make her more attractive to her husband). Perceiving his mother's sexuality as a threat to his own bid for her attention, the boy once again envisions a scenario in which he (rather than his father) would be the authority figure and would thus be in a position to right the injustices of the adult world—in this case, the mother's sexual attraction to the father: "I don't like it when mom dresses that way. . . . I'll grow up and ask her not to dress that way" (*Sobranie soch.*, vol. 3, 540).

198. Zholkovskii explains this paradox by remarking (*Mikhail Zoshchenko: poetika nedoveriia*, 124) that for Zoshchenko achieving independence—that is, taking matters into one's own hands—brings with it not only greater responsibility but greater vulnerability.

199. Likewise, in those instances where such a conflict is not at hand the young Zoshchenko nevertheless reaches the conclusion—as in the vignette entitled "So Simple"—that the world is somehow disappointingly, "unscientifically" organized: "I jerk the right rein and, suddenly, as if in a fairy tale, the horse runs to the right. But for some reason I am distressed, irritated. That simple. I thought it was much more

difficult to steer the horse. I thought that there was a whole science here, which had to be studied for years. But it's just nonsense" (*Sobranie soch.*, vol. 3, 531) (note that the word Zoshchenko uses, "nonsense," is the same as that used by various authority figures to describe Zoshchenko's writing).

200. Note that in the given instance the conflict is defused by sharing—a solution that the young Zoshchenko also uses to defuse a conflict with his father over a pudding in the vignette entitled "I'm Not Guilty." As Masing-Delic remarks, here the "irrational judgement 'from above' is overcome by the child's rational suggestion to share a pudding, the object of strife between father and son" ("Biology," 83).

201. Ibid., 53.

202. Irene Masing-Delic, "Gorky's Tutorship," 57.

203. Ibid., 53.

204. See Rachel May, "Superego as Literary Subtext," 120. See also Gregory Carleton, *The Politics of Reception*, 146–47.

205. Eric Naiman, "Diskurs, obrashchennyi v plot'," 630.

206. Ibid.

207. Jochen Hellbeck, "Writing the Self," 78.

208. As Zholkovskii notes (*Mikhail Zoshchenko: poetika nedoveriia*, 236): "If food embodies life, then, its disruption of its processes naturally serves as a sign of death. When Zoshchenko requires an image of existential prostration in the spirit of Pushkin's 'Like a corpse in the desert I lay,' he shifts it into the stomach: 'With a torn belly I rolled in my bed.'"

209. As I have tried to show, this particular fantasy is one that repeats itself, as the following episode (already discussed) in Zoshchenko's *povest' Mishel' Siniagin* demonstrates. Here, too, the image of losing one's innards and growing new organs is present (*Sobranie soch.*, vol. 2, 212): "It's not entirely clear whether this is true, but the author knows a certain girl who finished stenography courses last year who told him that in Africa there supposedly exist animals, like lizards, who when attacked by a larger creature eject part of their intestines and run away, in order to collapse in a safe place and lie in the sun until new organs grow."

210. Rainer Grübel, "Gabe, Aufgabe, Selbstaufgabe: Dicther-Tod als Opferhabitus," in *Welt Hinter Dem Spiegel: Zum Status des Autors in der russischen Literatur der 1920 bis 1950er Jahre*, ed. Klaus Städtke (Berlin: Akademie Verlag, 1998), 177.

211. Ibid. Smirnov also comments on the large number of Stalinist novels containing the word "light" (*Psikhodiakhronologika*, 283n579).

212. As Zolotonosov notes, the theme of the "person at his post" was one of the most popular motifs of the Stalinist '30s and was executed in a number of different media (*Slovo i telo*, 649). Cf. Zoshchenko's short story "Anna around the Neck," in which the author's alter ego is precisely a "person at his post."

213. Mikhail Zoshchenko, *Sobranie soch.*, vol. 3, 625, 689.

214. As G. N. Iakovleva notes ("Mifologiia preobrazheniia landshafta strany v sovetskoi kul'ture 1930-kh—nachala 1950-kh godov," *Sovetskoe iskusstvoznanie*, vyp. 27 [1990], 205), Stalin was often compared to the sun, no doubt underscoring his Apollinian aspect.

215. Tatiana Kadash, "Gogol' v tvorcheskoi refleksii Zoshchenko," 286.
216. Ibid.
217. Ibid., 287.
218. Gregory Carleton, *The Politics of Reception*, 155.
219. Ibid.
220. Ibid.

Chapter Three

Lev Kassil': The Soccer Match as Stalinist Ritual[1]

Zoshchenko's attempts to reform himself in such prominent works of the 1930s as *Youth Restored* or *Before Sunrise*—to reengineer the artist's ailing body and soul so as to emerge in the guise of a socialist "superwriter"—is in many ways emblematic of the period. As one contemporary scholar notes, Stalinist culture's relationship to suffering was ambivalent through and through. On the one hand, physical pain is shown to be central to the formation of a (masochistic) Stalinist self. On the other, the desire to negate the very phenomenon of suffering occupies a prominent place in the culture's imagination.[2] Similarly, much of contemporary scholarship has focused on the extent to which the literature of the Stalin period renounced the earlier pathos of Spartan collectivism in favor of a large-scale revalorization of private life. As surely as writers like Andrei Platonov, whose works portrayed the agony inherent in socialism's attempts to restructure reality, were forcibly resettled beyond the pale of Soviet literature, those authors more adept at embodying Stalinism's "optimistic tragedy" quickly saw their own stars rise. To a large extent, this shift coincides with sea changes at work in the culture at large. In contrast to the carefully cultivated asceticism of much of the previous decade, the Stalinist 1930s were distinguished by a new cult of wealth, by ubiquitous portrayals of the "unprecedented prosperity of the Soviet land."[3] Alongside the rhetoric of suffering and sacrifice, Stalinism praised the pleasures of everyday life. To be sure, the idea of tragic heroism survives in the proliferation of episodes that take up the notion of redemptive suffering, mutilation, or self-sacrifice. Yet at the same time the public sphere is replete with images of happiness, wealth, and prosperity, celebrating food, comfort, and even the traditional family ritual of New Year's.[4] Thus Korchagin's mortification of the flesh cohabits comfortably with the fleshiness of a Lyubov'

153

Orlova. The official cultivation of a new "leisure culture" is evident in every-thing from the proliferation of popular Hollywood-style Soviet musicals such as *Happy-Go-Lucky Guys* (1934), *Circus* (1936), *Volga-Volga* (1938), and *Radiant Path* (1940) to the fashion for dancing and dance classes.[5] Even the oft-maligned sphere of sexuality witnessed a rebirth, shifting from the earlier era of "revolutionary anorexia" to celebrations of fertility, and family.[6] And in the arts, as well, there is an equally ambitious rehabilitation and appropri-ation of the "great tradition of Russian culture." Thus in almost every way the 1930s mark a return to the traditional—what Sheila Fitzpatrick describes as a shift from a centrifugal model of culture to a centripetal one, from periphery to center.[7]

Caught between the utopia-building pathos of the past and the necessity of representing the present as a reified variant of the ideal future ("We were born to make fairy tales come true"),[8] many authors chose a path of ambivalent con-formity. In the case of Platonov, the shift from portraying (male) technical utopias or dystopias during the 1920s toward a distinct bias in favor of the (fe-male) body and biology echoes Stalinism's revalorization of private life.[9] In the work of Pasternak, Akhmatova, and Zoshchenko, as well, one discovers a new orientation toward "grassroots folksiness," as one contemporary critic puts it—an attempt to exchange deadly alienation for a sense of inclusion within the greater family of Stalinism.[10] Yet for all these authors the sense of inclusion is conditional, tempered by a latent inability or unwillingness to re-construct oneself completely. This is made manifest, among others, in the un-usual violence that invariably accompanies their attempts at self-reform. Thus even the comformist writer Vasily Azhaev, whose 1948 novel *Far From Moscow* portrays the pathos of socialist construction in glowingly positive terms, alludes to the high cost of "reconstruction" by situating the action of the work in the fictional "Adun" as opposed to the real-life "Amur."[11] Similarly, in a feuilleton published by Zoshchenko in 1935 entitled "The Fairy-Tale Life," the ideologically convalescent author acknowledges that reordering the body (politic) in accordance with the utopian ideal of complete mechanization can perhaps be achieved only by destroying the very body itself.[12]

By contrast, the work of such lesser contemporaries as Lev Kassil' is most interesting precisely for its remarkable ability to reconcile those contradictions that for more prominent authors remained unresolved. Curtailing the slack left by such overtly ambivalent authors as Isaac Babel, Kassil''s *The Goalkeeper of the Republic* (*Vratar' Respubliki*, 1939) seeks to merge the image of the (Apollinian) Jewish intellectual with the (Dionysian) Russian hero by situat-ing both within the extended Stalinist family of the 1930s. No less than the cul-ture's most visible heroes—whose function according to Katerina Clark lay in mediating various kinds of cultural oppositions such as highbrow versus lowbrow culture, or agitation versus affirmation of the status quo[13]—Stalin-era writers had to strike a delicate balance between criticism and praise. Platonov's famous "Pushkin is Our Comrade" (1937) provides a case in point. In it the author merges the opposed images of Peter the Great and Evgenii (of "The Bronze Horseman") in order to bring about a rapprochement between the lofty heights of state power and the "anarchic" individual. Likewise, in *Youth Restored* and *Before Sunrise*, Zoshchenko stresses the importance of resolving contradiction as a prelude to achieving physical and ideological health. This same mechanism is taken to its logical conclusion in Kassil''s *Goalkeeper of the Republic*. Prizing synthesis over disjuncture, the author effectively resolves the dilemma (posed by Isaac Babel's *Red Cavalry*) of the Jewish intellectual who attempts unsuccessfully to remake himself in order to gain admittance to the virile Russian collective. Yet unlike Babel's Lyutov, whose acceptance *by* and *of* the Cossack clan is never complete,[14] Kassil''s novel envisions a scenario in which such a merger is not only possible but desirable. Thus the author employs Stalinist myth as a means of achieving that which had earlier only been the subject of theoretical speculation.[15]

Known primarily as an author of books for children, Lev Kassil''s works portray the life of model individuals representing various walks of Soviet life. Although he began his career as a writer by working closely with Mayakovsky (in 1928 he even published a short sketch in *Novyi Lef* followed by excerpts from *Conduit*), Kassil' quickly became known as an author of children's literature. His autobiographical novels *Conduit* (1929) and *Shvambraniia* (1931) paint a grim picture of the tsarist school system as seen through the eyes of a child, while at the same time depicting the successes of the first Soviet vocational schools. Kassil' is also noteworthy as one of the few Jewish authors to portray pogroms in Russia after the revolution.[16] During much of the 1930s, Kassil' worked as a journalist, publishing sketches and feuilletons on various topics ranging from the construction of the Moscow metro to the heroism of such Stalin-era celebrities as Konstantin Tsiolkovskii, Valerii Chkalov, and others.

It was not until 1939 that Kassil' published his first nonautobiographical work. This was *Goalkeeper of the Republic*, composed between 1932 and 1937 and published by Sovetskii pisatel' in 1939. *The Goalkeeper of the Republic* can be placed alongside such other well-known works for children as Veniamin Kaverin's *The Two Captains* (1933–1934) or Arkady Gaidar's *The Fate of the Drummer* (1937–1938), the latter of which portrays a young boy's coming-of-age as coinciding with the killing of two imperialist spies. Likewise, Kassil''s *Goalkeeper* uses the seemingly innocuous genre of the adolescent adventure novel to tell an edifying tale of lifelong friendship as a thinly veiled allegory of Stalinist family values. The novel follows two childhood friends from their rivalry and friendship early in the years before the revolution through their separation during the stormy days of October up until their reunion sometime during the mid-to-late '30s. The first of the two friends is Evgenii Karasik, a slender-bodied journalist who is assigned to chronicle the heroic feats of a speedboat-racing, soccer-playing commune named Gidraer, which he later joins. Karasik functions throughout the novel as the "conscious" mentor or "father" figure for the novel's other protagonist, Anton Kandidov—an enormous, "spontaneous," *bogatyr'*-like figure who joins the Gidraer commune at Karasik's behest and then goes on to become the most famous goalkeeper in the Soviet Union and even Europe. The central conflict of the novel revolves around Kandidov's decision to leave the devoted commune/soccer team to take up a more prestigious position with the rival Magneto team on the eve of their foreign tour. Yielding to the natural expansivenes of his nature and an attendant desire for fame, Kandidov goes abroad and is quickly corrupted by new friends and foreign influences. Upon returning from Europe, he encounters his former comrades again—this time on the soccer field—where the Magneto team loses to Gidraer because of its lack of cohesion and, most importantly, because of Kandidov's rashly individualistic decision to leave his goalposts at a decisive moment in the game. Having lost both his reputation as an unbeaten or "dry" goalkeeper and his friends, Kandidov goes through a period of crisis and soul-searching, and after almost killing himself (he inadvertently leaves the gas stove on in his apartment), he is ultimately reunited with his best friend Karasik as well as with the members of the Gidraer commune.

Like many of the works written during this period, *Goalkeeper of the Republic* reflects a broader cultural preoccupation with borders. In particular, Kassil''s novel fuses the perceived need to transcend the boundaries of one's immediate biological family (and, indeed, of biology as such) with a ritualist reaffirming of the sacred borders that guard the Stalinist community against its imagined enemies from within and a genuine threat from without. The apparent contradiction between resurgent traditionalism and an actively anti-biological posture is—as I have tried to demonstrate elsewhere—characteristic of Stalinist culture's well-documented eclecticism. Indeed, it underscores the reality of competing metaphors that govern the twin realms of public consciousness and discourse during the period. As Mikhail Vaiskopf notes, Stalinist civilization employed a wealth of metaphors taken from the biological and agrarian realms, while at the same time continuing to profess the industrial/technocratic creed of the early revolutionary years.[17] It is this very syncreticism that produces the "mixed metaphor" of the great Stalinist family, a collective that at once affirms and transcends the traditional boundaries of the nuclear family. Yet ultimately one's primary allegiance was due to the state, within which biological families served as a mere stepping-stone on the path to greater community. Likewise, the pathos of reforging so prominent throughout the '30s presupposes not merely the transformation of the individual but his or her inclusion in the "broader Soviet family" at the expense of one's primary milieu.[18] Kassil''s *Goalkeeper* is no exception. Because of its focus on an ethnic minority (Karasik is Jewish), the novel might well be compared to Grigorii Aleksandrov's popular 1936 musical *Circus*. This film juxtaposes the myth of an all-inclusive Stalinist family (a black American child is accepted into an extended Soviet family that includes Russians, Ukrainians, Armenians, Jews, and others) against the exclusionary "antimyth" of the racially pure, Aryan clan projected by Nazi ideology. A somewhat more subtle creature, Kassil''s *Goalkeeper* nevertheless scrupulously reenacts the principle of dialectical synthesis that underwrote much of Stalinist culture's ideological pathos. Thus the extended family in *Goalkeeper* brings together the *bogatyr'*-like contemporary hero (most often an aviator, polar explorer, border guard, or Stakhanovite distinguished by "daring, defiance and high spirits")[19] with the intellectual outsider. Speaking more broadly, one might speculate that the imagery of Kassil''s novel, by attempting to fuse Jewish abstraction with Russian spontaneity or *stikhiinost'*, suggests a kind of Stalinist analogue to the Nazi myth of the Germanic superman.

The unlikely friendship between the Russian *bogatyr'* Kandidov and his Jewish mentor Karasik underscores one of the commonplaces of Stalinist mythology. Applicable to virtually any imaginable scenario, the Socialist Realist topos of pairing excessive sons with restraining father figures was sufficiently protean that it "could be translated, *mutatis mutandis*, into numerous lesser situations, in which any authoritative figure could play 'father' to a subordinate or assume some other paternalistic role."[20] This reflects, as Katerina Clark remarks, the Marxist-Leninist narrative of history, according to which both individual and society are located on a continuum that spans human development from its "spontaneous" beginnings to the triumphant attainment of complete knowledge at the pinnacle of history. Thus in the typical Socialist Realist text the hero's ascent to transcendent consciousness necessarily passes through the trauma of transgression as she or he moves from ignorance to sublime gnosis. Likewise, in Kassil''s *Goalkeeper of the Republic* the efforts of the Gidraer collective (as well as that of the parabolic narrative as a whole) are directed almost entirely at bringing a wayward and misguided Kandidov back into the fold of Stalinism's Great Family.

Kassil''s novel deviates only marginally from this paradigm by portraying the mentor himself as an outsider needful of being integrated into the commune. In other words, Karasik as Jewish intellectual is a "prodigal son" whose crime consists not only in having abandoned the collective but in having never belonged in the first place. In "Socialism without Shores," Katerina

Clark points out that the consciousness/spontaneity (or father versus son) dichotomy characteristic of most if not all Socialist Realist novels occurs not as
an immobile set of character functions but as a broad continuum, along which
protagonists are situated according to their relative degree of familial and political maturity vis-à-vis other characters and in keeping with the novel's
overall scope. Thus, in a work about children (or for children) an older, more
experienced or responsible boy who plays "father" to his younger friend(s)
may be accorded the same familial status as a party official in a more ambitious work.[21] In *Goalkeeper of the Republic* the mentor figure is neither a
stern party official nor a wise old man—he is a mere journalist—yet relative
to his enthusiastic but undisciplined counterpart he comfortably takes up the
role of the reproving father.

In his book *Parting with Narcissus: Experiments in Funeral Rhetoric*,
Aleksandr Gol'dshtein characterizes Kassil''s novel as a failed or "dystopian"
variant of Plato's *Republic* projected onto a contemporary (Stalinist) setting.
Failed, because while Kandidov represents a contemporary incarnation of
Plato's caste of guardians and Karasik a version of the philosopher king, the
desired fusion of strength and wisdom ultimately fails to materialize within
the repressive conditions of Stalinist totalitarianism.[22] A less recherché ex-
planation of the novel's ideological and mythological underpinnings (its
abundant classical references included) lies within the boundaries of Stalinist
culture itself, for much of Kassil''s *Goalkeeper* reads like a laundry list of
ideas, motifs, and myths typical for the period. Neither a carefully crafted cri-
tique of Stalinist utopianism nor a tale of disaffected heroes, Kassil''s largely
conformist novel appears to function like many of its Socialist Realist peers
as a "politicized variant of the *Bildungsroman*," one in which "the hero
achieves greater harmony both within himself and in relation to his society."[23]
Meanwhile, the protagonists' discomfort with their respective roles can easily be explained by recalling the literary and cultural stereotypes of the time.
Indeed, the novel as a whole appears much more concerned with producing a
discourse of control or containment than with spinning a cautionary tale about
the perils of Stalinism. Seduced by the temptation of inclusion in the transbiological family of the multiethnic Soviet Union, Kassil''s novel presents the
reader with an unabashedly conformist tale of loss and reintegration, of transgression and redemption. Thus those who are excluded from the collective
(either after having drifted away from it or by virtue of their "flawed" biological or ethnic inheritance) will ultimately be reincorporated into an all-
encompassing and benevolent body social.

The importance of containment as one of the central motifs of Kassil''s
Goalkeeper of the Republic is rivalled only by the novel's repeated allusions
to the natural (indeed even necessary) transgressiveness of Stalinist subjec-

tivity. In this *Goalkeeper* mirrors the conceptual switchbacks of Stalinist ideology as a whole. Here carnival excess, with its customary disregard for
norms and the status quo, goes hand in hand with a near pathological interest
in preserving and reaffirming the sanctity of various boundaries. Thus carni-
vals along with the very phenomenon of "carnival" became fashionable precisely during the mid-to-late 1930s (as part of Moscow's revamped image of
itself as a boisterous empire capital), existing in stark counterpoint to the reality of total surveillance and control that enveloped everyday life.[24] The
same marriage of polar opposites (i.e., of "spontaneousness" and "consciousness") governs the relationship between the two protagonists in Kassil''s
Goalkeeper. Thus Kandidov is a close cousin to the archetypal Stalinist
hero—the pilot. Brimming with energy, will, and determination, he is a *bogatyr'* poised to carry out heroic feats. Yet like these same fliers, he is sorely
lacking in discipline and self-control.[25] Both anarchical and uncontained, the
Russian hero is a picture-perfect illustration of Freud's claim that Russians
are "like water that fills any vessel but does not preserve the form of any one
of them."[26] Thus it is no accident that Anton Kandidov is associated with the
Volga river region. For the hero's Volga roots recall the archetypal image of
water as symbolizing an originary or chaotic state of being common to most
mythologies, including that of Stalinism.[27] At the same time, water proves
central to the culture's perception of itself as a powerhouse of vibrancy and
fertility. "Stalin's Moscow," writes Papernyi, was "saved by the Volga waters
from drying up, embellished with grandiose embankments, powerful foun-
tains, park reservoirs and boat docks," and was to become not Jerusalem or
Alexandria but Palmira.[28] Finally, with its qualities of breadth and freedom
the Volga came to symbolize the vast expanse of the country as a whole, as
attested to by such Stalin-era hit songs as "Song of the Motherland."[29]

Alongside the abundance of water imagery there is a discernable warming
trend within Stalinist culture, one which is proportional to the ideological
fervor of its inhabitants. Kassil''s conflicted protagonist echoes this split. He
is at once the impetuous or "spontaneous" son, as well as the future "emblem
of consciousness"—the fiery goalkeeper and protector of the republic who
will emerge triumphant at the end of the novel.[30] One can imagine that *Goalkeeper's* preoccupation with rehabilitating the "watery" Kandidov is not entirely fortuitous, for in 1937 Kassil' produced a brochure detailing the virtues
of the newly constructed Moscow-Volga Canal. Its practical benefits aside,
the Moscow-Volga canal was important as a an emblem of the culture's desire to reclaim the natural for the purposes of Bolshevik culture and civilization. In this regard, it was of a piece with the earlier metro project, which
Kaganovich had once described as "the twin brother" of the canal. Moreover, in both cases the technical and the anthropological dimensions of the

project are closely connected. By making Kandidov the emblem of the newly reconstructed socialist metropolis Kassil' seems to suggest that the project of reclamation concerns not only the city's waterways but its human inhabitants, as well.

To the extent that Stalinism's "struggle with the elements" presupposed an analogous reshaping of human nature, Kandidov's struggle in the novel is as much a contest to contain the "elemental" within himself as it is to harness nature per se. For this reason, *Goalkeeper* abounds in such juxtapositions as water versus fire, air/water/gas versus the willpower that restricts it, unbridled enthusiasm versus rational restraint, and the like. And if the hero's tagname (a clear allusion to Voltaire's simpleminded Candide) is any indication, Anton must do battle, first and foremost, with the treachery and chaos hidden in the depths of his own unreconstructed nature. Thus in addition to the larger-than-life qualities that recommend him as a cultural hero, Kandidov boasts a clear negative side, which manifests itself in the hero's perennial inclination to wander. At one point early in the novel Anton is shown walking along the banks of the Volga river parallel to a band of gypsies. The picturesque beauty of their nomadic lifestyle seduces Kandidov, leading him to describe his affinity for freedom and open spaces to a disapproving Karasik: "Maybe I'm a wanderer at heart myself, my father's grandfather wandered with the gypsies—maybe he found a sweetheart there or something—and so he went astray. He even took a new name. That's how we got our amazing last name."[31]

Kandidov's programmatically "split personality" first surfaces in a chapter entitled "Salvation on the Waters." Here the future hero saves a provincial Volga town from the effects of a flood of near Biblical proportions by organizing a soccer game, after which he mobilizes the entire populace to shore up the local dam. Despite what is ultimately a happy ending, however, Kassil''s narrative stresses precisely the element of lingering chaos that inheres in the very center of the cultural city. Extrapolating from this image, the reader invariably draws a parallel with the Stalinist subject, who, like the waterlogged landscape above, is forever at pains to master the hostile chaos within: "The river was besieging the town. Yet in the besieged town itself an act of great treachery was unearthed. The water that had hidden underground reared its head and moved to close ranks with the outside waters" (455). If we assume that Stalinist subjectivity represents the ultimate "work in progress"—that is, an ongoing project of self-purification and perfection—Kandidov's saving of the city from the flood waters symbolizes the first stage of his rehabilitation. Later this task will be taken up by his Jewish mentor, Evgenii Karasik. But for the moment the threat from the encroaching Volga waters forces Anton himself to curtail his own errant nature—to subdue the rebellious Sten'ka

Razin inside in order to save the city: "In moments like these he completely forgot about Sten'ka Razin, about whom he always thought when he rode the flat-bottomed boats carrying watermelons down the Volga" (128).

Throughout the 1930s the ritualized soccer match provided a convenient and compelling arena for the reforging pathos of the culture at large. In this sense, it was only one of several possible avenues of self-expression for Stalinism's narrative of overcoming nature. Just as the then-popular "Arctic myth metaphorically oriented the Soviet Union's perceptions of itself and the world around it,"[32] so, too, the soccer match served as a microcosm of society's struggles, encouraging the body social to continuously renew itself, while doing battle with its many enemies—both imagined and real. And it is precisely a soccer match that during the first part of *Goalkeeper* allows the citizens of the provincial town to shore themselves up (both literally and figuratively) against the encroaching Volga waters. Not accidentally, the soccer field where Kandidov organizes the game is located atop a dike. At the conclusion of the game the chairman of the Executive Committee reminds the spectators that just as Kandidov kept his goalposts "dry," so, too, in the Soviet Union each person must act as the goalkeeper of her or his city. In other words, every citizen must act to protect and reaffirm the boundaries of the socialist polis. This idea is taken to its logical conclusion at the end of the novel, where a now fully reformed Kandidov stands in front of his goalposts (*vorota* means both "goalposts" and "gate") that symbolically guard St. Basil's Cathedral and with it the whole of the Soviet land.

This image is the result of careful calculation. Stalinist culture understood the importance of endowing its heroes and monuments with a quasi-sacral aura. For instance, the marble that had been recovered in 1934 from the destroyed Christ the Savior Cathedral was—I would argue—not accidentally used to produce facading for the Moscow metro.[33] Likewise, Kassil''s Gidraer commune is intentionally located in the former Nikola-On–the-Island church.[34] Just as important, Anton Kandidov's rehabilitation toward the end of the novel is clearly linked to his status as a member of the Russian Orthodox community (as opposed to the Catholic West). Earlier in the work, during a trip to Rome, Kandidov is offered a position as the goalkeeper for the soccer team of the Vatican. The post would make him the earthly equivalent of St. Peter, who guards the gates to heaven, according to Christian tradition. The corrupt Vatican representative tries to entice Kandidov with money and by arguing that playing for a Catholic team should not present an obstacle to a Soviet citizen, since all Soviets are atheists. Of course, Anton indignantly refuses the offer. Yet it is only at the end of the work that Kandidov realizes (if only subconsciously) the danger implicit in straying from the "Russian church"—that is, from his ethnic and

ideological community. In a nightmare the same St. Peter tries to catch the
wayward goalkeeper in a net, just as the Vatican had tried to seduce him
away from the visiting Soviet team. Notably, Kandidov's reinstatement in
the commune at the end of *Goalkeeper of the Republic* is rife with unmistakable religious symbolism. Having rejoined his collective and thus symbolically returned to the fold of the Gidraer-cum-Orthodox Church, Kandidov ends the novel by playing a soccer match and manning the goalposts in
front of St. Basil's Cathedral. In this we see not only the rehabilitation of
the errant goalkeeper, but—more importantly—the ascendancy of Moscow
as the Third (socialist) Rome. By rejecting the corrupt Catholic West and
embracing Orthodoxy, the spirited Russian soccer player embodies not only
his personal choice but a larger historical reality. For it is now Moscow that
has replaced Rome in its aspiration to unite humankind within a single family. This is reflected, as one contemporary critic notes, in the wealth of contemporary portrayals of socialist Moscow as home to every inhabitant of the
vast country.[35] By the same token, it is Moscow that represents the utopian
city of the future, not the spiritually decrepit Rome.

The polar opposite of Kandidov is Evgenii Karasik—a kind of Stalinist
Pangloss to his Candide. In keeping with the well-documented tendency
within Socialist Realism to pair elemental sons with "conscious" father figures,[36] Karasik emerges as the perfect embodiment of the trope of containment, combining self-control with the Jew's proverbial capacity for abstract,
rational thought.[37] On still another level, Karasik might be seen as a reflection
of that part of Soviet culture which in its desire to reform human nature sought
to regulate even the murky depths of the unconscious (i.e., the watery Kandidov).[38] As a journalist and someone who is intimately familiar with the power
of the Word to shape the natural, he represents the wayward goalkeeper's antipode. Still, to the extent that Karasik is himself connected to water (his name
means "little carp" in Russian), he too must struggle to transcend the short-
comings of the natural. Thus the physically underdeveloped Jew and counterpoint to the charismatic Kandidov serves as a reminder of the limitations and
dangers of unrepentant biology. In this sense, it might well be said that Kassil''s novel was at least partially conceived as a means of reinscribing the intellectual into the Stalinist discourse of life-centeredness,[39] which in turn resembles the vitalist rhetoric of Nazism.[40] At the same time, it cannot be
overlooked that Karasik perfectly embodies Stalinist culture's masochistic
urge to bind and delimit the very biology it appears otherwise to praise.[41] And
it is this same mechanism that underwrites Zoshchenko's attempts in such
works as *Youth Restored* and *Before Sunrise* to neutralize the excesses of the
body through a progressive mechanization of human psychophysiology. Consider the following conversation, in which Karasik rejects what the wayward

Kandidov sees as the pull of the elements, while condemning Blok's famous response to the sinking of the Titanic ("The ocean is alive") as an affront to humanity.[42] For Karasik nature is a stepping-stone, not a goal in itself. His fascination is not with the slow-moving Titanic but with high-speed boats that seem to defy the law of gravity itself (in one instance, the narrator describes the Gidraer boat as having "wide, prostrated wings made of foam and spray"). And while speaking with a certain Professor Tokartsev, Karasik describes speed boats as a final and decisive challenge to the ancient reign of nature: "The speed boat, which finds support in its own speed, bearing within itself the principle of intensive influence on its environment, is closer to us in spirit than the extensive round boat held up by Archimedes's ancient formula and that stands in an inert relationship to the water."[43] Karasik's fascination with gravity-defying speedboats—that is, boats that negate their relationship to water—is symptomatic of the Jew's desire to transcend biology in order to gain access to the transbiological family of Stalinism. In addition, it mirrors other cultural fetishes. Among these is the image of the pilot, who throughout the period embodied critical aspects of the revolutionary project, such as the conquest of nature and the constitution of a new, ideal man.[44]

In a certain sense, Evgenii Karasik becomes that ideal man. It has been suggested that Stalinism minimizes or even negates the significance of various specialized or professional discourses, privileging instead the language of literature as a kind of all-encompassing superdiscourse.[45] As a journalist Karasik speaks to this core aspiration. Capable of wielding language in its most universal sense, he provides the perfect example of what might be called the Stalinist "antispecialist." In fields as disparate as filmmaking and industrial production, technicians were roundly rebuked for their "'wingless positivist' way of thinking," giving birth to a movement that advocated the "training of new cadres unburdened by any knowledge of 'old technical norms.'"[46] Kassil' provides an exemplary model of this in his 1935 *Miracle beneath Moscow*, where the Moscow party boss and head of the metro project L. M. Kaganovich proves able to solve the most complicated engineering problems precisely because of his *ideological* approach to technology.[47] Karasik, too, is representative of the new generation of Stalinist cadres. The author makes this clear in a conversation between Karasik and Professor Tokartsev, where the latter praises Karasik's nontechnical, philosophical understanding of technology: "And then, too, you approach technology in a philosophical manner, lucidly, historically."[48] In a related scene, during a conversation with a lawyer named Lasmin, an enthusiastic Karasik characterizes jurisprudence as a dying profession. According to the journalist, lawyers are like buoys that are necessary only to guide heavy round ships but are a mere hindrance to the new generation of more maneuverable speedboats. Although he is criticized by the lawyer for being a "leftist," Karasik's point is well taken. Under Stalinism legal discourse, which represents only one of many moribund "secular" languages (biology, physiology, and so on) aimed at circumscribing the realm of the possible, will be rendered obsolete via a new brand of Stalinist voluntarism:

> "Legal advisors are a dying profession," Karasik announced to Lasmin. "It's like being a buoy-keeper: they put out signs, markers indicating the shallow spots in our laws." "But we need buoy-keepers, too." "Speed-boats don't need buoy-keepers. Only round, deep-water ships need them." "That's going too far," said the offended Lasmin. "Maybe . . ." "You're an extremist," said Lasmin, "but I've got both feet on the ground, and the inventory I took . . ." "Forget your jurischemistry—inventory, record, census, shmensus." (135)

Karasik's unconcealed disdain for legalistic mumbo jumbo underscores one of the most important facets of Stalinist mythology. This was its near mystical faith in the power of the Word. Whether spoken or written, the word was prized not for its mimetic potential but for its ability to rewrite the very narrative of being. Yet in order for language to attain this lofty end it had to rise synergistically above its fledgling components. Only in the hands of a genuine "engineer of human souls" could it become more than a cold catalogue of isolated words, styles, and discursive techniques, recovering something of the Biblical sense of language as primordial logos. The fragment above mirrors this, deriding the lawyer's hopeless reliance on written norms as a betrayal of the Word's mystical calling. Thus the words that are derived from the verb "to write" (*pisat'*) are dismissed as legalistic alchemy ("jurischemistry")—as an attempt to confine the power of the word within the frozen boundaries of the letter. Here Lasmin's legalese is analogous to the deadening formalism that supposedly prevented many nonconformist artists/writers/musicians of the period from being able to view the world in all of its "vital totality and multifacetedness"—as "something living, an organic whole, impossible to dissect."[49] As unusual as it might seem, the most compelling example of the ideologically and artistically robust practitioner of the word (other than Stalin) is none other than Pushkin. And just as the figure of Pushkin served as the prototype for a new species of socialist Superbeing, so, too, the poet's inspired Word becomes an icon of Stalinism's epic narrative.[50] Thus it is no surprise that the young Karasik identifies himself with Pushkin once he takes up journalism and begins to write professionally. In an obvious nod to the official ideology's canonization of the nineteenth-century poet as a superman and a model Socialist Realist writer *avant la lettre*, Karasik alludes to his writerly ambitions using the famous Pushkinian dictum—"to kindle the hearts of men with the Word."[51] Likewise, the narrator remarks that as Karasik matures professionally, his writing becomes increasingly simple. Here again one hears more than a faint echo of the official campaign against formalism in the arts. As Mikhail Iampol'skii notes, the Socialist Realist writer could achieve mastery only by abandoning the enclosure of the studio and being "violently forced into the midst of seething life." Moving beyond the confines of traditional artistic form and practice, the author reemerges in the guise of "some kind of supersensory apparatus, capable of perceiving the world in all its vital totality and multifacetedness."[52] On a somewhat more sinister note, in his famous essays on language from 1934 Gorky remarks that frivolous linguistic play represents the first step toward ideological deviance.[53] Not surprisingly, Kassil''s Karasik becomes Pushkin-like precisely by abandoning the playful word games that had earlier preoccupied him in favor of a simpler, more robust style. And as if reminding the reader of the genuine danger of tolerating "loose lips," Kassil' has the mature Karasik curtail his friendship with the constantly punning Dimochka Shneis:

> From one day to the next he [Karasik] wrote more and more simply. The hunt for unusual images and stunning comparisons began to seem boring to him. . . . Now the the "word play," in which his former friend Dima was such a specialist, seemed tasteless and disgusting. Zhenia developed a taste for words. And words began to open up their entire meaning to him, fully and completely, without hiding anything.[54]

The writer's coming of age is accompanied by an obligatory sacrifice. Reflecting (if only symbolically) the masochistic ritual of self-mutilation that often parallels the Stalinist subject's entry into the larger community,[55] Karasik must paradoxically give up a part of himself in order to become whole. Thus Kassil' describes the journalist-writer's work—not accidentally, I would argue—in terms of cutting, shortening, and mutilating. Karasik reacts, for instance, with indignation to the fact that his sketches are "shortened and mutilated,"[56] yet he ultimately acknowledges the necessity of these painful procedures. In an still more telling example the young journalist notes of his freshly composed feuilleton that in wandering from one column to the next "it had to be cut to the bone" ["Надо было его резать с мясом"][57] Finally, even Karasik's name is shortened when he takes on the nom de plume of Evgenii Kar. Symptomatically, the strangely truncated moniker leaves no trace of Karasik's watery origins. Instead it suggests the Russian verb for "to punish" (*карать*). Not unlike Platonov or Zoshchenko, whose poignant evocations of Pushkin during this period invariably point up the high cost (in terms of physical suffering) of mastering the Word, Kassil''s Karasik achieves professional mastery by symbolically cutting himself off from his connection to the past.

Only then does he become "Pushkin-like," subsuming his now battered and exhausted body within the narrative of Stalinist vigilance:

> During these moments, when every joint sang and hummed in its own way from exhaustion, only now did Karasik feel that he possessed a small measure of responsibility for the peace and rest of the sleeping country. He was pleased to be on guard, that he was keeping vigil with the militiamen at their posts, who were freezing at the intersections.[58]

The word's importance as a fundamental structuring force in Stalinist mythology is made clear in the scene from *Goalkeeper* that describes Anton Kandidov's approach to the Stalinist capital. As the "first" and most important city in the land, Moscow is the mystical logos toward which the rest of the Stalinist landscape points. Beginning in 1933 the mythology of Moscow as the spiritual center of the new Soviet Union was actively cultivated in both poetry and prose, producing Moscow-centric works by numerous figures (including D. Bednyi, V. Kataev, S. Eisenstein, and others) and culminating in I. Shmelev's *The Year of Our Lord* (1927–1948), A. Platonov's *Happy Moscow* (1933–1936), and, finally, Bulgakov's *Master and Margarita* (1929–1940).[59] More than any other place 1930s Moscow posed as a testing ground for the Stalinist narrative of reforging and reconstruction. As the spiritual and ideological instigator behind this process, the Kremlin appeared to be nothing less than the center of the world. Triumphantly marked by Lenin's Mausoleum, which embodied socialism's victory over chaos and death, it was here that the fabled *axis mundi* lay.[60] For this reason literary and real-life heroes alike were drawn to it from every corner of the vast Soviet land.[61] Consider Grigory Alexandrov's popular 1936 musical *Volga-Volga*, whose heroes enter Moscow "as if it were Venice, sailing through wide canals on steamers, boats, skiffs, and yachts, and even by swimming."[62] Kassil''s larger-than-life Kandidov is no exception— save that he enters Moscow not by swimming but by rail. In his eyes the mythic stature of the capital is reflected in the very landscape that leads up to it. Here every village or town suggests an entry in a topological encyclopedia whose entries reveal a growing order of "presence" as one draws nearer to the "very capital itself." At the same time, the hero's movement towards the center prefigures the metamorphosis of the chaotic Volga dweller into a disciplined denizen of the Stalinist capital. Likewise, in Alexandrov's *Volga-Volga* one has the distinct impression that the newly constructed Moscow-Volga Canal models the metamorphosis of Dunya and her troupe of amateur musicians from the Volga into a disciplined musical ensemble that occurs at the conclusion of the film:

> The capital grew closer, as when one draws closer to a major article in an encyclopedia. First come the adjectives modifying the word, the derivations and

root-formations. Just imagine yourself leafing through the pages, looking for the word "England." English ailment, English literature, English salt, Anglicans, and finally England! But all of the sudden you encounter a footnote: "See Great Britain." The train leafed through the fields, striving to reach Moscow as quickly as possible. Already signs with the first syllable Moscow appeared on the cooperatives of the dacha stops—Mossel'prom, Mostorg. Through the suburbs, beyond the horizon one could already divine the main city itself, and every station was a footnote to it. (136)

In yet another key scene from the novel the social hierarchy of Stalinist society is cast in terms of the perceived power of various letters of the Russian alphabet. Each team member is assigned a single letter of the team's name ("Gidraerovtsy"). Confirming the ambiguous status of the (Jewish) intellectual vis-à-vis the more athletic members of the Gidraer commune, Karasik is given a jersey with the Russian letter "ы" emblazoned across it. As an outsider (a Jew) and therefore the "least" of the team's members he naturally ends up with the last letter in his name. More than this, the very structure of the letter seems to echo Karasik's ambiguous place within the team. The letter "ы" is, according to Karasik, a soft sign next to a stick, thus the protagonist's "softness" is placed side by side with his hardened resolve to remake his body and become a competent soccer player: "'Of course, I would never get a good letter,' Karasik said dejectedly, 'Damn it, of course, it's just like me to end up with the letter "ы" . . . a soft sign with a stick'" (235). By the same token, the scene above demonstrates the extraordinary extent to which the human body itself plays the part of a signifier within the *Gesamtkunstwerk* of Stalinism. We see this, among others, in the widespread practice of using bodies to spell out words or to illustrate important ideologemes. Thus during the popular physical culture parades of the time the bodies of individual participants were often used to suggest words, pictures, or even architectural monuments. Indeed, the practice of sadistically molding the body in order to lend it a "word-like" or statuary quality is everpresent in the artistic practice of the time.[63] Rodchenko's famous photograph of a human wheel taken on Red Square in 1938 provides the perfect case in point. Here "seven sportswomen in shorts and jerseys represent the spokes inside a giant wheel rolling through the square, thus literally realizing the saying 'The last spoke in the chariot.'"[64] Likewise, in the example above the Gidraer collective functions as a crucible in which socialist humanity is molded using the lettered bodies of individual soccer players. Among these the intellectual Jew is last though not least. And finally in Platonov's novel *Happy Moscow* the body is represented by the Russian letter "Я" with one of its limbs removed, as if to suggest the ritual mutilation without which the Stalinist subject could not come into being.

Such masochistic episodes represent the stock-in-trade of Stalinist fiction, according to Igor' Smirnov. They underscore the fact that for the Socialist Realist hero subjectivity is acquired through the *via negativa*. Here identity is paradoxically most present in its absence or loss.[65] A corollary of this is that the body in Socialist Realist texts regularly strives to occupy a position that is unlikely or even impossible with respect to the norm. Examples of this are easily adduced from the iconography of the period. The bas-relief of the Stalin's Stadium metro station provides a case in point. A simulacrum of a neo-Attic sculpture, the piece depicts a barefoot girl with a banner who appears to be magically hovering above the ground.[66] This curious image of levitation once again underscores Stalinist culture's aspiration to overturn the ancient force of gravity—an aspiration that not surprisingly lay at the very heart of the metro project.[67] Finally, the specifically masochistic aspect of the Stalinist "anti-body" is illustrated on the pages of the popular magazine *Gymnastics*. The photo études contained in the magazine typically portray at least two types of bodies, according to Zolotonosov: (1) the freely moving or ecstatic body, and (2) the disciplined body.[68] In the case of the latter type, a series of artistic photos done by Ir. Prokhorova merits particular attention. The étude shows a woman trainer sadistically sculpting the body of her seven-year-old pupil. Characteristically, the photo series ends with the trainer having successfully contorted the boy's body into a classical, statuary pose, even as the boy forces a pained smile for the camera.[69] Moreover, throughout the series the photographer consciously juxtaposes the young boy's grimaces with the smiles of pleasure exhibited by the woman.

The equally "masochistic" fantasy of transforming the slender-bodied Jewish intellectual into a soccer-playing dynamo—of overcoming his own physical limitations and by extension nature itself—is played out in Karasik's rigorous training routine, during which the would-be soccer player forces himself to perform maneuvers such as somersaults that are completely unnecessary in the game and leave his body

> covered with bruises. His legs hurt so much that when he had to put them on the bed with his arms. At night mamma Frumma sometimes heard strange soft knocking sounds on the floor coming from Karasik's room. It was Karasik who, having spread out his overcoat on the floor, was learning to do somersaults. Somersaults are completely unnecessary in soccer, but somehow Karasik had noticed that he was unable to do them, that he was afraid. So he made himself do somersaults. His shoulder-blades were completely covered with bruises. He flopped with his entire back against the coarse floor. (217)

The same masochistic impulse underpins Karasik's transformation at the end of the novel. Symptomatically, the protagonist's moment of glory comes at a point during the final match of the novel when he is crushed between two much larger players (Kandidov is one of them) in a so-called "box maneuver." And this, too, recalls a commonplace of Socialist Realist fiction. Demonstrating its deep roots in medieval Christian culture, with its linking of "mutilation, as a universal emblem of corporeal vulnerability and abjection, and holiness,"[70] Stalinism puts forth maiming as the most potent metaphor for self-transformation—as its paramount semantic gesture, so to speak.[71] And in this it merely reprises the mythocentrism of most traditional cultures. Thus while convalescing in a Moscow hospital Karasik reflects on the importance of wounds as a status symbol: "They called from the newspaper, from the committee. Karasik felt like a hero. Now everyone liked him. 'You suffered physically, were wounded,' say what you will, but it sounds good" (273). By undergoing a physical transformation (Karasik's "near-death" experience on the field merely consummates his earlier masochistic floor exercises) the hero parts with her or his profane, individualistic self in order to be accepted into the ideological and spiritual collective.[72]

Like his "conscious" counterpart, the "spontaneous" Kandidov also stands in need of remaking. And if Karasik represents the "disciplined" body in Zolotonosov's scheme, then Kandidov is surely the "freely moving, ecstatic body." The epitome of raw physicality and brute strength (a fact to which Kandidov himself frequently alludes),[73] the chaotic Volga transplant must be weaned from his own nature before he can finally become the feted goalkeeper of the republic. Strangely enough, a chance encounter with a group of blind men marks the beginning of Kandidov's transformation. Here again Kassil' makes good use of ancient cultural stereotypes—particularly, the image of the blind seer of the Judeo-Christian and classical traditions. Following in their footsteps, Kassil' elevates the visionary blind over their sighted but tragically unseeing counterparts. After losing the most important game of his life to his former family (i.e., the Gidraer team), Anton realizes the error of his ways from a conversation between several blind men riding in a street car. In this episode the platonic overtones of Kassil'"s *Goalkeeper of the Republic* (embodied in the image of the blind who emerge from their cave to behold the visionary sun of Stalinist truth) intersect with the transformational pathos of Pushkin's poem "The Prophet." As Jacques Derrida notes in connection with the Allegory of the Cave, Plato's geneaology of knowledge "relates the sensible sun, the cause of sight and the image of the eye—for the sun resembles the eye—the most 'helioform' of all sense organs—to the intelligible sun, that is, to the Good, just as the son is related to the father who has begotten him in his own likeness."[74] In *Goalkeeper,* too, the restoration of the unruly hero's vision depends on his ability not only to *see* the sun (i.e., to discern the intelligible as opposed to the phenomenal world) but to acknowledge his father, in this case, Stalin.[75]

Somewhat closer to home, the scene invokes yet another important subtext in the representation of blindness; namely, Pushkin's famous poem "The Prophet." And if the line "He touched my pupils and prophetic pupils opened up" specifically describes the shift from sight to insight, the poem as a whole portrays a radical reconfiguring of the body as prerequisite to serving as God's elect. As Gasparov notes, mutilation (and more specifically, symbolic castration) in Pushkin's poem enables the prophet's ability to truly *see*.[76] The same might be said of the rebellious Kandidov, who is repeatedly blinded by the sun while playing soccer against the rival Gidraer. Here the Stalinist soccer stadium provides an arena of contest not merely between rival teams but between the wayward son and his chastising father. In his reflections on Plato Derrida makes the point that the "absolute Good, the intelligible father" is one who "begets being as the visibility of being."[77] A similar argument could be made for Kassil''s portrayal of the high-stakes soccer match. For in the Stalinist polis the stadium functions as a place where the body social is maximally visible, endowing it with the ability to truly see — yet only at the cost of its own blinding.[78] Likewise, in Kassil''s *Goalkeeper* the unruly son must be blinded or castrated by the reproving sun (i.e., his father's all-seeing eye) as punishment for past transgressions. Thus during the second half of Magneto's match with Gidraer Kandidov is both literally and symbolically overcome by the patriarchal sun: "The low sun burnt and cut his eyes . . . The sun didn't allow him to get a good look around" (248). Notably, it is only after Anton has been punished in this manner that he is truly able to see, so that at the end of the novel the reformed son meets his father's gaze "without turning away."

Yet even before this scene it is clear that blindness begets insight. In a key moment in the novel one of the "visionary" blind men hints indirectly that the loss of a leg is preferable to spiritual blindness. Although the exchange of mobility for insight is clearly presented in a humorous key, its gravity from the standpoint of cultural and personal mythology should not be underestimated. Ultimately, the blind man's disability is precisely what valorizes him for Kassil'. Conversely, those who are sighted emerge as spiritual cripples. Their vision is, as Derrida writes, "too natural, too carnal, too external, which is to say, too literal." In order to be saved they must be "converted to interiority, their eyes turned toward the inside . . . the body and exteriority of the letter reproached."[79] Kassil''s narrative "reproach" of the body is played out in a similar fashion. In the following scene one of the blind men jokingly notes that the streetcar stop *ploshchad' Nogi-na* ["Have some legs" Square] should really be called *ploshchad' glaza-na* ["Have some eyes" Square]. Here the symbolic exchange of legs for eyes goes hand in hand with the hero's new-found ability to read allegorically — "past the exteriority of the letter" — and thus to glean the hidden connection between things.

The pock-marked blind man, with a fat nose ravaged by small-pox that looked like a thimble, was smiling out into space. "Nogina Square," said that conductor crisply, stressing the first syllable of "Nogina." "Dzha hear that? 'Nogi na!'" ["Have (Take) some legs"], said the affable blind man. "What do I need legs for? You should'a said, 'Have some eyes!' Eyes I could use. Got legs of my own . . ." Another time Anton would have simply thought to himself: "There's a spirited blind man." But today everything had particular meaning—people, houses, words. . . . And now Anton thought about how much more honest this blind man was than many of the seeing, who, without being able to divine the sun, assure you that it doesn't exist, thereby preventing others from seeing. The words of the blind man seemed to have an allegorical meaning, like the words of the prophet. Today Anton's eyes gleaned the secret connection between things.[80]

As Sergei Lobanov-Rostovsky points out, cultural representations of vision invariably waver between emphasizing the interior or the exterior dimensions of the eye. This fundamental ambivalence is anchored in the fact that the eyes are as capable of projecting light as they are of consuming it.[81] In certain texts and periods this ambivalence produces a relative overemphasis on the eyes as the instrument of the soul's vigilance—of its ability to provide "judicious surveillance of the body's domain." In such works vision emerges as the body's first line of defense against the "'headlong violence' by which the world tries to make 'breach and entrance' into the brain."[82] Lev Kassil''s *Goalkeeper* (with its thinly veiled references to Plato's *Republic*) provides an excellent case in point.[83] Not surprisingly, the narrative ambivalence surrounding vision becomes most acute when the fame-hungry Kandidov arrives in Moscow; for Moscow is both the ideological and mythological center of the socialist world (the internal or noumenal realm) and a gateway to capitalism (the external, phenomenal world).[84] Thus one of the first things that Anton sees after arriving is the garish display window of a travel bureau. A clear metaphor for the protagonist's own wayward vision, the travel bureau window depicts the eye not in its role as judge and guardian, but as a place where the world might make "breach and entrance into the brain." It is the aperture through which worldly pleasures and tastes threaten to corrupt the future Guardian's soul. In sharp contrast to the reigning myth of the (male) Stalinist hero whose penetrating gaze masters and dominates the visible cosmos,[85] Anton's vision is dangerously passive—perhaps even effeminate. Thus he is "breached" by the outside world rather than himself penetrating and mastering *it*. His polar opposite is the vigilant Karasik, who has also stood in front of the travel bureau on more than one occasion yet remains unmoved by its charms. Unlike his counterpart, the "philosopher king" sees reality through his mind's eye. Similarly, when Anton enters a hairdresser's salon, Kassil' emphasizes at length the large mirrors that lovingly reflect the protagonist's

gaze back onto himself. Like the earlier display window, the hairdresser's salon mirrors symbolize vision that is mired in the charms of the phenomenal
world. And it is no accident that what threatens to emasculate the hero is precisely a beauty salon. Like Plato's benighted prisoners of the cave, Anton is
enthralled by a false, *reflected* image:

> An enormous, brightly illuminated picture-window caught Anton's attention.
> Behind the mirror-like glass there hung posters that were naive and colorful, and
> reminded one of a Chinese lantern. This was the window of the Tourism Bureau.
> Beyond the glass in front of Anton there shone a tempting, radiant world—the
> dream of wanderers and travellers, broken down into the primitive colors of an
> ad. The window beckoned with all the charms of the world. . . . Anton stood in
> front of the window for a long time. He did not know that Karasik had stood in
> front of the same window on more than one occasion. "That's the most seduc-
> tive picture-window in the entire city," said Evgenii Kar of the window. . . . Not
> without a certain shyness Anton walked into the glass lobby of a beauty salon
> and strode into the room. Everything there shone. Anton walked in, enormous
> and reflected many times over. . . . For a long time the mirrors repeated him with
> surprise from head to foot. (137)

The same reproach of carnal, exterior vision is played out in the scene immediately preceding Kandidov's encounter with the four blind men. Fore-
shadowing the seer Filat's desire to exchange his legs for insightful eyes,
Kassil''s narrative underscores the connection between a dandy's flashy appearance and the unseeing eyes of those who are seduced by superficial lus-
ter and fashionable clothing. The passage begins by pointing out that "everyone looked at him [the dandy] . . . the girls occasionally looked at him through
the glass," and finally that "he was used to the fact that everyone stared at
him." As Kandidov (particularly his European shoes) becomes the center of
attention, gradually overshadowing the "impoverished stylishness" of the
dandy, the narrator notes that the would-be foreigner "was unable to tear his
eyes away from Anton's shoes."[86] The resulting humiliation at the hands (or
rather feet) of the giant Kandidov causes the vanquished fop to hide his own
nogi clad in "suddenly faded shoes" beneath the bench on which he is sitting.
Having realized the extent of his own transgression, a now-repentant Anton
appropriately serves as a living reproach to those whose gaze is drawn to
what lies "outside the goalposts" (i.e., that which is foreign). Anticipating the
episode to come, the narrative thus removes (if only from our field of vision)
the same feet/legs (*nogi* in Russian) that will later be traded for insight in the
blind man's speech. The symbolic dimming of the protagonist's sight culminates in the scene where Anton passes the same travel bureau that had earlier
caught his eye but which has since moved to another location. As if reflecting on the tragedy of his own undisciplined vision, Kandidov notices that not

only had the display window become dim but that flies were entangled in a
spiderweb next to the murky glass. Finally, in a conversation with a militiaman stationed next to the defunct travel bureau the travel-weary goalkeeper
warns against the seduction of sight. While the militiaman muses out loud
that it would be nice to *see* what sort of beauty the world has to offer, Anton
encourages his alter ego (earlier in the novel Kandidov had fantasized about
being a militiaman) not to be seduced away from his post. And not surprisingly, for *seeing* is one thing, while understanding (literally, "seeing-in" in
Russian) is another:

"Having a look? " Kandidov asked sympathetically.

"Yes, I just got promoted and they put me here. So, I look out of boredom, and
reflect during the evening hours. And I'm thinking, there's a great deal of beauty
in the world. Just look at the mansions. And palm trees in hot climes. The sub-
tropics. An attractive picture. Departing ships. Passengers and travelers. Everywhere one observes a great commotion. And I'm thinking I'd like to have a
look, see how life abroad is progressing. "

"I looked and had my fill of looking, " Anton said. "It looks good in pictures,but
in fact it's nothin' but trouble." (260)

Due in no small measure to the classical pretensions of the culture as a
whole,[87] the soccer stadium (at least in Kassil''s *Goalkeeper*) inhabits the
mythological center of the Stalinist polis. This impression is conveyed,
among others, by the spectators themselves, who in the first major match of
the novel are described by Karasik as sitting "in the classical poses of the
spectators in an amphitheater. 'This is how they must have sat in Aristro-
phanes's theater or on the benches of the coliseum'" (174). More importantly,
the match allows the body politic to ritually reenforce the boundaries that distinguish one's own ("our side") from that which is foreign, hostile, or Other.
In the Stalinist stadium both players and spectators come together in order to
engage in a mythic ritual of collective self-renewal. Thus the novel culminates in a pair of symbolically charged soccer matches, whose purpose is to
humiliate the renegade Kandidov so as to coax him like the prodigal son back
into the fold of his communal family. Figuratively speaking, the reunion of
the two friends Karasik and Kandidov at the end of the novel serves to
reestablish the equilibrium of nature and culture (or, speaking in Freudian
terms, of conscious and unconscious) that had been disrupted by Kandidov's
defection to the other side.

The soccer stadium where this takes place is both a mythological locus and
a model of the Stalinist state. Kassil''s fanciful description of the round soccer
ball that the referee carries makes this clear. More than a soccer ball, it is an
"orb . . . placed in the very center of the field, and it lay here, circumscribed by

a magic circle like Khoma Brut in Gogol's *Vii*."[88] Our impression of the soccer ball as the center of this mythological universe is bolstered by the fact that airplanes "were describing circles in the sky that were concentric in relationship to the white one, where the ball already lay in the center."[89] More importantly, the very construction of the soccer ball functions as a metaphor for the carefully maintained familial cohesion of the Stalinist state, emphasizing the struggle between the highly compressed air within (its spirited but unruly sons) and the tightly bound leather outside (the firm and reproving hand of the fathers): "The ball rang out from tension. Its highly compressed air was ready to burst out. But the tender rubber navel, through which a pump filled the ball with elasticity, was tied up, twisted, and tucked inside. The cruelly bound outer leather sphere was sewn together from sixteen segments that resembled biscuits."[90]

The match itself, which ends predictably with the victory of the communal Gidraer team over the individualist Magneto, underscores the paramount importance of the commune as *family*. In this instance, the smaller *rod,* or "clan," functions as a microcosm of the Stalinist family, or *rodina* ("motherland"). The rout of the Magnetovtsy in general and Kandidov in particular is due to the goalkeeper's rash decision to leave his post and thereby abandon his clan. Indeed, this act functions as a metaphor for Kandidov's life in general. Broadly speaking, his mistake lies in transgressing a series of overlapping boundaries/borders—first, the boundary separating Order/Culture/the Word from Chaos/Water (not for nothing does Karasik respond to his friend's decision to leave the commune by remarking on his dangerous "watery" nature: "Look out, Anton, you'll be carried off by the current. Where will you put ashore?" [210]); second, the boundaries of the small homeland of the Gidraer commune, and third and most important, the sacred boundaries of the socialist *rodina*. In each case, one transgression logically follows from the other. For the gesture of yielding to one's nature that Soviet/Stalinist ideology sought at all costs to curtail invites one to venture beyond the boundaries of the familial commune.[91] This in turn leads to a betrayal of the homeland as the most complete expression of family. Later Kandidov will summarize his mistakes by saying, "That's the problem, Ardal'on Gavrilovich. I'm living on the offside. I've gone past the line" (259). The now empty allure of this movement is best expressed in the image of the abandoned travel bureau. Exposing the capitalist West as both lusterless and rife with death, the narrative suggests the absent charm of everything that is *за границей* (the Russian word for "abroad" literally means "beyond the border"). Perhaps most importantly, Kassil''s narrative signals the closing of the traditional image of a "window to the West" associated with the Petersburg period of Russian history. The contemporary shift of the capital to Moscow as the new ideological and spiritual hub of the Soviet Union coincides with the country's increasing isolation from the world outside its own goalposts[92]:

> But even this window had grown dull. The militiaman Snezhkov stood by the familiar display window of the tourist office. The office, it seems, had moved into a different building. Soiled by flies, the posters were faded and warped, and the colors had grown yellow. A zig-zag-shaped crack cut across the glass. . . . It was dull in that lithographed world, and dead flies had become entangled in a spider-web next to the turbid glass. (260)

Kassil"s portrayal of the Gidraer soccer club as a microcosm of the Soviet family and the soccer stadium as its symbolic home echoes but also revises the strategy of one of the most important novels of the 1920s—Iurii Olesha's *Envy*. This novel represents, among others, the best-known attempt in Soviet literature to draw the contours of the new socialist family, using a ritualized sporting event (the soccer match) as its metaphoric equivalent. What both works have in common is the near-mythological struggle between an individualist and a collectivist ethos for the right to define the character of new Soviet humanity. In *Envy* the soccer match represents not only the victory of Volodia Makarov's Soviet-style collectivism in the public sphere but also the ignoble end of Nikolai Kavalerov's quixotic quest for a life of individual glory with Valia as its symbolic centerpiece. Put in spatial terms, Olesha's novel defines a realm of inclusion/exclusion that prevents Kavalerov and all that he represents from participating in the new world. At a decisive moment in the novel when the game momentarily comes to a stop, threatening to turn a serious soccer match into comic grotesque, Kavalerov finds himself mysteriously unable to pick up an errant ball and return it to its rightful owners. In a remarkable turnaround, the mocking Kavalerov himself becomes a comic figure—he is frozen like the soccer players and spectators a moment before—while Andrei Babichev quickly picks up the ball, "unfreezing" the transfixed stadium. Moreover, the effect of Andrei's overly serious posture in returning the ball is to overturn the comic principle represented throughout the novel by Nikolai (that is, words/gestures/actions deprived of practical or semantic motivation) in favor of Soviet-style pragmatism. Taking up the commonplace theme of the intelligent and his or her ambivalent relationship to postrevolutionary reality, the soccer match in *Envy* enacts the victory of the new Soviet family by marginalizing the world outside the mythological field of battle. Intensely ambivalent about the principles of fatherhood and family, Kavalerov is paralyzed by the "deep-seated urge to flee from fathers, reproduction, and family ties" and a competing pull toward these very institutions. As a result, during a decisive moment in the match, Kavalerov finds himself "'out of the game' (*vne igry*), always observing but never acting."[93] At the end of the match, the victors Andrei, Volodia, and Valia assume the status of the new socialist hegemons. Meanwhile, a vanquished Kavalerov inherits the role of the son in a parodic ménage à trois—one that closely resembles the Oedipal triangle he spends most the novel trying to escape.[94]

By contrast, Kassil''s *Goalkeeper*, written exactly one decade after *Envy*, is directed not so much at those outside the soccer field as it is at the players themselves. In this sense, the pathos of the novel chronicles a significant shift in the culture at large. As Jochen Hellbeck notes, the infamous purges of the mid-to-late '30s were more than a simple orgy of political repressiveness on the part of the Stalinist regime. As the private diaries of many a writer and ordinary citizen clearly illustrate, the political purges of the '30s induced many Soviets to enact the revolutionary call for self-transformation at a profoundly personal level, thus converting political ideology and mythology into a relationship of radical interiority.[95] The juxtaposition of good and evil (or inside and outside) earlier associated more or less exclusively with the political and social arenas now began to model the most intimate quarters of selfhood. An offshoot of this is the Stalinist stadium, which in Kassil''s *Goalkeeper* and in culture at large serves as an allegory of collective selfhood. Yet unlike Olesha's stadium with its clear demarcation of insiders versus outsiders, Kassil''s stadium-cum-amphitheater contains no bystanders—only the all-inclusive body politic within which the dichotomy of inside versus outside is played out in a purely intrinsic manner.[96] Rather than a watershed where the victors are neatly segregated from the vanquished, the Stalinist stadium becomes a place in which the entire polis is ritually reconstituted by purging itself of the "alien" or "foreign" element within. In this regard, it might well be seen as the official counterpart of Bakhtin's carnival body, the pathos and structure of which are precariously close to those surrounding the political purges of the same era.[97]

The paramount importance of the stadium for Kassil' is reflected not only in the sheer numbers of fans it holds but in the carefully articulated relationship between architecture and collective identity. Kassil''s soccer fans are crowded together so densely that one can no longer properly distinguish between stadium and spectator, or between players and fans. Recalling the abundant water imagery used throughout the novel, the stadium is likened to an enormous bathtub (the external form of which molds the watery chaos within). And the narrator notes of the undifferentiated masses of spectators that they "devoured the last empty spaces on the slopes of the cement foundation pit [*kotlovan*—which is derived from *kotel*, or "kettle"]," again evoking the image of water: "The overflow settled on the track, spilling out onto its curves" (559). Meanwhile, the *kotlovan* of the stadium structures and informs the "living matter" of the body politic. The city outside the stadium echoes this pattern, for Moscow is beset by spring flooding, yet its main river, the *Moskva-reka*, is rendered harmless by the grated parapets that guard and contain it.[98] Likewise, in Alexandrov's musical comedy *Volga-Volga*, the amateur talents of the carnivalesque *narod* are (by the end of the film) shaped into an orderly choir, just as the unpredictable Volga river is rationally channeled by the newly constructed Moscow–Volga Canal. This same rechanneling pathos is at the heart of Kassil''s *Goalkeeper*, where the very layout of the soccer stadium exemplifies the ideal synthesis of "spontaneousness" and "consciousness" that was the crux of Stalinism's dialectical worldview. Thus Kassil' notes of the Soviet soccer fan that he or she is "noisy, yet disciplined" (175). And in distinguishing between the boisterous southern stand and its more reserved northern part, Kassil' notes that the rotunda located in the middle of the stadium functions as a means of reconciling the conflicting opinions of both sides:

> The southern stand is blinded by sunlight and partiality. The round tribune does not suffer from such one-sidedness. Often it unites the opinions of the two stands and publically sums them up. Its spectators are loud mouthed, disrespectful, but fair in the proletarian way. The spirited and self-willed spectators of the round tribune rout equally for their own players and those of the other side. (175)

If the body politic in Olesha's *Envy* is established through an act of mythological separation (inside/outside, old/new, etc.), then Kassil''s *Goalkeeper* alludes evokes a kind of miraculous harmony between opposites—one that had been upset by the goalkeeper's defection from his lawful post. Meanwhile, the novel as a whole strives entirely toward the moment when the Stalinist polis will overcome its disunity and reenter a state of primordial oneness. It looks forward, in other words, to the moment when the goalkeeper-as-prodigal-son will reenter the communal fold. Before this, however, Kandidov briefly experiences the dilemma of those doomed to live in the capitalist West. As Hans Günther notes, official accounts of Soviet expeditions to the Arctic invariably attribute the success of pilots and explorers to their unbroken connection with the warmth and solicitude of the Motherland.[99] By contrast, the efforts of their Western counterparts such as Charles Lindbergh or the explorer Scott are portrayed as "lunatic" or even "insane." And the explorers themselves are "tragic loners," whose heroism is doomed to wither in the cold wasteland that is the bourgeois West.[100] By forsaking his homeland Kandidov unwittingly joins this camp. In a sense, the goalkeeper manqué is not unlike the mythological hero Anteus (note that Kandidov's first name is Anton). Characterized by Stalin in a speech given at the February-March plenum of 1937 as a kind of patron saint of Bolshevism,[101] Anteus was said to derive his strength in battle from his connection to the earth. Once removed from it, however, the ancient hero was easily defeated. Like all true Bolsheviks, whose strength according to Stalin flowed from their mythological connection to that same earth, Kandidov remains strong only if he is firmly tethered to his native soil. Thus after returning from his first wildly successful foreign tour the goalkeeper realizes that he must return to his origins, which is to say, to the Gidraer commune that had "nourished and raised him": "To hell with everything! Time to get back to my roots. I have to go to my own people. . . . Before its too late" (230).[102] As the narrator notes—symptomatically conflating the territory of the familial commune and that of the Soviet Union—"he [Kandidov] was irrepressibly drawn to familiar territory" (231). By contrast, the world outside one's goalposts ("outside of the game") emerges as no place at all, for despite its glitter and charm the capitalist West is devoid of the warming embrace of one's extended family. This becomes abundantly clear at the conclusion of the novel, where Kandidov's "individualist" team suffers a stunning upset at the hands of the Gidraer collective. Later the vanquished goalkeeper meets a militiaman to whom he confesses the sin of having strayed abroad. And here Kandidov fantasizes about a situation in which he would never again leave his post: "I'm envious of everything. Even that militiaman. He holds his ground; he has his post. But I'm scared just getting up every morning . . . I don't have my people around me" (259).[103]

As Aleksandr Etkind remarks in his book on Russian sectarian culture, while utopia had often been imagined in Russia in terms of a radical redistribution of wealth and property, its most extreme advocates—the "fanatics and poets" of communism—were inclined to view human sexuality as the more promising arena of utopian projecteering. In the words of one character from Andrei Platonov's 1929 novel *Chevengur*: "Every person has an entire imperialism in his lower parts." Sexuality and family, profit and property are inextricably bound, and together they constitute the undoing of communism.[104] Similarly, such late-nineteenth and early-twentieth-century Russian religious philosophers as Nikolai Fedorov, Vladimir Solov'ev, and Nikolai Berdiaev valorized eros only in its "ideal," purified aspect—which is to say, as a means of binding individuals into a larger spiritual unity. Paradoxically, copulation divided more than it unified because "in sexual congress 'difference' becomes most apparent at the very moment when the drive to obliterate it becomes most intense."[105] Most importantly for present purposes, Fedorov and others transformed the received image of woman as primarily sexual into the basis of a metaphysics that viewed women (with abhorrence) as the "cosmic, global carrier of the sexual element, of all that is elemental in sex," concluding that "the natural procreative element of sex is the female element."[106]

Similar ideas resurfaced with a vengeance in the 1920s in connection with broader societal fears about ideological purity and the potential loss of communal identity occasioned by Lenin's New Economic Policy. At the same time, post-October attempts at reforming the traditional family led (if only on the level of the revolutionary imagination) to what might be characterized as a "masculinization" of Soviet society. The substitution of affiliative male ties for "filial" or biological bonds manifested itself in literature as a shift toward emotionally and ideologically charged images of male comradeship and community.[107] And even as late as 1931 Iurii Olesha attempted to explain the paucity of female roles in contemporary plays by claiming that "'we live in a masculine time,'" and that "'the revolution is a masculine time, a time of settling men's accounts.'"[108] Despite the fact that by the mid-to-late '30s such imagery was largely a thing of the past, *Goalkeeper* (in its tender portrayal of Karasik and Kandidov's friendship) seems to look backward toward the all-male collectivism of the previous decade. To be sure, women are not entirely absent from the novel, yet they function mostly as a means of cementing the bonds of male friendship. Meanwhile, the novel's homoerotic overtones are evident from the very first page of the work; the 1939 edition of *Goalkeeper* begins with a quote from Walt Whitman's "When I Heard at the Close of Day" (Calmus 11), an open celebration of Platonic (i.e., homosexual) love.[109] Like the image of Tom stretched out next to Kory-Kory in Melville's *Typee* (or Ishmael sleeping next to Queequeg in *Moby Dick*), Whitman's poem evokes an idyll of male friendship and love. It looks lovingly forward to the moment when the lyric I's lover will be "sleeping by me under the same cover."[110] Likewise it can easily be argued that in *Goalkeeper* the image of Kandidov and Karasik sleeping next to each other on the same bed represents the ideal toward which the work as a whole is striving. The first such episode occurs during the early years of NEP. Disappointed by his heartthrob Tosia's decision to marry a *nepman*, Karasik seeks solace with Kandidov and the two spend the night sleeping together on the same cot:

> Karasik barely managed to wake Anton with his knocking. Anton was already asleep. He opened the door absolutely naked, went back into the room and sat down, scratching himself. The room was filled with the faint scent of his clean, well-proportioned body. . . . "Well, thanks Zhenia," he said, firmly pressing Karasik's shoulder. "Spend the night at my place, you take the wall and I'll sleep on the other side." Karasik lay down on the squeaky cot. Anton positioned himself on the other side. He lay there large and hot, his breathing strong and regular. . . . Zhenia listened to the life of that large body. (68)

A variant of this scene occurs at the end of the novel, at the moment when the estranged protagonists are finally reunited. As a sign of their renewed

friendship, Anton goes over to sit on Anton's bed, but quickly returns to his
own when several people unexpectedly enter the room: "Both were extremely
embarrassed upon seeing several people walk into the room. Anton dove under the blanket on his bed" (275). Of course, neither episode represents evidence of homosexuality as such in the work. Still, Kassil''s use of suggestive
detail along with the epigraph from Whitman's poem points toward a strong
homoerotic strain in *Goalkeeper*. This sort of homoeroticism is hardly unique
to Kassil''s novel, however. Olesha's 1936 screenplay *A Strict Youth*—to
name only one example—is replete with homoeroticism and thinly veiled homosexual imagery.[111] More generally, Zolotonosov argues for a strong homosexual element within Stalinist ideology and rhetoric as a whole.[112] Kassil''s
novel for adolescents is symptomatic of this tendency. Not unlike Whitman
who in the poems of the Calamus series anticipates a "'brotherhood of
lovers,'"[113] *Goalkeeper* seems to see the true fulfillment of socialist society's
potential in the promise of "comradely love." For the Soviet writer the renewed friendship of two best friends (as well as the reconciliation of fathers
and sons it clearly symbolizes) represents the sole guarantee of the health and
well-being of the Republic.

The only possible solution to the dilemma posed by the novel is to reunite
Karasik with Kandidov and thus to reintegrate the severed halves of the Stalinist polis. This Kassil' accomplishes at the end of *Goalkeeper* by having his
heroes share a hospital room, Karasik with a fractured rib and Kandidov recovering from a near-death experience.[114] The sense that the protagonists'
hospital stay represents a symbolic resurrection is evident in the narrator's description of that morning as being "unusually bright, happy, festive, as on
Easter when they were children" (273). Further developing the image of the
Stalinist city/stadium as the leather which securely (indeed, sadistically)
binds the volatile nature of its inhabitants, the author notes that the "spontaneous" Kandidov's blanket "surged on him like the sea." Meanwhile, the
more "conscious" Karasik is lovingly constricted by his hospital bandages:
"The pain died down shortly after the bandage was applied. He was tightly
bound and bandaged. The gauze constricted his breathing but the bandages
calmed him. In their density he sensed the safety of friendly embraces" (272).
Karasik's convalescence marks the folding of the Jewish intellectual into the
cauldron of Stalinist collectivity. At the same time, the novel's epilogue portrays the vestiges of Kandidov's "watery" chaotic nature as fully conquered
and contained. Indeed, the final scene of *Goalkeeper of the Republic* emphasizes not so much the predominance of water as it does fire, heat, and sunlight. Thus Red Square, where Kandidov plays his final and most important
match, seems to radiate pure heat, reflecting the ideological fervor of the socialist collective body:

A July day was burning Moscow. But, fire-resistant, the Muscovites advanced toward the square. The ash-colored dark blue spruce trees near the sacred wall were languishing in the swelter. Thick honey-like drops of pitch fell from the walls of the upper trade booths that were festooned with spruce boughs. The stars on the Kremlin towers, heated to the point of transparence and looking like they had been turned from blazing coal, burned through the sky. The cobblestones of the square were white-hot and it seemed odd that the drops of pitch didn't sizzle as they fell onto the stones. On Red Square it smelled like a hot mid-day in the forest. (279)

If on a philosophical plane the pathos of Stalinist ideology lay in its grandiose claim to be the ultimate resolver of all contradictions,[115] this same urge manifested itself on a more mundane level in a concerted effort on the part of the superstructure to clothe itself in the everyday pleasures, pastimes, and concerns of its base—that is, to furnish the airy spaces of '20s-style utopia with a smattering of bourgeois prosperity. In literature and in public discourse a new Stalinist sentimentalism merged (if only as metaphor) the domain of private life with a mythologized image of the country and its many peoples as an extended family, making it possible for fictional mothers to publish their children's first words on the pages of *Izvestiia* or a no less imaginary doctor to help (by radio) a simple woman deliver her first child in the barren wastelands of the Arctic.[116]

In both its desire to promote a kind of overarching synthesis—of everything and everyone—and its projection of core cultural myths, Lev Kassil''s *Goalkeeper of the Republic* attests to the power of Stalinist ideology. Stalinism presented itself as a society untroubled by boundaries (racial, ethnic, or biological), while at the same time attributing near mythological significance to an entire array of social, political, and geographical hierarchies/boundaries. In a significant discussion near the end of the novel, Anton denies that it is a faceless 1920s-style collectivism (*obezlichka*) that allowed the Gidraer team to triumph over Magneto, but rather a quasi-familial synthesis of individual freedom and collective belonging—a kind of Stalinist *sobornost'*: "Everyone feels his place. They play together and each in his own way" (261). Thus Kassil''s novel paints a picture of the Republic that emphasizes the constant (but ultimately synthesizable) tension between such opposites as enthusiasm and discipline, intellect and strength, or Jew and Russian. Unsettled by chaotic forces from within and threatened by fascism from without, the society enjoins its members to engage in an ongoing process of ideological self-discipline and self-renewal. The result is a vision of Stalinist society as a cohesive familial collective, held together by the drama of continuously and triumphantly retrieving its errant (male) member. Whether in its extravagant efforts to save stranded expedition members from certain death in the polar wastes, or in the purely imagined reunion of Kandidov and Karasik, Stalinist civilization envisioned itself as progressing toward a kind of mythological unity—toward the final resolution of every contradiction. Kassil''s novel for adolescents endeavors to put this ideal into practice. In the case of Evgenii Karasik (a Jew), the boundaries of biology are renegotiated so as to join the Apollinian intellectual to the Dionysian *bogatyr'*. Likewise, the "elemental" Kandidov is elevated above wayward nature (his own) to rejoin the collective whose sacred boundaries he had earlier transgressed. For both protagonists the Whitmanesque paean to friendship contained in the epigraph to the novel provides a compelling description of what is most important in the creation of Stalin's utopia:

> And else, when I carous'd, or when my plans were accomplish'd, still I was not happy; But the day when I rose at dawn from the bed of perfect health, refresh'd, singing, inhaling the ripe breath of autumn. . . . And when I thought how my dear friend, my lover, was on his way coming, O then I was happy.

NOTES

1. This chapter represents an expanded version of my article "The Soccer Match as Stalinist Ritual: Constructing the Body Social in Lev Kassil''s *Goalkeeper of the Republic*," *The Russian Review* 60, no. 1 (October 2001): 592–613.

2. Igor' Smirnov, *Psikhodiakhronologika*, 255.

3. Irina Gutkin, *The Cultural Origins of the Socialist Realist Aesthetic*, 99.

4. Aleksandr Gol'dshtein, *Rasstavanie s nartsissom: Opyty pominal'noi ritoriki* (Moskva: Novoe literaturnoe obozrenie, 1997), 162.

5. Sheila Fitzpatrick, *Everyday Stalinism*, 90. See also Randi Cox, "All This Can Be Yours!: Soviet Commercial Advertisting and the Social Construction of Space: 1928–1956," in *The Landscape of Stalinism: The Art and Ideology of Soviet Space*, ed. Evgeny Dobrenko and Eric Naiman (Seattle: University of Washington Press, 2003), 125–62.

6. Eric Naiman, *Sex in Public*, 292.

7. Katerina Clark, *Petersburg, Crucible of Cultural Revolution*, 283.

8. Quoted in Svetlana Boym, *Commonplaces: Mythologies of Everyday Life in Russia* (Cambridge, MA: Harvard University Press, 1995), 283.

9. Hans Günther, "Liubov' k dal'nemu i liubov' k blizhnemu," 310–11.

10. Aleksandr Zholkovskii, *Mikhail Zoshchenko: Poetika nedoveriia*, 310.

11. The word "Adun" clearly suggests the Russian word for "hell" (*ad*), as Lahusen notes (Thomas Lahusen, "Das Geheimnis des Adun. Rekonstruktion einer Geschichte," [*Wiener Slawistischer Almanach*, 1989], Bd. 24, 126).

12. M. Zoshchenko, *Sobranie soch. v 3-kh tomakh*, vol. 2 (Leningrad: Leningradskoe otdelenie, 1986), 394.

13. Katerina Clark, *Petersburg*, 283.

14. Eliot Borenstein, *Men without Women*, 92.

15. In *Sodom i psykheia: Ocherki intellektual'noi istorii Serebriannogo veka* ([Moskva: ITS-Garant, 1996], 29), Aleksandr Etkind notes that Lou-Andreas Salomé speculated on the beneficial results for Russian philosophy of a synthesis of Jewish abstraction and Russian artistic concreteness and picturesqueness. This project is made explicit, I would argue, in the name of the commune "Gidraer," which combines the idea of watery chaos with ethereal abstraction.

16. Efraim Sicher, *Jews in Russian Literature after the October Revolution* (Cambridge: Cambridge University Press, 1995), 80.

17. Mikhail Vaiskopf, *Pisatel' Stalin* (Moskva: Novoe literaturnoe obozrenie, 2001), 343.

18. Sheila Fitzpatrick, *Everyday Stalinism*, 75.

19. Ibid., 71.

20. Katerina Clark, *The Soviet Novel*, 129.

21. Katerina Clark, "Socialist Realism without Shores: Conventions for a Positive Hero," in *Socialist Realism without Shores*, 45.

22. Aleksandr Gol'dshtein, *Rasstavanie s nartsissom: Opyty pominal'noi ritoriki* (Moskva: Novoe literaturnoe obozrenie, 1997), 218–19.

23. Katerina Clark, *The Soviet Novel*, 17.

24. Mikhail Zolotonosov, *Slovo i telo*, 285.

25. Cf. Katerina Clark's discussion of the relationship between the "spontaneous" pilots and their "conscious" mentors (*The Soviet Novel*, 126).

26. Quoted in A. Gol'dshtein, *Rasstavanie s nartsissom*, 218.

27. S. A. Tokarev, ed., *Mify narodov mira: Entsiklopediia*, vol. 1 (Moskva: Sovetskaia entsiklopediia, 1991), 240.

28. V. Papernyi, *Kul'tura "Dva,"* 145.

29. Hans Günther, "Broad is My Motherland: The Mother Archetype and Space in the Soviet Mass Song," 86.

30. As Katerina Clark points out in "Socialist Realism without Shores," in the typical Socialist Realist novel a character's function is distributed between two aspects; his or her moral/political identity and his or her symbolic role in the Great Family. These two facets are never entirely separate, so the quality of "son-ness" that causes the character to be depicted as childish or overly "spontaneous" paradoxically functions as an indicator of the protagonist's potential to develop into an emblem of consciousness.

31. L. Kassil', *Vratar' Respubliki* (Moskva: Sovetskii pisatel', 1939), 60.

32. See John McCannon, "Positive Heroes at the Pole: Celebrity Status, Socialist-Realist Ideals and the Soviet Myth of the Arctic, 1932–39," *Russian Review* 56 (July 1997): 349.

33. M. Allenov, "Ochevidnosti sistemnogo absurdizma skvoz' emblematiku moskovskogo metro," *Iskusstvo kino*, no. 6 (1990): 84.

34. Aleksandr Gol'dshtein, *Rasstavanie s nartsissom*, 204.

35. N.V. Kornienko, "Moskva vo vremeni: (Imia Peterburga i Moskvy v russkoi literature 10—30-kh gg. XX v.)," in *Moskva v russkoi i mirovoi literature* (Moskva: nasledie, 2000), 235.

36. Katerina Clark, *The Soviet Novel*, 126–29.

37. In *Die Pathologiesierung des jüdischen Körpers: Antisemitismus, Geschlecht und Medizin im Fin-de-Siècle* ([Wien: Picus Verlag, 1997], 241), Klaus Hödl describes the prominence of similar stereotypes in turn-of-the-century Austrian and German characterizations of Jews, particularly in various pseudoscientific studies that supposedly demonstrated the Jews' "greater aptitude for the abstract and conceptual, for abstract logical deduction."

38. Thus A. Etkind remarks on Trotsky's interest in extending socialism's project of remaking nature to include human nature/psychology (*Eros nevozmozhnogo: Istoriia psikhoanaliza v Rossii* [Sankt-Peterburg: Meduza, 1993], 282).

39. Thus A. Gol'dshtein writes (*Rasstavanie s nartsissom*, 217): "It was necessary to remind the powers-that-be, who had just purged the country of murderers and saboteurs, about the possibility of a beneficial union of the Guardian with the loyal philosopher."

40. See Victor Klemperer, *LTI: Notizbuch eines Philologen* (Leipzig: Reclam, 1990), 153.

41. Thus in "Sotsrealizm: antropologicheskoe izmerenie" (*Novoe literaturnoe obozrenie*, 15 [1995]: 37), Igor' Smirnov argues that Socialist Realism's proverbial love for food, for instance, is rather the opposite: "The abudance of food so beloved in Socialist Realist painting is the opposite of food. In 'The Kolkhoz Holiday' (1937) by Plastov it lies untouched (instead of eating the kolkhoz farmers are looking at a portrait of Stalin). How do the people of Stalin era satisfy their hunger? Here are a couple of excerpts from *The Povest' About a Real Man*: 'Without reflecting for even a moment . . . about the fact that according to legend hedgehogs are considered unclean animals he quickly tore the scale-like foliage from the creature . . . With a blow of his knife Aleksei killed the hedgehog . . . and with pleasure (sic!) began to tear with his teeth the still warm, bluish, stringy meat that adhered closely to the bone . . . The small insects (the hero of *The Povest'* . . . is feeding on ants.—I.S.) fought back furiously. They covered Aleksei's hands, lips, tongue (food eating the person eating.—I.S.) with bites. They crept underneath his overalls and stung his body, but the stings were even pleasant to him (sic!).'"

42. L. Kassil', *Vratar' respubliki*, 194.

43. Ibid., 165–66.

44. Ibid., 127.

45. I. Smirnov, *Psykhodiakhronologika*, 275.

46. Irina Gutkin, *The Cultural Origins of the Socialist Realist Aesthetic*, 119.

47. L. Kassil', *Metro*, 14.

48. L. Kassil', *Vratar' Respubliki*, 166.

49. Mikhail Iampol'skii, "Censorship as the Triumph of Life," in *Socialism without Shores*, 169.

50. Irina Paperno, "Nietzscheanism and the return of Pushkin," in *Nietzsche and Soviet Culture: Ally and Adversary*, ed. Bernice Glatzer Rosenthal (Cambridge: Cambridge University Press, 1994), 227.

51. L. Kassil', *Vratar' Respubliki*, 77.

52. Mikhail Iampol'skii, "Censorship As the Triumph of Life," 169.

53. See Michael Gorham, "Mastering the Perverse: State Building and Language 'Purification' in Early Soviet Russia," Michael S. Gorham, *Slavic Review*, vol. 59, no.

1 (spring 2000): 150–53. What Gorham does not mention is that Gorky finds even the most innocent wordplay (in this case, wordplay that is suspiciously reminiscent of futurist *zaum'*) to be reprehensible because it "spoils" language. See M. Gor'kii, *Sobranie soch. v 30 t-kh*, t. 27 (Moskva: Khudozhestvennaia literatura, 1953), 167.

54. L. Kassil', *Vratar' Respubliki*, 81.

55. See Rainer Grübel, "Gabe, Aufgabe, Selbstaufgabe: Dichter-Tod als Opferhabitus," 177. See also Mikhail Iampol'skii, "Censorship as the Triumph of Life," 166.

56. L. Kassil', *Vratar' Respubliki*, 81.

57. L. Kassil', *Vratar' Respubliki*, 83.

58. L. Kassil', *Vratar' Respubliki*, 84.

59. N.V. Kornienko, "Moskva vo vremeni," 236.

60. M. Zolotonosov, *Slovo i telo*, 720. As an example Zolotonosov cites the following poem by Simonov (Ibid.): "Polnoch' b'et nad Spasskimi vorotami,/ Khorosho, ustavshi kochevat'/ I obvetrias' vsiakimi shirotami,/ Snova v tsentre mira postoiat'."

61. Thus, as Kornienko notes ("Moskva vo vremeni," 239), in *Happy Moscow* Platonov gathers together characters from the provinces, from Petersburg, and from Moscow in an attempt to survey the landscape of socialist construction.

62. Oksana Bulgakowa, "Spatial Figures in Soviet Cinema of the 1930s," trans. Jeffrey Karlsen, in *The Landscape of Stalinism: The Art and Ideology of Soviet Space*, eds. Evgeny Dobrenko and Eric Naiman (Seattle: University of Washington Press, 2003), 64.

63. M. Zolotonosov, *Slovo i telo*, 687. Note that Igor' Smirnov's claim (*Psikhodiakhronologika*, 254) that the masochistic body of the Stalinistic subject consistently occupies a place contrary to that of the norm is a direct result of this phenomenon.

64. Ibid.

65. I. Smirnov, *Psikhodiakhronologika*, 248.

66. M. Zolotonosov, *Slovo i telo*, 700.

67. Ibid., 702.

68. As Zolotonosov points out (*Slovo i telo*, 702), the bas-relief is not without a sexual component, since, according to Freud, dreams about flying invariably revolve around the seemingly miraculous character of erection.

69. M. Zolotonosov, *Slovo i telo*, 702.

70. Stephen Greenblatt, "Mutilation and Meaning," 223.

71. Of particular interest is the relationship, according to Greenblatt, between Christ's crucified body and the text in medieval Christianity. Christ's mutilated body is represented as a book, one which by virtue of its wounding achieves a kind of semantic plenitude: "This is, to be sure, an unusual book, not so much because it is flesh but because it has no blank spaces: '[T]here was no margent lefte in all thys booke, they was no voyd place, but every where it was eyther drawne with lynes, or els wrytten with letters, for these scourges fylled not onely his most precyous bodie with lynes drawne everie where, but also left many small Letters, some blacke, some blewe, some reade. . . . And for bycause no parte of thys book shoulde bee unwritten, hys head also was pearsed with sharpe thornes'" (Ibid., 223).

72. Katerina Clark, *The Soviet Novel*, 178.

73. As, for instance, in the following exchange (*Vratar' respubliki*, 145): "The room appeared unusually cramped to Karasik that evening. It was ready to burst at the seams. Anton's longshoreman's voice, his shoulders, the sweep of his arms and his height hardly were able to fit into it. Half-dressed, Anton stood in front of the mirror. . . . 'I'm big, Karasik! Damn, big as an ox.'"

74. Jacques Derrida, *Memoirs of the Blind*, trans. Pascale Ann-Brault and Michael Naas (Chicago: University of Chicago Press, 1993), 15.

75. Thus the high point of Anton's rehabilitation comes at the end of the novel when the hero's eyes meet those of Stalin, who is standing atop the mausoleum on Red Square: "Anton looked at the left wing of the mausoleum. A man in a grey service jacket and cap worn straight and pushed slightly forward was standing there. Without turning away, Anton looked him in the eye" (L. Kassil', *Vratar' Respubliki*, 279).

76. B. M. Gasparov, "Poeticheskii iazyk Pushkina kak fakt istorii russkogo literaturnogo iazyka," 246, 204.

77. The connection between Stalin and the sun was, as Zolotonosov points out (*Slovo i telo*, 736), a commonplace and has distinct sexual connotations.

78. A. Gol'dshtein, *Rasstavanie s nartsissom*, 208–9.

79. Jacques Derrida, *Memoirs of the Blind*, 19.

80. L. Kassil', *Vratar' Respubliki*, 263. Translation courtesy of Timothy D. Sergay.

81. Sergei Lobanov-Rostovsky, "Taming the Basilisk," in *The Body in Parts: Fantasies of Corporeality in Early Modern Europe*, eds. David Hillman and Carla Mazzio (New York: Routledge, 1997), 201–2.

82. Ibid., 202.

83. See A. Gol'dshtein, *Rasstavanie s nartsissom*, 217ff.

84. The ambivalence of the gateway is made particularly clear in a scene that occurs later in the novel. Echoing Stalinism's hypertrophied fear of contamination/penetration from the outside, Kandidov remarks: "When you think about it, the country is so big! But the goalposts are so small. . . . But for a ball that's enough" (186).

85. Viacheslav Kuritsyn, *Liubov' i zrenie*, 73. As Thomas Lahusen points out ("Novyi chelovek, novaia zhenshchina i polozhitel'nyi geroi, ili k semiotike pola v literature sotsialisticheskogo realizma," *Voprosy literatury*, no. 1 [1992], 195), the portrayal of the male versus female gaze in the literature of Socialist Realism emphasizes essentially opposite attributes. While the man's gaze is most often "thoughtful" or "penetrating," the woman's eyes are frequently described as "affectionate," "kindhearted," or "moist."

86. Ibid., 262.

87. See A. Gol'dshtein, *Rasstavanie s nartsissom*, 236.

88. Kassil"s reference to *Vii* is significant because it underscores the image of the mythological struggle between Good and Evil, in this case, between the *bogoslov*, or representative of God's word, and the evil *Vii*.

89. L. Kassil', *Vratar' Respubliki*, 242. The spatial model of the stadium in *Goalkeeper of the Republic* reproduces the spatial model of the Soviet Union, whose internal and external boundries were conceived as a series of concentric circles with Moscow in the middle (Hans Günther, *Der sozialistische Übermensch*, 168).

90. L. Kassil', *Vratar' respubliki*, 241. The image of the ball as a microcosm of the state echoes an earlier scene (142) in which Kandidov catches a globe and is described by his teammates as "Hercules with a globe."

91. See Etkind, *Sodom i psykheia*, 257.

92. See V. Papernyi, *Kul'tura "Dva,"* 63–66.

93. Eliot Borenstein, *Men without Women*, 141, 130.

94. Ibid., 183.

95. Jochen Hellbeck, "Writing the Self," 71.

96. A. Gol'dshtein, *Rasstavanie s nartsissom*, 206.

97. Aleksandar Mihailovic, *Corporeal Words*, 191.

98. "The Moscow river flowed beyond the parapet grating. It was grey, like an elephant in the zoo. And as in the zoo people tried to tease it. They stuck branches and sticks through the bars, threw apple cores and pebbles. They were afraid of the flood" (L. Kassil', *Vratar' Respubliki*, 230).

99. Hans Günther, *Der sozialistische Übermensch: M. Gor'kij und der sowjetische Heldenmythos* (Stuttgart: Verlag J. B. Metzler, 1993), 165.

100. Ibid.

101. M. Vaiskopf, *Pisatel' Stalin*, 188.

102. If Anteus's natural element is earth, Anton's is water, so that in returning to his Gidraer origins Kandidov remarks that it may be time for him to "get back in the water" (*Vratar' Respubliki*, 231).

103. Note that here Kandidov echoes Karasik, who earlier had also fantasized about the figure of the militiaman.

104. A. Etkind, *Khlyst*, 71.

105. Eric Naiman, *Sex in Public*, 31.

106. Ibid., 39.

107. Eliot Borenstein, *Men without Women*, 37.

108. Rimgaila Salys, "Understanding Envy," in Olesha's *Envy: A Critical Companion*, ed. Rimgaila Salys (Evanston: Northwestern University Press, 1999), 10.

109. As Byrne R. S. Fone notes [*Masculine Landscapes: Walt Whitman and the Homoerotic Text* (Carbondale: Southern Illinois University Press, 1992), 207], the poem seems to echo certain images in Plato's *Phaedrus*.

110. Ibid., 220.

111. Jerry Heil, "A Strict Youth, an Oneiric Literary/Film Fantasy: Restoration of the Cultural Memory and Beyond," *Russian Literature* 51 (2002): 169.

112. M. Zolotonosov, *Slovo i telo*, 636.

113. Byrne R. S. Fone, *Masculine Landscapes*, 258.

114. After having lost the match to the Gidraer team, Kandidov accidentally leaves the gas stove running in his apartment and is nearly killed.

115. Boris Groys, "Die gebaute Ideologie," 18.

116. Thus in "Obyknovennaia Arktika," (*Literaturnoe obozrenie*, 17 [1938]: 36), a certain M. Demidova writes that "it was the very first time that the doctor had sensed, up close, his great motherland, the friendly closeness of her peoples. He discovered the insignficance of the little world in which he had lived before. It was as if he had been born again at the age of fifty, after having felt that he was one of the members of the great friendly Soviet family."

Chapter Four

Conquering the Underworld: The Spectacle of the Stalinist Metro

"The metro is a world in itself—in the winter it's warm down there, cool in the sparkling clean. No Russian would dream of spitting on the metro's marble floor; he'd sooner spit on another passenger."

—Alexander Kaletski

The Stalinist body and body politic were forged through a complex process that envisioned the ideological formation of both individual and collective within a vast landscape of interconnected, mythologically charged locales, each of which had a central role to play in realizing the culture's grand narrative of social transformation. One such locale, as the previous chapter on Lev Kassil"'s *Goalkeeper of the Republic* has attempted to show, was the Stalinist stadium, where the unruly throng was ritually molded through its participation in the spectacle of the soccer match into an orderly and ideologically transparent body social. Even more than the stadium, however, one of the most compelling and enduring monuments to Stalinist culture's aspiration to give birth to a new brand of human being (my epigraph notwithstanding!) is to be found in the phenomenon of the Moscow metro. Without a doubt one of the boldest technological undertakings of the Stalinist '30s, the Moscow metro provides a perfect model of the culture's attempts to envision the communist society of the future. Alongside such other prominent metaphors of Stalinist utopian projecteering as the Belomor Canal project, the Moscow-Volga Canal, or the much publicized conquest of the Arctic by "Stalin's falcons,"[1] the mythology surrounding the Moscow metro spotlights what Clark describes as the fundamental literary and culture trope of high Stalinist culture; namely, the much publicized "struggle with nature."[2] At the same time, given the particularly rich cultural and symbolic connotations of the underground, it would seem apt to view the project as encompassing not simply nature as such but the specifically *human* nature which the bulk of revolutionary ideology (and its prerevolutionary antecedents) sought to transfigure. Perhaps not surprisingly, given Stalinist culture's easy appropriation of mythological (and specifically Christian) symbols,[3] the metro also embodied certain obvious elements of religious discourse, such that the finished construction might well be seen as a kind of Soviet holy site. Here the communist body social could receive its daily baptism in the font of Stalinist ideology and be continually, symbolically reborn.[4]

The Moscow metro (or "Kaganovich metro," as it was originally called) was as much an ideological project as it was an engineering feat.[5] As one contemporary scholar notes, such archetypal Stalinist rituals/sites as the physical culture parades, the many "parks of culture and rest" that dotted the former Soviet landscape, and even some public toilets were created with a view toward sculpting the body politic and initiating it into the new system of Stalinist ideology and mythology.[6] Without a doubt the Moscow metro was one of the most prominent of these locales. And as Mikhail Ryklin notes, the *discourse* of the Moscow metro was in many ways as important as the technological and engineering feats that attended its construction. Hence the rather ambiguous coloring of a phrase pronounced by L. M. Kaganovich at the triumphant opening of the first line of the metro: "'Our Soviet metropoliten is more than a technical structure.'"[7] A prominent locus within the map of Stalinist reconstruction, the Moscow metro was conceived as a place where the radiant contours of the future utopia could be experienced in miniature. The chapter that follows does not pretend to be a comprehensive account of the metro's history, since this work has already been done. Rather it offers a reading of the ideologically and mythologically saturated discourse that emerged from this very important project. This having been said, a brief summary of the history of the Moscow metro and the most significant aspects of its construction is necessary for a fuller understanding of the texts that follow.

As Dietmar Neutatz notes in his recently published monograph on the subject, if the construction of the Moscow metro began only in 1931, the idea of building it dates back to the end of the nineteenth century.[8] While plans for the construction of an underground were originally put forth by private firms around the turn of the century, they were quickly rejected by the Moscow municipal authorities. The latter deemed the idea premature and were also fundamentally opposed to the idea of licensing the construction and operation of public transportation to private entrepeneurs.[9] A decade later in 1911–1912 the Moscow city fathers agreed that the time had finally come for a metro. Yet they once again found themselves confronted with the necessity of licensing the project to private entrepeneurs, who were, in addition, backed by foreign firms and capital.[10] Likewise, in the 1920s the project failed to materialize due to financing difficulties. In contrast to earlier years, the new Bolshevik government showed no real signs of interest in the idea, while the relevant party officials kept their distance from the project due to the lack of available funding.[11] Any progress on the metro project was further complicated by the fact that during the "Cultural Revolution" years of 1928–1931 the party was still considering plans for the revolutionary reconstruction of Moscow. The question of the metro could not be decided until the shape of the future Metropolis had been definitively resolved.[12]

The issue was finally decided when the Moscow party chief L. M. Kaganovich used his considerable influence with the Politburo to move the project ahead. During the June party plenum (held from June 11–16, 1931) Kaganovich cited Moscow's increasingly acute transportation problems as the most pressing reason for building the metro. At the same time he placed his plan for a socialist underground in the context of the larger "General Plan for the Reconstruction of Moscow" that superseded earlier deurbanist ideas and was gradually expanded until 1935.[13] The decision was ultimately taken, as Neutatz informs us, not so much out of military considerations but for reasons of prestige and visibility. Still, it was not prestige alone that motivated the decision. Whereas in other countries the desire to overcome technological backwardness could be seen as a function of national pride, here it was clearly political ideology that played a dominant role. As the future "capital of the international proletariat and a showplace of socialism" the city of Moscow would have to build a metro that was more than just a means of transportation—the first ever *socialist* metro could be nothing less than "the best in the world."[14]

Despite such grandiose proclamations, the project was beset with numerous difficulties from its very inception. First among these was the problem of personnel. Pavel Pavlovich Rotert, the engineer chosen by the Council of People's Commissars in 1931 to head *Metrostroi* (the organization charged with constructing the underground), encountered considerable difficulties in assembling a qualified staff of technicians. Indeed, only several of Rotert's engineers had experience building a metro, as Neutatz remarks. In addition to these, there were several more who had at least seen a metro in their travels abroad.[15] This rather serious problem was exacerbated by the fact that *Metrostroi* was forced by political pressure from above to rush headlong into the process of construction—even before the final plans for the project had been completed.[16] Meanwhile, in the rhetoric that accompanied almost every step of the metro's construction this obvious shortcoming was quickly recast as its opposite: that is, great strength. For in the eyes of the Soviet leadership the experience of building the metro provided an object lesson in how the universal shortage of skilled technical personnel in the Soviet Union could be solved. As Stalin notes in a speech given to a group of metal workers in 1934, the problem of cadres can be solved only in one of two ways: "Either we start by training people . . . or we begin by immediately creating machines . . . so that we school our people in technology—create cadres—in the very process of producing and exploiting the machines. We have chosen the second path."[17] Stalin's utopian belief that qualified socialist workers could be conceived through a symbiotic relationship with the machine is illustrated in the bowels of the Moscow metro.[18] In this manner the underground emerged as one of the premier venues of Stalinist reforging. Here unskilled laborers were miraculously transformed into skilled workers through the production and manipulation of technology. At the same time (and here we see a perfect illustration of Stalinist culture's flexibility in negotiating contradictory propositions), the discourse of the Moscow metro does not shy away from denigrating the machine in favor of the metro workers' voluntarist zeal. Indeed, more often than not the worker's lack of technical know-how or of the proper equipment is promoted as a virtue, since it allows her or him to press beyond a mechanistic worldview into the realm of utopian construction proper. This, in turn, mirrors what a number of scholars have described as Stalinist culture's marginalization of technical and professional languages in favor of a single, quasi-religious or mythological superdiscourse.[19] Human beings, it was argued, are characterized by their ability to press beyond available norms into the realm of the fantastic and the miraculous. Man—not machine—is born to make the fairy tale come true.

Another significant obstacle to the construction of the metro concerned the character of the tunnels. In March of 1932 considerable controversy arose surrounding the issue of whether to build the underground using the Berlin method of open-trench digging or the English method of deep tunneling.[20] For strategic reasons (during wartime the tunnels "with their reinforced shielding and buttressed walls, would make excellent bomb shelters," Khrushchev writes)[21] and in order not to interrupt the traffic along the major thoroughfares, it was decided in 1933 to use the deep tunneling method throughout significant portions of the new metro. As with other facets of the construction, this aspect too has a considerable (if not overwhelmingly) symbolic significance, which is brought out in the numerous narratives that recount the heroic tale of the metro's building. In addition to deciding the question of open-trench digging or deep tunneling, the government was able to further resolve the underground crisis by postponing the finish date for the metro from January 1, 1934, to December 24, 1934. Finally, as Neutatz writes, Kaganovich and company provided *Metrostroi* with a more efficient organization (including a political component to the leadership in the person of E. T. Abakumov), at the same time that they began mobilizing thousands of Komsomol and communist members from Moscow factories and from around the country to work on the construction site.[22] The latter—particularly the Komsomol—were soon touted as the socialist vanguard of the metro.[23] They made up for their lack of technical expertise by bringing extraordinary amounts of energy and enthusiasm to the project, while at the same time providing the basis for a saga of labor feats and miracles crucial to the broader narrative of socialist transformation.

A certain amount of the mythology surrounding the construction of the metro is no doubt due to the fact that the lion's share of the actual building was carried out in the last year of construction—from April to October of 1934. Indeed, it was only through a massive increase in the number of workers and the amount of resources applied to the project that *Metrostroi* was able to make up for what had been neglected during the first two years of work. The technical problems that arose from these increased tempos caused the finish date to be pushed back to February 1935; however, by the beginning of February the first train was able to travel the entire line.[24] In the months that followed, further improvements were made and the metro was triumphantly opened to the public on May 15, 1935.[25]

While the grand opening of the first-ever socialist underground became a cause for public festivities, the phenomenon of the Moscow metro was broadly celebrated throughout literature and film as one of the most significant landmarks in the building of the new Stalinist utopia. As Boris Groys notes, "the metro-builder was declared the hero of the new culture," while "books, poems, novels and plays were written about the metro and its architects."[26] More importantly, the Moscow metro—which soon became the most compelling metaphor for the culture's aspiration to build the communist society of the future—echoes the utopian construction that marked Russia's entrance into modernity at the outset of the eighteenth century. For if Peter the Great's intention to transport the city of Saint Peter (i.e., Rome) to the banks of the Neva was itself less than fully utopian, the site chosen for the future city was not, according to Groys. Indeed, the choice of a swampy marsh as the location for Russia's first attempt at Westernization seems eerily apt in retrospect. As the least suitable *topos* (because unstable, chaotic, and fundamentally separate from the Russian soil), the swamp provided an ideal location for a city whose very purpose was to be negate the chronotope of pre-Petrine culture and history.[27] At the same time, it laid the foundation for an enduring narrative of struggle with nature that would animate Russia's utopian thinking well into the twentieth century.

The Moscow metro, built by Peter's self-proclaimed twentieth-century heir, is located in a supremely inhospitable place—deep underground. This, too, was no accident. As Groys points out, "a utopia requires a certain spatial isolation in order to be conceived and constructed in every detail, and in order

to be sheltered from . . . corruption by the everyday, imperfect world.[28] Moreover, in the utopian world of the underground there can be nothing "inherited,
traditional, self-evident, nothing that is not planned out."[29] Likewise, Mikhail
Ryklin remarks that the era that produced the metro discourse "approaches
history, the past and in general anything created by it with deep distrust. The
new world begins everything anew and on its own terms: everything inherited becomes suspect."[30] To be sure, one can argue with this characterization
of a culture whose claim to represent the crowning achievement of human
history is well known, yet the very remoteness of the Moscow metro from the
trials of surface life is noteworthy. And the fact that many of the stations were
constructed at the unheard-of depth of 20–30 meters beneath the surface—in
addition to its obvious pragmatic and military significance—spotlights the
largely utopian tenor of the project. Indeed, as Groys goes on to argue, the
Stalinist metro represents an even more consistent embodiment of the utopian
impulse than many of the projects conceived by the 1920s avant-garde. For
the avant-garde proved insufficiently dialectical in its approach to utopia,
overlooking the fact that a "total utopia" would necessarily include both
heaven *and* hell. Preoccupied as they were with the surface and the heavens,
their projects appear to have been "topian" rather than utopian.[31] By contrast,
it is only the Stalinist era (with its extraordinary passion for orchestrating a
Hegelian overcoming of opposites)[32] that endeavors to create heaven in the
very depths of hell.[33] Thus, Groys writes that "it was only the Stalinist epoch
that brought together Heaven into Hell and made possible a synthesis of both.
The product of this synthesis is the genuinely utopian city of Moscow, the underground Moscow, which is to say, the Moscow metro."[34]

In a similar vein, Mikhail Vaiskopf stresses the "barbarous syncretism" of
Stalinist civilization, a trait that enables a free modulation between industrial/
mechanical metaphors as well as their organic and biological equivalents
throughout the culture's ideological and mythological discourses.[35] The illu-
sionist pathos of the architecture and lighting of the Moscow metro underscores this by creating the paradoxical impression that the passenger is high
above the ground even when he or she is actually deep beneath the earth.[36]
This fact is invariably remarked upon in contemporary accounts.[37] By the
same token, the metro was to act as an *embodied* rapprochement of the real
and the ideal. "It was necessary," one recent critic writes, "not to conceal [its]
'undergroundness' as a fault and not to emphasize it as an advantage; rather
one had to create the illusion of being in a palace that in reality was located
underground but ideally was placed outside of any 'topos,' in an 'u-topos.'"[38]
It is presumably this same need to steer a course between the Scylla of natu-
ralism and the Charybdis of idealism that informs the following discussion of
several successful and not-so-successful designs for individual stations. In the

commemorative volume entitled *How We Built the Metro*, the well-known Stalin-era architect Kolli remarks on the extraordinary difficulty of his work as a metro architect. Echoing the pathos of synthesis that underlay not only the official doctrine of Socialist Realism but much of Stalinist culture, Kolli defines his task vis-à-vis the other participants in the project as one of discovering an elusive "unity of opposites."[39] Likewise, in laying out the design of particular stations the greatest challenge for the architect lay in "reconciling all of the supposedly irreconcilable contradictions."[40] Thus while some designs were rejected because of their "undergroundness,"[41] others were dismissed for their excessive formalism or because they suggested an unearthly, almost religious mysticism. A famous episode concerns L. M. Kaganovich's criticism of the artificial lighting proposed for the Hunter's Line and Palace of Soviets stations. Rejecting them because of their exaggeratedly mystical character—a quality that in fact constituted the very core of the metro project but which could not be *over*emphasized within the Stalinist doctrine of a synthesis of opposites—Kaganovich commands: "I want more realistic lighting. After all, these aren't temples but underground railroad stations!"[42]

If in the broadest sense the metro represents Stalinism's desire to embody the transcendent ideal within the realm of the real,[43] stylistically it proves no less "synthetic," assembling a broad array of periods and artistic forms within a single mythologically charged locus. Thus the stations of the Kaganovich metro bring together diverse materials, styles, and eras in such a way as to dissolve any sense of chronological distinctivness. This, in turn, mirrors Stalinist civilization's perception of itself as the absolute telos of world history — as heir to all its artistic and cultural wealth:[44] Finally, the utopian character of the metro's art and architecture was more or less guaranteed by a direct connection of both to the culture's most prominent visionaries. And one need hardly point out that the true architects of the utopian underground were none other than Kaganovich and Stalin.[45] For this reason the artistic sensibilities of the individual architects ultimately proved irrelevant to the project:[46] "In designing the metro stations the leadership wished to express its own collective taste. In this sense, as well, the metro was utopian. It was the work of cultural outsiders, of nonspecialists and nonartists who had no place in the traditional world and who therefore found their only opportunity for cultural self-fulfillment in the underground."[47]

The ideological and mythological character of the metro was such that it shared much in common with places of religious or cult worship. On a rather impressionistic note, one recent critic sees the "catacombs" of the finished metro as reminiscent of ancient pre-Christian ritual. Upon descending into the bowels of the earth, the passenger would revert to a state of archaic non-individuation and join with the collective through the warmth of Mother

Earth's womb.[48] In a somewhat different vein, the same author remarks that in terms of its cultural significance the *metropoliten* recalls the *Mitropoliia*, or head of the official Orthodox Church. Particularly significant is the fact that the institution of the *Mitropoliia* was branded by the unofficial church as a "creation of the underworld." By this logic Kaganovich could be cast as the devil, even as the metro became his diabolical church.[49] To be sure, such characterizations of what was—after all—a construction project might initially appear somewhat far-fetched. Yet if nothing else, they reflect the degree to which the metro as a discursive or rhetorical construct captivated (and continues to captivate) the imagination of a broader public. While contemporary critics might be inclined to see the metro in a diabolical light, there is every indication that within the Stalinist imagination the metro represented nothing less than a taste of heaven on earth. Thus even the act of entering it acquires a certain mythological or religious resonance in contemporary accounts. This quality is perhaps best captured in a children's book published by E. Tarakhovskaia in 1935—the same year that the metro was opened to the general public. In Tarakhovskaia's *M*, the trip underground is marked by a series of fairy-tale boundaries that the child must cross over in order to reach his destination—from the outward-radiating arches of the Red Gates station through the magical "turnstile–automat," down the "miracle staircase" (i.e., escalator) and finally into the lucid space of the underground itself.[50] And it could well be argued that the author's choice of a folktale idiom to describe the metro (for instance, the folktale phrase лестница-чудесница or "miracle staircase") is motivated not only by considerations of audience but by the sense of the metro as yet another of Stalinism's fairy-tales-come-true. Finally, the image of the underground as an almost magical creation is encapsulated in the cover drawing of Tarakhovskaia's book. The picture is of a giant, radiant letter "M" placed in relief against a starry night sky. Not so much a prosaic *metropoliten*, the cover drawing shows Stalinism's miracle underground assuming its rightful place at the center of a host of heavenly bodies, shedding light amid cosmic darkness.

Implicit in the gesture of "crossing over" is one of the oldest topoi in Western literature—the descent into the underworld. From Homer's Odysseus to Virgil's Aeneas and finally Dante's himself, epic literary travelers to the underworld have "crossed over" in order to gaze into the secret places of the soul (the "subterranean city" of the self)—in order, that is, to acquire spiritual insight through a mythological ritual of death and rebirth.[51] Likewise, in more contemporary works such as those of Victor Hugo and his contemporaries, the Paris underground is viewed both as a sacred space linked to the "cult of darkness and prophetic dreams"[52] and as a hellish antiworld, where human beings are turned into shades and become like the souls of the dead.[53] Thus while the gloomy underworld of the Paris sewers in Hugo's *Les Misérables* is consciously associated with the myth of Hades,[54] at the same time the cloaca appears—according to Mikhail Iampol'skii—as a kind of "sacred text, a text that can only be opened by the hand of God . . . or by the author, endowed with the ability to raise his all-seeing eye high above the surface of the earth."[55] This split is echoed in the juxtaposition of Jean Valjean's blindness with the superior vision of the author as Creator. Similarly, in the darkened tunnels of the Moscow metro the individual's initiation into the higher reality of the collective subjectivity requires a sacrifice or loss of individual(ized) vision, according to one author.[56]

A less mystical approach to the same Paris sewers/underground (yet one that shares much in common with the later metro and the reconstruction of Moscow) is found in the urban renewal projects undertaken by Emperor Napoleon III during the period of the Second Empire. As Donald Reid remarks, Napoleon III's prefect of the Seine, Baron Georges Haussmann, viewed reforming the water and sewage system of Paris as essential to overcoming the flawed legacy of the ancien régime, a legacy that had "culminated in the revolutions of 1830 and 1848."[57] Underscoring his intellectual debt to the utopian Saint-Simonism that underlay much of Second Empire social thought, Haussmann envisioned the city as a body whose vital arteries, organs, and orifices could be cleansed and reformed through a sweeping project of urban renewal: "'The underground galleries, organs of the large city, would function like those of the human body, without revealing themselves to the light of day. Pure and fresh water, light, and heat would circulate there . . . Secretions would take place there mysteriously and would maintain public health without troubling the good order of the city and without spoiling its exterior beauty.'"[58] As Reid goes on to remark, the symbolic role of the new sewer system in the restructuring of the capital was that of a civilizing agent. And if the earlier Paris "cloaca" suggested certain parallels with human anatomy (i.e., the intestinal, urinary, or generative canal), the more modern *sewer* was stripped of its anthropomorphic dimensions. It was a social construction rather than a quasi-anatomical outgrowth. In the passage from nature to culture the corporeal underground was thus transformed into an enlightened apparatus, one that could be subjected to constant scrutiny and surveillance.[59]

The distinction between cloaca and sewer in the rhetoric surrounding Haussmann's reformed underground is expressed, first and foremost, as the passage from natural body to enlightened mechanism. This gives rise to a further opposition: that of female anatomy and male supervision. Thus for the prominent public health expert Alexandre Jean-Baptiste Parent-Duchalet the cloaca represented nothing less than the architectural equivalent of the brothel.

More specifically, it was associated with the prostitute's (as yet unregulated) genitals. To be sure, both cloaca and vagina played an essential part in the "social economy of purgation," yet in order for that economy to function properly it was necessary that the state "impose rational order in these disorderly realms."[60] Thus if the early cloaca was perceived as a feminine realm, plagued by the unbridled folly of nature, the Second Empire's attempt to reclaim it underscored the advance of an entirely "'male,' technical rationality where nature was controlled rather than in control."[61] What had previously been opaque and therefore the object of purely fantastic, mythological imaginings was now rendered transparent—indeed, even pleasing to the eye. As Reid notes, in order to publicize its achievements in reclaiming the underworld, the sewer administration began (in 1867) offering tours that allowed the public to view a "second underground Paris."[62] And in stark contrast to what Victor Hugo had earlier described as a "'refuse heap'" for all the "'filthiness of civilization,'" where the very hierarchies that render society intelligible were dissolved,[63] the Second Empire sewers were conceived as a locus of exemplary order. No longer content to function à la Hugo as the city's *con*science, the newly reclaimed sewers were the brainchild of *science*—of the intellect's lucid and penetrating gaze: "The sewers were literally a spectacle of enlightenment. They were illuminated 'with some thousands of moderator lamps, each provided with its silvered reflector. . . . Rows of lamps that grow fainter and fainter in the distance, light up the vaulted gallery and cast their reflections in the black turgid waters at our feet.'" [64]

It might seem a logical stretch to compare the Paris sewers of the second half of the nineteenth century with the Moscow metro of the 1930s, yet ultimately there is much to recommend such a comparison. Indeed, Haussmann's reconstruction of Paris served not only as a point of comparison but as a cautionary tale for the contemporary Soviet project of rebuilding Moscow.[65] Moreover, at least one contemporary critic notes that by the beginning of the twentieth century the literary imagination had replaced the Leviathan of the cloaca with the labyrinth of the metro.[66] The fact that the metro plays a role structurally analogous to that of the earlier cloaca is made clear—among others—by the antipathy it evoked in many Russian emigres, who saw in the metro a metaphor for exile and death. It is presumably for this reason that such important 1920s expatriates as Shklovskii, Ehrenburg, Pasternak, and Nabokov scrupulously avoided any mention of the underground in their descriptions of life abroad.[67] By contrast, in his poem "A Bit of Utopia about Miss Metro," the archetypal Soviet poet Mayakovsky speaks of a future Moscow metro in glowingly positive terms—as a continuation of the 1920s utopian fantasies of settling the heavens.[68] Indeed, Mayakovsky's "A Bit of Utopia" is nothing if not prophetic. By symbolically moving the conquerors of the ether underground, the futurist poet anticipates the utopian push to colonize the underground that lay at the very heart of the Stalinist metro project. Yet, is not merely the religious/ mythological perceptions of the underground as a place of otherwordly mystery that Soviet ideology sought to dispel. Equally compelling was the utopian dream of rationalizing or "Bolshevizing" the benighted realm of the human unconscious, which since Freud (and earlier, Dostoevsky) had been mapped out in terms of the underground.[69] Thus Mayakovsky writes of the new Soviet *Metropoliten* as a model of life stripped of its shadowy underbelly: "через год/ без всякой тени/ прите/ в метролитене."[70] Perhaps the most unsettling portrayal of Soviet ideology's desire to reclaim the underworld or "sewer" of human nature is to be found in Andrei Platonov's unfinished novel *Happy Moscow*. In it the realm of the unconscious is structurally and thematically linked to the image of the underground—an underground that is quite literally being emptied of its base contents by the utopian architects of the Moscow metro. In stark contrast to Mayakovsky, however, Platonov casts doubt on communism's optimistic plans to rebuild the (subterranean) city of the soul. Thus the ultimate of utopian projects is entrusted (in words all too reminiscent of Trotsky's appeal to transform the human unconscious) to the novel's most ambiguous character, the quixotic surgeon Sambikin: "Now it is essential to understand everything because either socialism would succeed in penetrating the last hiding-place of a man's insides and releasing the pus that had accumulated there drop by drop over the centuries, or nothing new would happen" (*Happy Moscow*, 39).[71]

If Haussmann's reconstruction of the Paris sewer represents a quasi-utopian attempt to rationalize the bowels of the city-as-body politic, the Kaganovich metro seems no less ambitious in its desire to civilize the Moscow underground. In this it mirrors the larger Stalinist narrative of ideological rebirth and reclamation, which often equated reforging with an overhaul of the body's internal mechanism(s). Thus in the works of Andrei Platonov and Mikhail Zoshchenko the promise of revolutionary transformation is aimed, among others, at the stomach and digestive tract. Similarly, the Stalinist playwright Afinogenov depicted his ideological self-rehabilitation as similar to a "surgical intervention." Describing the events that led up to his spiritual rebirth (following his exclusion from the party in 1937), Afinogenov writes: "I put myself under the knife; I took out not only my stomach but the heart as well. I killed the self inside of me—and then a miracle happened: Having already given up all hope and preparing myself for my physical death, I suddenly understood and saw the beginning of something new, a new 'self.'"[72] A similar sense of life-and-death struggle animates the narratives that deal with the Moscow metro, many of which paint the process of building it in explicitly martial colors. And as in the case of the writer Afinogenov, war is waged not with any external enemy but with the "irrational" *internal* economy of the City itself. For despite its aspiration to become the capital of socialism and home to the world proletariat, Moscow of the early '30s still seems deeply mired in its parochial past via multiple layers of history and geology. The metro builders' heroic struggle to overcome this past—to "kill the self inside so that a miracle might happen"—is spotlighted in a short history of the Moscow metro entitled *The First Soviet Metro*. Here the author remarks that "the history and geology almost seem to have done everything possible to make the work as difficult as possible. History left the foundations of old buildings and fortress walls beneath the earth. It squeezed Moscow's streets into narrow crevices and connected them in absurd knots. And nature brought soil here that was like watery kissel, as well as a complex jumble of currents."[73]

If it is true that utopias can flourish only at a secure distance from the contaminating potential of profane space and time, it is not surprising that history (or more precisely, its material traces) poses a certain threat to the socialist metro. To be sure, the danger associated with these "traces" is invariably explained in practical terms; the foundations of old buildings and other residual structures can cause accidents or delay the construction of tunnels if their locations are not mapped out in advance. Yet the considerable symbolic potential of the past—that is, its ability to corrupt or contaminate the fledgling utopia of the underground—appears no less unsettling for the authors of the metro narrative. Highlighting the precarious closeness of a chaotic, preideological past to the Soviet present, the author of the *First Soviet Metro* remarks that the only thing separating the Sverdlov Square of today from the foul swamp of yesterday is a thin layer of asphalt.[74] Likewise in the Krestovskii market scene of his novel *Happy Moscow*, Platonov describes the prerevolutionary past as existing cheek by jowl with the communist present, as its indelible, undeniable shadow.[75] How, then, does the metro narrative (and more broadly, Stalinist culture) assuage its inevitable anxieties about the "foul swamp of yesterday"? In a sense, by reconfiguring the entire historical narrative. Not content to simply become the next layer in an endless series of strata stretching backward in time, Stalinist civilization recasts itself as the indisputable telos of human history and striving. It is, in other words, the alpha and the omega—the Third Rome, after which no others will follow.[76] Because Stalinism sees itself as sole claimant to the past, it is precisely the construction of the underground by Stalin, Kaganovich, and company that allows history to be fully documented, cataloged, and understood. Thus one contemporary proudly remarks that the ancient walls and fortresses of Moscow (as well as many other priceless archeological finds) were first discovered during the digging of the tunnels.[77] The implicit connection between the fledgling underground, which was to embody the very essence of the utopian future, with the riches of the Russian past merely buttresses the culture's claim to be the rightful heir to everything that precedes it. For this reason one can imagine that the triumphant mapping of the Moscow underground was not simply a practical project—though it was obviously that, as well.[78] By threading the jumble of the past through the filter of the utopian present, one produces a map that is living testimony to history's march toward self-fulfillment in socialism. As one recent critic remarks, Stalinist culture is, first and foremost, a culture of cartography. In it the map becomes a quasi-aesthetic object which permits its readers to view the steady progress of the real toward the ideal.[79] Thus the digging of the metro tunnels takes the science of cartography to a new level. Opening up layer after layer of history, the architects of the Moscow underground proved that all roads lead not to Rome but to the Third Rome deep beneath the surface of Moscow—that is, to the Kaganovich metro.

In keeping with the narrative of struggle against nature that underpinned nearly every front of socialist construction, by far the greatest threat to the Kaganovich metro comes from the city's mysterious underbelly. While it is true that conditions were indeed difficult—significant amounts of ground water and quicksand produced frequent cave-ins and flooding[80]—it is also true that the subsequent metro *narratives* invariably transform what was essentially an engineering problem into an epic contest with the hostile, untamed elements. In this they mirror the high pathos associated with Stalinism's conquest of the Arctic wastelands at the hands of the Cheliuskin and other expeditions.[81] While Arctic snow, ice, and sheer distance from the Motherland were the bogeymen of the Stalinist flier, for the architects of the Moscow metro the city's chaotic geology represents the greatest threat. Thus in *How We Built the Metro*, Kaganovich remarks that the builders "fought with nature, with the poor soils beneath Moscow" and that Moscow's "geology turned out to be pre-revolutionary, old regime."[82] And as in the case of the St. Petersburg myth, where the cultural capital seemed to arise as if by divine fiat from some primordial ooze, here, too, water symbolizes the originary chaos (amniotic fluid?) out of which the civilized metro will emerge. Other similarities suggest themselves, as well. For instance, the constant threat of encroaching flood waters, so compellingly described in Pushkin's *Bronze Horseman*, here becomes the threat of groundwater leakage. And the latter is not merely an obstacle; it is a menace forever threatening to undo the painstaking work of the intrepid builders. Moreover, if the (bodily) cave is most often associated with the "female and the maternal,"[83] the Moscow underground appears to symbolize that "feminine" and therefore fluid, unconscious realm which must be clothed in cement, granite, and marble in order to join together with the "masculine" city above. No doubt it is for this very reason that one of the few statues of the period to represent a genuinely masculine woman is of a Female metro builder. This statue (originally entitled "The Female Metro-Builder" and subsequently "For the Mastery of Technology") allegorizes the death of "feminine" nature at the hands of masculine technology and civilization, departing significantly from the mainstream of statuary of the time, which was more inclined to associate women with the earth, nature, and the *kolkhoz*.[84] By the same token, the finished metro—like granite Petersburg atop the swamp—radiates neither instability nor chaos, but the "epidemic of stasis" that was surely one of the defining moments of Stalinist civilzation.[85]

For both practical and ideological/mythological reasons, the theme of water occupies a prominent position within the larger metro narrative. As Neutatz points out, the technical problems associated with water were far from insignificant. Indeed, the mining methods that were initially used to construct the metro tunnels quickly proved unsuitable for digging in the water-bearing and quicksand-ridden Moscow underground. It was not until spring of 1933 that the problem was solved through the introduction of caissons—that is, watertight, highly pressurized chambers used for constructing tunnels underwater.[86] Yet this strictly *technical* problem acquires distinctly mythological overtones in the subsequent retelling of the metro's construction. Thus one contemporary describes water as the most fearsome enemy of the Moscow underground,[87] while almost every account of the period includes an enthusiastic mention of L. M. Kaganovich's lapidary admonition to the workers to build the tunnels dry, so that "it doesn't drip anywhere." [88] Typical for the metro narrative as a whole is Lopatin's *First Soviet Metro*, which juxtaposes the treacherous underground water with the cement walls used to isolate and contain it. Symptomatically, the author refers to this using images of "clothing"—a nod to the pathos of dressing (as opposed to that of disrobing or divestment) that distinguished the culture of the Stalinist period from its iconoclastic predecessor in the '20s.[89] This is hardly Lopatin's invention, though he makes more extensive and evocative use of it than most. Indeed, the metro narrative as a whole repeatedly refers to the process of isolating tunnel walls and appyling marble to them in terms of "dressing." One can easily imagine that this metaphor had not so much to do with a kind of architectural modesty on the part of Kaganovich and others as it did with Stalinist culture's acute preoccupation with stasis and the preservation of boundaries—in short, with hierarchy. For in addition to its obvious practical function the isolation and marble facading used throughout the underground (i.e., its "clothing") also functioned metaphorically as a protective barrier separating the fluid incontinence of Moist Mother Earth from the unchanging, immobile *eidos* of Stalinist civilization:[90]

> Subterranean water lies in wait for the tunnel at every step. It is necessary to fence oneself off from it with a sturdy wall. Truly impenetrable fortresses— immune to the pressure of the subterranean waters—must be erected. The tunnel has to be dressed in tough, water-proof clothing. The task of creating sturdy, impenetrable clothing for the subterranean metro corridors is perhaps even more important than the task of moving earth.[91]

Perhaps one of the most engaging portrayals of the Moscow metro as a microcosm of Stalinist culture's battle to reclaim the natural is to be found in Lev Kassil''s 1936 book *Miracle beneath Moscow*. Although best known as an author of books for children and adolescents, Kassil' also published a number of sketches and feuilletons dealing with a wide range of topics from the Moscow metro to the Moscow-Volga Canal. His *Miracle beneath Moscow* represents a vivid recasting of the most important cliches of the broader metro narrative and anticipates much of the imagery and thematics of Kassil''s later novel *Goalkeeper of the Republic* (1939).[92] The most important of these concerns the passage of the Stalinist subject from a state of physiological and psychological excess to one conscious restraint and is clearly prefigured in the pathos of transforming the underground that was the ideological core of the metro narrative. An additional (though surely accidental) similarity can be gleaned in the prototype of the conscious Jew who oversees the ideological rehabilitation of an excessive Other. In *Goalkeeper of the Republic* it is the Jewish journalist Karasik who plays intellectual mentor to his too-spirited Russian friend Kandidov. Meanwhile, in *Miracle beneath Moscow* Lazar' Kaganovich—the nearly superhuman symbol of reason's triumph and also a Jewish Bolshevik—conceives and carries out the miraculous transformation of the city's chaotic underground.

A central theme within the larger metro narrative concerns the issue of vision or visibility. The Stalinist ideological hero, according to Viacheslav Kuritsyn, is one who transforms space with his gaze, endeavoring to encompass the entire cosmos in his field of vision.[93] And within the poetics of Socialist Realism only those who fulfill a lofty demiurgic function are granted the gift of sight.[94] Hearkening back to the tradition that imagined the revolution as the engine of history,[95] such heroes typically combine the conqueror's all-powerful gaze with penetrating movement through space in an act of masterful "vision-from-the-train."[96] This situation is exemplified in one of the classic works of Socialist Realism—Vs. Azhaev's *Far from Moscow*. In it the hero Koshkin is shown traveling by rail to an important construction site in the Far East. The closer he draws to his destination, the more he is able to peer

through the clutter of random building materials and workers into the radiant future of socialist construction.[97] The odd person out is Andrei Platonov,
whose most memorable works of the '30s (i.e., *Dzhan* and *Happy Moscow*)
intentionally dim the overactive gaze of their visionary protagonists, such as
Nazar Chagataev and Semion Sartorius. In this one senses the author's growing preference for the stirrings of the invisible heart over the demands of a
masterful, all-seeing eye. By contrast, Lev Kassil''s work appeals openly to
the cultural mainstream. A *skophiliac* rather than *skopophobic* coloring predominates in such works as *Miracle beneath Moscow* or *Goalkeeper of the
Republic*. Echoing the strong current of neo-Platonism that underlay Stalinist ideology, Kassil' identifies vision—with its implict connection to the
Sun/Good/Truth in Platonic philosophy[98]—as the highest and most noble
among the senses.

If "vision-from-the-train" represents a key mythologeme within Stalinist ideology, what better place to envision its workings than in the depths of the
Moscow underground? As in the case of Haussmann's sewer, whose ultimate
goal was the rationalization of a chaotic body politic, the trains of the
Kaganovich metro serve not only as an efficient means of public transport but
to transport Stalinism's fantasy of total vision into the murky depths of the un-
derground-as-unconscious.[99] Yet on the most basic level, the metro narrative's
interest in vision and light underscores the broader culture's obsession with the
aesthetic—its desire to remake reality in the form of a grandiose *Gesamtkunstwerk*. And the Moscow metro stands as the most successful testimony to the
era's attempts at aesthetic engineering. A veritable feast for the eye, the sheer
beauty of the *metropoliten* is a fact that never fails to warrant mention in contemporary accounts. In one commemorative work, the authors describe the
underground as "solid, comfortable and beautiful," while the future, post-
reconstruction Moscow is envisioned as "the best and most beautiful city in the
world."[100] At the same time, the metro narrative's overemphasis on vision recalls the project of enlightment—of all-penetrating, masterful vision—that lay
at the core of Stalinist culture's fetishization of the eye.[101] Kassil''s account of
the metro, with its unusual emphasis on transparency, light, and vision throughout, only reinforces this. Accordingly, one of the very first images of *Miracle
beneath Moscow* (before the reader even enters the underground) includes a vision of the future, reconstructed Moscow *and* a playing out of the very act of
utopian *seeing*. Like Azhaev's Koshkin who is able to visualize the triumph of
socialism through the banal clutter of the present, Kassil' encourages his reader
to stroll with his mind's eye through the alleys of tomorrow:

> It has already become a cherished tradition during the October and May holi-
> days to display designs—projects for the future palaces, stadiums, institutes and

dormitories of socialist Moscow—in the display windows of the main streets. Spread out on Whatman paper and stretched onto frames, separated from our glances by nothing more than glass and a few future years, the splendor of socialism's capital of tomorrow takes part in the holidays of the present. In our mind's eye we stroll through new alleys that recede far into the depths of the future. We admire the granite giants of the future aeroports, the great stadium halls, brimming with sunlight and air. During these days the old Moscow houses appear transparent, and through them we clearly see their future stone, cement and marble successors.[102]

The ultimate object of this futuristic vision is none other than the finished metro itself. Having risen from of the depths of the underground, it realizes the utopian ideal set forth in the display case above, even as it redeems Stalinism's pledge of life as the fairy tale come true: "It is no longer a project, a design. . . . Descend down the running steps of any metro station . . . and you will see that the radiant landscape displayed in the festive picture windows is not an empty paper promise."[103] This is a far cry indeed from what came before. While the completed metro represents nothing less than a tribute to transparency and vision—"a model of technical mastery and (male) dominance"[104]—the unreconstructed Moscow underground is portrayed as irrational, opaque, and implicitly feminine. And the instinctive fear with which the (male) eye encounters the chaos of Moscow's underbelly is made clear in the following scene. Here Kassil''s narrator peers cautiously down from a watchtower into the first shaft of the metro: "Afterwards the bold, stunning plan set up the watchtowers of the future metro, and soon we peered curiously and with hidden fear into the 'First Hole' of the Moscow Metropoliten."[105] Notably, the still unfinished shaft betrays all the characteristics of primordial nature, here evoked by a rather transparent allusion to the female genitals. In keeping with this image, the tunnel appears blind, dark, and wet: "The tunnel was still blind. It was a blind alley. Water was dripping from the roof. From every side it was muffled, and seemed like the primordial swampy hole of the earth."[106] As in every other metro narrative, here, too, the greatest danger for the builders of the underground comes from the symbol par excellence of chaos—that is, from water.

More than the other metro authors, Kassil' goes out of his way to evoke the near-mythological dimensions of the contest between Moist Mother Earth and Bolshevik technology. The author writes, for instance, that the "slushy forces of quick-sand, the unstable quagmire-jellies attempted to swallow the tunnels."[107] And if we follow the logic of Kassil''s imagery, it quickly becomes apparent that the contest is between an inherently unstable, opaque nature (hence, its "blindness") and the lucid, differentiated realm of language and ideology.[108] Kassil's rather impressionistic portrayal of the original tunnels—and by extension, of the earth itself—as blind recalls a long line of pre- and postrevolutionary thought which juxtaposed "blind nature" with the "conscious," civilizing activities of mankind. Fedorov, for instance, claimed that humankind's instinctual life put it at the mercy of "blind" nature, preventing it from overcoming the vicious ("feminine") cycle of birth and death. Likewise, in his novella *Dzhan*, the onetime follower of Fyodorov Andrei Platonov likens the vegetative existence of the tribal Dzhan to a kind of primordial blindness that blocks its members from entering the current of universal history and thus from achieving "narratability" in language.[109]

Kassil''s *Miracle beneath Moscow* draws from the same tradition. Thus the possibility that the civilizing efforts of the metro builders might be swallowed up by the cavernous underground void must be understood in a figurative as well as a literal sense. To be sure, the danger of cave-ins and floods was a real one for the metro's engineers and builders. Yet in Kassil''s account this concrete threat acquires rich symbolism, recalling Stalinism's mythologized struggle with nature. This contest was—as I have already mentioned—gender specific. According to Zolotonosov, the metro project was overwhelmingly predicated on the "death of (feminine) nature and the triumph of civilization."[110] On a metaphorical level, then, woman was drawn into the subterannean tunnels of the *metropoliten* in order to transcend her own gender.[111] To a large extent, we can see this in the portraits of robust female workers that Zenkevich produced for Kassil''s *Miracle beneath Moscow*. These are, in many cases, women who differ from their male counterparts not so much in terms of size or strength but in their more pronounced hips or buttocks. Still, one of the most dramatic examples of such "cross-gendering" comes from a relatively late narrative devoted to the construction of the third metro line in 1944. While the predominance of women in the piece can easily be explained in practical terms (due to the war men were in short supply) their symbolic role in the narrative nevertheless remains unmistakable. Capable of working alongside men and, more importantly, sometimes even passing as men, the *metrostroevki* (or female metro builders) serve as yet another reminder of the construction project's core aspiration to clothe the feminine underground in the garments of male civilization, to transform the uncouth underground shaft into a civilized tunnel.[112] Consider the following episode in which the former parasol maker Ania becomes a tunnel digger à la Rosie the Riveter:

> The following story is told about Ania. Once comrade engineer Titov, who was very exacting and a real fault-finder, arrived at our sector . . . and asked Katamanin: "Who's that guy you got working on cement?" "What's wrong with

him," asked the brigadier. "Nothing at all. The opposite, in fact. He's got great technique.". . . "That's not a guy, it's a girl, one of the new ones, the parasol maker." "Impossible," said Titov with a dismissive gesture. They walked up to her. Ania took no notice. Carried away by the quick tempo of her work and the competition with her partner, smeared from head to foot in earth, she resembled an agile youth. "Atta boy!" the engineer exclaimed. "I serve the working people," Ania answered and on her dirty face that glistened with sweat a young girl's smile shone forth.[113]

The dramatic antipode to such narratives is to be found in Platonov's *Happy Moscow*. In the novel's cameo of the metro construction the underground emerges as a place of eternally reconstructed physicality, as a dark labyrinth that repels humankind's attempts to reclaim it in the name of civilization and technology. By the same token, the idea that feminine nature can be forcibly "cross-gendered" is overturned in Platonov's novel via multiple images of claustrophobic closure that accompany the female miner Moscow Chestnova's accident in the metro shaft. For no less than the utopian myth(s) surrounding St. Petersburg, the *canonical* metro narrative celebrates the "opening up" of Moscow's swampy underground onto the current of universal (i.e., Marxist-Leninist) history. And as in the case of St. Petersburg, here, too, the construction of a "spacious and lucid underground city" with "kilometer-long arterials" marks the inscription of Stalinist Moscow into a utopian narrative of transparency and openness.[114] Its title notwithstanding, Platonov's novel undermines any sense of historical optimism by turning the socialist construction site into a metaphysical black hole. And if Kassil''s heroic Vera Vorob'eva sets a record by moving 140 carts of earth,[115] Platonov's Moscow Chestnova sets no records at all. Quite the contrary, in fact, since she is seriously wounded by several carts that run over her leg in a "blind shaft." Morever, just as Platonov's underground arterials evoke history's dead end (and not the masterful "vision-from-the-train" mandated by Socialist Realism) the exhausted blood that pours from Chestnova's body symbolizes the eternal impoverishment of (human) physiology and, indeed, of the human condition: "Blood came out of her. On the snow and illuminated by a searchlight the blood appeared yellow, long since exhausted in the body."[116]

As in Lopatin's *First Soviet Metropoliten*, in Kassil''s *Miracle beneath Moscow* the obverse of Moist Mother Earth is to be found in the the technology used by the metro builders to stabilize the waters of Moscow's subterannean swamp. This miraculous transfiguration of fluid miasma into monumental statuary (with its obvious antecedent in the founding of St. Petersburg) echoes the narrative of chaos-made-cosmos that was reproduced throughout Stalinist culture. For an eloquent example one need look no further than the work of Sergei Eisenstein. In the draft plans for a film project about Moscow, Eisenstein portrays the historical progression from Ivan the Terrible to its Stalinist counterpart as a passage from the elements of water and earth ("feminine") to those of fire and air ("masculine"). And as Katerina Clark notes, the numerous images of water that populate Eistenstein's plans depict Russia as moving from "primeval sludge" to the "firmament of the authoritarian state."[117] The end result of this passage from "sludge" to "firmament" is the apotheosis of stasis that characterizes many metro stations but which is exemplified in Revolution Square, with its panoply of ideally ossified human figures.[118] Manizer's sculpted history represents the progress of Soviet society from the grizzled physiognomies of the revolution to its ideal instantiation in the "elegant, classically proportioned physiques" of the Stalinist present/future.[119] Likewise, in *Miracle beneath Moscow*, it is air (more precisely, the highly condensed air of the caissons and pneumatic drills) that allows the metro workers to win out in their struggle against the unstable "elements" of the underground. Meanwhile, Kassil' does not fail to mention the near phallic quality of the pressurized air, which symbolizes Bolshevik will and resolve: "liquid air and condensed Bolshevik will were set against the quicksand . . . the fluid soil was being frozen and through its crunchy stiffening the tunnel was built."[120] Elsewhere the same images of condensed air locked in mortal combat with the fluid underground anticipate the ultimate triumph of *cosmos* over *chaos*—of eternal "statuary" truth over ceaseless flux. Thus in *The First Soviet Metropoliten* the statue emerges as the symbol par excellence of Stalinism's "hard body." Describing the caissons used to dig the underground tunnels, the author writes: "The metal walls are very sturdy and are impervious to the pressure of the ground. Then the compressed air attacks the water, and the water withdraws. The air almost seems to press it back into the ground from which it came. It vigilantly guards the established border and dries the compartment."[121]

It might well be argued that the overwhelmingly "masculine" character of the metro rhetoric (e.g., its undisguised admiration for the power of the phallic drill over the retreating flesh of Mother Moist Earth) is such that it produces a certain homoeroticization of the narrative as a whole. This is particularly true in the case of Kassil's *Miracle beneath Moscow*. Hardly surprising, if one considers the unusual prominence of all-male collectives (and the resultant homoerotic overtones surrounding them) in the most significant literary works of the 1920s, such as those of Babel, Olesha, and Platonov. Indeed, even the vastly more traditionalist Stalinist '30s occasionally preserved a similar homoerotic pathos. Witness Lev Kassil''s *Goalkeeper of the Republic*, with its Whitmanesque praise of male camaraderie and friendship. Likewise, the metro project, with its aspiration to reclaim not only the underground but the very nature of the workers who labored to transform it,[122] is tailor-made to accommodate a rhetoric of homoerotic masculinity. Thus in *Miracle beneath Moscow* Kassil' writes of one female metro builder (Vera Vorob'eva) that she was able to work "steadfastly" alongside the best of her male counterparts (note that Kassil''s use of the word "steadfast" or *muzhestvenno* in Russian suggests both "courageously" and "manly").[123] More importantly, the author's rendering of the topos of the *sboika* (i.e., the triumphant coming together of two shafts to form a single tunnel) can easily be *reread* as evoking a homosexual act, especially if one considers the semantic resonance of the words *shakhta* and *shakhter* in contemporary Russian.[124] Not unlike other authors' descriptions of the same event,[125] Kassil''s piece reflects the extent to which the utopian brotherhood of the underground is predicated on a clear privileging of the male over the female, and thus tends to eroticize (whether consciously or not) this very visible and important encounter:

> The shafts, tunnels came towards each other underneath the capital, merging or "huddling together," as they say in the metro. And through an opening [*otverstie*, which means "opening, aperture, orifice, hole" in Russian] in the punctured layers people from one shaft greeted their comrades from the other, and, following an old miner's tradition, after a triumphant subterranean handshake, the engineers of the huddled shafts entered into each other's shafts.[126]

Kassil''s portrayal of what might be described as a utopian community of the underground mirrors the anthropological ideal of the metro project. Like such analogous undertakings as the White Sea Canal project,[127] the construction of a socialist metro was portrayed as a crucible in which a qualitatively new type of human being would be forged.[128] And, once again, a comparison with Haussmann's reconstruction of the Paris underground suggests itself. For here, too, the civilizing potential of the new sewer seemed to manifest itself in the reclaimed nature of its exemplary custodians—the sewermen. As Donald Reid notes, these denizens of the deep were idealistically viewed by many as the "embodiment of health, order, and civilization."[129] Roughly the same can be said of the new Kaganovich metro. While the major construction sites of the Stalin era functioned in general as a kind of halfway house for the rural population seeking to make the transition from agricultural to industrial labor, the Moscow metro quickly came to occupy a special place among such projects. Indeed, if the propaganda surrounding the metro is any indication, the "Arctic of the underground" possessed an almost magical power to turn ordinary workers into heroes of labor, even as the latter struggled to transform the ancient underground into a model of Stalinist civilization.[130] Describing not so much the workers of the underground as its future passengers, Il'f and Petrov portray the newly constructed metro as a show-place for the radiant world of the future.[131] This world is one in which technology and architecture merge to produce a new breed of Homo sapiens. And just as such traditional means of transportation as the trolley or the streetcar would be replaced by the ultramodern trains of the *metropoliten*, so, too, the magical underground would ultimately transform the very fabric of human relations, according to Il'f and Petrov. Using the palatial interiors of the metro as a metaphor for the luminous architecture of a new *socialist* humanity, the feuilleton (entitled simply "M") depicts the relations of passengers to one another as ideally transparent—as artistically, aesthetically sculpted.[132] The same principle applies to the metro's intrepid builders, who represent the first wave of avant-garde humanity to emerge from the bowels of the Moscow underground. This perception of the metro project as an unusually potent forge of the *Homo novus* occurs at the intersection of diverse myths. For Stalin, whose rural roots surely shaped his mythologically charged thought, everything important (whether good or bad) seemed to occur underground.[133] Indeed, according to archaic perceptions, the earth's womb was the locus where the spirits and embryos of all living beings are acquired.[134] Meanwhile, the ancient topos of the hero's trip to the underworld (with its suggestion of symbolic death and triumphant rebirth) surely stands in the foreground of the metro project's promise of ideological and spiritual renewal. Whether as womb or tomb, Stalinist culture reconfigures the underground as the ideal *u-topos* from which the new revolutionary cadres will emerge into a still-profane world. The near magical ability of the underground to bring forth such new men and women is eloquently evoked in the following description from *Miracle beneath Moscow*:

> From out of the wet, clay bowels and the shafts young men and women emerged onto the street. . . . They strode along the streets of the capital with the gait of conquerors, stepping firmly and in concert along the earth which they knew inside and out.[135]

Alongside the Stakhanovites, the metro builders quickly came to represent a special breed. Plucked from their positions in the more traditional sectors of production, metro workers were invariably forced to reinvent themselves by acquiring unusual skills or miraculously mastering unheard-of new technologies. Implicit in this is the same feverish desire to overcome physical and psychological limits that was the driving force behind Stalinism's voluntarist worldview.[136] Thus the most celebrated participants of the construction project (i.e., the Komsomol) were overwhelmingly associated with overturning traditional norms and thus seen as exemplary of the new revolutionary cadres that would emerge, as if by magic, from the depths of the underground. Paradoxically, it is precisely their youthful ignorance of traditional techniques and standards that renders the Komsomol best suited for the utopian enterprise of building the metro. As one contemporary critic notes, the discourse of the Moscow metro is one that humbles the specialized, purely technical knowledge of the engineer. Indeed, the "engineer's technical calculations are proclaimed obsolete beneath the pressure of the Bolshevik pace of work and Komsomol improvisations."[137] And there is no shortage of accounts in the metro narrative that describe the success of the Komsomol in achieving unheard-of results and thus overtaking the so-called *kadroviki* or "experienced workers." In his *First Soviet Metropoliten*, for instance, Lopatin describes a particular ten-day period at the beginning of which the inexperienced Komsomol are met with hostile, suspicious glances by the older workers. At the end of the period, however, the "beardless youth" emerge as victorious, having exceeded the norm for tunneling by 30 percent.[138] The author goes on to remark that the shaft workers began to suggest that it might not be a bad idea for the *kadroviki* to learn a thing or two from the Komsomol. Likewise, in the 1935 commemorative volume entitled *Stories of the Metro Builders*, E. T. Abakumov remarks that the older engineers had seriously misjudged the enthusiasm and energy of the Komsomol who represent a new breed of socialist Homo sapiens. Unlike their older counterparts, the new postrevolutionary generation proves able to master new skills and carry out feats of labor with unprecedented speed.[139] By the same token, every metro narrative invariably stresses the victory of the "youthful" Soviet technology over its Western counterpart. Thus the first "shield" used for tunneling in the adverse conditions of the Moscow underground is ordered from England. In short order, however, the older capitalist technology is replaced by a superior, entirely Soviet-made model.[140] Moreover, in a description which clearly juxtaposes the utopian new with the old, the authors remark on the relative superiority of the Soviet shield—manned by inexperienced, young engineers—over its English counterpart, which is run by experienced specialists.[141] Finally, in Bela Iles's short story "Fire in the Metro," an older Jewish engineer named Dimensheits is literally rejuvenated by his experience working on the metro, and in a symptomatic moment the author notes that Dimensheits (an old engineer) often learned how to work from his own subordinates.[142]

The preceding examples demonstrate the denigration of professional discourse characteristic of Stalinism, even as they point toward a phenomenon with much deeper cultural roots. The fetishization of youth within the rhetoric of the metro and, indeed, within the culture at large can be ascribed—at least partially—to Stalin's own pronounced gerontophobia.[143] The dictator's privileging of youth and inexperience over tradition is perhaps most visible in his promotion of a new brand of "socialist" science. Distinguished by its contempt

for traditional empirical methods, it excels à la Stakhanov in defining new, unheard-of norms. Thus Stalin describes the "miraculous" feats of daring and
brinksmanship carried out by the members of the Papanin polar expedition of
1937 by remarking: "Who does not know that Papanin and the Papaninites in
their practical work on a drifting ice floe overturned—in passing, and without
particular effort—the old notions about the Arctic as obsolete, and established
new ones adequate to the demands of true science."[144] Meanwhile, one cannot
help but detect in this paradigm a hint of the relatively old theme of Russia's
"newness" with respect to the culturally and technically more advanced West.
As Uspenskii points out, already the Metropolitan Hilarion in his *Sermon on
Law and Grace* compares Byzantium with the Old Testament figure of Hagar,
at the same time likening Russia to Sarah and the blessings of the New Testament. And later, following the fall of Constantinople, Russia's relative "newness" vis-à-vis its cultural and religious predecessors allowed the monk Filofei
to proclaim its status as the Third (and final) Rome.[145] Add to this the later
Stalinist incarnation of the Moscow-as-Third-Rome myth, which brings with
it an analogous juxtaposition of the "older" West (i.e., its traditional methods
of metro construction) with respect to the more radical, "new" technology and
labor techniques employed in constructing the Moscow metro.

As most critics seem to agree, Stalinist ideology represents an eclectic blend
of often competing rhetorical models. In it the agrarian/rural worldview continually vies with the myth of the machine, for instance. Similarly, technology
is simultaneously celebrated and denigrated. In the latter instance, it ceases to
function as a discrete realm and is subsumed within a larger literary or epic
mode.[146] In the metro narrative, this is most clearly evident in the portrayal of
such figures as L. M. Kaganovich. For unlike the vast army of anonymous architects, engineers, and workers who merely labor to build the metro, these officials (Kaganovich, above all) serve in quasi-priestly or prophetic capacity as
the sole intuitors and interpreters of the Party's utopian vision of the future.[147]
They are, in other words, the most complete and compelling incarnation of the
party's all-mighty Word. Or to put it another way, we might say that the Bolshevik leader—whether Kaganovich or Stalin—stands in the same relationship to his subordinates as does the absolute fullness of life vis-à-vis the petty
rules and norms of the formalist. Unlike the narrowly focused specialist, the
party leader exemplifies life in its epic sweep, a fact that is mirrored in the
nearly superhuman qualities with which each party leader is endowed. Thus in
one instance a mechanic named Rabinovich tells that after meeting
Kaganovich he was so overwhelmed by the breadth of the latter's knowledge
that he found himself unable to sleep that night.[148]

Given Kaganovich's status as the metro's spiritual father, it would seem
that nothing lies outside of his purview, nothing escapes his notice. Such su-

perhuman qualities ensure that the Bolshevik leader never fails to appear at the right moment in order to effortlessly resolve a conundrum that has stumped even his most competent engineers and architects.[149] This is due not so much to the latter's intelligence or perspicacity as to the mythological surplus of vision that the culture reserves for its most prominent heroes. Kassil' makes this abundantly clear in one of the episodes of *Miracle beneath Moscow* in which Kaganovich is shown riding in a metro car that is literally pulsating with light. And one can imagine that this light is nothing more than a physical manifestation of the "inner lucidity" which allows Kaganovich to penetrate even the most obscure aspects of the construction project. He is a light that cuts through the darkness. To use Kassil''s own colorful description, Kaganovich literally sees Moscow *through and through*: "Lazar Moiseevich stunned even the most prominent specialists with his exclusive knowledge of Moscow through and through. Precisely, through and through. He knew and remembered all the streets, all the directions of the tunnels, and faultlessly named the depth of the construction."[150]

What ultimately distinguishes Kaganovich from the host of technocrats surrounding him is thus his supernal vision. As the party's incarnation, he is able to view the project from a vantage point beyond that of immediate reality. Instead of the clutter of construction he sees the broader, epic narrative of socialist *re-construction*. In the following quote a certain engineer explains Kaganovich's omniscience as the result of his having mastered numerous, different languages. Yet one can easily see in this an allusion to the latter's access to Stalinism's grand narrative, which is the only "language" that supercedes all others: "Lazar Moiseevich also spoke to us using technical language. But he had a great advantage over the result of us. He had mastered several other languages, which we had only just begun to study."[151] In one of the most quoted examples of the Bolshevik leader's perspicacity, Kaganovich brilliantly solves the problem of tunneling beneath the Arbat radius. While numerous metro engineers discuss their plans for either deep tunneling (so as not to disturb the complex subterranean infrastructure of the Arbat) or open-trench digging (in order to save time), Kaganovich proposes a simple, ideologically prescient solution. Most importantly for our purposes, it is a solution that brings out the radically distinct nature of Moscow's socialist metro vis-à-vis its capitalist counterparts in the West. Unlike his engineer-specialists, who are slavishly beholden to the existing maps of Moscow, Kaganovich treats the city's confusing topography as an aesthetic phenomenon, transforming and simplifying it in accordance with socialism's grandiose remapping of reality.[152]

It was at this point that Lazar Moiseevich first gave voice to his idea that it was not absolutely necessary to tunnel beneath Arbat Street and Comintern Street.

"Isn't it all the same to the passenger travelling underground what he passes beneath, whether it's under houses, back-alleys, courtyards or under the street? It's
most important for him to enter the tunnel in a specific place that's convenient
and to exit from a similarly convenient place. What's the problem? We'll put the
stations on the squares and build the tunnels where it's most convenient for us,
close to the Arbat, but not necessarily under the street." Lazar Moiseevich told
us that he was always surprised that we, the workers of Metrostroi, were so in-
sistent on having the line go precisely under the street, despite the fact that it
caused so many problems. "That's natural for a capitalist city, where the owner
of this or that house is also the owner of the ground and would demand significant compensation for any violation of his ground. In our country the houses,
the courtyards and the ground are the property of the state.[153]

As has already been mentioned, the metro narrative comprises a fusion of
rhetorical models. The organic metaphor that governed significant aspects
of Stalinist myth does not by any means exclude the possibility of technological or industrial symbolism. Quite the opposite, in fact. As Vaiskopf
writes, Stalinist civilization "bore within itself . . . a strange mixture of
agrarian-biological pathos, imperial aesthetics, as well as the indestructible
industrial-technocratic utopianism of the revolutionary years."[154] While the
former emphasizes the need to overcome a mechanistic view of phenomena,
the latter spotlights technology (and above all, the machine) as the guiding
metaphor for the functioning of society.[155] A point of comparison might be
found in Zoshchenko's writing of the 1930s. In such works as *Youth Restored*, *The Sky-Blue Book*, or *Before Sunrise*, the author wavers endlessly
between a view of the universe as governed by machine-like "iron laws"
and a sense that these can be overturned by miraculous events (i.e., the so-
called "Kursk anomaly"). Similarly, the metro narrative oscillates between
a supremely vitalist stance and fascination for the Machine. To be sure,
Stalin's new cadres emerge like a new breed from the womb of Mother
Earth. Yet it is also true that "more and more often Bolshevik specialists are
'smelted' or even 'forged' in industrial centers."[156] This paradox characterizes both Marxist and later Bolshevik ideology. For just as in Marxist
dogma the grave-digger proletariat matures within the very womb of capitalism, so here the bowels of Mother Earth contain the means of nature's
transformation, in the form of coal, oil, and metal.[157] The same paradox
shapes Kassil"s *Miracle Beneath Moscow*, where in order to be reborn of
the Machine workers must first descend into the depths of the benighted underground: "But Metrostroi was a wonderful university — in both the technical and the general cultural sense. Descending beneath the earth, people
rose up in their own eyes and gradually mastered the heights of technology
and culture."[158]

In the decades following the opening of the Paris sewer at the end of the Second Empire, the Paris sewermen gradually became identified with the civilizing, enlightenment pathos of the new *tout a l'égout* itself. Paradoxically, it was those who descended into the underworld who would eventually come to embody the qualities of an ideal, rationalist order.[159] Similarly, under the leadership of Kaganovich and Stalin the Moscow underground of the 1930s gave birth to a new species of socialist superworkers, heroes who struggled to bring the light of reason into a benighted underworld. These new men and women were known as the *metrostroevtsy*:

> It is therefore quite natural that the building of the metro represents not only a technical achievement of our country but a gigantic human machine, which in addition to material objects also produces an object whose worth consists in the transformation of human beings. A forty thousand person collective . . . which serves as a forge that produces new human beings. This construction project raises our technology to an undreamt-of level, while at the same time raising human activity to an undreamt-of level.[160]

The triumph of the metro as the victory of reason and enlightenment over chaos represents the high point of any canonical metro narrative. This is made explicit (perhaps more than in any other account) in the climax of Kassil''s *Miracle beneath Moscow*. And as with every other celebration of the Moscow underground, here, too, the motif of light looms large. Its overabundance in this and every other account underscores not only the hyperenlightenment pathos of Stalinist culture but the latter's ambitious plan to reforge the murky "underground" of human nature.[161] Here one cannot help but recall Plato's cave allegory, in which the benighted prisoners of ignorance pass from the dark interior of the womb-like cave into the lucid realm of gnosis.[162] Likewise, Kassil''s account of the Moscow metro begins with the underground's first "blind tunnel" and culminates in a veritable orgy of light. To suggest that the Moscow underground resembles a womb is not as much of a stretch as it might appear at first glance. As Gilbert and Gubar note, Plato's characterization of the cave as a locus of chaos/nature mirrors the commonplace (within patriarchal culture) association of woman with her "cave-like anatomy." The critics go on to note that "like Plato's cave-dweller, . . . woman is a prisoner of her own nature, a prisoner in the 'grave cave' of immanence."[163] If, as one contemporary critic suggests, the metro passenger is plunged into a kind of mythic darkness in order to achieve "higher vision,"[164] in *Miracle Beneath Moscow* the primordial darkness of the metro tunnel is finally dispersed by a speeding train that is bathed in noumenal light. And it should come as no surprise that this train is carrying not just ordinary passengers but one of the most potent symbols of Bolshevik reason and technology—that is, L. M.

Kaganovich. If earlier Kassil''s emphasis had been on the blindness of the "vaginal" tunnel, now the image of the Stalinist train-as-phallus suggests not blindness but absolute transparency and vision—what Kuritsyn describes as the Bolshevik hero's all-encompassing "vision-from-the-train":

> We can never forget the night when we were able to take our first trip on the first train of the Moscow metro. I was waiting for it at Crimea Square station. Around two o'clock at night a train composed of four light cars, painted in bright olive and yellow colors, flew with a triumphant whistle forth from the tunnel which seemed to lose itself in infinity. Through the enormous glass panes of the train's windows we saw Kaganovich and the other leaders of the capital. Inside there was so much light that the car appeared prostrated by rays—by the soft waves of radiance coming from milky lamps that reminded one of sleeping car lamps.[165]

To be sure, Kassil''s extensive use of light and visual imagery in *Miracle beneath Moscow* reflects the prominence of such themes in the author's own work, as for instance in his *Goalkeeper of the Republic*, which deals extensively with visual problematics. At the same time, it suggests (as I have already noted) a much broader mythological underpinning. Among others, the prominence of light throughout the metro rhetoric is reminiscent of Stalinist Moscow's aspiration to become a kind of modern incarnation of Campanella's City of the Sun.[166] For evidence we need look no further than Lopatin's *The First Soviet Metropoliten*. Here Lopatin writes that unlike the cold and wintry city above, the scientifically engineered climate of the Moscow underground is sheltered from any change of seasons. Indeed, the temperature remains forever the same: "Here above, as before, the same penetrating cold wind, wet, sticky snow-flakes blind your eyes and creep under your collar. It is hard to believe that below your feet . . . everywhere, in the tunnels, on the platforms, and at the rows of turnstiles there reigns a climate that does not know a change of seasons."[167] Similarly, one contemporary speaks of the architecture of the metro as reflecting the "undimmed sun of the Stalinist epoch."[168] Meanwhile, the victory of Apollonian light over Dionysian darkness and chaos (in every metro narrative including Kassil''s *Miracle beneath Moscow*) reminds us of Stalinist ideology's core pathos. Whether in its promotion of supernal flight or in its urge to burrow into the opaque Moscow underground, the culture was fueled by a utopian drive to overturn the ancient gravity of human life—that is, to radically rewrite the book of physical and psychophysiological law. Kassil' and those of his contemporaries who participated in creating the metro myth clearly understood that the matter concerned not just building a functioning metro but constructing a utopia in the very bowels of Mother Earth. For this reason the Kaganovich metro would emerge as the antithesis of the gloomy subways of Europe and America, with their residual likeness to the human body (Kassil' describes the latter as having "gloomy orifices" and "black maws"). Indeed, the Moscow metro was the ultimate "anti-body." For it symbolized the transfiguring of the earth's carnival body into the ideal, statuary city:

> The light and airy palace-vestibule, with its light-blue vaulted ceiling covered with moulded honeycombs, beckons to the heights rather than underground. Here there is no hint of the murky words "underground," "basement," "cellar," or "catacomb." The entrance to the Moscow metro is not the gloomy maw or black orifice of the European undergrounds. It pours masses of light out into the Moscow night. . . . There's no hint that you've come a step closer to the center of the earth.[169]

A similar portrait can be found in Semion Kirsanov's poetic tribute to the metro simply entitled "M."[170] Here, too, the newly completed underground recalls the triumph of technology and civilization over feminine nature that was the stock-in-trade of Stalinist mythology. Invariably, this entails the same transformation of water into stone that the metro narrative had inherited from the myth of the founding of St. Petersburg: "I'm happy,/ that we,/ growing up,/ were able/ to raise/ from the mist,/ from the subterranean/ ravenous water/ the cold midnight/ of the dank underground caverns/ to noonday heights/ and rout/ the cold hordes/ of dampness/ and drown them in light/ ourselves growing up like marble."[171] More importantly, with the construction of the underground the possibility of paradise on earth (Stalinism's utopia realized) seems tantalizingly near, for the heavens themselves have descended into the depths of the Kaganovich metro: "We descended/ along the staircase/ downward/ and found ourselves/ it seemed to me/ up above!// It seems,/ that soon/ clouds will begin,/ to hang down/ from the columns/ and balconies."[172] This achievement is all the more impressive, according to Kirsanov, in light of the dire predictions of the Orthodox Church, which supposedly warned the metro builders that to descend into the netherworld was a sin. Quite the contrary, the netherworld has now been transformed into a place of exemplary culture and hygiene, according to Kirsanov: "The priests in their nasal voices/ in the flickering of the candle/ warned of the terrible/ underground hell,/ But there is no hell! . . ./ Rays of light shine,/ And Muscovites will start/ to come here/ as if to a lecture/ on hygiene."[173] Finally, in addition to spotlighting the superior qualites of the metro vis-à-vis the surface ("In a flash the train doors opened; . . . And it's not at all scary/ and even calmer,/ than on the street"), Kirsanov's poem reflects the almost mystical character of the letter "M" that marks the entrances to Moscow's underground. The Moscow metro, Kirsanov suggests, is more than a means of conveyance. The embodiment par excellence of Stalinism's utopian ideal, the metro is its own destination: "How quickly/ did we race through/ four sections./ And once again/ Open up the Moscow sky!/ And once again/ the letter 'M'/ strides/ on neon legs/ above evening Moscow."[174]

Like Kirsanov, Kassil"s *Miracle beneath Moscow* portrays the finished underground as more than a simple means of conveyance. Bathed in noumenal light that emanates from sources hidden deep in the ceiling and reflects off the abundant marble facading used throughout the stations, the eye of the metro *spectator* is granted a vision of the New World. Here it is genuinely difficult to believe that one is still underground:

> We are taking an amazing stroll through the new palaces of the Moscow underground. We stop for a long time at each station. The flashes of light from the trains dance in the marble tile. The staircases' balustrades, the light-blue tile, the porcelain blocks, the capitals, the bronze chandeliers, the arcs, cupolas and an ocean of light gushing forth from enormous, radiant chalices in the form of censers, or falling in cataracts from the plafonds, or given off by some invisible source hidden inside the enormous marble tulips. The ceilings of several stations, which are illuminated from below, resemble an enormous block of matte glass—weightless and supported by light-rays alone. . . . All of the structures delight the eye with their magnificent simplicity. They are contemporary in the very best sense of the word. They are magnificent in a manner befitting an era that has created such a marriage of strength and lightness, joy and self-assurance. It is impossible to believe that one is underground.[175]

To be sure, the overemphasis on light both in the metro itself and in the discourse about it reflects its status as a quasi-sacral space.[176] We see this—albeit indirectly—in Kaganovich's stern admonition to several metro architects to use less mystical (i.e., more realistic) lighting to illuminate the station interiors. The quasi-religious quality of the underground is brought out in more direct ways, as well. Thus one contemporary critic points out that some of the marble used in it had been recovered from the recently defunct Cathedral of Our Savior. Originally earmarked for the Palace of the Soviets, the same marble eventually ended up being used as facading for individual metro stations.[177] Likewise, in the commemorative work *How We Built the Metro*, a certain engineer tells of how the former Tikhon church had been converted into a cement factory in order to supply the first section of the construction site.[178] Still, if Kassil"s *Miracle beneath Moscow* is any indication, the orgy of light within the metro narrative is symptomatic, first and foremost, of Stalinist culture's fetishization of vision and of the supernal light that makes such vision possible.[179] This recalls what Foucault has described as the entire modern discourse of "penetrating vision," which by analogy with the Panopticon, or "seeing eye," seeks to render the entire body (social) transparent, reconfiguring its many parts as a continuous "object of knowledge."[180] At the same time, the metro narrative's obsession with light clearly evokes the Platonic inner vision that was an essential part of the culture's push to transcend the empirical netherworld. In either case, the Stalinist eye or vision-from-the-metro-train looms large as one of the most potent symbols of the culture's utopian aspiration to master the realm of the real.

Despite (or perhaps because of) their utopian overtones, such attempts at cleaning out the underworld of human nature are not always greeted with universal applause—especially from writers. Thus while Napoleon III's regime seemed in the eyes of many contemporaries to have effectively tamed the underworld, Victor Hugo was less than enthusiastic about the "Haussmannization" of Paris. Of the new, "enlightened" sewer, Hugo writes: "'Today the sewer is clean, cold upright, proper. It attains the ideal of what is understood in England by word 'respectable.' It is dull and presentable; in a straight line; one might almost say dressed to the nines. . . . One can almost see clearly in it. The mire is well-behaved.'"[181] Likewise, two of the Moscow metro's most prominent contemporaries—Mikhail Bulgakov and Andrei Platonov—included in their unpublished works (*The Master and Margarita* and *Happy Moscow*) a polemic with the "Kaganovichization" of Moscow. In marked contrast to the metro narrative described above, Platonov and Bulgakov put forth a vision of the underground that significantly undermines the official ideology's attempt to "empty out" the eternal labyrinth of the underworld. The most obvious polemic belongs to Platonov. In his unfinished novel *Happy Moscow*, the writer intentionally foregrounds the image of blindness as a counterpoint to Stalinist culture's promotion of all-encompassing (super)vision. And it is not accident, as I suggested earlier, that the novel's heroine Moscow Chestnova is simultaneously mutilated and transformed through her violent contact with the entrails of the "blind" underground, even as she labors in vain to clean out one of the tunnels of the new Moscow metro.[182] As in the earlier novella *Dzhan*, here, too, the marginalization of vision (and with it the protagonist's spiritual transformation) follows a shift in the latter's center of gravity from the eyes to the heart. Similarly, by the end of *Happy Moscow* the image of the revolution as a light cutting through the darkness (taken from the first line of the novel) is irretrievably compromised. The "dark man with a burning torch" who marks both the coming-to-consciousness of the heroine, Moscow Chestnova, as well as the beginning of the revolution, turns out to be none other than Komiagin, the least heroic of the novel's protagonists. Symptomatically, upon discovering his true identity, Moscow Chestnova refers to the former torchbearer of the revolution using the insulting epithet "a blind man in the nettles" (*Happy Moscow*, 113). Platonov's strategy in the novel is thus that of

symbolically blinding the revolution's intrusive, all-encompassing vision—
of castrating its desire to peer into the very bowels of the human organism
so as to illuminate the latter with the torch of reason and technology.[183 184]

Polemicizing with Malthus's vision of a humanity that would soon outgrow
its food supply, the nineteenth-century French socialist Pierre Leroux developed the idea of the "circulus"—that is, the theory that an individual's waste
could be used to produce the food necessary for that individual to live.[185] "'If
men were believers,'" Leroux writes, "'then instead of laughing . . . at socialism, they would profess with profound respect and veneration the doctrine
of the *circulus*. Each would religiously gather his dung to give it to the State,
that is to say the tax-collector, in place of a tax or personal levy.'"[186] Likewise, Karl Marx in volume III of *Das Kapital* identifies the squandering of
human waste as characteristic of capitalism.[187] And Victor Hugo—a personal
friend of Leroux—writes of the squandered capital of the Paris underground:
"The city spends its cloacas. Such that one can say that the great Prodigality
of Paris, its marvellous fete . . . its orgy, its gold flowing from full hands, its
splendor, its luxury, its magnificence, is its sewer." Similarly, in his *Happy
Moscow* Andrei Platonov takes up the cause of human waste, arguing with
Stalinism's brutal attempts to purge itself of the last remaining elements of social and ontological waste (the metro). Like Victor Hugo who endowed Leroux's idea of the *circulus* with artistic form, Platonov points to the integral
connection between filth and the human being in the grotesquely beautiful
body of Moscow Chestnova. Rather than simply being purged along with the
human beings who produce it, "filth" must be reclaimed and redeemed—it
must be incorporated back into the circle of life.

In many ways Platonov's polar opposite, Mikhail Bulgakov appears no less
critical of Stalinist culture's utopian attempt to master the underworld. As Anton Sergl' notes, Bulgakov's *Master and Margarita* provides an implicit
polemic with the official ideology's representation of the Moscow metro as
yet another argument in favor of its own atheistic worldview. If the Stalinist
conquest of the heavens by Chkalov and other famous fliers seemed to prove
the nonexistence of God, the exploration of the underworld by the metro
builders would finally demonstrate the absence of a devil. By contrast, Bulgakov's novel as a whole demonstrates the need for a more nuanced ontology,
one based on the principle of interpenetrating darkness and light. At least a
hint of this is given in the very name of Bulgakov's diabolical protagonist,
Woland. For here the "M" in "metro" seems literally to have been stood on
its head, as if to suggest a carnival overturning of the metro narrative's purist
ontology. Meanwhile, Bulgakov himself appears not to have been unaware of
the significance of this gesture. A famous photograph shows the author sporting a cap with a large letter "W" displayed on it—possibly an attempt to par-

ody the metro conductors' caps, which were prominently embellished with the letter "M."[188] The sense of a polemic is bolstered, as one Bulgakov scholar notes, in the image of the fictional Master's cap, which Margarita embroiders with the letter "M." By linking the ubiquitous "M" of the metro with its mirror image in the first letter of Woland's name, Bulgakov lays bare the ideological and mythological character of the larger metro narrative. At the same time, it can be argued that Bulgakov views the "infernal" trains of the Moscow underground as yet another sign of the apocalyptic collapse of history.[189] And in this he contradicts the canonical metro text (e.g., Kassil''s *Miracle beneath Moscow*), which sees the project as a reclaiming of the underworld in the name of Bolshevik science and reason.

Yet more than simply disproving the official culture's atheism or vividly evoking the demonic aspect of Bolshevik technophilia, Bulgakov's novel undermines the very conceptual core of the metro project itself. And given the Master's consistent association with the underground,[190] the case can easily be made for a much broader, philosophical argument with Stalinist ontology. The conceptual topsy-turvy both of Woland's Moscow and of Bulgakov's novel serves, I would argue, to negate Stalinism's naive belief that the first-ever socialist *metropoliten* would rationalize and definitively order the chaotic underground of human nature. Not unlike Dostoevsky's *Notes from the Underground* in its polemic with Chernyshevsky's rationalist utopia, Bulgakov's *Master and Margarita* adds a carnivalesque corrective to the metro architects' dream of turning the underworld into a paradise of Stalinist enlightenment. In sharp contrast to the metro builders' utopian dream of constructing a kingdom of pure light, Bulgakov's novel projects a thoroughly dialogic scenario—one in which light and darkness are unalterably twined to produce a vision of metaphysical chiaroscuro. The highest order of truth, the novel seems to suggest, exists in a realm outside the limiting ("this-worldly") categories of good and evil. This is certainly the case with the Master's novel. More importantly, the "devil" who sets in motion the action of the work appears throughout the work as a unity of opposites, as the "living dialectic of existence."[191] By the same token, the image of sunlight (frequently invoked during the period as a symbol of Stalin as well as of Stalinist culture's solar dimensions)[192] is rejected in the novel in favor of muted, lunar light. The harsh light of the Absolute in *Master and Margarita* is reserved for the "fanatical and limited Levy Matvei." By contrast, the thoroughly carnivalesque atmosphere associated with Woland and his suite represents the antipode of the philosophical monologism that underlay such utopian undertakings as the Moscow metro.[193] In a poignant indictment that could easily be applied to the metro architects' plan to redeem the underworld, Woland remarks to a fanatical Levy Matvei: "Do you want to strip the earth of all trees and living things

just because of your fantasy of enjoying naked light?"[194] To be sure, this is
not the blindness that overtakes the transformer-heroes of Platonov's *Happy
Moscow*. Yet like Platonov Bulgakov seems to suggest that the underbelly of
human nature can never be purged of its dark, ontological Other. The murki-
ness of human history and of human nature is best illustrated by none other
than Woland himself. Thus in her first meeting with him Margarita describes
Woland in a manner that emphasizes a mysterious cohabitation of darkness
and light: "On Woland's bare, hairless chest Margarita also noted a gold chain
with a finely carved scarab of dark stone that had some kind of writing en-
graved on the back. Next to Woland on the bed, on a heavy base, stood a
strange globe that seemed to be alive and was lit up on one side by the sun."[195]

The Moscow metro as an ideological project promised nothing less than
the total reclamation of human nature and history, and that within the fore-
seeable future. The finished structure aimed, among others, to provide a taste
of the new world of socialism that would soon emerge from beneath the clutter of the old. As Mikhail Ryklin notes, in the perfect underground world of
the metro there is "no death, no sabotage, no mutilation."[196] Indeed, even the
climate seemed close to perfect. "The air in it is close to hygienic norm and
is changed 6–7 times more often than in the other metros of the world."[197]
Finally, as one contemporary wrote of the new metro: "The time is not far
when the passenger, having ascended the granite stairs of the Moscow underground, will see him/herself in a new city—a city as well-built, comfortable and spacious as the marble city of the *metropoliten*. Soon in Moscow it
will be as nice as it is in the Metro beneath Moscow."[198] By contrast, Bulgakov's *Master and Margarita* casts a dark shadow on Stalinism's claim to
be producing a new species of socialist Homo sapiens. And here the novel
simply echoes the scepticism about the possibilities of transforming human
nature of such earlier works as *The Heart of a Dog* or *The Fatal Eggs*. In one
of the key chapters of the novel ("Black Magic and its Exposure") the devil
in the guise of Woland notes that, in fact, very little in human nature has
changed, even since the days of Christ and Pontius Pilate. Thus the shortsighted optimism of the comment above ("the time is not far when") is offset by the considerably larger temporal perspective of Bulgakov's Woland.
Socialist humanity, the devil opines, comprises the same mix of good and
evil, of greed and compassion, that it always had. Whatever the metro narrative's vision of a sparkling socialist underground might seem to symbolize, the view from *above* is no different than before: "'Well,' the latter
replied pensively, 'they are like people anywhere. They love money, but that
has always been true. . . . People love money, no matter what it is made of,
leather, paper, bronze or gold. And they are thoughtless . . . but, then again,
sometimes mercy enters their hearts . . . they are ordinary people . . . On the

whole, they remind me of their predecessors . . . only the housing shortage has had a bad effect on them.'"[199]

The Moscow metro, like such sibling works as the Belomor or Moscow–Volga canals, was one of the showcase projects of Stalinist construction undertaken during the latter half of the 1930s. Conceived by Kaganovich and others as an essential part of the socialist reconstruction of Moscow, the metro was an engineering feat of truly grandiose proportions. But it was also an ideological and aesthetic project, the equal of the most ambitious utopian dreams of the previous, revolutionary decade—and arguably the most consistent expression of Stalinism's push to reclaim reality in the form of a *Gesamtkunstwerk*. Yet if the utopian dreamers of the '20s set their sights exclusively on the surface or on the heavens, the metro architects of the '30s envisioned utopia in the very bowels of the earth. In many ways, it was to be the undoing of those mythological and cultural perceptions that had imagined the underground as a place of mystery and Gothic terror. Not unlike the Paris sewer, which was conceived as part of Haussmann's reconstruction of the French capital, the Kaganovich metro sought to rationalize the ancient labyrinth, replacing it with a shining monument to Stalinist civilization and technology. Lev Kassil''s *Miracle beneath Moscow* and P. Lopatin's *The First Soviet Metropoliten*, as well as a host of other metro narratives, embody the culture's desire to reclaim—both symbolically and practically—one of the most volatile arenas of the cultural imagination. A metaphor, among others, for Stalinist culture's desire to revamp human nature, the metro project was the subject not only of official encomia but of unofficial polemics. Thus Andrei Platonov's unfinished novel *Happy Moscow* spotlights the fate of a metro-building heroine named Moscow Chestnova, whose body is irreparably maimed by the very underground it labors to remake. Likewise, Bulgakov's *Master and Margarita* contains a thinly veiled polemic with the *metropoliten imeni Kaganovicha*. And like his idealistic but skeptical contemporary, Bulgakov rejects the official ideology's evocation of an underworld suffused with pure light. Human nature, he suggests, occupies the no-man's land between good and evil. Keenly aware of the mythological and ideological implications of building the "first ever socialist metro," Bulgakov responds to Kaganovich and comapny by turning the underground's ubiquitous "M" into a devilish "W," once more joining order to chaos, and darkness to light.

NOTES

1. Term quoted in Hans Günther, *Der sozialistische Übermensch*, 155.
2. Katerina Clark, *The Soviet Novel*, 100.

3. See Sheila Fitzpatrick, *Everyday Stalinism*, 75.

4. See Anton Sergl', "Katabazis kak poezdka na metro (Gumilev, Khodasevich, Maiakovskii, Brecht, Bakhtin i drugie: psikhoanaliz metro)," *Mesto pechati*, no. 3 (1993): 81.

5. Likewise, I. P. Smirnov remarks that the metro was an aesthetic project wholly in keeping with Stalinism's aestheticization of the whole of Soviet reality (*Psikhodi-akhronologika: istoriia russkoi literatury ot romantizma do nashikh dnei* [Moskva: Novoe literaturnoe obozrenie, 1994], 276): "Stalinist society is beautiful: it worships the perfect body (the cult of sports), it encourages the masses to engage in artistic activity, it embellishes structures that are in themselves utilitarian with sculptures (for instance, the sluices of canals). Even a simple ride in the metro was a kind of narrative. Riding from station to the next the passenger acquainted him/herself with the history of the revolution (cf., for instance, the Moscow subway stations dedicated to Kropotkin and Mayakovsky)."

6. Mikhail Zolotonosov, *Slovo i telo*, 573.

7. Mikhail Ryklin, "Metrodiskurs," in *Sotsrealisticheskii kanon* (Sankt-Peterburg: Akademicheskii proekt, 2000), 714.

8. Dietmar Neutatz, *Die Moskauer Metro*, 36–37.

9. Ibid., 572.

10. Ibid.

11. Ibid.

12. Ibid.

13. Ibid., 81.

14. Ibid., 85.

15. Ibid., 91

16. Ibid., 573.

17. Quoted in Mikhail Vaiskopf, *Pisatel' Stalin*, 346.

18. As Vaiskopf writes (*Pisatel' Stalin*, 346): "Stalin's cadres are conceived, so to speak, by the machine and develop in a close symbiosis with it."

19. See Vladimir Papernyi, *Kul'tura "Dva,"* 200; also Mikhail Ryklin, "Luchshii v mire. Diskurs moskovskogo metro 30-kh godov," *Wiener Slawistischer Almanach*, Bd. 38 (1996): 154.

20. Dietmar Neutatz, *Die Moskauer Metro*, 573.

21. Nikita Khrushchev, *Khrushchev Remembers*, ed. and trans. Strobe Talbot (Boston: Little, Brown & Co., 1970), 69.

22. Dietmar Neutatz, *Die Moskauer Metro*, 573.

23. As one contemporary chronicler of the metro remarks, the term "Metrostroi" was jokingly replaced by some with the word "Komsomolstroi" due to the high spirits and enthusiasm of the Komsomol brigades (P. Lopatin, *Pervyi sovetskii metropoliten* [Moskva: Moskovskii rabochii, 1935], 95).

24. Dietmar Neutatz, *Die Moskauer Metro*, 574.

25. Ibid.

26. Boris Groys, *Die Erfindung Rußlands*, 161.

27. Ibid., 157. The utopian origins of the city are reflected in the wealth of dystopian narratives from Pushkin to Belyi associated with Petersburg in Russian literature.

28. Boris Groys, *Die Erfindung Rußlands*, 156.

29. Ibid., 159.

30. Mikhail Ryklin, "Metrodiskurs," 714.

31. Ibid.

32. See I. P. Smirnov, "Sotsrealizm: antropologicheskoe izmerenie," 33.

33. This would explain the presence of pilots/parachutists in the metro. In his 1935 long short story entitled "Fire in the Metro," the Hungarian writer Bela Iles has a pilot named Cherkasov help fight a fire in the Metro ("Pozhar v metro," Oktiabr', no. 6 [June 1935]: 119). Similarly, the heroine of Andrei Platonov's unfinished novel *Happy Moscow* goes from working as a parachutist to working in the Moscow metro.

34. Boris Groys, *Die Erfindung Rußlands*, 159.

35. Mikhail Vaiskopf, *Pisatel' Stalin*, 343. In "Sotsrealizm: antropologicheskoe izmerenie," (32), Smirnov takes this characteristic a step further.

36. Mikhail Ryklin, "Luchshii v mire. Diskurs moskovskogo metro," 156–57.

37. It can be said without hesitation that every contemporary (canonical) account of the metro brings up this important point.

38. Mikhail Ryklin, "Luchshii v mire," 156.

39. *Kak my stroili metro*, ed. A. Kosarev (Moskva: Izd-vo "Istoriia fabrik i zavodov," 1935), 177–78.

40. Ibid.

41. Mikhail Ryklin, "Luchshii v mire," 156.

42. *Kak my stroili metro*, 207.

43. Boris Groys, *Die Erfindung Rußlands*, 160–61.

44. As Boris Groys writes (*Die Erfindung Rußlands*, 162): "In this manner, the entire past was taken over by the utopian present. All traditional artistic styles were released from their historical bindings and applied anew. Thus the past lost its distinction from the present and future; even in the depths of antiquity one saw only Stalin, Soviet flags and the people gazing optimistically into the future."

45. Ibid., 161.

46. This is implicit in the rather unusual situation that architects like Kolli found themselves in when they asked their superiors for guidance in designing individual stations, for no instructions were given. In a particularly symptomatic episode (described *in Kak my stroili metro*, 178) Kolli and several other architects are given just twenty-five days to build their respective stations and when they ask what kind of stations they are to build the laconic reponse is: "Beautiful stations." The architect's job in this instance is not simply to build "beautiful stations" but rather to carefully intuit the intention of the first architect of the land, that is, Stalin/Kaganovich. The situation described above is strikingly similar to that described in the following episode where Stalin admonishes artists to "write the truth"—again, not the external/statistical truth but one that confirms the artist's closeness to the ultimate source of all truth (i.e., Stalin) (Boris Groys, *Utopiia i obmen* [Moskva: Znak, 1993], 66): "This is the sense in which one must understand Stalin's famous demand of writers and artistic workers in general: 'Write the truth.' What is meant . . . is not the external, statistical truth but the internal truth of the artist's heart—his love for Stalin and faith in him."

47. Ibid.

48. Quoted in Anton Sergl', "Katabazis kak poezdka na metro (Gumilev, Khoda-sevich, Maiakovskii, Brecht, Bakhtin i drugie: psikhoanaliz metro)," *Mesto pechati*, 1993, no. 3: 63.

49. Quoted in Anton Sergl', "Katabazis kak poezdka na metro," 65.

50. E. Tarakhovskaia, *M* (Moskva: Izd-vo detskoi literatury, 1936), 3–6: "Ia vsegda ego uznaiu/ i ne sputaiu ni s chem:/ pogliadi, nad nim, kak znamia,/ znak metro—bol'shoe 'M.'/ Avtomat-turniket/ ne nuzhno brat' bileta,/ ni k chemu nam zdes' bilet!/ Bros' zheton, i nas za eto/ vmig propustit turniket./ Lestnitsa-chudesnitsa/ Nam shagat' po lestnitse/ nezachem s toboi!/ Lestnitsa-chudesnitsa/ bezhit sama soboi./ My s toboi ozhidali,/ chto pod nami temnota,/ chto pod nami, kak v podvale,/ chernota i dukhota,/ Zdes' svetlo, kak v polden' zharkii,/ i prostoren i vysok."

51. Anton Sergl', "Katabazis kak poezdka na metro," 66.

52. Ibid., 69. Similarly, Mikhail Iampol'skii notes (*Demon i labirint: Diagrammy, deformatsii, mimesis* [Moskva: Novoe literaturnoe obozrenie, 1996], 94) that in his *Salons et souterrains de Paris*, Joseph Méry equates the spatial configuration of the underground labyrinth with the mystical handwriting of God.

53. M. Iampol'skii, *Demon i labirint*, 87.

54. Anton Sergl', "Katabazis kak poezdka", 68.

55. M. Iampol'skii, *Demon i labirint*, 87.

56. Viacheslav Kuritsyn, *Liubov' i zrenie*, 76.

57. Donald Reid, *Paris Sewers and Sewermen: Realities and Representations* (Cambridge: Harvard University Press, 1991), 29.

58. Ibid.

59. Ibid., 36.

60. Ibid., 23.

61. Ibid., 41.

62. Ibid., 39.

63. Ibid., 21.

64. Ibid., 41. It might not be going too far to suggest here that the passage from cloaca to sewer—from (female) body to (male) mechanism—echoes what Sergei Lobanov-Rostovsky describes as the transformation of body into truth in modern (Renaissance and post-Renaissance) discourse. In "Taming the Basilisk" (200) Lobanov-Rostovsky speaks of the function of the anatomist's gaze as that which transforms flesh/the body into a body of knowledge, as that which reconstitutes the corpse as language. Likewise, in the case of the Paris sewer it is the enlightened gaze of the engineer that renders the mute belly of the earth accessible to intellect, even as the earth's body itself is subsumed within the intellect's "speaking eye."

65. Vladimir Papernyi, "Moscow in 1937," unpublished manuscript.

66. Anton Sergl', "Katabazis kak poezdka na metro," 70.

67. Ibid., 69–72.

68. Boris Groys, *Die Erfindung Rußlands*, 158.

69. Thus Trotsky refers to the unconscious that Soviet power aspires to rationalize and remake as "subterranean": "The blind element has settled most profoundly within economic relations, but man is chucking it out of there with the socialist organisation of the economy. It is in this manner that a fundamental overhaul of the institution of

family becomes possible. Finally, human nature is hidden in the deepest and darkest corner of the unconscious, the elemental, the subterranean. Is it not obvious that the greatest efforts of probing thought and creative initiative will be sent there?" (Quoted in A. Etkind, *Eros nevozmozhnogo*, 285).

70. Quoted in Anton Sergl', "Katabazis kak poezdka na metro," 75.

71. This connection is only bolstered by the fact that the figure of Kaganovich is at least implicit in the novel. As Natasha Drubek-Meier notes, in *Happy Moscow* the utopian engineer Bozhko is working precisely on plans for the reconstruction of Moscow and thus recalls Kaganovich and his "Za sotsialisticheskuiu rekonstruktsiu Moskvy i gorodov SSSR" ("Rossiia—pustota v kiskhakh mira," 264)—which included the metro project.

72. Jochen Hellbeck, "Writing the Self," 78.

73. Pavel Lopatin, *Pervyi sovetskii metropoliten* (Moskva: Moskovskii rabochii, 1934), 42.

74. Ibid., 28.

75. Andrei Platonov, *Happy Moscow*, 53.

76. Vladimir Papernyi, *Kul'tura 'Dva,'* 46.

77. A. Garri, "Rozhdenie metro," *Novyi mir*, no. 1 (1935): 171.

78. See Neutatz, *Die Moskauer Metro*, 95.

79. E. Dobrenko, "Iskusstvo sotsial'noi navigatsii (Ocherki kul'turnoi topografii stalinskoi epokhi)," *Wiener Slawistischer Almanach*, 45 (2000): 122.

80. Dietmar Neutatz, *Die Moskauer Metro*, 102.

81. Hans Günther, *Der sozialistische Übermensch*, 163.

82. *Kak my stroili metro: Istoriia Metro imeni L. M. Kaganovicha* (Moskva: Izd-vo "Istoriia fabrik i zavodov," 1935), xxvii.

83. Mary Russo, *The Female Grotesque*, 116.

84. M. Zolotonosov, *Slovo i telo*, 633.

85. M. Zolotonosov, *Slovo i telo*, 612. For this reason, it seems less than convincing to see the finished metro as a kind of carnival locus, whose defining characteristic is the carnivalesque erasure of boundaries and the ceaseless movement of the body politic, as some scholars have done. (See Anton Sergl', "Katabazis kak poezdka na metro," 86; Boris Groys, *Die Erfindung Rußlands,* 163).

86. Dietmar Neutatz, *Die Moskauer Metro*, 111.

87. P. Lopatin, *Pervyi sovetskii metropoliten*, 39.

88. See Dietmar Neutatz, *Die Moskauer Metro*, 493.

89. V. Papernyi, *Kul'tura "Dva,"* 93. Likewise in his 1932 essay "O literaturnoi tekhnike," Gorky writes that "all phenomena of nature are clothed by the work of our reason in words, formed into concepts" (*Sobranie soch. v 30 t-kh*, t. 26 [Moskva: Gosudarstvennoe izd-vo khudozhestvennoi literatury, 1953], 329), evoking the strict (hierarchical) opposition of the natural and cultural worlds characteristic of Stalinist culture as a whole. The frequency with which the same image of "clothing" is used in the metro narrative suggests a related preoccupation with hiearchy in the underground spaces of the Moscow metro: "The wisdom of the party and the government consists in the fact that the underground vestibules of the metro and the above-ground structures of the Moscow-Volga canal were dressed in the most costly, decorative materials" (quoted in

V. Papernyi, *Kul'tura "Dva,"* 93). In a related vein, it would seem to be no accident that in his 1935 story "Rasskaz o baniakh i ego posetiteliakh," (*Sobranie soch. v 3 t-kh*, vol. 3 [Leningrad: Khudozhestvennaia literatura, 1987], 361). Mikhail Zoshchenko describes a scenario in which his protagonist's reversion to a preideological, preconscious state is the direct result of losing his *clothing* in a bathhouse (water, chaos).

90. Similarly, in a book of verse about the Moscow metro ("Pesnia," *Metro: Pervaia pesnia: stikhi*, ed. A. Bezymenskii [Moskva: Profizadat, 1935]), G. Kostrov describes the all-important transition from nature to culture as a passage from instability (body) to stability (architecture/technology). In Kostrov's "Pesenka," the watery insides of the earth are literally filled with reinforced concrete. Of particular significance in this regard is the rhyming juxtaposition of *nutro* [*insides*] and *metro*—that is, of body and technology: "Glubinnym/ vodonosnym zhilam/ betonom zalili nutro,/ Chtoby/ luchshim v mire passazhiram/ Dat'/ Luchshii na zemle metro." Cf. the analogous juxtaposition in Kostrov's "Pervyi reis": "Davno li zdes'/ Byla zemlia,/ Syraia, staraia, tugaia . . . / Davno li zdes'/ Byla zemlia,/ No my prishli,/ I vot—pervyi reis/ V tonnele nashem/ Pervyi poezd."

91. P. Lopatin, *Pervyi sovetskii metropoliten*, 72.

92. In addition to the highly emphasized battle against nature/water and the prominence of a noumenal light in the finished metro stations, the list of obligatory cliches might include an enthusiastic description of a visit to the construction site by L. M. Kaganovich, the no less impressive ability.

93. Viacheslav Kuritsyn, *Liubov' i zrenie*, 73. In a related vein, Aleksandr Gol'dshtein speaks of the predominance of the theme of transparency in the literature of the Stalinist '30s, transparency which is closely connected to the sense that the world is completely knowable (*Rasstavanie s nartsissom*, 183).

94. A. Kretinin, "Moskva Chestnova i 'drugie,'" 290.

95. T. Seifrid, "Platonov kak proto-sotsrealist," in *"Strana filosofov" Andreia Platonova: problemy tvorchestva*, ed. N.V. Kornienko (Moskva: Nasledie i Nauka, 1994).

96. Viacheslav Kuritysn, *Liubov' i zrenie*, 74.

97. Viacheslav Kuritsyn, *Liubov' i zrenie*, 74. Likewise, in Platonov's novella *Dzhan*, Chagataev sees (selectively) only those scenes that conform to the stereotypical image of socialist construction. As Platonov writes (*Dzhan*, 344): "And right beyond such a station one could see various people digging the earth, laying something or building in order to prepare a place of life and shelter for those without it. Chagataev did not see empty, desolate stations where one could only live in exile."

98. Jacques Derrida, *Memoirs of the Blind*, 15.

99. In this regard, the overemphasis on light in nearly every canonical metro narrative suggests neither the quasi-religious light of "triumphant socialism (Mikhail Ryklin, "Luchshii v mire," 158), nor the utopian (because artificial) light of Lenin's famous dictum "Communism is Soviet power plus the electrification of the entire land" (Boris Groys, *Die Erfindung Rußlands*, 164).

100. L. I. Kovalev, *Moskovskii metropoliten: Sbornik otchetnykh dokumentov o stroitel'stve i puske pervoi ocheredi Moskovskogo metropolitena* (Moskva: Izdanie

MK, MGK VKP/b/ i Mossoveta: 1935), 14, 22. Likewise, in a brochure that he wrote for the newly constructed Moscow–Volga canal, Lev Kassil' describes the new canal motor ships by saying that "neither on the rivers of the USSR nor abroad . . . are there ships that are so beautiful and so distinct in terms of their exterior from the existing ones" (*Kanal Moskva–Volga: spravochnik–putevoditel'* [Moskva: SSSR narkomvod po eksploatatsii kanala, 1937], 58).

101. The culture's fetishization of the eye is implicit in the following essay by Gorky, in which the language purification campaign undertaken by the author in the mid-1930s echoes the broader culture's aspiration to remake the very depths of the human unconscious in the image of ideology ("O boikosti," *Sobranie soch. v 30 t-kh*, vol. 27, 155): "In our enormous country there still exist places that are poorly illuminated by the lights of October, dark places, where the population continues to use poorly integrated foreign words, formless words." In this regard, Zoshchenko's immodest faith in the ability of reason to illuminate even the most distant and darkened corners of the human unconscious—to make them visible to the enlightened eye—is symptomatic. Thus, in *Before Sunrise* he writes: "Earlier I suffered defeat in the dark, not knowing who I was battling with or how I should fight. But now, when the sunlight has illuminated the location of my duel, I have seen the pathetic mug of my enemy" (*Sobranie soch. v 3 t-kh,* vol. 3 [Leningrad: Khudozhestvennaia literatura, 1987], 626).

102. L. Kassil', *Metro*, 8.

103. Ibid.

104. As Lobanov-Rostovsky writes ("Taming the Basilisk," 199), in Platonic theory the world is engendered through a process of envisioning that is implicitly male: "The eye imposes form on the visible world, much as the male endows the flesh with spiritual form in classical theories of the act of sexual generation."

105. L. Kassil', *Metro*, 8.

106. Ibid. Note that the word *prorva* in Russian suggests a kind of hole or pit inside a swamp.

107. Ibid.

108. Cf. Julia Kristeva, *Powers of Horror*, 72.

109. Eric Naiman, *Sex in Public*, 30. See also Irene Masing-Delic, *Abolishing Death*, 86.

110. Mikhail Zolotonosov, *Slovo i telo*, 633.

111. As Zolotonosov remarks, the underground represents only one of several discrete realms (i.e., water, ether, earth) that Woman is allowed to penetrate as a means of achieving symbolic self-mastery. Thus, the critic argues, Woman is granted entrance into the male cosmos, at the same time that the very concept of the "feminine" is liquidated (*Slovo i telo*, 633).

112. That the pathos of the piece concerns mastering a feminine nature—whether through violent penetration or the reconfiguration of the female as male—is most evident in the following excerpt, where the male digger's pneumatic drill complete with its phallic lance seduces and conquers the virginal rock (the Russian word *tselik* here is nearly the same as the colloquial world for a virgin, or *tselka*, while the word *pika* clearly suggests the male member): "—Razve zhe v tselik naprolom tychus? Ia

prozhilku nakhozhu. V kazhdom tselike naidetsia prozhilka. . . . Vot ona! Molotok so smiagchennym zvukom legko vpivaetsia v prosloiku . . . I vot proiskhodit chudo. Litoi, spresovannyi izvestniak prikhodit v dvizhenie. Pika vgryzaetsia v porodu, i glyby, drognuv, spolzaiut i rushatsia k nogam molodogo rabochego" (E. Iakub, *Prokhodchik Katamanin* [Moskva: Moskovsksii bol'shevik, 1944], 14).

113. E. Iakub, *Prokhodchik Katamanin*, 15.

114. Ibid., 4–5.

115. L. Kassil', *Metro: Chudo pod Moskvoi*, 12.

116. A. Platonov, *Schastlivaia Moskva*, 41. As Heli Kostov notes (*Mifopoetika Andreia Platonova v romane "Schastlivaia Moskva"* [Helsinki: Dept. of Slavonic and Baltic Languages and Literatures, 2000], 221–24)], spatial interiors (e.g., apartments, houses) are typically marked as negative.

117. Katerina Clark, "Eisenstein's Two Projects for a Film About Moscow," unpublished manuscript. In this regard, it is perhaps no accident that in Eisenstein's draft plans for the film, workers under Peter the Great and the contemporary metro builders are shown as historical counterparts, and that the liberation of the laboring classes under Stalin coincides with the symbolic predominance of the element of air.

118. Mikhail Zolotonosov, *Slovo i telo*, 611.

119. Mike O'Mahony, "Going Underground: Palaces for the People on the Moscow Underground," unpublished manuscript.

120. L. Kassil', *Metro*, 9.

121. P. Lopatin, *Pervyi sovetskii metropoliten*, 52. Note that the same basic confrontation is reproduced throughout the various metro narratives with little or no variation. Thus in his 1944 piece *Prokhodchik Katamanin* (3–4), E. Iakub reproduces the same basic confrontation between Bolshevik resolve and the elements: "The underground army of builders of the Moscow metro laid kilometers of tunnels through shaky masses of quicksand. Tearing into the hard layers of rock, pressing back the advancing water-bearing soils, drawing off and fettering the subterranean rivers, Soviet people erected twenty-eight station-palaces. Deep beneath the city, beneath the brimming Moscow river they paved straight, multi-kilometer arterials dressed in watertight, cement shirts."

122. Thus, Zolotonosov remarks, the struggle to build the first socialist underground was at the same time an attempt to conquer "(feminine) nature," replacing it with (male) civilization (*Slovo i telo*, 633).

123. L. Kassil', *Metro*, 13.

124. V. M. Mokienko, T. G. Nikitina, *Bol'shoi slovar' russkogo zhargona* (Sankt-Peterburg: Norint, 2000), 685.

125. Cf. the following poem entitled "Encounter" from G. Kostrov's *Stikhi o metro* (21–22): "Zemlia/ i sekundy ne styla,/ Zakhvachennaia v oborot,/ Kogda my i s flanga/ I s tyla/ Kroshili tverdyni porod!/ V khodu molotki/ I skarpeli,/ V rabote/ Pruzhinit ruka . . ./ Stuchat melodichno kapeli,/ Spadaiushchie s verkhniaka! . . . / Vse blizhe i blizhe . . . / I ukho/ Uslyshalo:/ Gde-to poiut,/ I s rokotom,/ Burno i glukho/ Navstrechu/ Pnevmatiki b'iut!/ Zapomnil tu bodruiu zven' ia,/ I shorokh otbitoi zemli,/ Kogda/ Molodezhnye zven'ia/ Poslednie metry veli!/ Itog napriazhennogo boia—/ Otbita/ Posledniaia piad!/ I v ramu/ Sploshnogo zaboia/ Tovarishchi podali

piat'!/ Ne kleilis'/ S radosti rechi./ Kak ptitsy./ Sryvalis' slova!/ Takoi/ Udivitel'noi vstrechi/ Ni razu/ Ne znala bratva."

126. L. Kassil', *Metro*, 11.

127. Cynthia A. Ruder, *Making History for Stalin*, 144.

128. Dietmar Neutatz, *Die Moskauer Metro*, 334.

129. Donald Reid, *Paris Sewers and Sewermen*, 114.

130. Dietmar Neutatz, *Die Moskauer Metro*, 334.

131. Ibid., 558.

132. Il'ya Il'f and Evgenii Petrov, *Sobranie soch.*, t. 3 (Moskva: Khudozhestven-naia literatura, 1996), 277–79. Likewise, Raisa Orlova writes of the era that it was suffused with a spirit of universal transformation and change. Recalling her perceptions of the Stalinist '30s, she notes: " I had an unshakable faith that my existence between these old walls [in an apartment on Gorky Street] was merely a preparation for life. Life, properly speaking, would begin in a new and sparkling white house. There I would do exercises in the morning, there the ideal order would exist, there all my heroic achievements would commence . . . It was both possible and necessary to alter everything: the streets, the houses, the cities, the social order, human souls" (quoted in Sheila Fitzpatrick, *Everday Stalinism*, 64).

133. Ibid., 339.

134. M. Vaiskopf, *Pisatel' Stalin*, 337. Thus Stalin imagined the birth of the revolutionary avant-garde in terms of an endless, quasi-agrarian cycle of self-regeneration, where the old guard served as fertilizer for a new crop of party comrades.

135. L. Kassil', *Metro*, 9, 16.

136. As Mikhail Iampol'skii notes ("Censorship as the Triumph of Life," 167), the theme of life overcoming form was already well-established by the mid-'30s. Having emerged from the antiformalist campaign that began in the late '20s it produced a narrative template that could be broadly applied to various situations. For instance, in the realm of belles lettres, the artist is portrayed as locked in a heroic struggle with a host of petty norms and rules that prevents him from representing life in its epic fullness. Only by overcoming such restrictions does the artist realize his full potential.

137. M. Ryklin, "Luchshii v mire," 154. See also M. Ryklin, "Metrodiskurs," 714.

138. P. Lopatin, *Pervyi sovetskii metropoliten*, 96.

139. *Rasskazy stroitelei metro*, 56. Cf. also the section entitled "Skvoz' plyvuny" of the commemorative edition *Kak my stroili metro* (253), in which older, more experienced caisson workers are outworked by their younger Komsomol counterparts: "As a result of a lot of explanatory work and a well-organized technical training program the entire Komsomol group mastered production in short order. . . . But the older caisson workers . . . were quickly put on the back burner. For the old-timers a load of 400 tubs was a record, while the young caisson workers easily made a thousand. Moreover, the old shaft sinkers were used to working in conditions where the timbering didn't crack and the rock held itself up. It was different in the metro. You've got water on all sides, the wood timbering cracks. And so the old-timers left. This underscores the role of new workers in our production. The Komsomol members had incredible energy, and they put all their effort into mastering all the details of production and speeding it up.

And so in front of our very eyes you see a new type of worker being born: the conscious, energetic, active builder of socialism."

140. *Kak my stroili metro*, 222. See also L. Kassil', *Metro*, 11.

141. *Kak my stroili metro*, 222.

142. Bela Iles, "Pozhar v metro," *Oktiabr'*, no. 6 (1935): 120.

143. Mikhail Vaiskopf explains the dictator's contempt for the old (and concommitant obsession with the new) as an outgrowth of the most ancient (Nartian) stage of Caucasian culture, which included the festive, ritualized killing of the elderly (*Pisatel' Stalin*, 328).

144. Quoted in M. Vaiskopf, *Pisatel' Stalin*, 332.

145. B. A. Uspenskii, *Izbrannye trudy, t. 1 (Semiotika istorii, semiotika kul'tury)* (Moskva: Iazyki russkoi kul'tury, 1996), 324.

146. M. Ryklin, "Luchshii v mire," 154. See also I. P. Smirnov, *Psikhodiakhronologika*, 276.

147. Cf. in this regard the representation of Kaganovich (reproduced in Neutatz, *Die Moskauer Metro*, illus. 11) with a kind of saintly halo.

148. See L. Kassil', *Metro*, 15.

149. See *Rasskazy stroitelei metro*, 121.

150. L. Kassil', *Metro*, 14.

151. *Rasskazy stroitelei metro*, 121.

152. As Evgenii Dobrenko explains ("Iskusstvo sotsial'noi navigatsii," 120), this is typical of the Stalinist era's understanding of the map not as a visual or technical phenomenon but as part of the grand narrative of socialist restructuring.

153. *Kak my stroili metro*, 436.

154. M. Vaiskopf, *Pisatel' Stalin*, 343. In a similar vein, Mikhail Ryklin remarks on the sharp rift in the iconography of the metro stations between images of jubilation connected to various earth and fertility symbols, and the more "traumatic" images of urbanization and industrial labor ("Telo terrora: tezisy k logike nasiliia," 138–89).

155. Irina Gutkin, *The Cultural Origins of the Socialist Realist Aesthetic*, 112.

156. M. Vaiskopf, *Pisatel' Stalin*, 345.

157. Ibid., 344.

158. L. Kassil', *Metro*, 16.

159. Donald Reid, *Paris Sewers and Sewermen*, 120.

160. Quoted in Dietmar Neutatz, *Die Moskauer Metro*, 334.

161. Boris Groys, *Utopiia i obmen*, 44–45. Similarly, I. P. Smirnov notes that one of the most commonplace motifs in Socialist Realism is the light of knowledge (*Psikhodiakhronologika*, 283).

162. Not unlike the image of the underground/labyrinth, Plato's gnoseological allegory recalls what Kristeva describes as the rite of passage that accompanies the self-constitution of the "speaking" subject in opposition to the "phantasmatic power of the mother," (*Powers of Horror*, 100). Remarking on the symbolic significance of the ritual of circumcision in Judaism, Kristeva notes that "by duplicating and thus displacing through ritual the preeminent separation, which is that from the mother, Judaism seems to insist in symbolic fashion—the very opposite of what is 'natural'—that the

identity of the speaking being (with his God) is based on the separation of the son from the mother." Likewise, in Plato's allegory the subject accedes to language by passing from darkness to light in a manner that is not unlike the child's emergence from the womb.

163. Sandra M. Gilber and Susan Gubar, *The Madwoman in the Attic: The Woman Writer and the Nineteenth Century Literary Imagination*, 2nd ed. (New Haven: Yale University Press, 2000), 94.

164. Viacheslav Kuritsyn, *Liubov' i zrenie*, 79.

165. L. Kassil', *Metro*, 18.

166. Cf. V. P. Ilenkov's 1935 *Solnechnyi gorod*, in which, as Zolotonosov notes (*Slovo i telo*, 735), this desire is made quite explicit in the image of a utopian Park of Culture and Rest, where the sign "Let in the Sun" is prominently displayed. As Zolotonosov goes on to point out, the culture's promotion of a kind of Stalinist solar myth is evident in the "warming trend" (Papernyi's term) that influenced the art, architecture, and thinking of the period.

167. P. Lopatin, *Pervyi sovetskii metropoliten*, 124.

168. Quoted in M. Ryklin, "Luchshii v mire," 156.

169. *L. Kassil', Metro*, 18–19.

170. *Metro: sbornik, posviashchennyi pusku moskovskogo metropolitena*, ed. L. Kovalev (Moskva: "Rabochaia gazeta," 1935), 198–99.

171. Ibid., 201–2.

172. Ibid., 198. Cf. also Smirnov's remark (*Psikhodiakhronologika*, 254) that in Socialist Realism the body invariably comes to occupy a place entirely contrary to the norm. Here the sky and the earth have essentially switched places.

173. *Metro: sbornik, posviashchennyi pusku moskovskogo metropolitena*, 199.

174. Ibid., 201.

175. L. Kassil', *Metro*, 19.

176. See M. Ryklin, "Luchshii v mire," 158.

177. M. Allenov, "Ochevidnosti sistemnogo absurdizma skvoz' emblematiku moskovskogo metro," 84.

178. *Kak my stroili metro*, 436.

179. In this regard, it might be worth noting the enormous significance which was attributed to the problem of illumination at the contemporaneous VDNKh, as Mikhail Ryklin notes ("Mesto utopii. K istorii VSKhV-VDNKh-VVTs," unpublished manuscript, 3): "As in the Moscow metro, enormous significance at VDNKh was attributed to lighting, since in the evenings the exhibit became a place for public strolling, concerts, and amateur performances."

180. See Michel Foucault, *Discipline and Punish: The Birth of the Prison*, tr. Alan Sheridan (New York: Vintage Books, 1977), 226; Michel Foucault, *The Birth of the Clinic: An Archaeology of Medical Perception*, tr. A. M. Sheridan Smith (New York: Pantheon Books, 1975), 114.

181. Donald Reid, *Paris Sewers*, 48.

182. *Prokhod* (42) versus *prokhodit* (44).

183. The metaphor of "intrusion" as characteristic of Stalinist voluntarism is one that is initiated by Stalin himself in his famous speech to the All-Union Conference

of Soviet Industry Workers, where he notes: "It's time to have finished with the putrid policy of not intruding into production. It's high time to establish a new policy, more appropriate to the current period: *to intrude in everything*" (quoted in *Andrei Platonov: vospominaniia sovremennikov*, 323). The Moscow metro, one might
well argue, is one of the most potent symbols of this aspiration to "intruding into
everything." It is for this reason, I would argue, that in *Happy Moscow* Platonov
goes out of his way to discredit precisely Stalinist culture's intrusive desire to see
and know *all*. Thus Stalin's metaphor of "intruding in everything" is reproduced in
the surgeon Sambikin's project of literally entering into the human body in order
to recover its darkest secrets and to reclaim it. Even more than this, the intrusive
quality of the scientist's desire to see/know is implicit in the ambiguity of certain
verbs. In the following example, for instance, Sambikin's urge to "investigate" or
"go carefully into" (*vniknut'*) also suggests a violation of the other. Describing his
dream of discovering a secret substance within the human organism that could be
used to prolong the life of the living, Sambikin reflects: "Eto veshchestvo imeet
sil'neishuiu ozhivliaiushchuiu silu dlia zhivykh ustalykh organizmov. Chto eto
takoe—neizvestno. No my postaraemsia vniknut' " (*Schastlivaia Moskva*, Novyi
mir, 9 [1991]: 33). Platonov's use of the verb *vniknut'* portrays in an extraordinarily
ambiguous light the model of cognition (à la Foucault) that is predicated on a violent excavation of and objectification of the Other. The opposite of this is a kind
of knowledge based on sympathy for the other and identified with the heart, as in
the following example where Sartorius is so overcome by his love for Moscow that
he loses his ability to think. Symptomatically, in this episode the heart rises up
above the eyes: "But now he was not conscious of any thought at all because his
heart had risen up into his head and was beating there above his eyes" (*Happy
Moscow*, 56).

184. Platonov's interest in blindness here is more than a little reminiscent of his
prominent contemporary, Georges Bataille. According to Bataille, the traditional
Western conception of knowing, modelled as it is on metaphor's visual perception,
puts in place a fundamental disparity between subject and object. Cognition-as-
vision, Bataille argues, allows the self to constitute itself in blessed isolation from that
which it seeks to know, risking neither contact with nor contamination by the Other
(Denis Hollier, *Against Architecture: The Writings of Georges Bataille*, trans. Betsy
Wing [Cambridge: The MIT Press, 1989], 95). Realizing the limitations of this model,
in *L'Expérience intérieure, L'Histoire de œil*, and other works, Bataille posits the state
of "blindedness" as the sole alternative to the existing "intellectual edifice" (Patrick
Ffrench, *The Cut/Reading Bataille's "Histoire De L'Oeil"* [Oxford: Oxford University Press, 1999], 130). Such blindness, he suggests, "ruins the dialectic of vision,"
pressing the eye to "that point where the structure of the gaze implodes" (Denis Hollier, *Against Architecture: The Writings of Georges Bataille*, trans. Betsy Wing [Cam-
bridge: The MIT Press, 1989], 95). Likewise, in Platonov's *Happy Moscow*, those
who seek transcendence—such as the metro-building Moscow or the utopian engineer Sartorius—are subjected to the "castrating" gesture of blindness or physical mutilation, a gesture that forces them to confront the same underground they initially
sought to rise above. Ironically, at the end of the novel the parachutist and metro

worker, Moscow Chestnova, becomes simply "Musia," and her new name is not unlike the Russian word for "garbage" (*musor*). Similarly, the renowned engineer Sartorius ends the novel performing the most mundane and earthly of tasks—weighing and distributing food.

185. Donald Reid, *Paris Sewers*, 54.

186. Ibid., 55.

187. "So far as their utilization is concerned," Marx writes (quoted in *Paris Sewers*, 57), "there is an enormous waste of them in the capitalist economy. In London, for instance, they find no better use for the excretion of four and one-half million human beings than to contaminate the Thames with it at heavy expense."

188. Anton Sergl', "Katabazis kak poezdka na metro," 96.

189. E. A. Iablokov, *Khudozhestvennyi mir Mikhaila Bulgakova* (Moskva: Iazyki slavianskoi kul'tury, 2001), 162.

190. Ibid.

191. E. A. Iablokov, *Khudozhestvennyi mir Mikhaila Bulgakova*, 159.

192. M. N. Zolotonosov, *Slovo i telo*, 736.

193. Here it should be noted that Boris Groys sees both Bulgakov and Bakhtin as presenting not so much a democratic/dialogic alternative to the supposed monologism of Stalinist culture. Rather Groys argues that Stalinism as a cultural and philosophical entity is itself thoroughly carnivalesque. Thus he remarks that "every ideologized, truly monologic idealism invariably encountered defeat in Stalinist culture. The official ideology of the Stalin-era excludes any consistent logic, . . . even the strict logic of Marxism. Such logic is immediately condemned as formalism and moribund scholasticism, which is alien to the complexity of life." At the same time, according to Groys, Bakhtin and Bulgakov's preoccupation with the phenomenon of carnival represents not an alternative (dialogic) model, but rather an attempt on the part of both to neutralize the terror and fear associated with Stalinism, to engage it in a kind of relativizing dialogue which it was not capable of conducting itself (*Die Erfindung Rußlands*, 67). Here Groys seems to take his argument too far. That both Bakhtin and Bulgakov, along with other writers, were inextricably bound to the same system of thought that they resisted (Groys, *Die Erfindung Rulands*, 66, 72) should not obscure the important distinction between the genuinely dialogic character of both Bulgakov and Bakhtin's work. What Mikhail Vaiskopf has correctly defined as the syncretic or "compromise" character of Stalinist discourse—its ability to move freely and unobstructedly between logically contradictory propositions or metaphors (*Pisatel' Stalin*, 343) represents not so much genuine dialogism as it does a kind of philosophical opportunism or double-dealing. Indeed, such visible projects of the Stalin era as the Moscow metro—their stylistic syncretism aside—seem overwhelmingly predicated on the notion of realizing the utopian ideal of absolute stasis, and not on the kind of philosophical dialogism that underlay the work of such authors/philosophers as Platonov, Bulgakov, or Bakhtin.

194. Mikhail Bulgakov, *The Master and Margarita*, trans. Diana Burgin and Tierna O'Connor (New York: Vintage Books, 1995), 305.

195. Ibid., 217.

196. Mikhail Ryklin, "Metrodiskurs," 719. This is, of course, an exaggeration on Ryklin's part. As Vladimir Papernyi notes (*Kul'tura "Dva,"* 163): "The texts of Culture II assert that saboteurs: 'threw rocks into the metro shafts' and 'shoved nails into pumps' during the building of the metro, while spreading rumors that people who worked in the caissons 'lost their ability to engage in sexual activity.'"

197. Ibid.

198. Quoted in Mikhail Ryklin, "Metrodiskurs," 719.

199. Mikhail Bulgakov, *The Master and Margarita*, 104.

Conclusion

Stalinist Bodies on Display

In his 1994 novel *The Life of Insects* Viktor Pelevin deftly compares a group of furiously dancing post-Soviet youth, who in their own way are searching for the deeper meaning of life, to a dump where plaster statues gathered from Parks of Culture and Rest throughout the country are unceremiously abandoned. The flashing strobe light mounted above the dance floor creates the eeriest of impressions. The gyrating dancers (who like all the characters in the novel are actually insects) are transformed into a series of freeze frames, each of which resembles a different Park of Culture and Rest adorned with an identical complement of lifeless statuary. Published only several years after the breakup of the Soviet Union, Pelevin's novel portrays the country's quest for a new identity against the backdrop of suddenly fallen idols and discarded myths. That Pelevin should use this rather macabre fusing of bodies and superannuated statues to symbolize the state of contemporary society is puzzling only to the non-Russian reader. For it evokes in terms instantly recognizable to almost any inhabitant of the former Soviet Union the extreme fragmentation of the post-Soviet body politic by symbolically deconstructing one of its most cherished and commonplace icons: the Stalin-era statue.

Indeed, even a cursory glance at the cultural landscape of the Stalinist period reveals the era's uncommon fascination with statuary and sculpture of various kinds. The Soviet pavilion of the 1939 World's Fair in New York, designed by Iofan and meant to reflect the as yet unconstructed Palace of Soviets, was no exception. Distinguished not only by the remarkable speed with which it was assembled, the pavilion was embellished with a wealth of statuary. The wings of the building portrayed the twin faces of Stalinist heroism, with one side devoted to the civil war and the other to industrialization. Most importantly, the pavilion was topped by a giant statue—measuring 24 meters in height and weighing 30 tons—of a worker holding up a red star.[1] And finally the Palace of Soviets itself, which when built, "would be the highest building on earth, higher than the Great Pyramid of Cheops, higher than Cologne Cathedral or the Eiffel Tower, taller than the highest skyscraper in New York," was to be "surmounted by a statue of Lenin, measuring 328 feet."[2] As Zolotonosov points out, sculpture was without a doubt one of the dominant (if not the dominant) culture code of the Stalinist period.[3] Whether in the newly constructed metro or in the numerous Parks of Culture and Rest, such sculpted bodies provided a statuary microcosm of Stalinist society. Every aspect of official ideology and mythology could, in a sense, be gleaned from this broad array of embodied postures and gestures, gestures which represented such all-important Stalinist mythologemes as "the leader," "childhood," "the mother," and so on.[4] More importantly, since the overarching metaphor of social cohesion was that of the social or collective body, these sculptures ultimately served as the most concise expression of what the society as a whole was endeavoring to produce. One might say, in other words, that in the image of the statue lay the keys to a new kind of uniquely Stalinist subjectivity. And from here it is no stretch to see such bodies as endowed with a distinct and even powerful erotic appeal.[5] Thus in a contemporary short story by Yuri Buida, a tippling Dostoevsky enthusiast who works as a watchman at a Park of Culture and Rest finds love and ultimately death in the arms of the famous Girl with an Oar who has miraculously come to life.[6]

If the Stalinist statue-body was representative of a world in which the dream of communism had been neatly reproduced in plaster and stone, the actual bodies of living human beings were quite another matter. Here the struggle to realize the ideal of utopia found was complicated by the retrograde character of the material to be transformed: i.e., human psychophysiology. This is powerfully expressed in Platonov's most important work of fiction from the 1930s—the unfinished novel *Happy Moscow*. In it the author repeatedly suggests that the historical novelty of communist ideology must be weighed against the eternal recalcitrance of (human) nature—an unequal contest if ever there was one! And in a key episode of the novel Platonov juxtaposes the linear narrative of Stalinist ideology ("on the streets and squares a modest Stalin watched over all the open roads, . . . life stretched into . . . the distance from which there was no return") with the eternal *round* of human existence. Thus at the Krestovskii market one finds coats that during the revolution had passed through so many hands that the "*circumference/meridian* of the earth's sphere was too small to measure their path between . . . humans."[7] The very curve of the earth's surface, the author hints, suggests a model of human history as *eternal return* that belies the revolution's facile pathos of futuricity.

Despite the considerable challenges involved in Stalinism's revolutionary project, there seems to have been no shortage of Soviet citizens willing to participate in what amounted to a collective ritual of psychophysiological reconstruction. This is hardly surprising, since the latter were simply internalizing or realizing the metaphors that governed vast, highly visible swaths of public discourse. And unlike the perennially pessimistic hero of Platonov's 1929 novella *The Foundation Pit* who muses that "a man will make a building and unmake himself,"[8] many Stalin-era subjects understood only too well the connection between the forging of iron and steel and the forging of the self. Among a host of such projects, the Moscow metro stands out as one of the most memorable. As with other similar undertakings, the construction site of the first-ever socialist metro served the dual purpose of taming the benighted underworld even as it transformed backward (human) elements into model worker-citizens. Thus in one account we are told that the construction of the Moscow subway is like "a gigantic human machine, which in addition to material values produces yet another value that lies in the transformation of human beings."[9] This was to be true not only for the builders of the metro, but for those who would one day travel through the bowels of a reclaimed underground. The former—often unskilled laborers or recent arrivals from the country—would typically be potrayed as having acquired several specializations while working underground, at the same time that they raised their educational level by participating in various organized cultural activities.[10] As to how the metro might change the human countenance of its passengers, one could only speculate—and some writers did. The prominent satirical duo of Il'f and Petrov described the subway as the antidote par excellence to the chaotic, overcrowded crucibles of *nekul'turnost'* so familiar from the short stories of Zoshchenko. In the gleaming socialist underground, the authors opined, "gentleness of manners, an uncommon politeness and even joviality would triumph. 'Did I bump you with my elbow, granny?' 'Oh no, my dear! Why your elbow is at least a meter away.'"[11] Likewise, in his diary entries for the year 1938 Yurii Olesha draws a clear connection between one of the models of Soviet humanity (i.e., Mayakovsky) and the Moscow subway. Anthropomorphically merging the metro with the man, Olesha writes of the subway station that bore the poet's name: "Once those arcs appeared to me to be gigantic armholes in someone's waistcoat. The very next instant I knew what the station represented. 'Mayakovsky's steel jacket,' my imagination whispered to me.' How nice. Now he who wore a yellow jacket can appear before us in the steel jacket of a giant."[12] Finally, distant echoes of the metro's former glory can be felt even today. In his recent film *Moscow* (2000), Aleksandr Zel'dovich has his protagonists take an excursion through the capital city, in which the subway is described as its most important monument. Yet in stark contrast to the anthropological ideal of the '30s, the metro of today embodies the pervasive emptiness that has enveloped Moscow after the end of empire. In one of the most disturbing scenes in the film, an empty subway car provides the backdrop for a passionless sexual encounter between two of the film's protagonists.

The "forge of the new man," the Moscow metro was itself a kind of ideal body, symbolizing in the very process of its construction the arduous struggle against (human) nature that would one day engender the New Man. Still, in order to become that "ideal body" the Moscow underground had to expunge any trace of its connection to the natural or "feminine" that was its origin. And here the Stalinist ritual of "forging" or *perekovka* mirrors the more fundamental process whereby language and culture themselves are born. As Kristeva notes, the phenomenon of language—predicated as it is on a fundamental gesture of separation—comes about only at the expense of the archaic maternal authority it suppresses. Here the undifferentiated self is reshaped into "a *territory* having areas, orifices, points and lines, surfaces and hollows, where . . . the differentiation of proper-clean and improper dirty, possible and impossible, is impressed and exerted."[13] Likewise, the benighted Moscow underground could be inscribed into the broader narrative of Stalinist utopianism only by surgically detaching it from the belly of "Moist Mother Earth" (*mat' syra-zemlia*). This idea is repeatedly implied—if not explicitly invoked—in numerous contemporary accounts of the metro's construction. In them the eternal threat of encroaching groundwaters coupled with Lazar Kaganovich's inspired admonition to the workers to build the metro "so that it doesn't drip anywhere" (*chtoby nigde ne kapalo*) serves only to underscore the extent to which the metro narrative was ultimately predicated on the death of the feminine. Nowhere is this more visible than in Lev Kassil''s 1935 poetic tribute to the Moscow subway entitled *Metro: Chudo pod Moskvoi*. And there can be no mistaking the symbolic thrust of the author's "before" and "after" descriptions, which portray the metamorphosis of unreconstructed body into sculpted monument. Thus the "wet, clayey bowels" of Mother Earth mentioned at the beginning of *Metro* are miraculously transformed into the glass and marble wonder which serves as a window into Moscow's socialist future: "Beyond the mirrored windows of the subway cars one after another panoramas of underground palaces flit by. Our metro car carries us through yesterday's future which has become today's present. And each one of us senses that the marble splendor of tomorrow's socialist Moscow is sprouting up and growing right in front of us."[14]

The pathos of creating a collective Stalinist body is no less at stake in the same author's (i.e., Lev Kassil''s) well-known 1939 novel for adolescents *The Goalkeeper of the Republic*. Ethnically an outsider—Kassil' was Jewish—his own relationship to the primarily Russian collective body politic could not but have been complicated. And his novel, which portrays a Jewish journalist's attempts to become part of a soccer-playing, speedboat-racing collective called Gidraer, alludes to this dilemma. Yet viewed in its entirety, the work ultimately resolves the vexing conundrum of insider versus outsider—of Jewish versus Russian body—by appealing to the myth of the Great Stalinist Family. Transethnic, even transbiological, the Stalinist notion of the Soviet Union as an extended family recast the relationship between citizens and their leader in openly patriarchal terms.[15] Kassil''s *Goalkeeper* uses this mythology as a means of overcoming what had been one of the central artistic dilemmas of the previous decade: that is, that of the intellectual outsider vis-à-vis the revolutionary collective. In this regard, the novel clearly invites comparison with the vastly superior and more well-known *Red Cavalry* cycle by Isaac Babel, a work that takes up but ultimately refuses to resolve the opposition between Jew and Cossack—old world and new. As much a product of the decade in which it was written as it is the creation of Babel's particular sensibilities, the *Red Cavalry* cycle ends with a murky tangle of irreconcilables. Thus the frail physique of the Jew Bratslavsky is juxtaposed with the robust physiology of two well-endowed Cossack women who drag his expiring body across the floor. Likewise, the personality of the narrator Lyutov is precariously stretched between the "storms of my imagination" and an ancient (Semitic) body poorly equipped to contain them.[16] In Kassil''s *Goalkeeper,* written more than a decade after the *Red Cavalry*, the (eternal) return of the repressed is declared defunct, in order to make way for Stalinism's more optimistic narrative of historical progress. By the same token the rational Jew and the "spontaneous" excessive Russian are folded together in a synthesis of Apollonian and Dionysian that mirrors the culture's ambitious push to reconcile everything with everything. The result is a situation in which even the "eternal" body of the Jew-cum-outsider proves susceptible to revision—to a radical historical rewriting. As in the case of the Moscow metro, where the murky (feminine) underground is transformed into a model of (masculine) culture and light, so, too, Kassil''s *Goalkeeper* challenges the very laws of psychophysiology, confidently demonstrating that the frail Jew and the robust Russian are not as incompatible as they had once seemed. In the cauldron of collectivity that was the Stalinist soccer stadium, this conundrum simply disappears. Thus what Zoshchenko might have referred to as a "Kursk anomaly" becomes reality in Stalinism's all-encompassing narrative of the fairy tale come true.

The Stalinist push to forge a common psychophysiology is no less profoundly reflected in the work of two authors whose oeuvres were instrumental in lending a voice to the postrevolutionary everyman: that is, Mikhail

Zoshchenko and Andrei Platonov. Despite the fact that both writers had unambiguously tethered their fates to the revolution, attempting to honestly portray its progress toward producing the New Man, both Platonov and
Zoshchenko repeatedly ran afoul of the literary-critical establishment. For
Zoshchenko this lack of acceptance by the literary powers-that-be could not
but have been particularly devastating. For despite his own deep-seated
doubts about the revolution's ability to qualitatively change human nature,
Zoshchenko undertook just such a project with respect to himself in much of
his writing of the 1930s. Thus a sense of fiction as autotherapeutic cure runs
through Zoshchenko's *Youth Restored* (1934), as well as many of the writer's
short stories and feuilletons of the '30s, culminating in the ambitious *Before
Sunrise* (1943)—to my knowledge, the only Stalinist self-help book to have
ever been produced. The first of these—*Youth Restored*—can and probably
should be understood as a private, literary variant of the highly visible public
construction projects such as the infamous White Sea Canal, one of the most
important goals of which was to reclaim socially backward or undesirable elements of the body politic. This is all the more evident, if we consider that in
1934 Zoshchenko published a short story depicting the putative rehabilitation
of a criminal through forced labor at the White Sea Canal—a story which not
accidentally bore the same title as the much larger *Youth Restored* published
that same year.[17]

As one might expect, the problem for Zoshchenko in *Youth Restored* lay in
the inevitable rift between theory and practice, between the author's relatively
straightfoward intention to portray the protagonist Volosatov's rehabilitation
and the lingering sense of human nature as fundamentally incorrigible. Thus
Youth Restored leaves the reader with a sense of almost surreal ambivalence;
in a year or two, we are told, the convalescent Volosatov will certainly be
bending "horseshoes with his left arm if for some reason he doesn't die."[18]
Such ambivalence does not, however, prevent Zoshchenko from continuing
to fantasize about the possibility of turning his frail Old World physique into
a model of statuary Bolshevik perfection. In a biographical piece about a proletarian woman named Ann Lavrent'evna Kas'ianova we see Zoshchenko
imagining the possibility of a sexual union between the epically proportioned
Aniuta—just as Lyutov had fantasized about becoming a Cossack or Evgenii
Karasik about playing soccer—and a frail officer (clearly, a stand-in for
Zoshchenko himself). Lamenting the absence of such sturdy women among
his own set, Zoshcenko's double remarks: "'Aniuta, he says, it's extremely
unfortunate that among our higher society there aren't any women like you. . . .
And I, he said, would probably be completely cured of my melancholy if I
took up with a person such as yourself.'"[19] Of all his attempts at belletristic
self-healing, it is certainly the much maligned *Before Sunrise* that emerges as

most "successful." Yet here, too, the author's victory is surely Pyrrhic, won at the cost of forgetting or censoring out vast swaths of his own past. In *Before Sunrise* Freud's eternal return of the repressed is neatly blocked using a mixture of Pavlov's "more scientific" theory of conditioned response and the Stalinist narrative of ascendant consciousness. Ultimately, the result for Zoshchenko himself, however, was not the longed-for transformation but the obsessed, half-mad writer about whom Kornei Chukovskii wrote in 1937: "a great man, but crazy. His madness is self-healing."[20]

Like Zoshchenko Andrei Platonov dreamed of a future utopia in which the bodies of *men* would no longer be haunted by the specter of feminine nature (in short, of biology) that had previously prevented access to the "kingdom of consciousness." Yet unlike his contemporary, Platonov nurtured such ideas only at the very outset of his career as a writer—in the early '20s—after which the very image of Woman that had been banished from utopia would loom increasingly large. Indeed, as the utopian (male) collectivism imagined in the poetry of the *Proletkul't* became an obligatory ritual within the mythology of the Stalinist '30s, Platonov himself recoiled from the body beautiful in order to embrace a broad poetics of corporeal and cognitive grotesque. As early as 1934, when the writer traveled to Central Asia with one of the then-popular writers' brigades, we see a shift away from the previous longing for ontological purity that is utopia toward an acceptance of the fundamental (im)purity of human existence. In his notebooks from the year 1934, Platonov repeatedly draws attention to that which has been excluded in Western (and, indeed, Stalinist) culture's civilizing narrative. In these elliptical, often opaque entries what stands out is the writer's refusal to differentiate between the clean and the unclean, between history-as-narrative and that which seems unnarratable or ahistorical. Thus in one entry, Platonov simply notes: "The doctor: 'Life is filled with false events, while the real events are unknown.'"[21] And in the same vein the author elsewhere offers us a curious image of defecation as fact—as an activity or pastime: "She [Dzhumal'] felt so dreary that she would go off to defecate, even if she didn't want or need to, just to have something to do."[22] Alongside a growing interest in the (un)clean, Platonov's writing from the mid-'30s on increasingly accords the image of Woman pride of place. In such works as *Dzhan*, *Happy Moscow*, and others, women (or men who aspire to be them) take on the important function of *embodying* the very utopia that previously could only be imaginatively evoked or abstractly inferred. Yet unlike Stalinism's utopia found, realized as it was by surgically altering the body politic, in his *Happy Moscow* Platonov envisions a utopia of all-inclusion; one that embraces filth, sickness, and decrepitude on a par with purity and health. As an antidote to Stalinism's adoration of the statue Platonov holds up the lame and battered body of his heroine

Moscow Chestnova. A paradoxical mix of transcendence and immanence, her body radiates immortality precisely in those moments when it appears most mortal—as, for instance, during defecation or after a near-fatal accident in the Moscow metro. The Stalinist ideal of corporeality was one which could be easily gleaned from the abundant statuary that adorned the culture's exterior and interior spaces—whether in the many Parks of Culture and Rest, the newly constructed Moscow metro, or finally in the interior realm of individual psychophysiology. Platonov's response in such works as *Happy Moscow* and others was—to borrow a disconcertingly Stalinist phrase—optimistically tragic, for it pointed to the inherently paradoxical situation of *embodied* humanity, unalterably anchored in the chthonic underworld even as it strives ceaselessly upwards.

NOTES

1. Mariia Chegodaeva, *Dva lika vremeni: 1939 odin god stalinskoi epokhi* (Moskva: Agraf, 2001), 37.

2. Sona Stephan Hoisington, " 'Ever Higher': The Evolution of the Project for the Palace of Soviets," *Slavic Review* 62, no. 1 (spring 2003): 65.

3. M. Zolotonosov, *Slovo i telo: Seksual'nye aspekty, universalii, interpretatsii russkogo kul'turnogo teksta XIX–XX vekov* (Moskva: Ladomir, 1999), 582.

4. Ibid., 587.

5. See M. Zolotonosov, *Slovo i telo*, 578.

6. Yuri Buida, *The Prussian Bride*, tr. Oliver Ready (Sawtry: Dedalus LTD, 2002), 40.

7. A. Platonov, *Schastlivaia Moskva*, in *Strana filosofov Andreia Platonova: problemy tvorchestva* (Moskva: "Nasledie," 1999), 95.

8. A. Platonov, *Iamskaia sloboda*, (Voronezh: Izd-vo im. E. A. Bolkhovitinova, 1999): 176.

9. Editorial board of "Istoriia metro." Statement made by chairman Kulagin during a discussion of the manuscript, August 13, 1934, GARF R-7952/7/269, bl. 1.

10. Dietmar Neutatz, *Die Moskauer Metro*, 334–35, 369.

11. Il'ia Il'f and Evgenii Petrov, *Sobranie soch. v 5 t-kh*, vol. 3 (Moskva: Khudozhestvennaia literatura, 1996), 278.

12. Yurii Olesha, ed. V. Gudkova, *Kniga proshchaniia* (Moskva: Vagrius, 1999)

13. Julia Kristeva, *Powers of Horror*, 72.

14. L. Kassil' and B. Zenkevich, *Metro*, 21.

15. Evgenii Dobrenko, "Sotsrealizm i detstvo," in *Sotsrealisticheskii kanon* (Sankt-Peterburg: Akademicheskii proekt, 2000), 35.

16. Isaac Babel, *Soch. v 2 t-kh*, vol. 2 (Moskva: Khudozhestvennaia literatura, 1990), 129.

17. See Cynthia A. Ruder, *Making History for Stalin*, 82–83.

18. Mikhail Zoshchenko, *Sobranie soch. v 3-kh t-kh*, v. 3 (Leningrad: Khudozh-estvennaia literatura, 1987), 79.

19. Leslie Milne, "Tema 'zdorov'ia v povesti Mikhaila Zoshchenko 'Vozmezdie,'" in *XX vek i russkaia literatura: Sbornik nauchnykh statei* (Moskva: Rossiiskii gosu-darstvennyi gumanitarnyi universitet, 2002), 156.

20. K. Chukovskii, *Dnevnik 1930–1969* (Moskva: Sovremennyi pisatel', 1994), 154.

21. A. Platonov, *Zapisnye knizhki: Materialy k biografii*, ed. N. V. Kornienko (Moskva: "Nasledie," 2000), 148.

22. Ibid., 144.

Bibliography

Anninskii, L. "Otkrovenie i sokrovenie: Gor'kii i Platonov." *Literaturnoe obozrenie* 9 (1989): 3–21.

Babel', Isaak. *Sochineniia v 2-kh t-kh*. Moskva: Khudozhestvennaia literatura, 1990.

Bahr, Hans-Dieter. *Die Sprache des Gastes: eine Metaethik*. Leipzig: Reclam Verlag, 1994.

Bethea, David. "Literature." *The Cambridge Companion to Modern Russian Literature*. Ed. Nicholas Rzhevsky. Cambridge: Cambridge University Press, 1998.

Boime, Alfred. *The Magisterial Gaze: Manifest Destiny and American Landscape Painting, c. 1830–1865*. Washington, DC: Smithsonian Institution Press, 1991.

Booker, Keith, and Dubravka Juraga, *Bakhtin, Stalin, and Modern Russian Fiction: Carnival, Dialogism, and History*. Westport, CT: Greenwood Press, 1995.

Borenstein, Eliot. *Men without Women: Masculinity & Revolution in Russian Fiction: 1917–1929*. Durham: Duke University Press, 2000.

Boym, Svetlana. *Commonplaces: Mythologies of Everyday Life in Russia*. Cambridge: Harvard University Press, 1995.

Bulgakov, Mikhail. *The Master and Margarita*. Trans. Diana Burgin and Katherine Tiernan O'Connor. New York: Vintage International, 1996.

Bulgakov, Sergei. *S. N. Bulgakov: sochineniia v 2-kh tomakh*. Vol. 1. Moskva: "Nauka," 1993.

Bullock, Phillip Ross. "Andrei Platonov's *Happy Moscow*: Stalinist Kitsch and Ethical Decadence." In manuscript.

Brel', Sergei. "Kul'turnye konteksty 'zhivogo–nezhivogo' A. Platonova." In *Strana filosofov Andreia Platonova: Problemy tvorchestva*, *vyp. 4*, 239–45. Moskva: IMLI RAN "Nasledie," 2000.

Carleton, Gregory. *The Politics of Reception: Cultural Constructions of Mikhail Zoshchenko*. Evanston, IL: Northwestern University Press, 1998.

Chalmaev, V. *Andrei Platonov: k sokrovennomu cheloveku*. Moskva: Sovetskii pisatel', 1989.

Clark, Katerina. "Eisenstein's Two Projects for a Film About Moscow." Unpublished manuscript.

———. *Petersburg: Crucible of Cultural Revolution*. Cambridge: Harvard University Press, 1995.

———. "Socialist Realism and the Sacralizing of Space." *The Landscape of Stalinism: The Art and Ideology of Soviet Space*. Ed. Evgeny Dobrenko and Eric Naiman. Seattle: University of Washington Press, 2003.

———. *The Soviet Novel: History as Ritual*. 3rd edition. Bloomington: Indiana University Press, 2000.

Cockrell, R. "Conquest or Coexistence: The View of Nature in Early Platonov." Unpublished paper delivered at BASEES Twentieth-Century Studies Conference, Mansfield College, Oxford, 15–16 September 1999.

Cooke, Brett. *Human Nature in Utopia: Zamyatin's "We."* Evanston, IL: Northwestern University Press, 2002.

Cox, Randi. "All This Can Be Yours! Soviet Commercial Advertising and the Social Construction of Space, 1928–1956." *The Landscape of Stalinism: The Art and Ideology of Soviet Space*. Ed. Evgeny Dobrenko and Eric Naiman. Seattle: University of Washington Press, 2003.

Debiuzer, L. "Nekotorye koordinaty faustovskoi problematiki v povestiakh 'Kotlovan' i 'Dzhan.'" In *Andrei Platonov: mir tvorchestva*, 320–29. Comps. N. V. Kornienko and E. D. Shubina. Moskva: Sovremennyi pisatel', 1994.

———. "Tainopis' v romane *Schastlivaia Moskva*." In *Strana filosofov Andreia Platonova: Problemy tvorchestva, vyp. 4, iubileinyi*, 630–39. Moskva: IMLI RAN "Nasledie," 2000.

Demidova, M. "Obyknovennaia arktika." *Literaturnoe obozrenie* 17 (1938): ????

Derrida, Jacques. *Memoirs of the Blind*. Trans. Pascale Ann-Brault and Michael Naas. Chicago: University of Chicago Press, 1993.

Dobrenko, Evgenii. "Iskusstvo sotsial'noi navigatsii: ocherki kul'turnoi topografii stalinksoi epokhi." *Wiener Slawistischer Almanach* 45 (2000): 93–134.

Drubek-Meier, Natasha. "Rossiia—'Pustota v kishkakh' mira. *Novoe literaturnoe obozrenie* 9 (1994): 251–68.

Dufourmantelle, Anne, and Jacques Derrida. *Of Hospitality*. Trans. Rachel Bowlby. Stanford: Stanford University Press, 2000.

Epstein, Mikhail. "Charms of Entropy." In *Russian Postmodernism: New Perspectives on Post-Soviet Culture*, ed. Mikhail N. Epstein, Alexander A. Genis, and Slobodanka M. Vladiv-Glover, 423–55. New York: Berghan Books, 1999.

Etkind, A. *Eros nevozmozhnogo: Istoriia psikhoanaliza v Rossii*. Sankt-Peterburg: Meduza, 1993.

———. *Khlyst: sekty, literatura i revoliutsiia*. Moskva: Novoe literaturnoe obozrenie, 1998.

———. *Sodom i psykheia: ocherki intellektual'noi istorii Serebriannogo veka*. Moskva: ITS-Grant, 1996.

Fitzpatrick, Sheila. *Everyday Stalinism: Ordinary Life in Extraordinary Times: Soviet Russia in the 1930s*. New York: Oxford University Press, 1999.

Florenskii, Pavel. *Stolp i utverzhdenie istiny: Opyt pravoslavnoi feoditsei v dvenadt-sati pis'makh*. Paris: YMCA, 1989.

Fone, Byrne R. S. *Masculine Landscapes: Walt Whitman and the Homoerotic Text*. Carbondale: Southern Illinois University Press, 1992.

Foucault, Michel. *The Birth of the Clinic. An Archaeology of Medical Perception*. Trans. A. M. Sheridan Smith. New York: Pantheon Books, 1975.

———. *Discipline and Punish: The Birth of the Prison*. Trans. Alan Sheridan. New York: Vintage Books, 1977.

French, Patrick. *The Cut: Reading Bataille's Histoire de L'Oeil*. Oxford: Oxford University Press, 1999.

Garri, A. "Rozhdenie metro." *Novyi mir* 1 (1935): 107–35.

Gasparov, Boris. "Poeticheskii iazyk Pushkina kak fakt istorii russkogo literaturnogo iazyka." *Wiener Slawistischer Almanach* 27 (1992).

Gilbert, Sandra M., and Susan Gubar. *The Madwoman in the Attic: The Woman Writer and the Nineteenth Century Literary Imagination*, 2nd ed. New Haven: Yale University Press, 2000.

Goldberg, Jonathan. *Writing Matter: From the Hands of the English Renaissance*. Stanford: Stanford University Press, 1990.

Gol'dshtein, Aleksandr. *Rasstavanie s nartsissom: Opyty pominal'noi retoriki*. Moskva: Novoe literaturnoe obozrenie, 1997.

Gorham, Michael. "Mastering the Perverse: State Building and Language 'Purification' in Early Soviet Russia." *Slavic Review* 59, no. 1 (spring 2000): 132–53.

Gorky, M. *Sobranie soch. v 30 t-kh*. Vol. 27. Moskva: Khudozhestvennaia literatura, 1953.

Greenblatt, Stephen. "Mutilation and Meaning." In *The Body in Parts: Fantasies of Corporeality in Early Modern Europe*, eds. David Hillman and Carla Mazzio, 221–41. New York: Routledge, 1997.

Grose, Richard B. "Zoshchenko and Nietzsche's Philosophy: Lessons in Misogyny, Sex and Self-Overcoming." *The Russian Review* 54, no. 3 (July 1995): 352–64.

Groys, Boris. *Die Erfindung Rußlands*. München: Carl Hanser Verlag, 1995.

———. "Die gebaute Ideologie." In *Tyrannei des Schönen: Die Architektur der Stalinzeit*. Ed. Peter Noever. München: Prestel, 1994.

———. *Utopiia i obmen*. Moskva: Izd-tvo Znak, 1993.

Grübel, Rainer. "Gabe, Aufgabe, Selbstaufgabe: Dicther-Tod als Opferhabitus." In *Welt Hinter Dem Spiegel: Zum Status des Autors in der russischen Literatur der 1920 bis 1950er Jahre*, ed. Klaus Städtke, 139–204. Berlin: Akademie Verlag, 1998.

Gutkin, Irina. *The Cultural Origins of the Socialist Realist Aesthetic: 1890–1934*. Evanston: Northwestern University Press, 1999.

Günther, Hans. "Arkhetipy sovetskoi kul'tury." In *Sotsrealisticheskii kanon*, ed. Hans Günther and Evgenii Dobrenko, 743–84. Sankt-Peterburg: Akademicheskii proekt, 2000.

———. "'Broad is My Motherland': The Mother Archetype and Space in the Soviet Mass Song." *The Landscape of Stalinism: The Art and Ideology of Soviet Space*, 77–95. Seattle: University of Washington Press, 2003.

———. *Der sozialistische Übermensch: M. Gor'kij und der sowjetische Helden-mythos.* Stuttgart: J. B. Metzler, 1993.

———. "Liubov' k dal'nemu i liubov' k blizhnemu: Postutopicheskie rasskazy A. Platonova vtoroi poloviny 1930-kh gg." In *Strana filosofov Andreia Platonova: problemy tvorchestva, vyp. 4, iubileinyi,* 304–12. Moskva: IMLI RAN, "Nasledie," 2000.

Hansen-Löve, Aage A. "Von der Dominanz zur Hierarchie im System der Kunstformen Zwischen Avantgarde und Sozrealismus." *Wiener Slawistischer Almanach,* 47 (2001): 7–35.

Haynes, John. *New Soviet Man: Gender and Masculinity in Stalinist Soviet Cinema.* Manchester: Manchester University Press, 2003.

Hegarty, Paul. *Georges Bataille: Core Cultural Theorist.* London: SAGE Publications Ltd., 2000.

Heil, Jerry. "A Strict Youth, An Oneiric Literary Film Fantasy: Restoration of the Cultural Memory and Beyond." *Russian Literature* LI (2002): 161–187.

Hellbeck, Jochen. "Stalin-Era Autobiographical Texts: Working: Struggling: Becoming." *The Russian Review* 60 (July 2001), no. 3.

———. "Writing the Self in the Time of Terror." In *Self and Story in Russian History,* eds. Stephanie Sandler and Laura Engelstein, 69–93. Ithaca: Cornell University Press, 2000.

Hellebust, Rolph. *Flesh to Metal: Soviet Literature and the Alchemy of Revolution.* Ithaca: Cornell University Press, 2003.

Hödl, Klaus. *Die Pathologisierung des jüdischen Körpers: Antisemitismus, Geschlecht und Medizin im Fin-de-siècle.* Wien: Picus Verlag, 1997.

Hollier, Denis. *Against Architecture: The Writings of Georges Bataille.* Trans. Betsy Wing. Cambridge: The MIT Press, 1989.

Horujy, Sergei. "Ulysses in the Russian Looking-Glass." *Joyce Studies Annual,* ed. Thomas F. Staley, 68–157. Austin: University of Texas Press, 1998.

Hutchings, Stephen. "Remembering of a Kind: Philosophy and Art, Miscegenation and Incest in Platonov's *Dzhan." Russian Literature* 51 (2000): 49–72.

Iablokov, E. "Gorod platonovskikh polovinok: 'Pushkinskii' podtekst v kinostsenarii 'Otets-mat'." In *Strana filosofov Andreia Platonova: Problemy tvorchestva, vyp. 4, iubileinyi,* 700–9. Moskva: IMLI RAN, "Nasledie," 2000.

———. *Khudozhestvennyi mir Mikhaila Bulgakova.* Moskva: Iazyki slavianskoi kul'-tury, 2001.

Iakub, E. *Prokhodchik Katamanin.* Moskva: Moskovskii rabochii, 1944.

Iampolski, Mikhail. "Censorship as the Triumph of Life." In *Socialist Realism Without Shores,* eds. Thomas Lahusen and Evgeny Dobrenko, 165–77. Durham: Duke University Press, 1997.

———. *Demon i labirint: (Diagrammy, deformatsii, mimesis).* Novoe literaturnoe obozrenie, 1996.

Iampol'skii, Mikhail, and Aleksandr Zholkovskii. *Babel'/Babel.* Moskva: Carte Blanche, 1994.

Il'f, Ilya, and Evgenii Petrov. *Sobranie soch.* Vol. 3. Moskva: Khudozhestvennaia literatura, 1996.

Iles, Bella. "Pozhar v metro." *Oktiabr'* 6 (1935): 112–25.

Kadash, Tat'iana. "Gogol' v tvorcheskoi refleksii Zoshchenko." In *Litso i maska Mikhaila Zoshchenko*, 279–90. Moskva: Olimp/PPP, 1994.

Kassil', L. *Kanal Moskva–Volga: Spravochnik-putevoditel'*. Moskva: Narkomvod, 1937.

———. *Vratar' Respubliki*. Moskva: Sovetskii pisatel', 1939.

Kassil', L., and B. Zenkevich. *Metro: Chudo pod Moskvoi*. Moskva: Gos. izd-vo "Khudozh estvennai literaturra," 1936.

Kharms, Daniil. *Menia nazyvaiut Kaputsinom: Nekotorye proizvedeniia Daniila Kharmsa*. Moskva: MP "Karavento," "Pikment," 1993.

Klemperer, Victor. *LTI: Notizbuch eines Philologen*. Leipzig: Reclam, 1990.

Koch-Lubouchkine, Marina. "The Concept of Emptiness in Platonov's Fourteen Little Red Huts and *Dzhan*." *Poetics: The Journal of the British Neo-Formalist Circle* 26 (autumn 2001): 83–95.

Kornienko, N. V. "Moskva vo vremeni: (Imia Peterburga i Moskvy v russkoi literature 10—30-kh gg. XX v.)." In *Moskva v russkoi i mirovoi literature*, 210–47. Moskva: "Nasledie," 2000.

———. "Proletarskaia Moskva zhdet svoego khudozhnika: k tvorcheskoi istorii romana." In *Strana filosofov Andreia Platonova: Problemy tvorchestva, vyp. 3*, 357–72. Moskva: "Nasledie," 2000.

Kosarev, A. *Kak my stroili metro*. Moskva: Izd-vo "Istoriia fabrik i zavodov," 1935.

———. *Rasskazy stroitelei metro*. Moskva: Izd-vo "Istoriia fabrik i zavodov," 1935.

Kostov, Heli. *Mifopoetika Andreia Platonova v romane "Schastlivaia Moskva."* Eds. Arto Mustajoki, Pekka Pesonen, and Jouko Lindstedt. Helsinki: Slavica Helsingiensia, 2000.

———. "Oppozitsiia dushi i tela v romane *Schastlivaia Moskva*." In *Strana filosofov Andreia Platonova: Problemy tvorchestva, vyp. 3*, 152–58. Moskva: "Nasledie," 1999.

Kostrov, G. *Metro: Pervaia pesnia: stikhi*. Ed. A. Bezymenskii. Moskva: Profizdat, 1935.

Kovalev, L. I. *Moskovskii Metropoliten: Sbornik otchetnykh dokumentov o stroitel'stve i puske pervoi ocheredi Moskovskogo metropolitena*. Moskva: Izdanie MK, MGK VKP/b/ I Mossoveta: 1935.

Kretinin, A. "Moskva Chestnova i 'drugie.'" In *Strana filosofov Andreia Platonova: Problemy tvorchestva, vyp. 3*, 288–98. Moskva: "Nasledie," 1999.

Kuritsyn, Viacheslav. *Liubov' i zrenie*. Moskva: Solo Aiurveda, 1996.

Kristeva, Julia. *The Kristeva Reader*. Ed. Toril Moi. New York: Columbia University Press, 1986.

———. *The Powers of Horror: An Essay on Abjection*. Trans. Leon S. Roudiez. Columbia: Columbia University Press, 1982.

Krushchev, Nikita. *Khrushchev Remembers*. Trans. and ed. Strobe Talbot. Boston: Little, Brown & Co., 1970.

Lahusen, Thomas. "Das Geheimnis des Adun. Rekonstruktion einer Geschichte." *Wiener Slawistischer Almanach* 24 (1989): 115–26.

———. *How Life Writes the Book. Real Socialism and Socialist Realism*. Ithaca: Cornell University Press, 1997.

———. "Novyi chelovek, novaia zhenshchina i polozhitel'nyi geroi, ili k semiotike pola v literature sotsialisticheskogo realizma." *Voprosy literatury* 1 (1992): 184–205.

LeBlanc, Ronald. "Gluttony and Power in Olesha's *Envy.*" *The Russian Review 60* (April 2001): 220–37.

Lih, Lars T. "Melodrama and the Myth of the Soviet Union." In *Imitations of Life: Two Centuries of Melodrama in Russia*, eds. Louise McReynolds and Joan Neuberger, 178–207. Durham: Duke University Press, 2002.

Livers, Keith. "Scatology and Eschatology: The Recovery of the Flesh in Andrei Platonov's *Happy Moscow.*" *Slavic Review* 59, no. 1 (2000): 154–81.

———. "The Soccer Match as Stalinist Ritual: Constructing the Body Social in Lev Kassil''s *Vratar' Respubliki.*" *The Russian Review* 60, no. 1 (October 2001): 592–613.

Lobanov-Rostovsky, Sergei. "Taming the Basilisk." In *Fantasies of Corporeality in Early Modern Europe*, eds. David Hillman and Carla Mazzio, 195–217. New York: Routledge, 1997.

Locher, Jan Peter. "Rasskaz Platonova 'Takyr' i tema vostoka." In *Strana filosofov Andreia Platonova: problemy tvorchestva, vyp. 4, iubileinyi*, 289–95. Moskva: IMLI RAN, "Nasledie," 2000.

Lopatin, P. *Pervyi sovetskii metropoliten.* Moskva: Moskovskii rabochii, 1934.

Maston, Jeffrey. "Is the Fundament a Grave?" In *The Body in Parts: Fantasies of Corporeality in Early Modern Europe*, eds. David Hillman and Carla Mazzio. New York: Routledge, 1997.

Masing-Delic, Irene. *Abolishing Death: A Salvation Myth of Twentieth Century Russian Literature.* Stanford: Stanford University Press, 1992.

———. "Biology, Reason and Literature in Zoshchenko's *Pered vosxodom solnca.*" *Russian Literature VIII* (1980): 77–101.

———. "Gorky's Tutorship and Zoshchenko's 'Metamorphosis.'" *Russian Studies in Literature* 33, no. 2 (spring 1997): 49–59.

Matveeva, I. "Simvolika obraza glavnoi geroini." In *Strana filosofov Andreia Platonova: Problemy tvorchestva, vyp. 3.* Moskva: Nasledie, 1999.

May, Rachel. "Superego as Literary Subtext: Story and Subtext in Mikhail Zoshchenko's *Before Sunrise.*" *Slavic Review* 55 (spring 1996): 106–24.

McCannon, John. "Positive Heroes at the Pole: Celebrity Status, Socialist-Realist Ideals and Soviet Myth of the Arctic, 1932–39." *The Russian Review* 56 (July 1997): 346–65.

———. "Tabula Rasa in the North." The Landscape of Stalinism: The Art and Ideology of Soviet Space, eds. Evgeny Dobrenko and Eric Naiman, 240–60. Seattle: University of Washington Press, 2003.

Mihailovic, Alexander. *Corporeal Words: Mikhail Bakhtin's Theory of Discourse.* Evanston: Northwestern University Press, 1997.

Mokienko, V. M., and T. G. Nikitina. *Bol'shoi slovar' russkogo zhargona.* Sankt-Peterburg: Norint, 2000.

Murashov, Iurii. "Pis'mo i ustnaia rech' v diskursakh o iazyke 1930-kh godov: N. Marr." In *Sotrealisticheskii kanon*, 599–607. Sankt-Peterburg: "Akademicheskii proekt," 2000.

Naiman, Eric. "Andrei Platonov mezhdu dvukh utopii." *Novoe literaturnoe obozrenie* 9 (1994): 233–46.

———. "Communism and the Collective Toilet: Lexical Heroes in Platonov's *Happy Moscow.*" *Poetics: The Journal of the British Neo-Formalist Circle* 26 (autumn 2001): 96–109.

———. "Diskurs, obrashchennyi v plot': A. Zamkov i voploshchenie sovetskoi sub"ektivnosti." In *Sotsrealisticheskii kanon*, 625–38. Sankt-Peterburg: Akademicheskii proekt, 2000.

———. "The Inadmissibility of Desire." *Russian Literature* 23 (1988): 319–67.

Neutatz, Dietmar. *Die Moskauer Metro: von den ersten Plänen bis zur Grossbaustelle des Stalinismus.* Köln, Weimar, Wien: Böhlau Verlag, 2001.

Olesha, Iurii. *Romany, rasskazy, stat'i, p'esy, vospominaniia, Ni dnia bez strochki.* Sankt–Peterburg: Kristall, 1999.

O'Mahoney, Mike. "Going Underground: Palaces for the People on the Moscow Underground." Unpublished manuscript.

Paperno, Irina. "Nietzscheanism and the Return of Pushkin." In *Nietzsche and Soviet Culture: Ally and Adversary*, 211–32. Cambridge: Cambridge University Press, 1994.

———. "Pushkin v zhizni cheloveka Serebriannogo veka." In *Cultural Mythologies of Russian Modernism: From the Golden Age to the Silver Age*, eds. Robert P. Hughes and Irina Paperno. Berkeley: University of California Press, 1992.

Papernyi, V. *Kul'tura "Dva."* Ann Arbor: Ardis, 1985.

———. "Moscow in 1937." Unpublished manuscript.

Plamper, Jan. "The Spatial Poetics of the Personality Cult." In *The Landscape of Stalinism: The Art and Ideology of Soviet Space*, eds. Evgeny Dobrenko and Eric Naiman. Seattle: University of Washington Press, 2003.

Platonov, Andrei. *Iamskaia sloboda.* Voronezh: Izd-vo im. E. A. Bolkhovitinova, 1999.

———. *Izbrannoe.* Moskva: Moskovskii rabochii, 1966.

———. "Pushkin i Gor'kii." In *Andrei Platonov: sobranie sochinenii.* Vol. 2. Moskva: "Sovetskaia Rossiia," 1985. 300–321.

———. *Schastlivaia Moskva. Novyi mir* 9 (1991): 9–76.

———. *Schastlivaia Moskva, povesti, rasskazy, lirika.* Moskva: Gud'ial Press, 1999.

———. *Vospominaniia sovremennikov: materialy k biografii.* Comps. N. V. Kornienko and E. D. Shubina. Moskva: Sovremennyi pisatel', 1994.

———. *Vzyskanie pogibshikh: povesti, rasskazy, p'esa, stat'i.* Comp. M. A. Platonova. Moskva: "Shkola"–Press, 1995.

———. *Zapisnye knizhki: Materialy k biografii.* Ed. N. V. Kornienko. Moskva: IMLI RAN, 2000.

Podoroga, V. "Golos vlasti i pis'mo vlasti." In *Totalitarizm kak istoricheskii fenomen*, 108–11. Moskva: Filosofskoe ob-vo SSSR, Vses. assotsiatsiia molodykh filosofov, 1989.

Poltavtseva, Natalia. "Tema 'obydennogo soznaniia' i ego interpretatsii v tvorchestve Platonova." In *Strana filosofov Andreia Platonova: problemy tvorchestva, vyp. 4*, 271–81. Moskva: IMLI RAN "Nasledie," 2000.

Pushkin, Aleksandr. *Zolotoi tom: sobranie soch.* Ed. B. Tomashevskii. Moskva: "Imidzh," 1993.

Rosenthal, Bernice. "Sotsrealizm i Nitssheanstvo." In *Sotsrealisticheskii kanon*, 56–69. Sankt-Peterburg: Akademicheskii proekt, 2000.

Reid, Donald. *Paris Sewers and Sewermen: Realities and Representations.* Cambridge: Harvard University Press, 1991.

Ruder, Cynthia A. *Making History for Stalin: The History of the Belomor Canal.* Gainesville: University Press of Florida, 1998.

Russo, Mary. *The Female Grotesque: Risk, Excess and Modernity.* New York: Routledge, 1994.

Ryklin, Mikhail. "Luchshii v mire: Diskurs moskovskogo metro 30–kh godov." *Wiener Slawistischer Almanach* 38 (1996): 153–69.

———. "Mesto utopii." K istorii VSKhV-VDNKh-VVTs. Unpublished manuscript.

———. "Metrodiskurs." In *Sotsrealisticheskii kanon*, 814–29. Sankt-Peterburg: "Akademicheskii proekt," 2000.

———. "Telo terrora: (Tezisy k logike nasiliia)." *Voprosy literatury* 1 (1992): 130–47.

Salys, Rimgaila. "Understanding Envy." In *Olesha's Envy: A Critical Companion*, 4–43. Evanston: Northwestern University Press, 1999.

Scatton, Linda Hart. *Mikhail Zoshchenko: Evolution of a Writer.* Cambridge: Cambridge University Press, 1993.

Seifrid, Thomas. "Pisat' protiv materii: o iazyke *Kotlovana* Andreia Platonova." In *Andrei Platonov: mir tvorchestva*, 303–319. Moskva: Sovremennyi pisatel', 1994.

———. "Platonov kak proto-sotsrealist." In *Strana filosofov Andreia Platonova: problemy tvorchestva.* Moskva: "Nasledie," 1994.

———. "Smradnye radosti marksizma: zametki o Platonove i Batae." *Novoe literaturnoe obozrenie* 32 (1998): 48–59.

———. "Platonov, Socialist Realism, and the Avant-Garde." In *Laboratory of Dreams: The Avant-Garde and Cultural Experiment*, eds. John Bowlt and Olga Matich, 235–44. Stanford: Stanford University Press, 1996.

———. *Andrei Platonov: Uncertainties of Spirit.* Cambridge: Cambridge University Press, 1993.

Semenova, S. "Voskreshennyi roman Andreia Platonova: Opyt prochteniia *Schastlivoi Moskvy.*" *Novyi mir* 9 (1995): 209–26.

Sergl', Anton. "Katabazis kak poezdka na metro: (Gumilev, Khodaseevich, Maiakovskii, Brecht, Bakhtin i drugie: psikhoanaliz metro)." *Mesto pechati* 3 (1993): 58–104.

Shimak-Reifer, Jadwiga. "V poiskakh istochnikov platonovskoi prozy." *Novoe literaturnoe obozrenie* 9 (1994): 269–75.

Shtange, Galina Vladimirovna. "Remembrances." In *Soviet Diaries of the 1930s: Intimacy and Terror*, eds. Véronique Garros, Natalia Korenevskaya, and Thomas Lahusen; trans. Carol A. Flath, 167–205. New York: The New Press, 1995.

Sicher, Efraim. *Jews in Russian Literature after the October Revolution.* Cambridge: Cambridge University Press, 1995.

Slattery, Dennis Patrick. *The Wounded Body: Remembering the Markings of Flesh.* Albany: State University of New York Press, 2000.

Smirnov, I. *Psikhodiakhronologika: istoriia russkoi literatury ot romantizma do nashikh dnei.* Moskva: Novoe literaturnoe obozrenie, 1994.

———. "Sotsrealizm: Antropologicheskoe izmerenie." *Novoe literaturnoe obozrenie* 15 (1995): 29–43.

———. "Sotsrealizm: Antropologicheskoe izmerenie." In *Sotsrealisticheskii kanon*, eds. Hans Günther and Evgenii Dobrenko. Sankt-Peterburg: Akademicheskii proekt, 2000. 16–30.

Spiridonova, I. "Uznik: Obraz Sartoriusa." In *Strana filosofov Andreia Platonova: problemy tvorchestva, vyp. 3*, 303–11. Moskva: "Nasledie," 1999.

Szymak-Reifer, J. "V poiskakh istochnikov platonovskoi prozy: Zametki perevodchika." *Novoe literaturnoe obozrenie* 9 (1994): 269–75.

Tarakhovskaia, E. *M.* Moskva: Izd-vo detskoi literatury. 1936.

Tokarev. S. A. *Mify narodov mira: Entsiklopediia.* Moskva: Sovetskaia enstiklopediia, 1991.

Tolstaia-Segal, E. "Ideologicheskie konteksty Platonova." In *Andrei Platonov: mir tvorchestva.* Comps. N. V. Kornienko and E. D. Shubina. Moskva: Sovremennyi pisatel', 1994.

Tolstaia-Segal, E. "Naturfilosofskie temy Platonova." *Slavica Hierosolymitana*, 4 (1979).

Uspenskii, B. A. *Izbrannye trudy.* Vol. 1, *Semiotika istorii, semiotika kul'tury.* Moskva: iazyki russkoi kul'tury, 1996.

Vaiskopf, Mikhail. *Pisatel' Stalin.* Moskva: Novoe literaturnoe obozrenie, 2001.

Vasiliev, Vladimir. *Andrei Platonov: ocherk zhizni i tvorchestva.* Moskva: Sovremennik, 1990.

Vernitski, Anat. "Christian Motifs in Platonov." *Australian Slavonic and East European Studies* 14, nos. 1–2 (2000): 61–73.

Viugin, V. Iu. "Obshchee delo A. Platonova: motif voskreseniia v rasskazakh 30-kh—40-kh godov." *Russian Literature* 46 (1999): 267–87.

Walker, Clint. "Happy Moscow and the Bronze Horseman." *Poetics: Journal of the British Neo-Formalist School* 26 (autumn 2001): 119–67.

White, Hallie. "Sequence and Plot in Andrei Platonov's *Chevengur.*" *Slavic and East European Journal* 42, no. 1 (spring 1998): 102–17.

Zalkind, S. *Ilya Mechnikov: His Life and Work.* Moscow: Progress Publishers. 1959.

Zholkovskii, A. "Dusha, dal' i tekhnologiia." In *Andrei Platonov: mir tvorchestva*, comps. N. V. Kornienko and E. D. Shubina, 373–96. Moskva: Sovremennyi pisatel', 1994.

———. *Mikhail Zoshchenko: poetika nedoveriia.* Moskva: Shkola: iazyki slavianskoi kul'tury, 1999.

———. "The Obverse of Stalinism." In *Self and Story in Russian History*, eds. Laura Engelstein and Stephanie Sandler, 46–48. Ithaca: Cornell University Press, 2000.

Zolotonosov, M. *Slovo i telo: seksual'nye aspekty, universalii, interpretatsii russkogo kul'turnogo teksta XIX-XX vekov.* Moskva: Ladomir, 1999.

Zoshchenko, Mikhail. *Iz arkhiva pechati: Mikhail Zoshchenko.* Ed. M. Z. Dolinskii. Moskva: Izd-vo "Knizhnaia palata," 1991.

———. "Karusel'." *Drezina* 1 (May 1923).

———. "Serenada." *Chudak* 4 (1929).

———. "Skazka zhizni." *Krokodil* 35/36 (1935).

———. *Sobranie sochinenii v 3-kh tomakh*. Leningrad: Khudozhestvennaia Literatura. Uteratira, 1985.

———. "Stradaniia molodogo Vertera." *Krokodil* 1 (1933).

Zhurbina, E. "Puti istseleniia." In *Vospominaniia o Mikhaile Zoshchenko*. Sankt-Peterburg: Khudozhestvennaia Literatura, 1995.

Index

Abakumov, E. T., 192, 211
Aeneas, 196
Afinogenov, Aleksandr, 8–9, 18, 93, 100–101, 127, 199–200
Against Architecture: The Writings of Georges Bataille (Hollier), 234n184
Akhmatova, Anna, 13, 66
Alexandria, 159
Alexandrian Heron, 52
Alexandrov, Grigorii, 6; *Circus*, 6, 31, 47, 157; *Volga–Volga*, 20, 166, 177
androgyny, 45, 49
Anteus, 177
Apollonian, 20, 97, 102, 182, 216, 241
Arbat Street, 213–14
Archimedes, 52–53, 163
Arctic, 161, 181, 189, 201, 208, 212
"The Aristocratic Lady" (Zoshchenko), 129
Aristophanes, 173
Aristotle, 71
avant-garde, 11; autoerotic ideal of, 13, 41
Avvakum, 3
Azhaev, Vasilii, 95, 98, 104; *Far From Moscow*, 203–4

Babel, Isaac, 19, 208; *Red Cavalry* cycle, 19, 43, 107, 155, 241

Bahr, Hans-Dieter, 38
Bakhtin, Mikhail, 2, 7, 32–33, 45; dialogism, 14, 71
Baltic–White Sea Canal, 16, 95–96, 116, 126, 189, 209, 223, 242
Baptism, 190
Barker Eddy, Mary, 97
Bataille, Georges, 78n70; role of filth in works of, 30–31; *The Story of the Eye*, 30, 71
bazaar, 32, 38–39
Bedny, Demian, 2, 166
Beethoven, Ludwig von, 50
Belomor. *See* Baltic–White Sea Canal
Belyi, Andrei, 100
Berdiaev, Nikolai, 45, 50, 64, 178
Berlin, 192
Bethea, David, 39
Bildungsroman, 158
"A Bit of Utopia about Miss Metro" (Mayakovsky), 198
blindness, 34–35, 50, 61, 74, 169–72, 197, 205–7, 215–16, 219–20, 222, 226n69, 234n184
Blok, Aleksandr, 135
body, 1, 3, 6; grotesque, 8, 57; Jewish, 156, 167; purification of, 58, 63, 99; rationalization of, 93–94, 100–101, 116, 105, 111, 118–20, 162, 199;

257

statuary, 7, 8, 21, 56, 121, 167–68, 190, 208, 237–38, 244; woman's, 5, 29–30, 33, 51, 57, 59, 68, 72, 201

bogatyr', 157, 159, 182

Boime, Alfred, 74n33

Booker, Keith, 149n179

Borenstein, Eliot, 12, 28, 43

Brel', Sergei, 85n165

Brik, Osip, 13

The Brothers Karamazov (Dostoevsky), 59, 84n146, 98

Buida, Yurii, 238

Bulgakov, Mikhail, 3, 21, 63, 119; *Heart of a Dog*, 63, 222; *The Master and Margarita*, 2, 166, 219–23

Bulgakov, Sergei, 60, 86n168

Butler, Judith, 73n13

Calamus Series (Whitman), 180

Campanella, Tommasso, 216

Candide, 160

capitalism, 214

Carleton, Gregory, 143n68, 149n183

carnival, 6–7, 159

"Carousel" (Zoshchenko), 144n87

cartography, 201

Cassiday, Julie A., 141n56

castrates. See *Skoptsy*

Central Asia (vis-à-vis Europe), 31, 39–40

chaosmos, 64

Chapaev, Vasilii, 6

Chekhov, Anton, 102

Cheliuskinites, 120

Chernyshevsky, Nikolai, 221

Chkalov, Valerii, 155, 220

Christ the Savior Cathedral, 161, 218

chthonic, 47

Chukovsky, Kornei, 95, 124, 139, 243

circle (as image), 64, 103, 105

circulus. See Leroux, P.

Clark, Katerina, 19–20, 24n48, 47–48, 87n189, 143n86, 208, 230n117; spontaneousness versus consciousness paradigm, 27, 104,

157–58, 183n30; struggle against nature narrative, 97, 189; symbolic wounding, 66, 112

cloaca, 197–98

Cologne cathedral, 238

Comintern Street, 213

compassion, 55–56

Conduit (Kassil'), 155

Cooke, Brett, 118

corporeality. *See* body

Council of People's Commissars, 191

Cultural Revolution, 191

The Cut/Reading Bataille's "Histoire De L'Oeil" (Ffrench), 234n184

Dante, Alighieri, 196

Dead Souls (Gogol), 123–24

Demidova, N., 187n116

Derrida, Jacques, 38, 169–70

devil, 196, 220–21

dialectic, 53, 65–67, 113

Dionysian, 20, 97, 102, 104, 182, 216, 241

dirt, 30–31, 42, 54–62, 68, 220, 243

Dneprostroi, 9, 64

Dobrenko, Evgenii, 124, 232n152

Dostoevsky, Fedor, 45, 55, 59, 66, 124, 199, 221

Drubek-Meier, Natasha, 26n109, 82n119, 227n71

Dubravka, Juraga, 149n179

Dufourmantelle, Anne, 38

Ehrenburg, Ilya, 5, 198

Eiffel Tower, 238

Eisenstein, Sergei, 166, 208

"engineer of human souls," 139

eros (as impediment to Communism), 12–13, 50, 178

Eternal Feminine. *See* Solov'ev, Vladimir

Etkind, Aleksandr, 3, 80n99, 178, 183n15, 184n38

Everday Stalinism (Fitzpatrick), 231n132

excrement, 57, 60–62. *See also* dirt

"Fairy-Tale Life" (Zoshchenko),
147n150
The Fatal Eggs (Bulgakov), 222
The Fate of the Drummer-Boy (Gaidar),
155
"Father-Mother" (Platonov), 45
Ffrench, Patrick, 234n184
Filofei, 211
Fillipovich, Danila, 3
Finnegan's Wake (Joyce), 71
"Fire in the Metro" (Iles), 211, 225n33
Fitzpatrick, Sheila, 231n132
Flaubert, Gustav, 60
flight (as mythologeme in Stalinist
culture), 46–49, 97, 122, 159, 163
Florenskii, Pavel, 82n120
food, 54, 56, 60, 118, 137–39
Foucault, Michel, 218
Freud, Sigmund, 18, 97, 129, 136, 159,
199, 243
Fromm, Erich, 28–29
Fyodorov, Nikolai, 44, 51, 68, 72, 133,
178, 206

Gaidar, Arkadii, 155
"Galoshes and Ice-Cream"
(Zoshchenko), 143n85, 144n90
Gastev, Aleksei, 4, 92
Geller, Leonid, 148n161
*General Plan for the Reconstruction of
Moscow*, 191
gerontophobia, 211
Gesamtkunstwerk, 8, 15, 100, 204, 223
Gilbert, Sandra, 215
gnosis, 215
Goethe, Johann Wolfgang, 103, 107,
124–25
Gogol, Nikolai, 15, 94, 123–25, 127,
139, 174
Goldberg, Jonathan, 88n207, 100,
146n129
Gol'dshtein, Aleksandr, 5, 26n99, 158,
184n39, 228n93
Gorham, Michael, 184n53
Gorkii Prospekt, 135

Gorky, Maksim, 16, 35, 48, 66–68, 124,
134–35, 165, 229
gravidan. *See* Zamkov, Aleksei
Greenblatt, Stephen, 185n71
Grosz, Elizabeth, 4
Groys, Boris, 11, 21, 65, 129, 145n106,
193–94, 225n44, 228n99, 235n193
guard. *See* sentinel (mythologeme in
Socialist Realism)
Gubar, Susan, 215
Gumilevskii, Lev, 67
Günther, Hans, 79n86, 111, 177, 186n89
Gurvich, A., 70
Gymnastics (Soviet magazine), 168

Hagar, 212
Happiness (Pavlenko), 66
Haussmann, Baron Georges, 197–98,
204, 209
Hegarty, Paul, 30, 37
Hellbeck, Jochen, 8–9, 93, 112, 130, 176
Hellebust, Rolf, 93, 140n13
hierarchy, 202
Hilarion, Metropolitan, 212
Hillman, David, 3
Hodel, Robert, 82n127
Hödl, Klaus, 184n37
Hollier, Denis, 234
holy fool, 39, 57
Homer, 196
homoeroticism, 180, 209
Horujy, Sergei, 85n166
hospitality, 38
Hugo, Victor, 196, 198, 219–20
Hunter's Line (metro station), 195
Hutchings, Stephen, 32, 36, 81n106,
83n131

Iablokov, Evgenii, 80n99
Iakovleva, G. N., 151n214
Iakub, E., 230n112
Iampol'skii, Mikhail, 165, 197, 226n52,
231n136
iconoclasm, 10
Iles, Bella, 211

Il'f, Ilya, 210, 239
immortality, 56, 59, 70–71
Inber, Vera, 93–94
"Incident on the Volga" (Zoshchenko),
    109, 142n68
Irigaray, Luce, 73n13
Iron Flood (Serafimovich), 92
"Iron Messiah" (Kirillov), 92
Ivan the Terrible, 208
Izvestiia (newspaper), 61, 181

Jerusalem, 159
Jesus, 32–33, 35, 39, 67, 133, 222
Joyce, James, 60, 71

Kaganovich, Lazar' Moiseevich, 20, 61,
    124, 163, 190–92, 195–96, 200–203,
    211, 213, 216, 223, 239
Kaganovich metro, 190, 201, 204, 208,
    223
Kaletski, Alexander, 189
Kant, Immanuel, 38, 92
Kapel'nitskaia, Ol'ga, 88n201
Das Kapital (Marx), 220
Kassil', Lev, 10; *Goalkeeper of the
    Republic*, 19, 155–82, 186n73,
    186n75, 186n84, 187n90, 187n98,
    187n102, 189, 203–4, 216, 240;
    Miracle beneath Moscow, 61, 66,
    163, 203–4, 206–10, 213–18, 240
Kataev, Valentin, 166
Kaverin, Veniamin, 155
Kazakov, I. N., 112
kenoticism, 67. *See also* suffering
Kharms, Daniil, 63, 72
Khlysty (religious sect), 3
Khrushchev, Nikita, 192
Kirillov, Vladimir, 92
Kirsanov, Semen, 217
Koch-Lubouchkine, Marina, 79n82,
    79n84
kolkhoz, 202
Komsomol, 61, 192–93, 210–11
Korchagin, Pavel. *See* Ostrovsky,
    Nikolai
Kornienko, N. V., 185n61

Kosarev, A.: *How We Built the Metro*,
    195, 218, 222n46; *Stories of the
    Metro-Builders*, 211, 231n139
Kostov, Heli, 230n116
Kostrov, G., 228, 230
Kovalev, L. I., 228n100
Kremlin, 166
Kretinin, A., 84n145
Kristeva, Julia, 29, 34, 60, 71, 73n12,
    82n120, 232n162, 240
Kronverskii Prospekt. *See* Gorkii
    Prospekt
Kuritsyn, Viacheslav, 74n35, 186n85, 203

Lenin, Vladimir Il'ich, 32–33, 179
Lenin Mausoleum, 166
Leroux, P., 220
Les Misérables (Hugo), 197
Lezhnev, A., 109
The Life of Insects (Pelevin), 237
light (as mythologeme in Socialist
    Realism), 137, 213, 215, 218, 221
Lih, Lars T., 5, 22n20, 114
Lindbergh, Charles, 177
Lissitzky, El, 11
Literary Leningrad (journal), 16, 96
Literaturnaia gazeta (newspaper), 88n205
Lobanov-Rostovsky, Sergei, 74nn31–32,
    171, 226n64, 229n104
logos, 164, 166
Lopatin, Pavel (*The First Soviet Metro*),
    200, 201–2, 208, 211, 216, 223,
    224n23, 230n121
Lunacharsky, Anatoly, 53

M (Il'f and Petrov), 210
"M" (Kirsanov), 217–18
M (Tarakhovskaia), 196
Malashkin, Sergei, 110
"Man in a Case" (Chekhov), 102
Mandel'shtam, Osip, 1, 31
Manizer, M. G., 22
Marx, Karl, 220, 235n187
Marxist-Leninism, 157, 207, 214
Masing-Delic, Irene, 98–99, 119, 123,
    135, 142n60, 150n192, 150n196

masochism, 102, 106, 153, 168
Masten, Jeffrey, 86n169
May, Rachel, 143n68, 149n183
Mayakovsky, Vladimir, 13, 155, 198–99
Mazzio, Carla, 3
Mechnikov, Ilya, 63, 119
Medvedev, Aleksandr. *See* Azhaev, Vasilii
Men (all-male utopia), 12, 52, 179
Merkurov, S. D., 123
"Mesto utopii. K istorii VSKh–VDNKh–VVTs" (Ryklin), 233n179
metaphor (versus metonymy), 36
metonymy, 37, 49
Metro: A Novel of the Moscow Underground (Kaletski), 189
Metrostroi, 191, 193, 214
Mifopoetika Andreia Platonova v romane "Schastlivaia Moskva" (Kostov), 230n116
Mikhailovich, Tsar Aleksei, 3
misogyny, 5, 12
Mitropoliia, 196
Moby Dick (Melville), 179
monologism, 7, 15
"Montage of Life" (Azhaev), 95, 98
Moscow, 166; as New Jerusalem, 48; as Third Rome, 162, 200, 201, 210
Moscow metro, 2, 15, 20–21, 46, 60, 119, 124, 155, 159, 161, 168, 189–223, 239, 244; as unconscious, 204–5; as underground paradise, 21, 190, 216–17, 222; as underworld, 196, 198, 210
Moscow-Volga canal, 20, 159, 166, 177, 189, 203, 223
Moses, 32
Moskovskii metropoliten: Sbornik otchetnykh dokumentov o stroitel'stve i puske pervoi ocheredi Moskovskogo metropolitena (Kovalev), 228n100
Moskva (Zel'dovich), 239
Moskva-reka, 177

Mother (image of), 44
Mother Earth, 21, 47, 51, 119, 196, 203–4, 207–8, 214, 239
Mother Volga (Panferov), 66
Mukhina, Vera, 14, 31, 43
Murashov, Yury, 94

Nabokov, Vladimir, 198
Naiman, Eric, 5, 17, 22nn15–18, 73n15, 83n135, 84n149, 85n159, 87n184, 88nn198–99
Napoleon III, 197
narod, 177
Nazi ideology, 157, 162
negative theology, 41, 57
NEP (New Economic Policy), 12, 179
Nest of Gentry-Folk (Turgenev), 108
Neutatz, Dietmar, 190–93, 202
Neva (river), 193
New Adam. *See* resurrection (theme of)
New Man, 16, 96, 137, 163, 189, 210, 240
New Testament, 211
"New Times," 146n123
New York World's Fair, 237
Nietzsche, Friedrich, 97
Notes From the Underground (Dostoevsky), 221
Novyi Lef, 155

"O boikosti" (Gorky), 229n101
obezlichka, 181
October Revolution, 99, 107, 123
Odysseus, 196
Oedipal, 51, 98–102, 108, 110, 129, 131–34, 176
Olesha, Yurii, 19, 67, 208, 239; *Envy*, 43, 175–76, 179; "A Stern Youth," 67, 113, 180
Opekushin, Aleksandr, 123
Orlova, Liubov', 153–54
Orlova, Raisa, 231
Orthodoxy (Russian), 161
Ostrovsky, Nikolai, 70, 92–93, 111, 127, 137, 153
"Outside" (Zoshchenko), 118

Palace of Soviets, 218, 238
Palace of Soviets (metro station), 195
Palmira, 159
Panferov, Fedor, 66
Pangloss, 162
panopticon, 218
Papaninites, 212
Papernyi, Vladimir, 159, 227n89
Parent-Duchalet, Jean-Baptiste
     Alexandre, 197
Paris, 196–97, 215, 219–20, 223
Paris sewer, 196–98, 215
Parks of Culture and Rest, 6, 237–38,
     244
*Parting With Narcissus: Experiments in
     Funeral Rhetoric* (Gol'dshtein), 158
Pasternak, Boris, 13, 198
Patriarch Nikon, 3
patriarchy, 10, 31, 71
Pavlenko, Petr, 66
Pavlov, Ivan, 18, 129, 243
Pelevin, Viktor, 237
Peter the Great, 46, 131–32, 155, 193
Petersburg (Belyi), 100, 131
Petrov, Evgenii, 210, 239
Philosophy of the Common Cause
     (Fyodorov), 133
Plato, 158, 169, 171–72, 215
Platonov, Andrei, 1, 13, 21, 89n211,
     119, 153, 165, 208, 242; "About the
     First Socialist Tragedy," 35, 37, 46,
     49, 53, 75nn41–42, 81n119; "Among
     Animals and Plants," 56, 71;
     "Antisexus," 12, 41; biophilia, 14,
     29, 41–45; *Chevengur*, 11, 27–29,
     41–42, 44, 178; "Clay House in the
     Uezd Garden," 45, 55; dialogism, 15,
     35–36, 64, 68; *Dzhan*, 14–15, 32–44,
     57, 62, 67, 71, 74n36, 75nn39–40,
     75n42, 76n45, 76n51, 77n62, 78n68,
     91, 204, 206, 219, 228n97, 243; *The
     Foundation Pit*, 27–28, 41–42, 50,
     62, 239; *Happy Moscow*, 10, 14–15,
     31, 41, 43, 45–72, 76n47, 78n71,
     82n125, 82n128, 83n139, 84n146,
     84n150, 85n162, 86n167, 86n172,
     87n177, 91, 100, 107, 112, 118,
     122–23, 166, 167, 199, 200, 204,
     207, 219, 222, 223, 235n184, 238,
     243, 244; mutilation in, 66–68,
     70–71; *Notebooks*, 30, 76n55, 77n62,
     78n66, 78n75, 80n91, 84n149,
     87n183, 243; "Pushkin and Gorky,"
     36, 123; "Pushkin is Our Comrade,"
     37, 42, 80n100, 155; "The River
     Potudan'," 29, 51–59, 62, 71, 76n55,
     81n101, 83n130, 88n200; "The Soul
     of the World," 29–30, 46, 68;
     "Takyr'," 58, 68, 84n152
Politburo, 191
Poltavtseva, Natalia, 84n148
Pontius Pilate, 222
Popov, V., 92
Prokhodchik Katamanin (Iakub), 230n112
Prokhorova, I., 168
Proletkul't, 4, 12, 27, 243
Prometheus, 32, 47, 53, 122, 135
Protestant Ethos (Max Weber), 4
purges, 8; internalization of, 9, 101, 113,
     115, 176
Pushkin, Aleksandr, 66, 68, 70, 71, 123,
     135, 164–65; "The Bronze
     Horseman," 21, 42, 100, 131, 155,
     201; "The Prophet," 137, 170
Putearmeets. See "The Soldier of the
     Tracks"
Pyramid of Cheops, 238

raskol, 3
Razin, Sten'ka, 160
Red Gates (metro station), 196
Red Square, 167, 181
Red Virgin Soil (journal), 42
Reid, Donald, 197–98, 209
The Republic (Plato), 158, 171
resurrection (theme of), 94, 101, 112,
     123, 137, 199
Revolution Square (metro station), 208
Rodchenko, Aleksandr, 167
rodina, 174

Romanshyn, Robert, 3
Rome, 161, 162, 193, 201
Ronen, Omry, 2, 22n4
Rotert, Pavel, 191
Rottenburg, Abraham, 16, 96, 126
Russo, Mary, 47, 81n110
Ryklin, Mikhail, 190, 194, 222, 228n99, 232n154, 233n179, 236n196

sacrifice, 33, 36, 59, 66, 68, 73n29, 153, 165, 197
sadism, 103, 105, 113, 106–7, 167–68, 180
Saint-Simonism, 197
Sarah, 212
Scatton, Linda Hart, 128, 141n29, 149n180,
schism. See *raskol*
Scott, Robert F., 177
Second Empire, 197–98, 215
Seifrid, Thomas, 73n14, 77n56
Semenova, Svetlana, 87n176
Seneca, 124–25
sentinel (mythologeme in Socialist Realism), 108, 121, 138
Serafimovich, Aleksandr, 92
"Serenade" (Zoshchenko), 109
Sergl', Anton, 220
"Sermon on Law and Grace" (Hilarion), 212
sexuality, 4, 12; women as embodiment of, 27, 178
Shklovskii, Viktor, 198
Shmelev, I., 166
shockworkers. See Stakhanovites
show trials, 7
Shurpin, Fedor, 33
Shvambraniia (Kassil'), 155
"The Sixth Tale of Belkin," 123
Skoptsy (religious sect), 3, 4
Slag and Steel (Popov), 92
Slattery, Dennis Patrick, 22n5
Smirnov, Igor', 14, 65, 81n117, 83n129, 86n174, 88n193, 106, 137, 145n110, 146n122, 148n168, 149n171,

151n211, 168, 184n41, 224n5, 232n161, 233n172
sobornost', 181
soccer (as mythologeme in Stalinist culture), 161, 170, 173–76, 180–81, 189
Socialist Realism, 14, 71, 137; coming-to-consciousness narrative, 32, 46, 115–116, 157, 159; mutilation in, 17, 59, 126, 165, 166–67, 169–70, 180; reforging narrative, 59, 64, 92–93, 96, 128, 130, 192, 239–40; struggle against nature narrative, 17, 46, 97, 160, 169
"The Soldier of the Tracks," 95
Solov'ev, Vladimir, 5, 45, 50, 91, 178
"Song of the Motherland," 159
Sophia (Divine Wisdom), 29; Moscow Chestnova as, 48
The Sorrows of the Young Werther (Goethe), 103
Stakhanovites, 16, 37, 95, 122, 157, 210–11
Stalin, Iosif, 46, 66, 82n125, 104, 122–23, 130, 169, 177, 192, 195, 200, 210–12, 215, 233n183; as "father of nations," 6, 33–34
Stalinism, 6; denigration of technology, 163, 192, 210–12; eclecticism of, 11, 156, 212; masochism, 20, 167–68; revalorization of traditional values during, 14, 43–44, 153; synthesis of opposites, 14, 31, 66, 177, 181–82, 194–95; technophilia, 11, 156, 192, 212, 214, 221; transbiological family narrative, 6, 19, 44, 155–58, 163, 174–75, 241; transformationalist narrative, 52, 55, 103, 123, 162; utopia found, 10, 14, 32, 34, 42, 100; writing in, 94, 100, 123–25, 134, 162, 164, 205
"Stalin's falcons," 189
Stavsky, Vladimir Petrovich, 1, 95
St. Basil's Cathedral, 161–62

"The Story About Baths and Their Patrons" (Zoshchenko), 143n83, 146n124, 228n89

St. Peter, 161–62

St. Petersburg, 121, 174; as utopian locus, 21, 201–2, 207

suffering, 40, 54, 66–67, 124

sun, 120, 138–39, 151n214, 169–71, 180, 204, 216, 221, 229n101, 233n166

Sverdlov Square, 200

symbolists, 5

"A Tale About Bathhouses and Their Patrons" (Zoshchenko), 114

Tarakhovskaia, E., 196, 226n50

"Thy Neighbor's Hand"(Zoshchenko), 99

time" linear, 40; cyclical, 40, 62

Tolstoy, Lev, 124–25, 136

transgendering, 31, 206; in works by Platonov, 44–45

Trotsky, Lev, 52, 54, 199, 226n69

Tsiolkovskii, Konstantin, 155

Tullius, Servius, 102

Turgenev, Ivan Sergeevich, 108, 134

Turkmenistan. *See* Central Asia (vis-à-vis Europe)

Tverskaya (street), 135

Two Captains (Kaverin), 155

Typee (Melville), 179

Ul'ianov, Anatolii, 93–94

Uspenskii, Boris, 212

Vaiskopf, Mikhail, 11, 156, 213, 224n18, 232n143

Vatican, 161

Venice, 166

via negativa, 168

Vii (Gogol), 174, 186n88

Virgil, 196

vision, 170–73; as metaphor for dominance, 33, 36, 171, 203–4, 207, 219

vitalism, 162, 164–65, 214

"Voice of the Father" (Platonov), 71

Volga, 159

Voltaire, 160

voluntarism, 164

water (theme of), 10, 21, 54, 82n120, 97–98, 110–11, 114, 118–20, 121–22, 125, 129, 132–33, 159–63, 176–77, 197–98, 201–3, 205–8, 217, 228n90, 228n92, 230n120, 231n139, 240

We (Zamiatin), 118

"We Grow Out of Iron" (Gastev), 92

Weber, Max, 4

West (capitalism), 171–72, 177–78

Westernization, 193

White, Hallie, 86n173

Whitman, Walt, 179–80

women: as biology, 5, 12, 24n60, 29, 40, 46, 50, 121–22, 129, 144n92, 178–79; death of, 5, 202, 206, 215, 229n111, 243; as synthesis of immanence and transcendence, 14–15, 29–30, 31, 38, 40–44, 46–51, 59, 68, 72, 243

World Soul. *See* Sophia (Divine Wisdom)

The Year of Our Lord (Shmelev), 166

Zalkind, S., 87n179

Zamiatin, Evgenii, 118

Zamkov, Aleksei, 9, 16–18, 93, 95–96, 136

Zel'dovich, Aleksandr, 239

Zenkevich, B., 206

Zholkovsky, Aleksandr, 17–18, 66, 76n53, 94, 96–97, 118, 130, 140n6, 142n68, 143n75, 143n79, 145n114, 147n138, 147n149, 148n152, 150n198, 151n208

Žižek, Slavoj, 8

Zolotonosov, Mikhail, 7, 24nn60–61, 85nn153–54, 85n160, 87n181, 108, 121, 143n68, 151n212, 168, 180,

185n60, 185n63, 185n68, 186n77, 206, 227n85, 229n111, 230n122, 233n166

Zoshchenko, Mikhail, 2, 15, 63, 66, 70, 119, 165, 199, 241–42; "Anna around the Neck," 120–22; *Before Sunrise*, 16–18, 91–92, 94, 96–98, 100–101, 110–11, 115, 117, 122, 128–39, 142n58, 149n188, 150nn193–94, 150n197, 150n199, 151n200, 153, 155, 162, 213, 242–43; "The Hand of Thy Fellow Man, 116–17; "How Much Does a Person Need," 104–5, 115; "The Lights of the Big City," 101, 116–18, 120, 146n134; "The Lower Depths," 112, 127; *Mishel' Siniagin*, 112, 151n209; scientific body, 70, 92–94, 96, 100–101; *Sky-Blue Book*, 11, 16, 92, 97, 100, 103–4, 109–10, 114, 127, 144n91; "Story of a Re-forging," 16, 95–96; "The Story of the Student and the Diver," 109–11, 144n111; "The Sufferings of the Young Verter," 101–8; *Youth Restored*, 9, 16–17, 91–92, 95, 97, 100, 111, 117–18, 122–27, 129, 139, 144n92, 147n142, 153, 155, 162, 213, 242

Zvezda (journal), 15–16, 96

Zweig, Stefan, 97

About the Author

Keith A. Livers is Assistant Professor at the University of Texas at Austin, where he teaches Russian literature, culture, and language. His research and publishing concerns twentieth-century Russian literature and film, with a strong emphasis on authors of the Stalinist and post-Soviet periods. He holds a Ph.D. from the University of Michigan.